DATE DUE

JY			
NO 13 01			

DEMCO 38-296

COGNITION

CONCEPTUAL AND
METHODOLOGICAL ISSUES

COGNITION

CONCEPTUAL AND
METHODOLOGICAL ISSUES

HERBERT L. PICK, JR.

PAULUS VAN DEN BROEK

AND DAVID C. KNILL

EDITORS

AMERICAN PSYCHOLOGICAL ASSOCIATION, WASHINGTON, DC

Washington, DC 20002

Copies may be ordered from the
APA Order Department
P.O. Box 2710
Hyattsville, MD 20784

This book was typeset in Century Condensed by Harper Graphics, Waldorf, MD.

Printer: Edwards Brothers, Inc., Ann Arbor, MI
Cover designer: Minker Design, Bethesda, MD
Copyeditors: Cynthia L. Fulton and Cathe Ballay
Production coordinator: Cynthia L. Fulton

Library of Congress Cataloging-in-Publication Data

Cognition: conceptual and methodological issues / Herbert L. Pick, Jr.,
    Paulus van den Broek, and David C. Knill, editors.
        p.   cm.
    "Result of a conference. The Study of cognition: conceptual and
    methodological issues ... held in February and March 1991 at the
    University of Minnesota."—Pref.
    Includes bibliographical references and index.
    ISBN 1-55798-165-5 (acid-free paper)
    1. Cognition—Congresses.   2. Perception—Congresses.
    3. Thought and thinking—Congresses.   4. Learning, Psychology
    of—Congresses.   I. Pick, Herbert L.   II. Broek, Paulus Willem
    van den, 1955–   .   III. Knill, David C.
    BF311.C54873   1992
    153—dc20   91–45909
                                                                    CIP

Printed in the United States of America
First edition

APA Science Volumes

Best Methods for the Analysis of Change: Recent Advances, Unanswered Questions, Future Directions

Cognition: Conceptual and Methodological Issues

Cognitive Bases of Musical Communication

Conceptualization and Measurement of Organism–Environment Interactions

Hostility, Coping, and Health

Organ Donation and Transplantation: Psychological and Behavioral Factors

The Perception of Structure

Perspectives on Socially Shared Cognition

Researching Community Psychology: Issues of Theory and Methods

Sleep and Cognition

The Suggestibility of Children's Recollections: Implications for Eyewitness Testimony

Taste, Experience, and Feeding

Through the Looking Glass: Issues of Psychological Well-Being in Captive Nonhuman Primates

APA expects to publish volumes on the following conference topics:

Cardiovascular Reactivity to Psychological Stress and Cardiovascular Disease
The Contributions of Psychology to Mathematics and Science Education
Developmental Psychoacoustics
Emotion and Culture
Lives Through Time: Assessment and Theory in Personality Psychology From a
     Longitudinal Perspective
Maintaining and Promoting Integrity in Behavioral Science Research
Psychological Testing of Hispanics
Stereotypic Behavior
Temperament: Individual Differences in Biology and Behavior

As part of its continuing and expanding commitment to enhance the dissemination of scientific psychological knowledge, the Science Directorate of the APA established a Scientific Conferences Program. A series of volumes resulting from these conferences is jointly produced by the Science Directorate and the Office of Communications. A call for proposals is issued several times annually by the Science Directorate, which, collaboratively with the APA Board of Scientific Affairs, evaluates the proposals and selects several conferences for funding. This important effort has resulted in an exceptional series of meetings and scholarly volumes, each of which individually has contributed to the dissemination of research and dialogue in these topical areas.

The APA Science Directorate's conference funding program has supported 22 conferences since its inception in 1988. To date, 13 volumes resulting from conferences have been published.

Wayne J. Camara, PhD   Virginia E. Holt
Acting Executive Director   Scientific Conferences Manager

Contents

Part Three: Learning in the Larger World

Afterword

Contributors

Daniel C. Dennett, Department of Philosophy, Tufts University

Eleanor Gibson, Center for Research in Learning, Perception, and Cognition, University of Minnesota

Robert Glaser, Learning Research and Development Center, University of Pittsburgh

James J. Jenkins, Department of Psychology, University of South Florida

Paul E. Johnson, Department of Information and Decision Sciences, University of Minnesota

Walter Kintsch, Institute of Cognitive Sciences, University of Colorado

David C. Knill, Department of Psychology, Univeristy of Minnesota

Laura E. Kochevar, Department of Information and Decision Sciences, University of Minnesota

Dominic W. Massaro, Program in Experimental Psychology, University of California, Santa Cruz

Douglas L. Medin, Department of Psychology, University of Michigan

Ulric Neisser, Department of Psychology, Emory University

Herbert L. Pick, Jr., Institute of Child Development, University of Minnesota

David Premack, University of Pennsylvania and Ecole Polytechnique, CREA, Paris

Naomi Quinn, Department of Anthropology, Duke University

Herbert A. Simon, Department of Psychology, Carnegie Mellon University

Claudia Strauss, Department of Anthropology, Duke University

David M. Thau, Department of Psychology, University of Michigan

M. T. Turvey, Center for the Ecological Study of Perception and Action, University of Connecticut, and Haskins Laboratories

Paulus van den Broek, Department of Educational Psychology, University of Minnesota

Imran Zualkernan, Department of Information and Decision Sciences, University of Minnesota

Preface

R ecent years have seen a number of exciting developments in the field of cognitive psychology. Change has taken place so rapidly, in fact, that there has been little time to reflect on the variety of underlying conceptual, philosophical, and meta issues that have arisen. Many of the technological and methodological advances have generated their own conceptual issues. We hope that this book will provide an opportunity for those involved in this dynamic field to step back and gain perspective on some of these issues.

The goal of this volume is not primarily to present empirical data. It is to raise conceptual and metatheoretical concerns against the background of relevant empirical investigations. For this reason, the contributors intentionally represent a variety of specific content domains.

Three fundamental questions are addressed in the chapters that follow: What kinds of behavior constitute the domain of cognition? How do we conceptualize the knowledge base underlying cognitive processes such as thinking, perceiving, and remembering? What are the implications of different methodological techniques for our understanding?

The chapters of this volume are based on papers originally presented at a conference, The Study of Cognition: Conceptual and Methodological Issues, organized by the University of Minnesota Center for Research in Learning, Perception, and Cognition. The conference was held in February–March 1991 in celebration of the center's 25th anniversary. The intellectual atmosphere at the conference was further stimulated by the participation of a number of formal discussants, including Patricia Bauer, Irving Biederman, Anne Pick, William Charlesworth, Wade Savage, and Ulrich Neisser. We hope this book will both reflect the breadth of the formal and informal exchanges that took place at that conference and encourage further productive dialogue on the issues raised.

Herbert L. Pick, Jr.
Paulus van den Broek
David C. Knill

Acknowledgments

T he conference that served as the occasion for the initial presentation of the chapters in this volume could not have been held without the participation of a number of organizations and people. It is a pleasure to acknowledge their help.

Major financial support was provided by the American Psychological Association (APA) under the Scientific Conference Program of its Science Directorate and by the Wilson Learning Corporation of Edina, Minnesota. The support, encouragement, and advice of Virginia Holt of the APA and Brad Lashbrook of the Wilson Learning Corporation are very much appreciated.

Supplementary financial support was provided by a number of University of Minnesota sources: the College of Liberal Arts Scholarly Conference Fund, the Graduate School, the Continuing Education and Extension Program Innovation Fund, the Cognitive Science Graduate Minor Program, and the Center for Research in Learning, Perception, and Cognition. The advice and support of Associate Dean Judith Lambrecht of the College of Education, Dean Robert Holt of the Graduate School, and Associate Dean Frederick Asher were most helpful.

The persistent hard work of the office staff of the Center for Research in Learning, Perception, and Cognition was instrumental at every phase of the conference. Molly Kelliher, executive secretary, as well as Christie Geiger and Erin Jewett, participated from the generation of the initial letters applying for support, through the extensive correspondence with the participants, to the actual logistics of running the conference itself.

The professional conference liaison personnel from the University of Minnesota Continuing Education and Extension, Lisa Brienzo and Chris Carlstrom, helped immensely with organizational logistics during all phases of the conference. They saved us from a number of mistakes that we know about and probably from many of which we are unaware.

The planning and organization of the conference was carried out by a student–faculty "special events" committee. In addition to the editors of this volume, the committee included Kirsten Condry, John Hummel, Lisa Isenberg, Leslie Schwandt, Elizabeth

Strickland, Richard Thurlow, and Lisa Travis. For over a year and a half they attended an endless series of meetings and performed innumerable thankless as well as appreciated tasks. The committee was aided considerably during the planning stages by the advice and encouragement of Randy Fletcher, Bruce Overmier, and Albert Yonas. Many other faculty consulted with the committee from time to time, and their contributions are gratefully acknowledged.

During the conference itself, the following pre- and postdoctoral students acted as hosts for visiting graduate students: Patty Gould, Douglas Gentile, Louise Hertsgaard, Elizabeth Husebye, Eryn O'Brien, Isabelle Schallreuter, Leslie Schwandt, and Kip Smith. Their generosity is much appreciated.

Any success of this volume is due to the hard work of all these individuals.

Introduction

Herbert L. Pick, Jr., Paulus van den Broek, and David C. Knill

I n the beginning, psychology was primarily cognitive psychology. The classical structural perspective that dominated the origins of psychology in the latter half of the 19th century was characterized by introspective analysis of our thought processes during problem solving (Humphrey, 1948). The psychophysical emphasis of the period had a cognitive tone to it, with the distinction between sensation and perception implying a cognitive component. Indeed, Helmholtz's concept of unconscious inference was an unblushing resort to cognitive processes to explain perception. Even the early clinical concerns were not free of a strong cognitive bias. Freud's unconscious motivation exercised its influence on thought processes as revealed in hypnosis and reflected in free-association reports. These approaches maintained their cognitive orientation when transported to America, as reflected, for example, in Titchener's and James's writings.

As is well-known, this orientation changed with the advent of behaviorism. Even within behaviorism, however, there were a few countervailing trends, such as Holt's (1915) analysis of response and cognition and Tolman's (1932) purposive behaviorism. Nevertheless, by 1940 a very noncognitive behaviorism clearly dominated at least American psychology. (Skinner's *The Behavior of Organisms* was published in 1938 and Hull's *Principles of Behavior* in 1943.)

World War II marked a radical change in perspective on thinking about and investigating cognitive processes. It is interesting to speculate on the causes of this shift. From within psychology, it might have been a simple cyclic variation. However, from outside psychology, the cognitive demands of military tasks pointed to a complexity of human performance that was not accounted for by behavioristic learning theory. These cognitive requirements were reflected in all kinds of activities from test performance of candidates for highly skilled tasks, such as flying combat planes, to detection of radar and sonar targets to linguistic communication in noise. At the same time, theoretical and physical models such as cybernetics (Wiener) and information theory (Shannon) were developed for some of these complex activities, and the first primitive computers were used in gun fire control. Whatever the reasons, many important conceptual developments can easily be traced to that period. Shortly after the war, interest was further stimulated by the study of topics such as computers and intelligence (Turing, 1950), automated pattern recognition (Selfridge, 1959), limitations of human information processing (Broadbent, 1958), and the relation of cognition and action (e.g., Miller, Galanter, & Pribram, 1960). Neisser (1967) provided an integration of the emerging view with his *Cognitive Psychology*.

The modern evolution of the study of cognition, however, had barely begun. Since that postwar period, among other influences, Piaget's work on developmental epistemology temporarily assumed a dominant role in the study of cognitive development. The work of ethologists such as Tinbergen and Lorenz gave impetus to careful and naturalistic observation of behavior. Chomsky's revolutionary work in linguistics not only reshaped that field but called into question our ideas about human learning, thinking, and problem solving. James Gibson proposed a different concept of information and made psychologists aware of the invariants that underlie both the perception of spatial layout and the stability of the perceptual world, which, in turn, facilitate guidance of behavior.

Throughout this period, the increasing availability, power, and use of computers not only provided a powerful research technology but, perhaps more importantly, reinforced the computational metaphor for cognitive processes. Marr's computational approach to visual perception is an elegant example of the power and generativity of such analyses. Now, the computational approach to the study of cognition is increasingly informed and constrained by the explosion of knowledge from the domain of neuroscience and connectionist modeling.

Insights derived through modern technological advances have led to such rapid development of the field that cognitive psychologists have been obliged to reformulate the questions they seek to answer. Participants at the 1991 Minnesota Study of Cognition conference sought the answers to three fundamental questions that are of central relevance to researchers today: First, what kinds of behavior constitute the domain of cognition? Neisser (1976) himself surprised the cognitive field with his book *Cognition and Reality*, in which he rejected the then-current information processing approach to the study of cognition, arguing instead for an approach more faithful to cognitive behavior as it actually occurs. Since then, a number of scholars from a variety of perspectives have made similar arguments. One relevant concept is that of *situated cognition*, which emphasizes the interaction of the social context and the cognitive problem. Currently, a strong impetus in that direction, especially in relation to cognitive development, is the revival of interest in the ideas of Vygotsky, who posited that the very formation of the child's mind is accomplished in social interaction. Another perspective emphasizes the relation of cognitive problem solving and emotion.

A second basic question was how to conceptualize the knowledge base underlying cognitive processes such as thinking, perceiving, and remembering. What is the nature of conceptual knowledge itself? A lively research area is concerned with the distinction between characteristic and defining properties of concrete concepts. The issues become even thornier when one considers abstract concepts such as that of object itself, causality, space, time, probability, justice, and kindness. How is knowledge organized? One issue centers on the extent to which cognition is modularized. There have been provocative discussions of the modularity of content domains (e.g., language and space). There have also been other bases proposed for the organization of knowledge, such as that captured by the distinctions between declarative and procedural knowledge and between semantic and episodic memory. Researchers generally agree that knowledge is represented in some form but disagree on the nature of that representation. Anderson's (1978) influential article in the *Psychological Review* showed that the argument as to whether certain kinds of information are represented in analog or propositional form is not resolvable. However, he went on to argue that different processes or operations can be defined on different representations (Anderson, 1983), and there continues to be considerable interest in this issue.

A third fundamental question concerned the implications of different methodological techniques for understanding cognition. A variety of new methods have been introduced during this period of rapid change in the study of cognition. These range from a modern mental chronometry to protocol analyses to connectionist computer modeling. They include comparative approaches across species, ages, cultures, and various types of pathology. There is even a new cognitive psychometrics. These methodological innovations are not theory or concept neutral. For example, describing a knowledge structure in terms of a semantic network derived from protocol analysis presupposes a great deal about cognitive processes. Such a description disposes one toward an information processing cognitive theory.

The volume is organized into three parts. Part 1, Relation Between Organism and Environment, addresses in traditional terms issues of perception and action. The focus in Part 2, Aspects of Thinking, is on the way in which knowledge is organized and processed. These chapters address processes of reasoning, memory, and representation. Part 3, Learning in the Larger World, extends the concerns of the first two parts to learning and applications of the study of cognition. This organization is quite arbitrary. An exciting feature of the chapters is the extent to which they address related problems from different perspectives and in different contexts.

A central issue that recurs in part 1 is the relation between categorization and perception. To what extent is perception structured by a priori categories? There seems to be agreement that perception is subject to constraints, but there is disagreement on where these constraints originate and at what levels they operate. In the area of speech perception, Jenkins reviews in chapter 1 the evidence that some categorization is present at birth and discusses how it is modified by linguistic experience. He leaves open the question of the levels at which such categorization operates. Dennett addresses in chapter 2 the constraint of "filling in" and illustrates the phenomenon by examples of many illusions. Although he argues that the mechanism is more likely a "finding out" than a filling in one, he nevertheless sees it as a construction on the sensory information. In chapter 3, Massaro clearly places the operation of categorization on the cognition end of a sensory–perceptual cognitive continuum. Although they differ in where they see constraints imposed on perception, these three authors take a fundamentally constructivist view to perception. In contrast, influenced by James Gibson, Turvey explains in chapter 4, as much as possible, perception and action in a nonconstructivist way. He places the constraints in the physical world and in the interaction of the organism with the physical world.

In part 2, Simon (chapter 5) and Kintsch (chapter 6) both describe activities involved in aspects of thinking. In so doing, they develop somewhat different characterizations of the domain of thinking. Simon identifies two traditions in research on thinking: reasoning and problem solving. He finds that research on reasoning has roots in logic and language, whereas research in problem solving has roots in artificial intelligence approaches to game playing and to search activities. He also suggests that a metaphor of perceiving or "seeing" can be a powerful one for understanding some aspects of thinking. In his characterization, Kintsch considers a dimension of cognition extending from perception at one end of the continuum to problem solving at the other. Kintsch is concerned not with differentiating reasoning from problem solving but rather with explicating the process of comprehension (of text), which he places at an intermediate position on the perception–problem solving continuum. His construction–integration model provides a concrete example of how prior knowledge and textual input interact to yield comprehension. Whereas Simon and Kintsch are concerned primarily with cognitive processes, Medin and Thau (chapter 7) and Premack (chapter 8) are concerned with the nature of cognitive categories and concepts. Medin and Thau use their own research area of categories to make very general conceptual and methodological points about cognitive psychology. Among their substantive conclusions is that constraints in category formation can be found by considering the functions that they serve for an organism. Premack addresses the origins of very abstract concepts in ontongony and phylogeny (e.g., What are the conceptual primitives of infants and nonhuman primates?). Premack proposes that there are innate conceptual species-specific primitives such as notions of object, intention, causality, and representation. Infants of any species possess all the basic conceptual primitives of the adult. The difference between infants and adults exists in what can be done with those concepts.

Part 3 provides examples of the extension of many of the previous issues to aspects of learning and practical situations in the larger world. Gibson (chapter 9) and Glaser (chapter 10) both investigate the current status of learning. Gibson focuses on perceptual learning by infants, emphasizing, as she has in the past, that perceptual learning is a selective process. However, her current view places much more stress on an ecological analysis of perceptual learning. She focuses in particular on the affordances of the events, objects, and layout of the world to infant learning. She asks what the information is for these affordances and how infants become sensitive to it. Glaser reviews progress in the integration of cognitive research and the psychology of learning in the form of instructional psychology. He examines this integration in terms of four components relevant to a "prescriptive theory of learning": the state of competence to be achieved, the initial state and prior competence, the conditions of learning, and the assessment of learning outcomes.

In chapter 11, Strauss and Quinn discuss a domain not usually considered a form of cognitive learning, namely, the acquisition of cultural understanding. They point out the conceptual similarity between the acquisition of this form of information and that of more traditional learning tasks such as language learning. However, they describe empirically how acquisition of the understanding of a cultural concept such as marriage is quite different from other types of learning. In so doing, they pose the general question of how cultural understanding is acquired.

Siegel (Chapter 12), although primarily addressing an issue in the philosophy or metatheory of science, also reviews the history of learning theoretic analyses of stuttering behavior. His main thesis is that the theoretical models or stories of researchers do not operate in a vacuum. New conceptual analyses not only open up possibilities for practical actions by clinical practitioners but also can impose inhibiting constraints. It is important that the theoretician be aware of these influences. This bridge between theory and practice is vividly exemplified in chapter 13 by Johnson, Kochevar, and Zualkernan, who use an analysis of expert problem solving in semiconductor manufacturing to illustrate their general framework for understanding and studying expertise. Their general framework is a scheme for considering in a given task environment the relations between the goals and actions of a problem solver (semantic fit) and between the available information and cognitive capacities (structural fit). The development of the semantic and structural fits in expertise seems analogous to Gibson's development of sensitivity to the affordances of the environment.

In conclusion, Neisser (Afterword) highlights two conceptual schemes reflected in the chapters and central to current cognitive psychology: the ecological and information processing perspectives. He suggests approaching direct perception from the ecological perspective and "higher" cognitive processes from the perspective of information processing.

Several issues unite all of the chapters. One is a methodological concern—a particularly strong focus in Medin and Thau's and Massaro's chapters. They urge that ideas be tested by constructing and contrasting alternative models. Evaluation is also a central aspect of Kintsch's chapter. Interestingly, Kintsch stresses the value of qualitative along with, or as a substitute for, quantitative evaluation of his cognitive architecture. The issue of generalizability of models across tasks is raised in chapters by Jenkins, Massaro, and Kintsch, all of whom consider this an important virtue of a model given that it is unlikely that the human mind has entirely different procedures for every task. At the same time, Simon as well as Johnson, Kochevar, and Zualkernan warn against the danger of assuming excessive similarity of mechanisms and strategies across tasks.

A more general methodological quality reflected in the chapters is the broad range of experimental and theoretical tools used in the study of cognition. These tools include the traditional experiment of experimental psychology and protocol analysis as used by Johnson, Kochevar, and Zualkernan, as well as the survey and interview of sociology and social psychology as used by Strauss and Quinn. The chapters also reflect the development and application of new methodologies, in particular, those drawn from nonlinear dynamics, as exemplified by Turvey. The tools of this domain are of great interest not only for analysis of perception–action systems but also for the development of connectionist modeling. Moreover, nonlinear dynamics has provided a novel descriptive framework, extending the conceptualizations of a broad range of mental processes.

The second theme that unites the chapters is an emphasis on ecological constraints. This is, of course, not surprising in the chapters by Turvey and Gibson, both of whom acknowledge the strong influence of James Gibson's ecological approach. It is only slightly surprising in the chapters by Jenkins and Neisser, who have previously acknowledged their indebtedness to Gibson. It is more surprising in the chapters by Medin and by Johnson, Kochevar, and Zualkernan. In his discussion, Neisser suggests that "direct" perception be studied from Gibson's ecological perspective (akin to what Turvey refers to as *holonomic*) and that other aspects of cognition (e.g., categorization, problem solving, etc.) be studied from an information-processing perspective (based on nonholonomic principles). However, as Turvey points out, the nonholonomic systems are subject to holonomic or ecological constraints. Furthermore, it may be the case that computational approaches such as that of Koenderink (1986) are beginning to link holonomic and nonholonomic conceptualizations.

The term *ecological*, as James Gibson used it and as reflected in these chapters, means more than an everyday or common occurrence. However, an ecological analysis in the abstract sense does indeed imply an analysis that is relevant to everyday activities and events. This is probably why the study of cognition is beginning to make exciting progress in understanding complex everyday activities such as instruction (Glaser), expert systems (Johnson, Kochevar, and Zualkernan), and social institutions (Strauss and Quinn). Overall, the chapters in this book present a picture of cognitive psychology almost a century and a half after the inception of psychology as a self-conscious field. It is a picture of cognitive psychology again playing a pervasive role throughout the whole field. This central position occurs by virtue of abstract concepts and theoretical analyses that are not domain specific but apply to all aspects of mental processes. These analyses gain power by virtue of their application to all aspects of human endeavor from the very mundane to the most complex.

References

Anderson, J. R. (1978). Arguments concerning representations for mental imagery. *Psychological Review, 85,* 249–277.

Anderson, J. R. (1983). *The architecture of cognition.* Cambridge, MA: Harvard University Press.

Broadbent, D. E. (1958). *Perception and communication.* Elmsford, NY: Pergamon Press.

Holt, E. B. (1915). *The Freudian wish and its place in ethics.* Philadelphia: Winston.

Hull, C. L. (1943). *Principles of behavior.* New York: Appleton-Century-Crofts.

Humphrey, G. (1948). *Directed thinking.* New York: Dodd, Mead.

Koenderink, J. J. (1986). Optic flow. *Vision Research, 26,* 161–180.

Miller, G. A., Galanter, E., & Pribram, K. H. (1960). *Plans and the structure of behavior.* New York: Holt, Rinehart & Winston.

Neisser, U. (1967). *Cognitive psychology.* New York: Appleton-Century-Crofts.

Neisser, U. (1976). *Cognition and reality.* San Francisco: Freeman.

Selfridge, O. G. (1959). Pandemonium: A paradigm for learning. In D. V. M. Blake & A. M. Uttley (Eds.), *Proceedings of the Symposium on the Mechanism of Thought Processes.* London: HMSO.

Skinner, B. F. (1938). *The behavior of organisms.* New York: Appleton-Century-Crofts.

Tolman, E. C. (1932). *Purposive behavior in animals and men.* New York: Appleton-Century-Crofts.

Turing, A. M. (1950). Computing machinery and intelligence. *Mind, 59,* 433–460.

PART ONE

Relation Between Organism and Environment

The Organization and Reorganization of Categories: The Case of Speech Perception

James J. Jenkins

T he 1960s were revolutionary times. Students at the University of Minnesota's Center for Research in Learning, Perception, and Cognition—of which I was part of the original staff—could be recognized by the books they carried: a copy of Kuhn's (1962) *Structure of Scientific Revolutions* in one hand and Chomsky's (1957) *Syntactic Structures* in the other. We were trying to break away from the stimulus–response (S-R) conceptions that confined both theory and experimentation. The general topic of categorization, for example, did not then exist in the psychological literature. A Kantian notion of innate categories was so far out of tune with the zeitgeist that Boring (1950) gave Kant's philosophy only one paragraph in his *History of Experimental Psychology*: "Thus we may pass over Kantian philosophy for the excellent reason that it does not bear with sufficient directness on our subject matter" (p. 238).

It is difficult to recapture the state of experimental psychology 25 years ago: E. J. Gibson had not yet written her book *Perceptual Learning and Development* (E. J. Gibson, 1969; when she did, one of her colleagues expressed amazement that there was enough known to write a book about it), and J. J. Gibson had not yet published *The Senses Considered as Perceptual Systems* (J. J. Gibson, 1966). There were no studies of infant speech perception. There was almost no information about infant visual capabilities. The general field discussed today was still unnamed; Neisser had not yet published *Cognitive Psychology* (Neisser, 1967). Newell and Simon's (1972) *Human Problem Solving* was still 7 years in the future. Glaser was seriously pursuing programmed learning. Premack had completed his attack on simple notions of reinforcement (by means of the "Premack principle") and was just beginning to work with the chimpanzee Sarah. Kintsch was doing experiments in verbal learning. And Turvey was a graduate student just deciding to pursue psychology.

On the other hand, there were clear signs of the change of direction. Miller, Galanter, and Pribram's (1960) book, *Plans and the Structure of Behavior* was required reading as the most radical theoretical book of its time. And the wave of the future could be seen in Feigenbaum and Feldman's (1963) *Computers and Thought*, which made available a score of basic articles, ranging from Turing's (1950) "Computing Machinery and Intelligence," through Newell, Shaw, and Simon's (1957) logic machine article, to Hunt and Hovland's (1961) model of human concept formation.

Reading *Computers and Thought* (Feigenbaum & Feldman, 1963) today, however, reveals one pervasive and important bias of the period. Consider, for example, Turing's view of human nature in 1950.

> Instead of trying to produce a programme to simulate the adult mind, why not rather try to produce one which simulates the child's? If this were then subjected to an appropriate course of education one would obtain the adult brain. Presumably the child's brain is something like a notebook as one buys it from the stationer's. Rather little mechanism, and lots of blank sheets. (Mechanism and writing are from our point of view almost synonymous.) *Our hope is that there is so little mechanism in the child brain that something like it can be easily programmed* [italics added]. (p. 31)

John Locke could hardly have said it better.

In another context in the same article, however, Turing (1950) made a different, but related, point. He realized that if there were internal structure in a machine or program, it might be very difficult to determine what it was. In rebuttal to the claim that a machine could only produce predictable, routine behavior, he argued,

> But this does not seem to be the case. I have set up on the Manchester computer a small programme using only 1,000 units of storage whereby the machine supplied with one sixteen-figure number replies with another within two seconds. I would defy anyone to

learn from these replies sufficient about the programme to be able to predict any replies to untried values. (pp. 28–29)

From our current vantage point, we can see the dilemma clearly. If the machine (the child) has a great deal of structure and if that structure is arbitrary, capricious, or unsystematic, we may never be able to discover it. Turing chose the alternative—that the structure is essentially simple. Today, we have been driven to the position that the structure is complex; that is, the child comes to us (and must come to us) with preset sensitivities, dispositions, tendencies, capacities, abilities, and the like. If we are not willing to accept the notion that there are strong constraints on the organism, we cannot be optimistic about the possibility of success in psychology. A very important change in psychology in the past 25 years is just this realization that we (as organisms) must embody an elaborate set of constraints to acquire the complex behavior that we do, and we (as psychologists) must assume that these constraints are in some sense reasonable, orderly, and discoverable.

What might the constraints on the human organism be? At this point, we see the field branching into two different types of theories: *Modular theories* argue that as members of our species, we are born with special-purpose "devices" to accomplish tasks in given domains. One example might be a module devoted to the processing of speech signals. This might be characterized as the "speech-is-special" view. (See Mattingly & Studdert-Kennedy, 1991, for an extended treatment of this view.) *Process theories* postulate the development (usually through interactions of maturation and experience) of certain general processes that apply in many domains to perform similar tasks. One example might be the ability to create complex, multidimensional categories. In this view, the categorization of speech signals is just a particular instance of the general process at work. (See, e.g., Cohen, in press.)

Rather than attempt to choose between such theories, I will discuss speech perception as a particular, ecologically important case in which we are gaining new insights into both the origin and modification of perceptual categories. This topic is interesting for two reasons: first, because it is an important problem in a species-specific behavior domain and second, because this area has seen startling developments in the past 25 years.

Categories in Speech Perception

Evidence over the past 20 years from the studies of Moffitt (1971) and of Eimas, Siqueland, Jusczyk, and Vigorito (1971) to those of Werker (1989) and of Kuhl (1990) is congruent with the radical claim that preverbal infants can detect most, if not all, of the acoustic cues that distinguish phonetic categories in any language of the world. At the same time, infants do not appear to be responsive to those same kinds of physical differences in speechlike stimuli that do not mark phonetic distinctions in the world's languages. These findings are captured in the notion that infants are *language-universal perceivers.* Other studies over the same 20-year span, from Goto (1971) to Logan, Lively, and Pisoni (1991), make it clear that the ability to distinguish phonetic categories is not readily available to adults who are asked to differentiate phonetic distinctions that are different from those made in their own language. We may capture this situation by calling these adults *language-specific perceivers.*

The change in loss of phonetic-discrimination performance is clear in a classic pair of studies, both published in 1975. In the first, Miyawaki, Strange, Verbrugge, Liberman, Jenkins, and Fujimura (1975) studied the perception of /r/ and /l/ by American and Japanese adults. They found that Japanese adults could not reliably discriminate synthetic tokens of /ra/ and /la/, although the Japanese were not different from American listeners in discriminating the acoustic cue that served to differentiate /ra/ and /la/ when presented in isolation in a nonspeech context.

The experimenters first developed a series of 13 synthetic speech stimuli. The syllable at one end of the series was modeled after a good instance of an American-English syllable /ra/. The syllable at the other end of the series was modeled after an American-English /la/. The stimuli at the beginning and end of the series are shown in Figure 1. For intermediate synthetic syllables, moving along the series from /ra/ to /la/, the third formant (i.e., the third resonance of the vocal tract), originated at a higher frequency, starting at a position about 167 Hz (cycles per second) higher for each step. All other acoustic parameters of the stimuli were held constant. The change in the transition of the third formant was the only difference among the stimuli.

When American listeners were asked to identify the stimuli in terms of /r/ or /l/, they produced the result shown in Figure 2. Somewhere between the seventh and eighth stimuli, the syllables began to sound like /la/ to the American listeners and continued to sound like /la/ to the end of the series.

American and Japanese listeners were then tested for their ability to discriminate syllables taken from the series. The items to be discriminated were three steps apart (e.g., Stimulus 1 paired with Stimulus 4, 2 with 5, 3 with 6, etc). Thus, all discrimination pairs differed in the third formant frequency onset by the same amount in terms of physical acoustics. The results are shown in Figure 3.

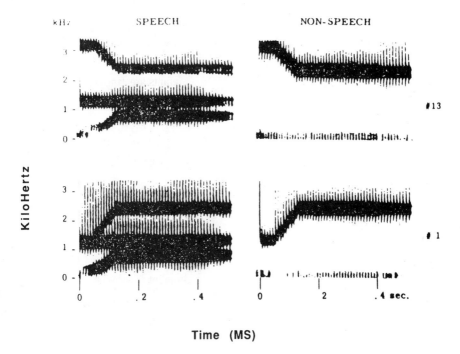

Time (MS)

FIGURE 1 Spectrograms of synthetic stimuli showing endpoints of the speech and nonspeech series. (The 1st and 13th members of the 13-step series heard as changing from /ra/ to /la/ in the speech case and as rising and falling glides in the nonspeech case. Adapted from Miyawaki et al., 1975. Used by permission.)

The overall results for American listeners show the typical findings of categorical perception; that is, the pooled identification function showed a sharp break (called the *phonetic category boundary effect*) from /r/ to /l/ identifications between the sixth and eighth stimuli. At the same time, the discrimination function showed a peak of relatively accurate discrimination for pairs across the category boundary (i.e., for pairs whose members were from different phonetic categories) but relatively poor performance within the phonetic categories (i.e., pairs whose members were from the same phonetic category). This finding is typically found for discrimination among consonants; it shows, surprisingly, that discrimination was little better than absolute identification. This means that American listeners readily detected the acoustic difference in the third formant when it marked the difference between phonetic categories but failed to detect a difference of the

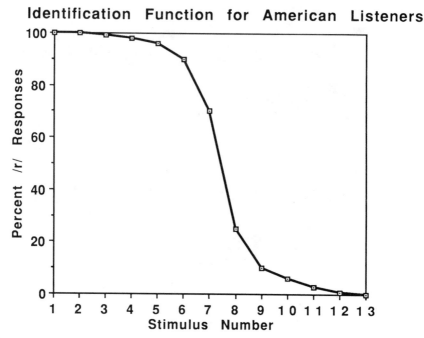

FIGURE 2 Identification function for American listeners. (American listeners hear syllables as /ra/, changing abruptly to /la/, between Stimuli 5 and 8. (Adapted from Miyawaki, et al., 1975. Used by permission.)

same physical magnitude when it fell within a speech category. (See Liberman, Cooper, Shankweiler, & Studdert-Kennedy, 1967, and Repp, 1984, for discussions of categorical perception of speech.)

In sharp contrast, the pooled Japanese discrimination function for these synthetic speech stimuli was relatively flat, only slightly above chance, and showed no discrimination peak in the vicinity of Stimuli 6, 7, and 8. This suggests that the Japanese listeners' difficulty with /r/ and /l/ was not merely a labeling or a production problem. As surprising as it may seem to a speaker of American English, the Japanese listeners did not hear the difference between the /r/ and /l/ that is so readily apparent to the American ear.

Finally, subjects were asked to discriminate between items taken from the isolated third formant series, the nonspeech series. The results are shown in Figure 4. Both the American and Japanese listeners showed highly accurate discrimination of all comparison

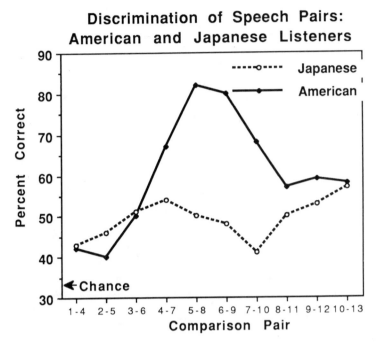

FIGURE 3   Discrimination of speech pairs by native speakers of American English and of Japanese. (The former showed good discrimination between syllable pairs across the phoneme boundary; the latter did not. Adapted from Miyawaki et al., 1975. Used by permission.)

pairs. This means that performance on the speech-syllable discrimination test was not a result of some physical inability to discriminate the relevant acoustical differences but, rather, that these differences did not function as meaningful cues when they were in the acoustic complex of speech.

The second classic study was conducted at the same time. Eimas (1975) used the identical synthetic stimuli to examine infants' sensitivities to differences in the syllables. Using a conditioning technique to test infants' discrimination of a sound change from one stimulus to another, Eimas showed that 2- and 3-month-old American infants discriminated synthetic speech syllables that crossed the American adult /r/–/l/ phonetic category boundary but did not discriminate syllables from within a phonetic category. That is, the infants discriminated Stimulus 5 and Stimulus 8 but did not discriminate Stimulus 1 and Stimulus 4 (both of which adults labeled /r/) or Stimulus 9 and Stimulus 12 (both of

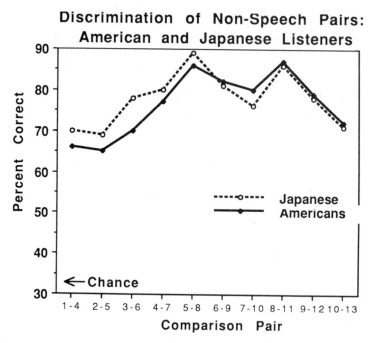

FIGURE 4 Discrimination of nonspeech pairs by native speakers of American English and of Japanese. (Both showed good discrimination of nonspeech pairs of glides. Adapted from Miyawaki et al., 1975. Used by permission.)

which adults labeled /l/). When Eimas tested infants' discrimination of the isolated third formant stimuli (the nonspeech condition), the infants did not discriminate between any of the stimulus pairs.

Although these data cannot support the notion that infants perceive the speech sounds in a truly categorical manner, they do support the interpretation that there is an innate sensitivity to acoustic differences in speech patterns that are used in languages to distinguish phonetic categories. If one assumes (as I do) that all normal human infants have essentially the same sensory equipment, it is reasonable to suppose that Japanese infants have the same innate sensory capabilities as American infants. The lack of exposure to a language with the /r/–/l/ distinction (as was the case for Japanese adults) must, then, markedly affect the individual's perception of these complex sounds later in life.

The findings of these two studies raise the following questions about origins of speech categories and the developmental course of the ability to discriminate speech sounds: First, how shall we describe the kinds of perceptual abilities that infants possess? Second, how are those abilities modified over time by children's experience? Third, in the case of adults learning a second language, can the process be reversed and, if so, what kind of training will accomplish the task? In what follows, I will briefly address each of these questions.

Infant Capabilities

Over the past 20 years, there has been a proliferation of studies of the speech perception abilities of the human infant. These studies have been reviewed recently by several different investigators who are active in the field (e.g., Aslin, Pisoni, & Jusczyk, 1983; Best, in press; Eimas, Miller, & Jusczyk, 1987; Kuhl, 1987). I will not attempt what they have already done so well but will point out what I take to be three major findings.

First, phoneme boundary effects in discrimination are routinely found in perceptual studies of young infants. Remarkably, they may be present even from the moment of birth. These effects have been found for every phonetic contrast that has been tested thus far. This implies, of course, that there is preattunement to the phonetically relevant aspects of the acoustic signal. Presumably, this is what enables infants to "break into" the speech stream that is around them, that is, to start to parse and differentiate classes of speech sounds in ways that will become linguistically meaningful.

Second, slightly older infants (by at least 6 months of age) readily display equivalence classification of discriminably different instances of phoneme classes. Striking examples are furnished by Kuhl (1979, 1983), who showed that infants could easily discriminate a variety of instances of the production of the vowel /a/ spoken by different voices but could also discriminate categorically between different versions of /a/ versus different versions of /i/, thus generalizing to the correct phonetic type classification in the midst of obvious token variation. Werker (1989) and Best (in press) have similarly shown that 6-month-olds can do this even for categories in languages to which they have not been exposed.

Finally, Kuhl and Meltzoff (1982, 1984) showed that 4- to 5-month-old infants could detect cross-modal similarities in visual and auditory speech signals. This was demonstrated by the fact that infants attended to a video of a face repeating a vowel that was currently being presented auditorially rather than the same face synchronously saying a vowel that was not being heard.

Overall, the evidence for phonetic boundary effects is quite compelling, and the evidence for the rapid formation of equivalence classes both intramodally and intermodally is very promising. Long before they begin to produce speech, children seem to be attuned to potential speech boundaries and seem capable of forming linguistically relevant perceptual categories.

Modification Over Time by Experience

A critical question is, When does this universal pattern of speech perception change to the language-specific pattern? Two major sources of information are available concerning the modification of these initial sensitivities and skills: studies of the loss of the ability to discriminate or categorize foreign speech sounds over time and studies of children and adults introduced to a new language community.

Studies of Infant Loss

First, consider the fate of nonnative distinctions in the natural course of development of the monolingual child. The investigator who has done the most compelling research on this subject is Werker (1989). In a recent series of studies using natural speech stimuli, Werker and her colleagues gathered data on speech perception from different age and language groups (Werker, Gilbert, Humphrey, & Tees, 1981; Werker & LaLonde, 1988; Werker & Tees, 1983, 1984). This research provides strong evidence that a "reorganization" of speech perception occurs by the infant's first birthday.

The research tested speech contrasts from English, Hindi, and Salish (a Canadian-Indian language). (None of the Hindi or Salish contrasts used in the study were phonemic in English.) In both cross-sectional and longitudinal studies involving subjects 6 to 12 months old, Werker and her colleagues showed that infants growing up in English-speaking homes lost their ability to differentiate the non-English consonant contrasts; at 6 months they could do so, but by age 11–12 months, the English-learning infants no longer differentiated the Hindi and Salish contrasts, although they continued to perform well on the English contrast. (Not surprisingly, 12-month-olds from Hindi- and Salish-speaking environments continued to discriminate the Hindi and Salish contrasts, respectively.) The investigators concluded that perceptual reorganization takes place as children start to learn the phonological structure of their first language. This reorganization appears to occur by the end of the first year, about the same time that children typically begin to produce their first words.

Recent work by Kuhl (1990, 1991) using new and sensitive techniques involving generalization from "prototypic" and "nonprototypic" synthetic vowels showed that language-specific prototype effects can be seen in infant vowel perception at the age of 6 months. Figure 5 illustrates Kuhl's technique. Adults were asked to judge the "goodness" of synthesized vowels that were distributed in a psychophysically calibrated vowel space. A vowel with high goodness ratings was judged to be a good prototype; a vowel with

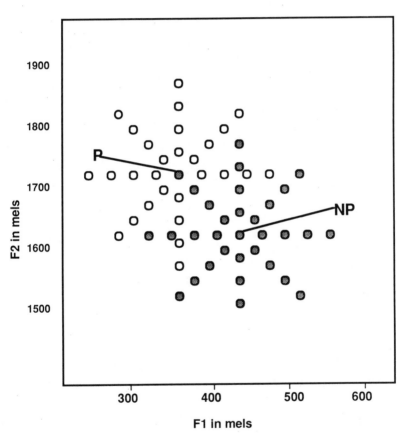

FIGURE 5   Kuhl's speech prototypes. (The /i/ prototype [P] is perceived to be more similar to its surrounding variants than the /i/ nonprototype [NP] is in relation to its variants, even though distance is controlled in the two cases. F1 and F2 are the frequencies of the first and second major resonances of the vocal tract, respectively. These resonances are called *formants*. Adapted from Kuhl, 1990. Used by permission.)

poor ratings was judged to be a nonprototype. Kuhl conducted conditioning procedures with infants using either the prototype or the nonprototype. Subsequent generalization testing showed that infants responded to more distant instances surrounding the prototype than they did to instances surrounding the nonprototype (Grieser & Kuhl, 1989). Kuhl viewed the prototype as a perceptual magnet that attracts surrounding examples to itself. (In the past, it would have been said that this stimulus showed greater "stimulus generalization.") Regardless of what it is called, the effect is clear and, Kuhl said, robust.

Because vowel systems differ radically (but in a semicontinuous fashion) from one language to another, this experiment offered an opportunity to study the emergence of language-specific skills in a quantitative fashion. A question that remained was how early the prototypes are differentiated in the behavior of infants growing up in different language communities.

To answer this question, Kuhl (1990) tested Swedish and American infants under exactly the same conditions. Because of the differences in Swedish and American vowel systems, it was possible to use two synthetic vowels, one of which was a prototype for American listeners and a nonprototype for Swedish listeners and another that was a nonprototype for American listeners and a prototype for Swedish listeners. The results were compelling. Kuhl wrote:

> The direction of the effect was consistent with the hypothesis that language experience even in the first 6 months of life, alters infants' phonetic perception. American infants demonstrated the prototype effect for stimuli surrounding the English vowel prototype. Swedish infants reversed this pattern; they demonstrated the effect for the Swedish vowel prototype. (p. 747)

Later Experience

Another question concerns the effects of later experience of children and adults with a new language community. Here, one finds both "experiments of nature" and instructional studies. Common experience suggests that at least some adults can learn to perceive and produce the phonemes of a second language as a function of massive amounts of practice and exposure to speaker–listener interactions in the language. In the case of the Japanese perception of /r/ and /l/, MacKain, Best, and Strange (1981) have provided relevant data. Their study examined identification and discrimination abilities of Japanese adults in the United States who had different amounts of experience with American English.

MacKain et al. (1981) divided native Japanese speakers into two groups on the basis of three criteria: length of time they had lived in the United States, amount of intensive conversational English training, and amount of interaction with native speakers of American English. They also tested a group of native speakers of American English for comparative purposes. The results of their study are shown in Figure 6. For native American English speakers, the findings were again typical of those showing categorical perception. The pooled identification function showed an abrupt crossover at the phonetic category boundary, and the discrimination functions showed marked peaks of relatively accurate discrimination in the neighborhood of that boundary.

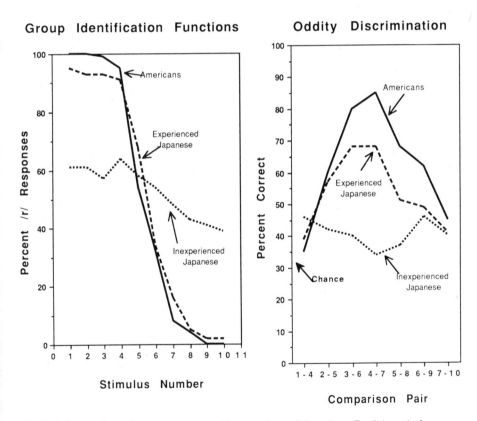

FIGURE 6. Speech perception by native speakers of American English and of Japanese with different amounts of experience. (American listeners and experienced Japanese listeners showed a steep identification boundary and good discrimination; the less experienced Japanese did not. Adapted from MacKain, Best, & Strange, 1981. Used by permission.)

In sharp contrast, the group of native Japanese speakers who had little experience with and instruction in spoken English showed identification functions that were nearly flat; that is, they responded little better than chance when they tried to identify the synthetic stimuli as *rock* or *lock*.

On the other hand, the native Japanese speakers with intensive conversational training and more exposure to and interaction with native speakers of American English produced fairly sharp boundaries on their identification functions. Their ability to identify and discriminate these synthetic syllables was only slightly different from that of the native American English speakers. MacKain et al. (1981) concluded that "the results are most encouraging, for they demonstrate that native Japanese speakers learning to converse in English as adults can achieve phonetic categorization of /r/ and /l/ that approximates the categorization behavior of native English speakers" (p. 387).

In another example, Williams (1980) examined children's perception of stimuli varying in voice onset time (e.g., the difference in English between /b/ and /p/). Williams studied native speakers of Puerto Rican Spanish who were learning English as their second language in the United States. (Spanish and English differ in the timing of the voicing boundary.) The children varied in both age (8–10 vs. 14–16 years old) and amount of exposure to English (0–6 months, 1.5–2 years, and 3–3.5 years).

The boundaries in identification functions for all the children fell between the boundaries observed for monolingual English speakers and monolingual Spanish speakers. The boundaries for Spanish-speaking children with more exposure to English were shifted more toward the English monolingual crossover. Also, within groups with equal amounts of exposure to English, the shifts toward English boundary values were greater in the younger children than in the older children, although this trend was not statistically reliable. Thus, as in the study by MacKain et al. (1981), the amount of language experience appeared to be an important factor influencing the modification of speech perception during the course of second-language learning. Whether age at which this exposure is experienced is a factor is still open to question (see Flege & Eefting, 1987, for some positive data).

In a remarkable study, Tees and Werker (1984) found that exposure to Hindi in the first 2 years of life (with no subsequent exposure) affected college performance in learning Hindi phonetics. Specifically, college students with such early experience learned to perceive the Hindi dental versus retroflex contrasts after only 2 weeks of study in their beginning Hindi course. Students without such early exposure were not able to perceive the most difficult Hindi contrast even after a full year of Hindi instruction.

If one were forced to give an opinion at this point, it would be reasonable to say that rather great amounts of exposure to, or intensive instruction in, a new language may be necessary for most adults to acquire nativelike facility in perception of new speech sounds. It also seems likely (although not proved as yet) that the earlier such experience is obtained, the better the final result. (These oversimplified generalizations ignore the complications introduced when one considers the variety of relations that may exist between the phonemic contrasts present in the first language and the new phonemic contrasts required in the second language. One must also note the complication of the very large individual differences that have routinely been found in these investigations. See Best, in press, and Best & Strange, in press, for a consideration of these issues and some hypotheses concerning the sources of second-language learning difficulties.)

Perceptual Training in the Laboratory

Overall, the experiments in laboratory training have broadened our horizons in several ways and sensitized us to a variety of variables, but, to date, they have had only limited success. A brief review will reveal some of the lessons learned so far and, perhaps, hint as to the directions to pursue.

The first lesson is that even successful laboratory training may not transfer to new materials. For example, Strange and Dittmann (1984) attempted laboratory training of the /r/–/l/ distinction with eight native speakers of Japanese. They used a synthetic stimulus series (from *rock* to *lock*) in an extensive course of discrimination training. Training involved a same/different discrimination task in which listeners attempted to discriminate series members against a "standard /r/" and a "standard /l/." Listeners received immediate feedback on each trial over an extensive training period (14 to 18 sessions with a total of approximately 2,500 training trials).

Gradual but substantial improvement in discrimination performance was observed during the course of training. Seven of the eight subjects showed generalization of training to more demanding identification and oddity discrimination tasks. Five out of seven subjects showed improvement on pre- and posttraining tests on a *rake–lake* synthetic series (but to a lesser extent than on the training materials). The effects of training did not generalize, however, to identification of natural productions of words containing initial /r/ and /l/.

Strange and Dittmann (1984) concluded that modification of perception of the /r/–/l/ contrast in adults appears in general to be "slow and effortful." They recommended that future studies should be designed in such a way that subjects learn to abstract the relevant parameters which differentiate the phonemes while ignoring the acoustic and phonetic contextual variations that are not distinctive with respect to the contrast. This would include training of the contrast with more than one set of stimuli and in more than one phonetic context. (p. 141)

Further training studies of /r/ and /l/ discrimination are being conducted. Logan et al. (1991), for example, recently summarized their work in this area. Briefly, these investigators trained native Japanese speakers on the perception of /r/ and /l/ with identification procedures rather than with discrimination procedures. In addition, their training materials were real words spoken by several different speakers (instead of synthetic stimuli) and included words with /r/ and /l/ in several different syllabic and phonetic contexts. An overview of their results is shown in Figure 7.

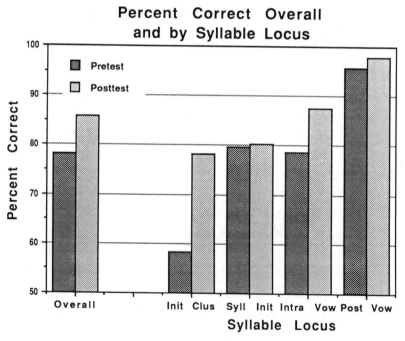

FIGURE 7.   Native Japanese speakers' scores on identification of /r/ and /l/ before and after training. (Improvement as a function of the syllabic context in which the phoneme appeared. Adapted from Logan et al., 1991. Used by permission.)

This study illustrates several typical findings. First, Logan et al. (1991) found an overall improvement in identification of about 8% (from about 78% on the pretest to about 86% on the posttest) as a result of 3 weeks of training. Second, the error rates for the subjects were different for different syllabic environments. (Even at the beginning there were very few errors in the perception of postvocalic /r/ and /l/, but perception of /r/ and /l/ in initial consonant clusters was almost at chance.) Third, the amount of improvement was different for different syllabic contexts. They found no improvement in the perception of initial /r/ and /l/ (e.g., *rock* vs. *lock*), which remained at about 80% correct. The largest improvement (from about 59% to about 79% correct) was in the identification of /r/ and /l/ in the context of a word-initial consonant cluster (e.g., *glass* vs. *grass*), the context for which identification was poorest in the pretests.

Another notable study of language training is that of Jamieson and Morosan (1986), which was the first study using synthetic training materials that was successful in demonstrating transfer to natural language examples. These investigators focused on teaching a difficult English voicing contrast to native French speakers (the difference between the *th* sound in *thigh* and in *thy*). They began identification training with extreme examples of pre- and postvoicing and gradually approached the English boundary as training progressed. This study, as well as others that have examined training in voicing (McClaskey, Pisoni, & Carroll, 1983; Pisoni, Aslin, Perey, & Hennessy, 1982; Tees & Werker, 1984), illustrates yet another facet of the problem, namely, that not all speech contrasts are of the same kind or of the same degree of difficulty. Timing differences, which furnish a robust cue to voicing contrasts, may be more accessible than the spectral differences that accompany contrasts in manner or place.

Complications

It is difficult to express concisely all of the issues involved in appraising our knowledge of perceptual training of speech contrasts. I find it useful to return to the tetrahedral model that I advanced some years ago (Jenkins, 1979). The model reminds us that experimentation in any cognitive domain must consider four major sources of factors that interact to determine the outcome of any particular study: (a) stimulus materials (e.g., natural vs. synthetic speech, the specific phonemic contrast involved, syllabic and phonetic contexts), (b) criterial tasks (e.g., identification, discrimination, single words, running speech), (c) orienting tasks (e.g., instructions, cognitive strategies, training regimes, identification, discrimination), and (d) differential characteristics of the subjects (e.g., particular native language, age, early experience, degree of experience with the nonnative language). Space does not permit me to develop these ideas here. A more detailed discussion of these factors can be found in Jenkins, Strange, and Polka (in press) and Strange (1990).

Conclusion

The evidence from developmental perception studies shows that prelinguistic infants are able to detect all or most of the differences in speech sounds that function to define phonetic classes in the languages of the world. This implies that infants are universal perceivers. By 1 year of age, however, it appears that infants have specialized so that they differentiate only the speech sounds that are important in the language that they are learning naturally. One view with which I currently tend to agree is that infants develop equivalence classes that serve to sharpen some of the natural boundaries and to suppress other boundaries that interfere with the equivalences or are simply irrelevant to them. With continued experience, categorization in terms of these abstract equivalence classes is highly practiced and brought to a state of automaticity. I think it is likely that the more isolated this process and the longer its duration, the harder it is for the individual to acquire a new set of distinctions that is incompatible with the first set (all other things being equal). The complete time course is not yet clear; the data at present are only suggestive. The field is rich with research problems and fortunate in having powerful techniques to find answers to these problems.

It is currently an open issue whether the picture that we see in the development of speech perception is at all like that in other domains. Banks and Krajicek (1991), in the recent *Annual Review of Psychology*, discussed Biederman's proposal regarding fundamental components for the recognition of visual objects under the provocative title "A 'Phonology' for Object Recognition." Can we take this seriously and turn the resources and techniques of speech perception research and developmental psychology loose on Biederman's "geons"? When looking at the proposal in detail, the parallels are not too close, but the suggestion is stimulating nonetheless.

Parallel research, of course, may come full circle and speak to the generality or specificity of the operators or the modules that various theorists are prone to propose. From my point of view, however, I would settle at this point for careful programs of descriptive research on the development and modification of perceptual categories in all domains. I think that it is time we gave Kant his turn in influencing the history of psychology.

References

Aslin, R. N., Pisoni, D. B., & Jusczyk, P. W. (1983). Auditory development and speech development in infancy. In M. M. Haith & J. J. Campos (Series Eds.), *Handbook of child psychology: Vol. 2. Infancy and developmental psychobiology* (4th ed., pp. 573–688). New York: Wiley.

Banks, W. P., & Krajicek, D. (1991). Perception. In M. R. Rosenzweig & L. W. Porter (Eds.), *Annual review of psychology* (Vol. 42, 305–331). Palo Alto, CA: Annual Reviews.

Best, C. T. (in press). The emergence of language-specific phonemic influences in infant speech perception. In H. C. Nussbaum & J. Goodman (Eds.), *The transition from speech sounds to spoken words: The development of speech perception.* Cambridge, MA: MIT Press.

Best, C. T., & Strange, W. (in press). Effects of language-specific phonological and phonetic factors on cross-language perception of approximants. *Journal of Phonetics.*

Boring, E. G. (1950). *A history of experimental psychology.* New York: Appleton-Century-Crofts.

Chomsky, N. (1957). *Syntactic structures.* The Hague: Mouton.

Cohen, L. B. (in press). Infant attention: An information processing approach. In M. J. Weiss & P. R. Zalazo (Eds.), *Newborn attention: Biological constraints and the influence of experience.* Norwood, NJ: Ablex.

Eimas, P. D. (1975). Auditory and phonetic coding of the cues for speech: Discrimination of the [r–l] distinction by young infants. *Perception & Psychophysics, 18,* 341–347.

Eimas, P. D., Miller, J. L., & Jusczyk, P. W. (1987). On infant speech perception and the acquisition of language. In S. Harnad (Ed.), *Categorical perception* (pp. 161–195). Cambridge, England: Cambridge University Press.

Eimas, P. D., Siqueland, E. R., Jusczyk, P., & Vigorito, J. (1971). Speech perception in infants. *Science, 171,* 303–306.

Feigenbaum, E. A., & Feldman, J. (1963). *Computers and thought.* New York: McGraw-Hill.

Flege, J. E., & Eefting, W. (1987). Production and perception of English stops by native Spanish speakers. *Journal of Phonetics, 15,* 67–83.

Gibson, E. J. (1969). *Principles of perceptual learning and development.* New York: Appleton-Century-Crofts.

Gibson, J. J. (1966). *The senses considered as perceptual systems.* Boston: Houghton Mifflin.

Goto, H. (1971). Auditory perception by normal Japanese adults of the sounds "L" and "R." *Neuropsychologia, 9,* 317–323.

Grieser, D., & Kuhl, P. K. (1989). Categorization of speech by infants: Support for speech-sound prototypes. *Developmental Psychology, 25,* 577–588.

Hunt, E. B., & Hovland, C. I. (1961). Programming a model of human concept formation. *Proceedings of the Western Joint Computer Conference, 19*, 145–155.

Jamieson, D. G., & Morosan, D. E. (1986). Training non-native speech contrasts in adults: Acquisition of the English /θ/–/ð/ contrast by francophones. *Perception & Psychophysics, 40*, 205–215.

Jenkins, J. J. (1979). Four points to remember: A tetrahedral model of memory experiments. In L. S. Cermak & F. I. M. Craik (Eds.), *Levels of processing in human memory* (pp. 429–446). Hillsdale, NJ: Erlbaum.

Jenkins, J. J., Strange, W., & Polka, L. (in press). Not everyone can tell a "rock" from a "lock": Assessing individual differences in speech perception. In R. V. Dawes & D. Lubinski (Eds.), *Assessing individual differences in human behavior*. Minneapolis: University of Minnesota Press.

Kuhl, P. K. (1979). Speech perception in early infancy: Perceptual constancy for spectrally dissimilar vowel categories. *Journal of the Acoustical Society of America, 66*, 1668–1679.

Kuhl, P. K. (1983). Perception of auditory equivalence classes for speech in early infancy. *Infant Behavior and Development, 6*, 263–285.

Kuhl, P. K. (1987). Perception of speech and sound in early infancy. In P. Salapatek & L. B. Cohen (Eds.), *Handbook of infant perception* (Vol. 2). San Diego, CA: Academic Press.

Kuhl, P. K. (1990). Toward a new theory of the development of speech perception. In *Proceedings of the International Conference on Spoken Language Processing* (Vol. 2, pp. 745–748). Kobe, Japan: Acoustical Society of Japan.

Kuhl, P. K. (1991). Human adults and human infants exhibit a "prototype effect" for speech sounds: Monkeys do not. *Perception & Psychophysics, 50*, 93–107.

Kuhl, P. K., & Meltzoff, A. (1982). The bimodal perception of speech in infancy. *Science, 218*, 1138–1141.

Kuhl, P. K., & Meltzoff, A. (1984). The intermodal representation of speech in infants. *Infant Behavior and Development, 7*, 361–381.

Kuhn, T. S. (1962). *The structure of scientific revolutions*. Chicago: University of Chicago Press.

Liberman, A. M., Cooper, F. S., Shankweiler, D. P., & Studdert-Kennedy, M. (1967). Perception of the speech code. *Psychological Review, 74*, 431–461.

Logan, J. S., Lively, S. E., & Pisoni, D. B. (1991). Training Japanese listeners to identify English /r/ and /l/: A first report. *Journal of the Acoustical Society of America, 89*, 874–886.

MacKain, K. S., Best, C. T., & Strange, W. (1981). Categorical perception of English /r/ and /l/ by Japanese bilinguals. *Applied Psycholinguistics, 2*, 369–390.

Mattingly, I. G., & Studdert-Kennedy, M. (Eds.). (1991). *Modularity and the motor theory of speech perception*. Hillsdale, NJ: Erlbaum.

McClaskey, C. L., Pisoni, D. B., & Carroll, T. D. (1983). Transfer of training of a new linguistic contrast in voicing. *Perception & Psychophysics, 34*, 323–330.

Miller, G. A., Galanter, E., & Pribram, K. (1960). *Plans and the structure of behavior*. New York: Holt.

Miyawaki, K., Strange, W., Verbrugge, R. R., Liberman, A. M., Jenkins, J. J., & Fujimura, O. (1975). An effect of linguistic experience: The discrimination of /r/ and /l/ by native speakers of Japanese and English. *Perception & Psychophysics, 18*, 331–340.

Moffitt, A. R. (1971). Consonant cue perception by twenty- to twenty-four week old infants. *Child Development, 42*, 717–731.

Neisser, U. (1967). *Cognitive psychology*. New York: Appleton-Century-Crofts.

Newell, A., Shaw, J. C., & Simon, H. (1957). Empirical exploration with the Logic Theory Machine. *Proceedings of the Western Joint Computer Conference, 15*, 218–239.

Newell, A., & Simon, H. (1972). *Human problem solving*. Englewood Cliffs, NJ: Prentice-Hall.

Pisoni, D. B., Aslin, R. N., Perey, A. J., & Hennessy, B. L. (1982). Some effects of laboratory training on identification and discrimination of voicing contrasts in stop consonants. *Journal of Experimental Psychology: Human Perception and Performance, 8*, 297–314.

Repp, B. (1984). Categorical perception: Issues, methods, findings. In N. J. Lass (Ed.), *Speech and language: Vol. 10. Advances in basic research and practice* (pp. 243–335). San Diego, CA: Academic Press.

Strange, W. (1990, November). *Learning non-native phoneme contrasts: Interactions among subject, stimulus, and task variables*. Paper presented at ATR Workshop on Speech Perception and Production, Kyoto, Japan.

Strange, W., & Dittmann, S. (1984). Effects of discrimination training on the perception of /r–l/ by Japanese adults learning English. *Perception & Psychophysics, 36*, 131–145.

Tees, R. C., & Werker, J. F. (1984). Perceptual flexibility: Maintenance or recovery of ability to discriminate non-native speech sounds. *Canadian Journal of Psychology, 38*, 579–590.

Turing, A. M. (1950). Computing machinery and intelligence. *Mind, 59*, 433–460.

Werker, J. F. (1989). Becoming a native listener. *American Scientist, 77*, 54–59.

Werker, J. F., Gilbert, J. H. V., Humphrey, K., & Tees, R. C. (1981). Developmental aspects of cross-language speech perception. *Child Development, 52*, 349–353.

Werker, J. F., & LaLonde, C. E. (1988). Cross-language speech perception: Initial capabilities and developmental change. *Developmental Psychology, 24*, 672–683.

Werker, J. F., & Tees, R. C. (1983). Developmental changes across childhood in the perception of non-native speech sounds. *Canadian Journal of Psychology, 37*, 278–286.

Werker, J. F., & Tees, R. C. (1984). Cross-language speech perception: Evidence for perceptual reorganization during the first year of life. *Infant Behavior and Development, 7*, 49–63.

Williams, L. (1980). Phonetic variation as a function of second-language learning. In G. H. Yeni-Komshian, J. F. Kavanagh, & C. A. Ferguson (Eds.), *Child Phonology: Vol. 2. Perception* (pp. 185–215). San Diego, CA: Academic Press.

CHAPTER 2

"Filling In" Versus Finding Out: A Ubiquitous Confusion in Cognitive Science

Daniel C. Dennett

B ooks and articles on cognitive science frequently state that the brain does a lot of "filling in"—(note the scare quotes). My claim is that this is *not* a safe bit of shorthand, or an innocent bit of temporizing, but a source of deep confusion and error. The phenomena described in terms of "filling in" are real, surprising, and theoretically important, but it is a mistake to conceive of them as instances of something being filled in because the vivid phrase *filling in* always *suggests* too much—sometimes a little too much but often much too much. The following examples should illustrate my point.

Many experiments have demonstrated the existence of apparent motion, or the phi phenomenon. If two or more small spots separated by as much as 4 degrees of visual angle are briefly lit in rapid succession, a single spot will seem to move. Nelson Goodman once asked Paul Kolers whether the phi phenomenon would persist if the two illuminated spots were different in color, and if so, what would happen to the color of "the" spot as "it" moved. Would the illusion of motion disappear and be replaced by two separately flashing spots? Would the illusory "moving" spot gradually change from one color to another, tracing a trajectory through the color solid? The answer, when Kolers and von Grünau (1976) performed such experiments, was striking: The spot seemed to begin moving and then change color abruptly in the middle of its illusory passage toward the second location.

As Goodman described the phenomenon, "each of the intervening places along a path between the two flashes is *filled in* [italics added] . . . with one of the flashed colors rather than with successive intermediate colors" (Goodman, 1978, p. 85). This seems to raise metaphysically vertiginous problems about time. As Goodman wondered, "How are we able . . . to fill in the spot at the intervening place-times along a path running from the first to the second flash *before that second flash occurs?*" (p. 73).

How indeed is this possible? Eccles (1977) went so far as to say that to explain such effects, one must admit that "the self-conscious mind . . . plays tricks with time" (p. 364)—real Twilight Zone stuff—backwards causation and all that.

However, according to Libet (1981), there is an uncontroversial precedent of *spatial* filling in: "There is experimental evidence for the view that the subjective or mental 'sphere' could indeed 'fill in' spatial and temporal gaps" (p. 196). Libet (1985) suggested as an example "the neurologically well-known phenomenon of subjective "filling in" of the missing portion of a blind area in the visual field" (p. 567).

This is not just neurologically well-known; almost everybody knows that the blind spot in each eye is "filled in" by the brain. There is also auditory "filling in." When one listens to speech, gaps in the acoustic signal can be "filled in"—for instance, in the "phoneme restoration effect" (Warren, 1970). Jackendoff (1987) put it this way:

> Consider, for example, speech perception with noisy or defective input—say, in the presence of an operating jet airplane or over a bad telephone connection. . . . What one constructs . . . is not just an intended meaning but a phonological structure as well: one "hears" more than the signal actually conveys. . . . In other words, phonetic information is "filled in" from higher-level structures as well as from the acoustic signal; and though there is a difference in how it is derived, there is no qualitative difference in the completed structure itself. (p. 99)

When one reads text, something similar (but visual) occurs. As Baars (1988) put it, "We find similar phenomena in the well-known 'proofreader effect,' the general finding that spelling errors in page proofs are difficult to detect because the mind 'fills in' the correct information" (p. 173).

Margolis (1987), in *Patterns, Thinking and Cognition*, added an uncontroversial commentary on the whole business of "filling in": "The 'filled-in' details are ordinarily correct" (p. 41).

These authors are not alone. Who among us has not felt the temptation to speak of the brain "filling in" one gap or another? And many have succumbed to the temptation in print: Some writers use scare-quotes, some use italics, and some use the term neat, without apology or warning. But even those who wield the phrase without a warning label (e.g., Goodman, 1978) often make it clear by other stylistic devices that they realize that there is something faintly misleading or in-need-of-further-elaboration, or maybe just plain wrong, about this way of speaking. They suggest that it is, at best, a useful shorthand. I think it is worse than that.

The tacit recognition that there is *something* suspect about the idea of "filling in," if taken literally, is manifested in the following passage from Hardin's (1988) book *Color for Philosophers*:

> Consider the receptorless optic disk, or "blind spot," formed where the bundle of optic fibers leaves the retina for the brain. We recall that this area is only 16 degrees removed from the center of vision. It covers an area with a 6 degree visual diameter, enough to hold the images of ten full moons placed end to end, and yet there is no hole in the corresponding region of the visual field. This is because the eye-brain fills in with whatever is seen in the adjoining regions. If that is blue, it fills in blue; if it is plaid, we are aware of no discontinuity in the expanse of plaid. (p. 22)

Hardin just could not bring himself to say that the brain fills in the plaid because this suggests, surely, quite a sophisticated bit of "construction," like the fancy "invisible mending" one can pay good money for to fill in the hole in one's herringbone jacket: All the lines line up, and all the shades of color match across the boundary between old and new. It seems that filling in blue is one thing—all it would take is a swipe or two with a cerebral paintbrush loaded with the right color—but filling in plaid is something else, and it is more than he can bring himself to assert.

But as Hardin's (1988) comment reminds us, we are just as oblivious of our blind spots when confronting a field of plaid as when confronting a uniformly colored expanse, so whatever it takes to create that oblivion can as readily be accomplished by the brain in either case. As Hardin said, "We are aware of no discontinuity." But if the brain does not have to fill in the gap with plaid, why should it bother filling in the gap with blue? In neither case, presumably, is "filling in" a matter of *literally* filling in—of the sort that would require something like paintbrushes. No one, surely, thinks that "filling in" is a matter of the brain's actually going to the trouble of covering some spatial expanse with pigment (or some temporal expanse with acoustical vibrations). The real, upside-down image on the retina is, of course, the *last* stage of vision at which there is anything colored in the unproblematic ways that reflective physical surfaces are colored. Because there is no *literal* mind's eye, there is no use for pigment in the brain. Still, one may be inclined to think that there is something that happens in the brain that is in some important way analogous to covering an area with pigment, otherwise one would not want to talk of "filling in" at all. As Jackendoff (1987) said, speaking of the auditory case, "One 'hears' more than the actual signal conveys" (p. 91)—but note that still he put *hears* in scare-quotes. What could it be that is *present* when one "hears" sounds filling silent times or "sees" colors spanning empty spaces? It does seem that *something* is *there* in these cases, something the brain has to *provide* (by "filling in"). What should one call this unknown whatever-it-is? I propose calling it *figment*. The temptation, then, is to suppose that there is something, made out of *figment*, that is *there* when the brain "fills in" and not there when it does not bother "filling in."

Put so baldly, this hunch will inspire few if any converts. The whole idea of figment looks ridiculous (if I have done my job well). It *is* ridiculous. There is no such stuff as figment. The brain does not make figment; the brain does not use figment to fill in the gaps; figment is just a figment of my imagination. And I suppose that you are all inclined to agree. What, then, *does* "filling in" mean? What *could* it mean if it does not mean filling in with figment? To put it bluntly, if there is no such medium as figment, how does "filling in" differ from *not bothering to fill in*?

It will help to find a sane view if one considers two different ways in which the following representations might be filled in. Figure 1 has information about shapes but no information about colors. Figure 2 has information about colors as well, in the form of a numbered code. For instance, one can tell that two different regions are the same color by determining that they are assigned the same number—the sort of discrimination job a computer is good at. If one were to take colored crayons or pens and fill in the regions with the indicated colors, one would have another way in which color information could be filled in—with real color, real pigment. An obvious question is whether the regions in Figure 2 as it stands are "filled in" or not. In one sense, they are, because any procedure that needs to be informed about the color of a region can, by mechanical inspection of that region, extract that information. This is purely informational filling in, and the system is entirely arbitrary, of course. One can readily construct infinitely many functionally equivalent systems of representation involving different coding systems or different media. Computer graphics systems such as CAD systems, for instance, represent the colors

FIGURE 1   Parrot without labels.

of regions in such a fashion. The regions are represented as ordered n-tuples of points in a virtual three-space ("connect the dots," in effect).

If one makes a colored picture on one's PC using PC-Paintbrush, when one stores the picture on a disk, a compression algorithm does something similar: It divides the area into like-colored regions and stores the region boundaries and their color number in an "archive" file rather than storing the color value at each pixel in a bit map, the alternative illustrated in Figure 3. A bit map is yet another form of color-by-numbers, but by explicitly labeling each pixel, it is a form of roughly continuous representation—the roughness a function of the resolution of the pixels. A third way of storing the image on one's computer screen would be to take a color photograph and store the image on, say, a 35mm slide.

These are importantly different representational systems. In the case of the 35mm slide, there is actual dye, literally filling in a region of real space. This, like the bit map, is a continuous representation of the depicted spatial regions (continuous down to the grain of the film, of course). But unlike the bit map, color is used to represent color. (A color

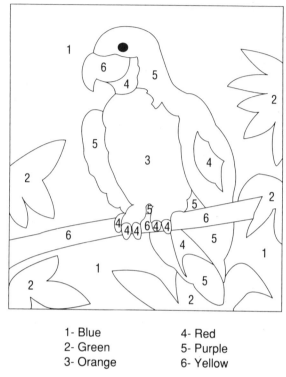

1- Blue   4- Red
2- Green   5- Purple
3- Orange   6- Yellow

FIGURE 2   Parrot with "color-by-number" labels.

negative also uses color to represent color but in an inverted mapping.) Videotape is another medium of roughly continuous representation, but what is stored on the tape is not literally images but recipes for forming images. A bit map is also not literally an image but is just an array of values, another sort of recipe for forming an image. An archive file storing the results of a compression algorithm is still another recipe for forming an image, and it can be just as accurate, although it forms the image by generalizing over regions, labeling each region only once.

Here, then, are three ways of "filling in" color information: color-by-colors, color-by-bit-map, and color-by-numbers. Color-by-numbers is in one regard a way of "filling in" color information, but it achieves its efficiency, compared with the others, precisely because it does *not* bother filling in values explicitly for each pixel.

```
1111111111111111111111111111111111111111111111111
1111111111111111111111111111111111111111111111111
1111111111111111111155551111111111111111111111111
11111111111111111155555555551111111111111111111111
111111111111111115555●555551111111111111111111111
1111111111111116666666644555511111111111111222222
1111111111111666666666445555511111111111111122222
1111111111111666666664445555511111111111112222222
1111111111111661114444455555511111111112222222222
111111111111111111133333335555555511111111111122222
111111111111111111133333333335555555555111111122222222
111111111111111155533333333333335555555511111111122222
1111111111111155553333333333333355555555111111222222
11111111111111155553333333333333335554555551112221122
111111112221115555333333333333355544555551111111122
11112222221111555533333333333333355444455551111111122
12222222211111555533333333333333355444455511111111111
222222221111111555533333333333333355444455511111111111
22222221111111111555533333333333333355554455511222222
2222222111111111155553333333333333355555555112222222
2222222211111111115555333333333333555555555666662222
2221122211111111111153333533333336666666666666622212
1222111111111111111166433336643466666666666661111122112
11111111666666666666444446644464455555555111211112
1666666666666666111111111115555444555555111111111
6666666666111111111111111115555444445555551111111111
6666111122111111111111111111155445554455511111111111
111122221111111111111111111111545555555512222211111
1222222211111111111112222222111225555555522222222111
22222222222211111111122222222212222255555222222221
2222222222222221111111112222222222222222222211111111
2222111222221111111111111112222222222222222211111111
```

FIGURE 3   Parrot as bit map.

Computers code for colors with numbers in registers, and no one thinks that the brain uses numbers in registers to code for colors. But that is a red herring; numbers in registers can be understood to stand for any system of magnitudes, any system of vectors, that a brain might use as a "code" for colors; it might be neural firing frequencies, or some system of addresses or locations in neural networks, or any system of physical variations. Numbers in registers have the useful property of preserving *relations* between physical magnitudes while remaining neutral about any "intrinsic" properties of such magnitudes. Although numbers *can* be used in an entirely arbitrary way to code for colors, they can also be used in nonarbitrary ways to reflect the structural relations between colors that have been discovered. The "color solid" is a logical space ideally suited to a numerical treatment—any numerical treatment that reflects the betweenness relations, the oppositional and complementary relations, and so on. Certainly, the more we learn about how the brain codes colors, the more powerful a *numerical* model of human color vision we will be able to devise.

The trouble with describing the brain as "coding" for colors by using intensities or magnitudes of one thing or other is that it suggests to the unwary that eventually these codings have to be *decoded* to get "back to color." (This is as if the brain might store color information about a parrot once seen in the form shown in Figure 2 but then arrange to have the representation "decoded" into "real colors" on special occasions.) No one takes the idea seriously, of course. Everyone recognizes that I introduced the idea of *literally* filling in the color-by-numbers parrot with pigment as a sort of joke, to remind you of a sort of limiting case view that nobody takes seriously. But to make sure, consider the phenomenon of *neon color spreading* (van Tuijl, 1975).

If the gray lines in Figure 4 were bright red, one would see a pink glow filling in the region of the ring, following the subjective contours. The pink seen would not be a

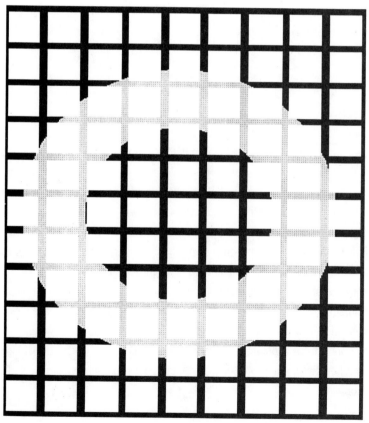

FIGURE 4   van Tuijl (1975) neon color spreading.

result of pink smudging of the figure or light scattering. The pink glow would be an entirely internal phenomenon; in other words, there would be no pink on one's *retinal* image (just the red or deep pink lines). How might this illusion be explained? Presumably, one brain circuit, specializing in shape, is (mis)led to distinguish a particular bounded region (the ring with its "subjective contours" or the Ehrenstein circle), while another brain circuit, specializing in color but rather poor on shape and location, comes up with a color discrimination (e.g., Pink #97) with which to "label" something in the vicinity, and the label gets attached (or "bound") to the whole region (see Figure 5). Why these particular discriminations should occur under these conditions is still controversial, but the controversy concerns the causal mechanisms generating the mislabeling of the region, not the further "products" (if any) of the visual system.

I suspect, however, that some will feel dissatisfied with this model of what happens in the neon color spreading effect. It stops short at an explanation that provides a labeled color-by-numbers region: Does that recipe for a colored image not have to be *executed* somewhere? Does not Pink #97 have to be "filled in"? After all, one might be tempted to insist (on seeing the illusion) that one *sees* the pink. (One certainly does not

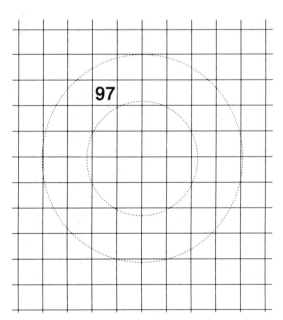

FIGURE 5   Pink #97 region label.

see an outlined region with a number written in it.) The pink one sees is not in the outside world (it is not pigment or dye or "colored light"), so it must be "in here"—pink figment, in other words.

If one were to insist that one thought that somewhere in the brain there is a roughly continuous representation of colored regions—a bit map—such that "each pixel" in the region has to be labeled "Color #97" (see Figure 6), this would at least be an empirical possibility that one could devise experiments to explore. The question would be, Is there a representational medium here in which the value of some variable parameter (the intensity or whatever that codes for color) has to be transmitted across or replicated across the relevant pixels of an array, or is there just a "single label" of the region, with no further "filling in" or "spreading out" required? That is a good empirical question, and I will not prejudge it. (It would certainly be impressive, for instance, if the color could be shown under some conditions to spread slowly in time—bleeding out from the central red lines and gradually reaching out to the subjective contour boundaries.) But that is an unresolved empirical question about whether the representational medium is captured by something like Figure 5 or by something like Figure 6. It is not a question about whether there is anything filled in with figment.

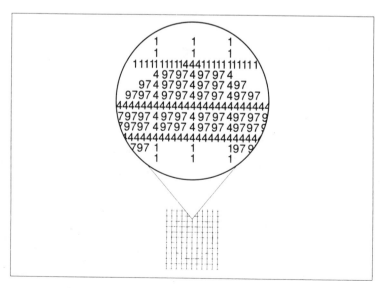

FIGURE 6   Pink #97 as bit-mapped region.

With some different models of filling in with which to work, I return to the first case, the phi phenomenon with the midcourse color switch. What might "filling in" come to in this case, and what are the alternatives?

First, I want to be clear about just how vivid the experience is for subjects. In studies by Kolers and von Grünau (1976) using these stimuli, even on the first trial (i.e., without conditioning), subjects reported seeing the color of the moving spot switch in midtrajectory from red to green—a report sharpened by the experimenters' use of a pointer device that subjects retrospectively, but as soon as possible "superimposed" on the trajectory of the illusory moving spot. Such pointer locations had the content: "The spot changed color right about *here*" (p. 330). In other words, it was not just that the subjects said retrospectively, that they guessed or surmised that the spot must have changed color suddenly somewhere along the path; they claimed to *recall* the color change, and they *pointed to* the place on the trajectory where it seemed to them to have happened.

Does that not *establish* that there has to have been a (roughly) continuous representation of the moving spot, a representation generated by the brain somehow and somehow interposed between the representations it was "given" by the two stimuli? No, it does not. All it establishes is that soon after the brain discriminates the second stimulus, it arrives at the interpretation that a single object has been in motion, with a color change occurring just about *there*. (You understood the sentence I just spoke—I did not *have* to draw you a picture. The brain does not have to draw itself pictures either if it can understand its own interpretations.)

Note that I am not saying that there *could not* be some form of continuous brain representation of the spot at successive place-times, as Goodman puts it, but just that there *need not* be on the evidence so far considered. It does *not* follow from the undeniable fact that it *seems* to the subject as if there has been continuous motion of the spot (with an abrupt midcourse color change). This is a crucial pivot point in a host of arguments. To review, consider the argument one might pose regarding a subject in Kolers and von Grünau's (1976) experiment:

1. It definitely does seem to the subject as if there has been continuous motion of the spot from left to right.

So, on standard materialist assumptions, it follows that

2. There has been representation of some sort in the subject's brain of the spot being (or having been) in continuous motion. But it does *not* follow that

3. there has been continuous (or even roughly continuous) representation of the motion of the seeming spot by means of a succession of "frames" or something like that.

The sentence

4. *The moon goes round the earth in an elliptical orbit* is a representation of the moon as being in continuous motion, but it is not itself a continuous or even roughly continuous representation of the moon's motion. A continuous representation is not needed to represent motion as continuous, and as color-by-numbers shows, a homogeneous representation is not needed to represent a property as homogeneous. In general, one can not read the properties of a representational medium directly off the properties represented by it. But often it is tempting to make this illicit inference.

When people learn of the color phi phenomenon, I find that their first impromptu model posits something like a delay loop for the representation of the actual stimuli (the red and green spots) so that the brain has time, in a sort of editing studio somewhere between the eyes and "consciousness," to interpolate a few frames to "fill in" the temporal and spatial gap between the two stimuli (Frames A and B) with some meaningful transition (see Figure 7). Goodman succumbed to this temptation. The idea is that these interpolated frames must be provided by the brain for the eventual *presentation* to . . . to whom? To the audience in the Cartesian Theater. But this supposed presentation process is entirely gratuitous. Why should the brain bother *making* Frames C and D if, down in

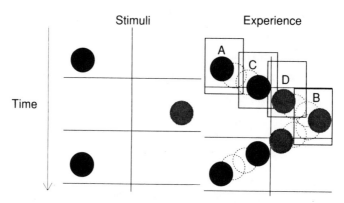

FIGURE 7   Color phi with Frames A, B, C, and D.

the editing studio, it has already arrived at the interpretation of the stimuli as an instance of motion-with-color-change? For whose benefit would all this painting be done? There is no further act of interpretation needed, and indeed, there is no one in the brain to look at Frames C and D.[1]

The brain engages in interpretation or discrimination all the time, at all levels, but there is a natural tendency to think of all interpretation as *deferred* until it can be done "in consciousness" (by the Self, presumably). And *if* interpretation were so deferred, then it would stand to reason that the interpretations accomplished by the Self would have to be based on something "in consciousness." Thus, people are attracted to the idea of the brain having to provide that basis in some sort of re-presentation (in a relatively uninter- preted format) of the data on which it has already based its interpretations. There is a tendency, in other words, to think of "filling in" as something the brain has to do to pro- vide the Self with the evidence—the "sense data," to speak in antique terms—on which to make judgments.

But the question of whether the brain "fills in" in one way or another is not a ques- tion on which introspection by itself can bear because introspection provides us—the subject as well as the "outside" experimenter—only with the content of representation, not with the features of the representational medium itself. For evidence about that, one would need to conduct further experiments.[2]

For some phenomena, one can already be quite sure that the form of representa- tion is a version of color-by-numbers, *not* a version of bit mapping. Consider how the brain must deal with wallpaper, for instance. Suppose you walk into a room and notice that the wallpaper is a regular array of hundreds of identical sailboats, or portraits of Marilyn Monroe. Obviously, you do not foveate, and do not have to foveate, each of the identical images in order to see the wallpaper *as* hundreds of identical images of Marilyn Monroe. Your foveal vision identifies *one* or a *few* of these and somehow your visual system just generalizes—arrives at the conclusion that the rest is "more of the same." We know that the images of Marilyn that never get examined by foveal vision *cannot* be identified by parafoveal vision—it simply lacks the resolution to distinguish

---

[1] In their article "Time and the Observer: The Where and When of Consciousness in the Brain," Dennett and Kinsbourne (in press) show that this delay-loop editing hypothesis is worse than gratuitous; it is contradicted by behavioral evidence about reaction times.

[2] For instance, Shepard and Cooper's (1982) initial experiments with the mental rotation of cube diagrams showed that it cer- tainly seemed to subjects that they harbored roughly continuously rotating representations of the shapes that they were imag- ing, but it took further experiments that probed the actual temporal properties of the underlying representations to provide partial confirmation of the hypothesis that subjects were actually doing what they thought they were doing.

Marilyn from various Marilyn-shaped blobs. Nevertheless, what you see is not wallpaper of Marilyn in the middle surrounded by various indistinct Marilyn-shaped blobs; what you see is wallpaper composed of hundreds of identical Marilyns. Now, it is a virtual certainty that *nowhere in the brain* is there a representation of the wall that has high-resolution bit maps that reproduce, Xerox-wise, the high-resolution image of Marilyn that you have foveated. The brain certainly would not go to the trouble of doing *that* filling in. Having identified a single Marilyn, and having received no information to the effect that the other blobs are *not* Marilyns, it *jumps to the conclusion* that the rest are Marilyns and *labels* the whole region "more Marilyns" without any further rendering of Marilyn at all. Of course, it does not seem that way to you. It seems to you as if you are actually seeing hundreds of identical Marilyns. And in one sense, you are: There are, as I said, hundreds of identical Marilyns on the wall, and you are seeing them. What is *not* the case, however, is that there are hundreds of identical Marilyns represented in your brain. The brain just represents *that* there are hundreds of identical Marilyns.

Experiments with wallpaper would no doubt show a lot about the generalization powers of vision. By making small or great variations in the pattern of repetitions, and seeing how gross the failures of generalization have to be before subjects notice, one can learn about the powers of discernment and the conditions of generalization. (In fact, in your youth you already participated in such informal experiments. Recall the picture puzzles in which your task is to discover which two clowns, in the row of apparently identical clowns, are the twins. This is usually a slow and difficult visual task.)

It is now understandable how one can be oblivious to one's blindspot, even when looking at a plaid surface. The brain does not have to "fill in" for the blind spot because the region in which the blind spot falls is already labeled. If the brain received contradictory evidence from some region, it would abandon or adjust its generalization, but *not getting any evidence* from the blind-spot region is not the same as *getting contradictory evidence*. The absence of confirming evidence from the blindspot region is no problem for the brain; because the brain has no precedent of getting information from that gap of the retina, it has not developed any epistemically hungry agencies demanding to be fed from that region. Among all the homunculi of vision, not a single one has the role of coordinating information from that region of each eye, so when no information arrives from those sources, no one complains. The area is simply neglected.

In other words, all normally sighted people "suffer" from tiny bit of "anosognosia"; they are (normally) unaware that they are receiving no visual information from their blind spots. The difference between normal people and sufferers of pathological neglect or other forms of anosognosia is that some of their complainers have been killed. (Kinsbourne, 1980, called them "cortical analyzers.")

This suggests a fundamental principle, which can be applied more widely to cases of putative filling in, namely, the thrifty producer principle: If no one is going to look at it, don't waste effort providing it.[3]

The brain's job is not "filling in." The brain's job is *finding out.*[4] Once the brain has made a particular discrimination (e.g., of motion or of the uniformity of color in an area), the task of interpretation is done; no further presentation of the "evidence" on which it is based is required, and hence no further *rendering* of the evidence for the benefit of the "judge." Applying the thrifty producer principle, it is clear that any further representations with special representational properties would be gratuitous. But it certainly does not seem that way from the "first-person point of view." Consider the following spuriously compelling line of reasoning:

1. For something to seem to happen, something else must really happen; namely, a *real seeming-to-happen* must happen. (This is just a tautology, of course.) For example, for something to seem red to somebody, a real seeming-red-to-somebody must happen.

2. But a real seeming-red-to-somebody cannot *just* consist in somebody judging or thinking that something seems red.

(Why not? Because there is a difference between a subject [merely] *judging* that something seems red and something really or actually seeming red to the subject.)

3. So one must posit something *extra* to be the "immediately apprehended" grounds for the judgment, or perhaps, even, to be the *object* of the judgment. This something extra is the phenomenon of *the occurrence of subjective red,* the instantiation of a special (and mysterious) sort of property.

The flaw in this argument comes in Step 2. I can understand what somebody would be asserting who said,

---

[3] Sometimes it is less costly for the brain to refrain from "filling in." Minsky (1975, 1985) drew attention to the ubiquity of defaults in our representational system—"Tommy kicked the ball to Billy"—now, was the ball (in your mind) a soccer ball, a beach ball, was it red? This is a genuine form of (informational) "filling in," not to be confused with gratuitous rendering needed to "prevent gaps" in the representation.

[4] Kinsbourne (1990) first suggested the slogan "Finding out versus filling in" at the ZiF conference on the Phenomenal Mind, May, 1990, Bielefeld.

"I don't just *say* that it seems pink to me; it *really does seem* pink to me."

This is naturally interpreted as an avowal of sincerity, a denial that one's words on this occasion are merely mouthed, not meant. But the argument above depends on making sense of the following variation:

"I don't just *think* (or judge, or believe) that it seems pink to me; it *really* seems pink to me."

What on earth could the difference be? I submit that this speech has no coherent interpretation—or at least, the burden of proof is on those who claim that this is not nonsense.

What is so wrong, finally, with the idea of "filling in"? It suggests that the brain is *providing* something when in fact the brain is *ignoring* something; it mistakes *the omission of a representation of absence* for *the representation of presence*. And this leads even very sophisticated thinkers to making serious mistakes. It led Goodman (1978), Eccles (1977), and Libet (1981), among others, to some bizarre metaphysical speculations on "backwards projection." And it led Edelman (1989) to make the following claim: "One of the most striking features of consciousness is its continuity" (p. 119). This is utterly wrong. One of the most striking features of consciousness is its *dis*continuity. Another is its *apparent* continuity. One makes a big mistake if one attempts to explain its *apparent* continuity by describing the brain as "filling in" the gaps.

References

Baars, B. (1988). *A cognitive theory of consciousness.* Cambridge, England: Cambridge University Press.

Dennett, D. C., & Kinsbourne, M. (in press). Time and the observer: The where and when of consciousness in the brain. *Behavioral and Brain Sciences.*

Eccles, J. C. (1977). Part II. In K. Popper & J. C. Eccles (Eds.), *The self and its brain* (pp. 227–424). Berlin: Springer Verlag.

Edelman, G. (1989). *The remembered present: A biological theory of consciousness.* New York: Basic Books.

Goodman, N. (1978). *Ways of worldmaking.* Brighton, Sussex, England: Harvester.

Hardin, C. L. (1988). *Color for philosophers: Unweaving the rainbow.* Indianapolis, IN: Hackett.

Jackendoff, R. (1987). *Consciousness and the computational mind.* Cambridge, MA: MIT Press.

Kinsbourne, M. (1980). Brain-based limitations on mind. In R. W. Rieber (Ed.), *Body and mind: Past, present and future* (pp. 155–175). New York: Academic Press.

Kolers, P. A., & von Grünau, M. (1976). Shape and color in apparent motion. *Vision Research, 16,* 329–335.

Libet, B. (1981). The experimental evidence for subjective referral of a sensory experience backwards in time: Reply to P. S. Churchland. *Philosophy of Science, 48*, 182–197.

Libet, B. (1985). Subjective antedating of a sensory experience and mind-brain theories: Reply to Honderich (1984). *Journal of Theoretical Biology, 144*, 563–570.

Margolis, H. (1987). *Patterns, thinking and cognition.* Chicago: University of Chicago Press.

Minsky, M. (1975). A framework for representing knowledge (Memo No. 3306). Cambridge, MA: AI Lab, MIT.

Minsky, M. (1985). *The society of mind.* New York: Simon & Schuster.

Shepard, R. N., & Cooper, L. A. (1982). *Images and their transformations.* Cambridge, MA: MIT Press.

van Tuijl, H. F. J. M. (1975). A new visual illusion: Neonlike color spreading and complementary color induction between subjective contours. *Acta Psychologica, 39*, 441–445.

Warren, R. M. (1970). Perceptual restoration of missing speech sounds. *Science, 167*, 392–393.

CHAPTER 3

Broadening the Domain of the Fuzzy Logical Model of Perception

Dominic W. Massaro

Introduction

T his chapter describes a theoretical framework, the fuzzy logical model of perception (FLMP) and applies it to several aspects of speech perception. In contrasting this framework with other frameworks, such as the well-accepted one of categorical perception, I use a number of prescriptions that I have proposed for psychological inquiry (Massaro, 1987). I begin with a brief description of the theoretical framework, the FLMP, and its application to speech perception by ear and eye.

A Theoretical Framework for Speech Perception

Speech perception is a human skill that rivals our other impressive achievements. Even after decades of intense effort, speech recognition by machine remains far inferior to human performance. The central thesis of the present framework is that there are multiple sources of information supporting speech perception, and the perceiver evaluates and integrates all of these sources to achieve perceptual recognition. There are four central assumptions to the FLMP: (a) Each source of information is evaluated to give the degree to which that source specifies various alternatives, (b) the sources of information are evaluated independently of one another, (c) the sources are integrated to provide an overall degree of support for each alternative, and (d) perception identification follows the relative degree of support among the relevant alternatives.

Well-learned patterns are recognized in accordance with a general algorithm, regardless of the modality or particular nature of the patterns (Massaro, 1987). The FLMP has received support in a wide variety of domains and consists of three operations: feature evaluation, feature integration, and decision. Continuously valued features are evaluated, integrated, and matched against prototype descriptions in memory, and an identification decision is made on the basis of the relative goodness of match of the stimulus information to the relevant prototype descriptions. Figure 1 illustrates the three stages involved in pattern recognition.

Central to the FLMP are summary descriptions of the perceptual units of the language. These summary descriptions are called *prototypes* and contain a conjunction of various properties called *features*. A prototype is a category, and the features of the prototype correspond to the ideal values that an exemplar should have if it is a member of that category. The exact form of the representation of these properties is not known and may never be known. However, the memory representation must be compatible with the sensory representation resulting from the transduction of the audible and visible speech. Compatibility is necessary because the two representations must be related to one another. To recognize the syllable /ba/, the perceiver must be able to relate the information provided by the syllable itself to some memory of the category /ba/.

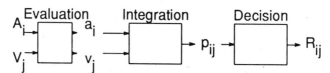

FIGURE 1   Schematic representation of the three operations involved in perceptual recognition. (The sources of information are represented by uppercase letters. Auditory information is represented by A_i and visual information by V_j. The evaluation process transforms these sources of information into psychological values [indicated by lowercase letter a_i and v_j]. These sources are then integrated to give an overall degree of support for a given alternative P_{ij}. The decision operation maps this value into some response [R_{ij}], such as a discrete decision or a rating.)

Prototypes are generated for the task at hand. In speech perception, for example, we might envision activation of all prototypes corresponding to the perceptual units of the language being spoken. For ease of exposition, consider a speech signal representing a single perceptual unit, such as the syllable /ba/. The sensory systems transduce the physical event and make available various sources of information called *features*. During the first operation in the model, the features are evaluated in terms of the prototypes in memory. For each feature and for each prototype, featural evaluation provides information about the degree to which the feature in the speech signal matches the featural value of the prototype.

Given the necessarily large variety of features, it is necessary to have a common metric representing the degree of match of each feature. The syllable /ba/, for example, might have visible featural information related to the closing of the lips and audible information corresponding to the second and third formant transitions. These two features must share a common metric if they are eventually going to be related to one another. To serve this purpose, fuzzy truth values (Zadeh, 1965) are used because they provide a natural representation of the degree of match. Fuzzy truth values lie between 0 and 1, corresponding to a proposition being completely false and completely true, respectively. The value .5 corresponds to a completely ambiguous situation, whereas .7 would be more true than false and so on. Fuzzy truth values, therefore, can represent not only continuous, rather than just categorical, information, but they also can represent different kinds of information. Another advantage of fuzzy truth values is that they couch information in mathematical terms (or at least in a quantitative form). This allows the natural development of a quantitative description of the phenomenon of interest.

It should be noted that fuzzy truth values are not probabilities, although both lie between 0 and 1. To say that "a penguin is a bird to degree .85" is not the same as saying that "the probability that a penguin is a bird is .85." The former represents some measure of the degree to which the concept *penguin* matches the concept *bird*, whereas the latter gives the probability that any given penguin exactly matches the concept *bird*. Thus, equivalent numerical values can correspond to different psychological representations. Although the FLMP might be mathematically equivalent to Bayes's theorem (Massaro & Friedman, 1990), the two formalizations are not equivalent psychological models.

Feature evaluation provides the degree to which each feature in the syllable matches the corresponding feature in each prototype in memory. The goal, of course, is to determine the overall goodness-of-match of each prototype to the syllable. All of the features contribute to this process, and the second operation of the model is called *feature integration*. That is, the features (actually the degrees of matches) corresponding to each prototype are combined (or conjoined in logical terms). The outcome of feature integration consists of the degree to which each prototype matches the syllable.

The third operation during recognition processing is decision. During this stage, the merit of each relevant prototype is evaluated relative to the sum of the merits of the other relevant prototypes. This decision operation is modeled after Luce's (1959) choice rule, called a *relative decision rule* (RGR) by Massaro and Friedman (1990). In pandemoniumlike terms (Selfridge, 1959), we might say that it is not how loud some demon is shouting but rather the relative loudness of that demon in the crowd of relevant demons. This relative goodness-of-match gives the proportion of times the syllable is identified as an instance of the prototype. The relative goodness-of-match can also be mapped into a rating judgment indicating the degree to which the syllable matches the category. An important prediction of the model is that one feature has its greatest effect when a second feature is at its most ambiguous level. Thus, the most informative feature has the greatest impact on the judgment.

The FLMP describes how multiple influences come together to influence behavior. Expanding an example from Jackendoff (1988), one can illustrate this principle in the domain of perceptual organization. It is known that similarity in shape and size and proximity in distance contribute to perceptual grouping. Each row of five objects in Figure 2 illustrates some degree of grouping that separates the two objects on the left from the three objects on the right. In the first row, the grouping is supported by size. In the second row, the grouping is supported by proximity. The grouping in the third row is stronger than that in the first two rows because it is supported by both proximity and size. The grouping is diminished in the fourth row because the influences of proximity and size are opposed to one another. These examples illustrate how multiple influences come together to influence perception.

The FLMP confronts several important issues in describing speech perception. One issue has to do with whether multiple sources of information are evaluated in speech perception. Two other issues have to do with the evaluation of the sources in that we ask whether continuous information is available from each source and whether the output of evaluation of one source is modified by the other source. The issue of categorical versus continuous perception also applies to the output of the integration process. A question about integration is whether the outcomes passed on by evaluation are integrated into

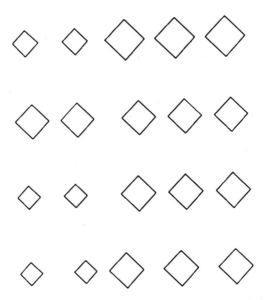

FIGURE 2   Four rows of objects varying in shape, size, and proximity. (See text for the description of the perceptual grouping within each row.)

some higher order representation. If the two sources of information are integrated, it is important to determine the nature of the integration process.

A Prototypical Experiment

An expanded factorial design offers the potential of addressing important issues in speech perception. I describe an experiment manipulating auditory and visual information in a speech perception task. The novel design, illustrated in Figure 3, provides a unique method to address the issues of evaluation and integration of audible and visible information in speech perception. In this experiment, five levels of audible speech varying between /ba/ and /da/ are crossed with five levels of visible speech varying between the same alternatives. The audible and visible speech also are presented alone, giving a total of 35 (25 + 5 + 5) independent stimulus conditions.

A five-step /ba/ to /da/ auditory continuum was synthesized by altering the parametric information specifying the first 80 ms of the consonant–vowel syllable. Using an animated face, control parameters were changed over time to produce a realistic articulation of a consonant–vowel syllable. By modifying the parameters appropriately, an analogous

Visual

	/ba/	2	3	4	/da/	None
/ba/						
2						
3						
4						
/da/						
None						

Auditory

FIGURE 3 Expansion of a typical factorial design to include auditory and visual conditions presented alone. (The five levels along the auditory and visible continua represent auditory and visible speech syllables varying in equal physical steps between /ba/ and /da/.)

five-step /ba/ to /da/ visible speech continuum was synthesized. The presentation of the auditory synthetic speech was synchronized with visible speech for the bimodal stimulus presentations. All of the test stimuli were recorded on videotape for presentation during the experiment. Six unique test blocks were recorded, with the 35 test items presented in each block.

Five college students were tested in the experiment. Subjects were instructed to listen and watch the speaker and to identify the syllable as either /ba/ or /da/. Each of the 35 possible stimuli were presented a total of 12 times during two sessions, and the subjects identified each stimulus during a 3-s response interval.

The points in Figure 4 give the mean proportion of identifications across subjects. The identification judgments change systematically with changes in the audible and visible information sources. The likelihood of a /da/ identification increased as the auditory speech changed from /ba/ to /da/, and analogously for the visible speech. Each source had a similar effect in the bimodal conditions relative to the corresponding unimodal condition. In addition, the influence of one source of information was greatest when the other source was ambiguous.

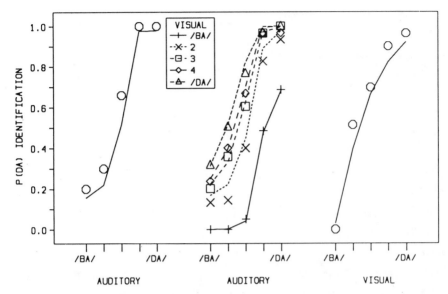

FIGURE 4 Observed (points) and predicted (lines) proportion of /da/ identification for the auditory-alone (left panel), the factorial auditory–visual (center panel), and the visual-alone (right panel) conditions as a function of the five levels of the synthetic auditory and visual speech varying between /ba/ and /da/. (The lines give the predictions for the fuzzy logical model of perception.)

Applying the FLMP, both sources were assumed to provide continuous and independent evidence for the alternatives /ba/ and /da/. Defining the onsets of the second and third formants (F_2 and F_3, respectively) as the important auditory features and the degree of initial opening of the lips as the important visual feature, the prototype for /da/ was slightly falling F_2–F_3 and open lips. The prototype for /ba/ was defined in an analogous fashion: rising F_2–F_3 and closed lips.

Given a prototype's independent specifications for the auditory and visual sources, the value of one source cannot change the value of the other source at the prototype matching stage. The integration of the features defining each prototype was evaluated according to the product of the feature values. If aD_i represents the degree to which the auditory stimulus (A_i) supports the alternative /da/ (i.e., has slightly falling F_2–F_3) and vD_j represents the degree to which the visual stimulus (V_j) supports the alternative /da/ (i.e., has open lips), then the outcome of prototype matching for /da/ would be $aD_i vD_j$, where the subscripts i and j index the levels of the auditory and visual modalities, respectively.

The outcome of integration would be computed in an analogous way for the other relevant alternatives.

The decision operation would determine their relative merit leading to the prediction that

$$P(/\text{da}/|A_iV_j) = \frac{aD_i vD_j}{\Sigma} \tag{1.1}$$

where Σ is equal to the sum of the merit of all relevant response alternatives.

The important assumption of the FLMP is that the auditory source supports each alternative to some degree, as does the visual source. Each alternative is defined by ideal values of the auditory and visual information. Each level of a source supports each alternative to differing degrees represented by feature values. The feature values representing the degree of support from the auditory and visual information for a given alternative are integrated following the multiplicative rule given by the FLMP. The model requires five parameters for the visual feature values and five parameters for the auditory feature values, for each response alternative.

The FLMP was fit to the individual results of each of the 5 subjects. The quantitative predictions of the model were determined using the program STEPIT (Chandler, 1969). The model is represented to the program in terms of a set of prediction equations and a set of unknown parameters. By iteratively adjusting the parameters of the model, the program minimizes the squared deviations between the observed and predicted points. The outcome using STEPIT is a set of parameter values that, when put into the model, come closest to predicting the observed results. Thus, STEPIT maximizes the accuracy of the description of each model. The goodness-of-fit of the model is given by the root mean square deviation (*RMSD*)—the square root of the average squared deviation between the predicted and observed values.

The lines in Figure 4 give the average predictions of the FLMP. The model provides a good description of the identifications of both the unimodal and bimodal syllables (an average *RMSD* of .0731 across the individual subject fits). Figure 5 shows the best fitting parameters for each subject. As can be seen in Figure 5, the parameter values differed for the different subjects but for each subject changed in a systematic fashion across the five levels of the audible and visible synthetic speech.

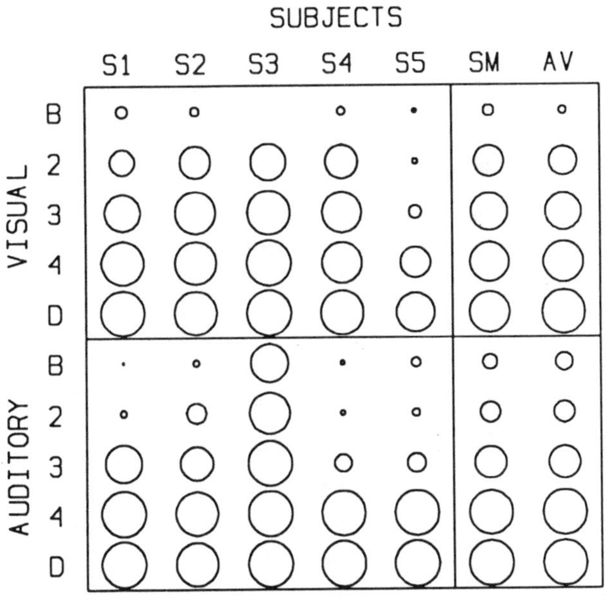

FIGURE 5 Parameters values for 5 subjects, the subject mean (SM), and the average (AV) of the 5 subjects for the support of the response alternative /da/ as a function of the five levels along the visual and auditory speech continua. (The parameter value is given by the area of each circle.)

The meaningfulness of the parameter values justify an important distinction between information and information processing. The parameter values represent how informative each source of information is. The integration and decision algorithms specify how this information is processed. This distinction plays an important role in locating several sources of variability in this inquiry. It is my contention that the variability in information is analogous to the variability in predicting the weather: There are just too many previous contributions and influences to allow an exact quantitative prediction. In addition, small early influences can lead to dramatic consequences at a later time (e.g., the butterfly effect in chaos theory). However, once this variability was accounted for (e.g., by estimating free parameters in the fit of the model), we were able to provide a convincing description of how the information was processed and mapped into a response. Although we could not predict a priori how /ba/-like was a particular level of audible or visible speech for a given individual, we could predict how the two sources of information were integrated. In addition, the model does take a stand on the evaluation process in that it assumes that the sources of information are evaluated independently of one another.

Prescriptions for Psychological Inquiry

The information-processing approach is an established and accepted paradigm that has generated a variety of valuable models and experimental tasks, but current research within this domain might profit from a set of prescriptions that could easily be formulated as general guidelines, independent of theory. The first set of prescriptions concerns theoretical and experimental principles of scientific inquiry. Investigators should follow the principles of falsification and strong inference. In the falsification framework, developed by Popper (1959), experimental tests decide whether a hypothesis or theory survives. If a theory survives experimental tests, it should not be discarded. On the other hand, if the experimental tests falsify conclusions drawn from the theory, then the theory should be rejected or modified accordingly.

Expanding on Popper's (1959) approach, Platt (1964) developed the concept of *strong inference.* Rather than test a single hypothesis, the scientist should test multiple hypotheses. Each experimental test would be designed to eliminate (or in Popper's words, falsify) as many of these hypotheses as possible. The results of the experimentation would allow the generation of new hypotheses that could be subjected to further tests. Using this strategy, a scientist could not easily confirm a single pet hypothesis. In addition, at least one of the multiple hypotheses under test should fail and therefore be rejected.

Carrying out research in this manner ensures that the research is theory driven. Not only should theories guide our research, but theories should be articulated in formal or quantitative form. Verbal theories are too ambiguous and not easily distinguished from one another. Strong inference generates precise experiments and a fine-grained analysis of the results. Viable hypotheses usually make highly similar predictions, and they can be differentiated only in highly constrained and sometimes artificial (laboratory) situations. When the opposing predictions of the hypotheses differ only quantitatively and not qualitatively, only precise quantitative analyses of the results are informative.

A second set of prescriptions involves analyzing and manipulating additional well-known variables having to do with individual variability. These variables differ from the typical independent variables that are aimed at influencing psychological processes and are usually considered to be orthogonal to the questions of interest. Individual variability plays a central role in evolutionary theory and inquiry, and psychology—the study of behavior that has necessarily evolved—should be no different. A third set of prescriptions involves analyzing and manipulating additional well-known variables having to do with the tasks. Finally, it is important to study and predict the dynamics of information processing.

My observations are much more optimistic than those of Jenkins (1979), who pointed out that generalizations about memory processes will have to include interactions among four variables: subjects, materials, orienting tasks, and criterial tasks. However, interactions are usually thought of as qualifications of the main effects. For example, dissociations in memory research are usually used to qualify explanations based on a single memory mechanism, rather than to illuminate how mnemonic processing occurs. What I have found, however, is that with the appropriate process model, the interactions allow more, rather than less, generality. Like Jenkins (1980), I advocate a close interaction between experimental investigations and model development.

Falsification and Strong Inference

The principles of falsification and strong inference are central to scientific inquiry. Without this research strategy, it is impossible to reduce uncertainty about the mechanisms involved. More important, testing opposing hypotheses for the experimental investigations helps offset a confirmation bias. The failure to use falsification and strong inference is apparent in the study of categorical perception. Categorical perception occurs when changes along the stimulus continuum are not perceived continuously but in a discrete manner. Listeners are supposedly limited in their ability to discriminate among different sounds belonging to the same phoneme category. The sounds within a category are only identified absolutely, and discrimination is possible for only those sounds that can be identified as belonging to different categories.

Consider the seminal study carried out by Liberman, Harris, Hoffman, and Griffith (1957). The authors generated a series of 14 consonant–vowel syllables ranging from /be/ to /de/ to /ge/ (/e/ as in *gate*). The syllables were used in identification and discrimination tasks. The results were used to test the hypothesis that listeners can discriminate the syllables only to the extent that they recognize them as belonging to different phoneme categories. The hypothesis was quantified to predict discrimination performance from identification judgments. The authors took the correspondence between the observed and predicted results as evidence for the hypothesis, and this has been the major source of support during the past three decades. As an example, Repp (1984) concluded that "the perception of these syllable initial stops was invariably quite categorical" (p. 282).

The persistent observation that the observed discrimination is better than that predicted identification has never been seen as embarrassment for the theory nor has it ever led to consideration of an alternative view. My proposal is that Liberman et al. (1957) failed to consider alternative hypotheses, beginning an unfortunate tradition in this research. No effort has been made to evaluate the actual goodness-of-fit between the predicted and observed results or to contrast this hypothesis with alternative hypotheses. In fact, one can simply formulate the null hypothesis that predicts chance performance at each condition (Massaro, 1987). This null hypothesis gives roughly the same goodness-of-fit as does the categorical model (Massaro, 1987). Clearly, the authors' conclusion that the results were evidence for categorical perception was not justified.

With hindsight, the confirmation bias used in categorical perception research seems difficult to understand. Unfortunately, this realization has not led to an immediate reconsideration of the idea. Thus, the work of Eimas (1985) and Bornstein (1987) are recent examples of failures to incorporate falsification and strong inference concerning the issue of categorical perception. In both cases, the authors failed to consider the possibility that other descriptions provide equally good or better accounts of the phenomena of interest. The latest treatise, on the Haskins approach to speech perception, still failed to consider alternatives to categorical perception (Mattingly & Studdert-Kennedy, 1991).

The relation between discrimination and identification performance has been a central source of evidence for categorical perception. As stated previously, however, investigators did not test alternative theories. Massaro (1987) contrasted the predictions of the classical categorical model with the FLMP in the discrimination/identification paradigm. In this comparison, which confronted the categorical model on its home turf, the FLMP gave a superior prediction of the observed results.

Testing Among Alternative Models

Given the value of falsification and strong inference, it is essential to contrast one model with other models that make alternative assumptions. Given the present state-of-the-art, we must formalize our hypotheses and theories in specific models that make quantitative predictions. Hintzman (1991) also advocated the use of formal models in scientific inquiry but was content with qualitative predictions. However, formal models cannot be distinguished from one another on qualitative grounds alone. Hintzman pointed out how exemplar models can also produce outcomes that were previously thought to be necessarily limited to prototype models. This is true but still leaves the issue of discriminating between these two classes of models. Success in this enterprise requires quantitative predictions and a fine-grained analysis of the results. Hintzman demanded explanatory value from models, not just their ability to predict data. However, the history of science has seemed to show that explanatory value is more a sign of taste than substance, and what has seemed explanatory at one stage has been viewed as curve fitting at a later time when new formal models are discovered and tested.

An important alternative to the FLMP is the theory of categorical perception, which Massaro (1987) formalized as the categorical model of perception (CMP). The model assumes that only categorical information is available from the auditory and visual sources and that the identification response is based on separate decisions given to the auditory and visual sources. Given the /da/–/ba/ identification task, the visual and auditory decisions could be /ba/–/ba/, /ba/–/da/, /da/–/ba/, or /da/–/da/. If the two decisions concerning a given speech event agree, the identification response can follow either source. When the two decisions disagree, it is assumed that the subject will respond with the auditory decision on some proportion p of the trials and with the visual decision on the remainder $(1 - p)$ of the trials. The weight p reflects the relative dominance of the auditory source.

The probability of a /da/ identification response, $P(/\text{da}/)$, given a particular auditory/visual speech event, $A_i V_j$, would be

$$P(/\text{da}/|A_i V_j) = (1)\ aB_i\, vB_j + (p)\ aB_i\, (1 - vB_j) \qquad (2.1)$$
$$+ (1 - p)(1 - aD_i)vD_j + (0)(1 - aD_i)(1 - vD_j),$$

where subscripts i and j index the levels of the auditory and visual modalities, respectively. The aD_i value represents the probability of a /da/ decision given the auditory level i, and vD_j is the probability of a /da/ decision given the visual level j. The value p reflects the bias to follow the auditory source. Each of the four terms in the equation represents the likelihood of one of the four possible outcomes multiplied by the probability of a /da/ identification response given that outcome.

Some advocates of categorical perception might respond that this model is not representative of their notion of categorical perception. This is a reasonable response, but the advocates must then propose a testable model in its place. In fact, the theory implicated by the CMP is not inconsistent with previous notions of categorical perception. For example, advocates of categorical perception have based their conclusions on auditory speech perception. That is, auditory speech is putatively perceived categorically. It does not seem unreasonable to assume that auditory speech in bimodal speech perception is categorically perceived. In fact, McGurk and MacDonald (1976) originally interpreted their results in this way: Voicing and manner were determined by auditory speech, and place was determined by visible speech. Advocates of categorical perception must specify how the auditory and visual information is combined. Until they do, the CMP is the best known exemplar of categorical perception.

An additional inducement for testing the CMP against empirical results is that this model actually represents two other theories of speech perception. Equation 2.1 can be reduced to Equation 2.2, which shows that the model also quantifies a weighted averaging model and a single channel model.

$$P(/\text{da}/|A_i V_j) = (p) \, aD_i + (1 - p) \, vD_j \qquad (2.2)$$

The weighted averaging model is exactly analogous to the FLMP in every respect except for the integration algorithm (Massaro, 1987, Chapter 7). The sources of information are added, which means that the contribution of a given source of information is independent of its ambiguity. The parameter p in Equation 2.2 indexes the overall weight given the auditory source; however, the integration is always additive. In the FLMP, on the other hand, the least ambiguous source has a greater impact on the final percept.

Equation 2.2 also formalizes a single-channel model, the central assumption of which is that the percept is based on a single source of information. The percept is determined by either the auditory or the visual source of information, but not both. The determining source can change from trial to trial. The parameter p indexes the proportion of trials determined by the auditory source.

To fit this model to the results, each unique level of the auditory stimulus requires a unique parameter aD_i, and analogously for vD_j. The modeling of /da/ responses thus requires five auditory parameters plus five visual parameters. The additional p value would be fixed across all conditions and responses. Thus, we have a fair comparison to the FLMP that requires one fewer parameter than the CMP. The CMP was fit to the individual results in the same manner as that of the FLMP. Figure 6 gives the average observed results and the average predicted results of the CMP. As can be seen in Figure 6, the CMP gave a poor description of the observed results. The *RMSD* was .1134, compared with the average *RMSD* of .0731 for the FLMP. Given that the CMP represents three different hypotheses, its falsification is a particularly informative outcome.

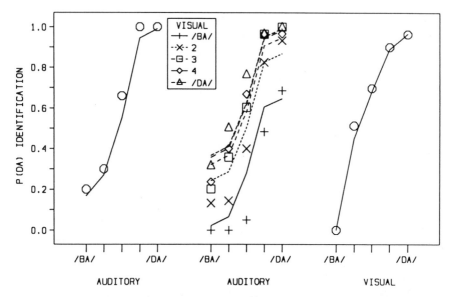

FIGURE 6   Observed (points) and predicted (lines) proportion of /da/ identification for the auditory-alone (left panel), the factorial auditory–visual (center panel), and the visual-alone (right panel) conditions as a function of the five levels of the synthetic auditory and visual speech varying between /ba/ and /da/. (The lines give the predictions for the categorical model of perception.)

The good fit of the FLMP also provides evidence against categorical perception because the assumptions of the FLMP would contradict those of any categorical perception model. The FLMP assumes that continuous, not categorical, information is available both from the separate sources of information and from the outcome of integration of all sources. The good description given by the FLMP makes it less likely that a model with opposing assumptions would provide an equally good fit. Thus, although it is possible that another model is mathematically equivalent to the FLMP, it is less likely that the model could embody assumptions that are opposite those of the FLMP.

It is also important to determine the falsifiability of models. I am certainly sensitive to this issue, having been concerned about the falsifiability of connectionist models with hidden units (Massaro, 1988). It is necessary to show that the FLMP can be falsified. I see the contrast between the FLMP and the CMP as particularly fair because the latter model has one additional free parameter. Kanevsky (1989), on the other hand, observed that the FLMP might have an advantage because its predictions are more complex than those of the CMP. The CMP predicts additive results, whereas the FLMP predicts nonadditive results. Although this is true, I have not been able to determine why this is necessarily an a priori advantage for the FLMP. On the basis of simulated results and model fits, it is clear that the FLMP can be falsified by additive data in the same manner that the additive model can be falsified by nonadditive data.

The Demise of Categorical Perception

It has become obvious that categorical perception is a belief that will not die or fade away easily. Many textbooks and tutorial articles also state that speech is perceived categorically (J. R. Anderson, 1990; Eimas, 1985; Flavell, 1985; Miller, 1981). However, I have argued that previous results and more recent studies are better described in terms of continuous perception—a relatively continuous relation between changes in a stimulus and changes in perception (Massaro, 1987).

There are severe weaknesses in previous evidence for categorical perception. One approach—the traditional one used throughout the almost three decades of research on categorical perception—concerns the relation between identification and discrimination. In the typical experiment, a set of speech stimuli along a speech continuum between two alternatives is synthesized. Subjects identify each of the stimuli as one of the two alternatives. Subjects are also asked to discriminate among these same stimuli. The results of such experiments have been interpreted as showing categorical perception because discrimination performance is reasonably predicted by identification performance (Studdert-Kennedy, Liberman, Harris, & Cooper, 1970). It turns out that this relation between identification and discrimination provides no support for categorical perception for two reasons. First, the categorical model usually provides an inadequate description of the relation between identification and discrimination, and it has not been shown to provide a better description than continuous models. Second, even if the results provided unequivocal support for the categorical model, explanations other than categorical perception are possible (Massaro, 1987; Massaro & Oden, 1980).

As described in the previous section, evidence against categorical perception comes from a direct experimental comparison between categorical and continuous models of perception. Subjects asked to classify speech events independently varying along two dimensions produce identification results consistent with the assumption of continuous information along each of the two dimensions. A model based on categorical information along each dimension gives a very poor description of the identification judgments. In other research, we asked subjects to make repeated ratings of how well a stimulus represents a given category (Massaro & Cohen, 1983). The distribution of the rating judgments to a given stimulus is better described by a continuous model than a categorical one. The best conclusion is to reject all reference to categorical perception of speech and to concentrate instead on the structures and processes responsible for categorizing the world of speech.

Most readers will remain unconvinced as long as no satisfying explanation is given for the sharp category boundaries found in speech perception research. However, it is only natural that continuous perception should lead to sharp category boundaries along a stimulus continuum. Given a stimulus continuum from A to not A that is perceived continuously, goodness(A) is an index of the goodness-of-fit of Variable A to the Category A. The left panel of Figure 7 shows goodness(A) as a linear function of Variable A.

An optimal decision rule in a discrete judgment task would set the criterion value at .5 and classify the pattern as A for any value greater than .5. Otherwise, the pattern is

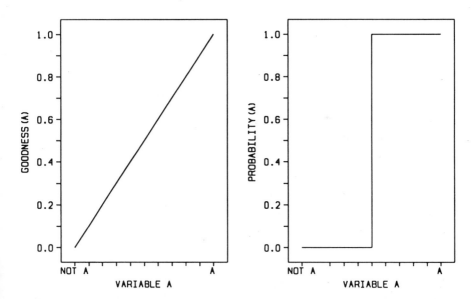

FIGURE 7   Left panel: The degree to which a stimulus (Variable A) represents the category A, called GOODNESS(A), as a function of the level along a stimulus continuum between not A and A. Right panel: The probability of an A response, Probability(A), as a function of the stimulus (Variable A) if the subject maintains a decision criterion at a particular value of GOODNESS(A) and responds A if and only if the GOODNESS(A) exceeds the decision criterion.

classified as not A. Given this decision rule, the probability of an A response would take the form of the step function shown in the right panel of Figure 7. That is, with a fixed criterion value and no variability, the decision operation changes the continuous linear function given by the perceptual operation into a step function. Although based on continuous perception, this function is identical to the idealized form of categorical perception in a speech identification task. It follows that a step function for identification is not evidence for categorical perception because it can also occur with continuous information.

If there is noise in the mapping from stimulus to identification, a given level of Variable A cannot be expected to produce the same identification judgment on each presentation. It is reasonable to assume that a given level of Variable A will produce a normally distributed range of goodness(A) values, with a mean directly related to the level of Variable A and a variance equal across all levels of Variable A. If this is the case, noise will influence the identification judgment for the levels of Variable A near the criterion value more than it will influence the levels further away from the criterion value. Figure 8 illustrates the expected outcome for identification if there is normally distributed noise with the same criterion value assumed in Figure 7.

If the noise is normal and has the same mean and variance across the continuum, a stimulus, the mean goodness of which is at the criterion value, will produce random classifications. The goodness value will be above the criterion on half of the trials and below the criterion on the other half. As the goodness value moves away from the criterion value, the noise will have a diminishing effect on the identification judgments. Noise has a larger influence on identification in the middle of the range of goodness values than at the extremes because variability goes in both directions in the middle and only inward at the extremes. This differential effect of noise across the continuum will produce an identification function that has a sharp boundary. Thus, the hypothetical subject giving this result appears to show enhanced discrimination across the category boundary when, in fact, discrimination was constant across the continuum. The shape of the function resulted from noise at the decision stage.

This example shows that categorical decisions made on the basis of continuous information produce identification functions with sharp boundaries, previously taken to indicate categorical perception. Strictly speaking, of course, categorical perception was considered present only if discrimination behavior did not exceed that predicted from categorization. However, one should not be impressed with the failure of discrimination to exceed that predicted by categorization if the discrimination task resembles something

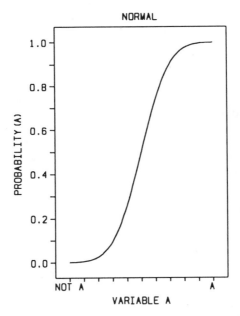

FIGURE 8 Probability(A) as a function of Variable A given the linear relation between GOODNESS(A) and Variable A and the decision criterion represented in Figure 7 but with normally distributed noise added to the mapping of Variable A onto GOODNESS(A).

more akin to categorization than discrimination. That is, subjects will tend to rely on identification labels in discrimination tasks if the perceptual memory is poor (Massaro, 1987).

At the theoretical level, it is necessary to distinguish between sensory and decision processes in the categorization task. What is central for our purposes is that decision processes can transform continuous sensory information into results usually taken to reflect categorical perception. A finding of relatively categorical partitioning of a set of stimuli in no way implies that these stimuli were perceived categorically. Tapping into the process in ways other than simply measuring the identification response reveals the continuous nature of speech perception. Perceivers can rate the degree to which a speech event represents a category, and they can discriminate among different exemplars of the same speech category. Werker (1991) has demonstrated remarkable changes in speech categorization as a function of development and native language. She and others (Kuhl, 1990) have found age-related changes in the sensitivity to nonnative contrasts. These changes are not necessarily evidence for categorical speech perception, however. As Werker (1991) stated, "The fact that adults can still discriminate the nonnative contrasts under certain testing conditions indicates that maintenance is operating at the level of linguistic categories rather than auditory abilities" (p. 104). In addition, reaction times (RT) of identification judgments illustrate that members within a speech category vary in ambiguity or the degree to which they represent the category (Massaro, 1987).

Although speech perception is continuous, there may be a few speech contrasts that qualify for a weak form of categorical perception. This weak form of categorical perception would be reflected in somewhat better discrimination between instances from different categories than between instances within the same category. As an example, consider an auditory /ba/ to /da/ continuum similar to one used in the current experiments. The F_2 and F_3 transitions are varied in linear steps between the two endpoints of the continuum. The syllable /ba/ is characterized by rising transitions and /da/ by falling transitions. Subjects might discriminate a rising transition from a falling transition more easily than they might discriminate between two rising or two falling transitions even though the frequency difference is identical in the two cases. Direction of pitch change is more discriminable than exact magnitude of change. This weak form of categorical perception would arise from a property of auditory processing rather than from a special characteristic of speech categories. Thus, similar results are found in humans, chinchillas, and monkeys as well as in nonspeech analogs (e.g., Kuhl, 1987; Pastore, 1987). However, it is important to note that discrimination between instances within a category is still possible, and although a weak form of categorical perception might exist for a few categories, most do not appear to have this property. Hence, what is required is an explanation of continuous rather than categorical speech perception.

Psychology and the speech sciences seem reluctant to give up the notion of categorical perception perhaps, in part, because of phenomenal experience. Our phenomenal experience in speech perception is that of categorical perception. Listening to a synthetic speech continuum between /ba/ and /pa/ provides an impressive demonstration of this. Students and colleagues usually agree that their percept changes qualitatively from one category to the other in a single step or two with very little fuzziness in between. (I have had similar experiences, hearing certain German phonological categories in terms of similar English ones.) Phenomenal experience, however, is not enough to confirm the existence of categorical perception. As noted by Marcel (1983), phenomenal experience might be dependent on linking current hypotheses with sensory information. If the sensory information is lost very quickly, continuous information could participate in the perceptual process but might not be readily accessible to introspection. Reading a brief visual display of a word might lead to recognition even though the reader is unable to report certain properties of the type font or even a misspelling of the word. Yet the visual characteristics that subjects cannot report could have contributed to word recognition. Analogously, continuous information could be functional in speech perception even if retrospective inquiry suggests otherwise. As in most matters of psychological inquiry, we must find methods to tap the processes involved in cognition without depending only on introspective reports.

Dennett (chapter 3) clarifies an important distinction between "filling in" and finding out as descriptions of a variety of experiences such as the apparent motion in the phi phenomenon. The issue for Dennett is whether it is correct to say that the sensory system accomplishes these outcomes by filling in. That is, the sensory system accomplishes an outcome identical in the phi phenomenon to that of continuous motion. It has been reported that the color of the moving object changes in midstream when a red dot at one location is alternated with a green dot at another location. Does the visual system fill in to give us the impression of a continuously moving dot that changes color? Dennett argues very forcefully that our impressions go beyond the information given but that our sensory systems do not—that is, they do not fill in.

Dennett's philosophical argument is highly relevant to categorical perception. In the categorical perception viewpoint, there seems to be significant filling in. Categorical perception accomplishes at the sensory/brain level a direct correspondence between some representation and our impression. Categorical perception supposedly occurs because the sensory/perceptual system blurs any stimulus differences within a category and perhaps sharpens stimulus differences between categories. Categorical perception in the context of filling in occurs when one perceives two different speech events as belonging to the same category because the speech-is-special module makes them equivalent at the sensory/perceptual level. Categorical perception also seems to predict filling in because sensory processing supposedly occurs in a manner that renders the stimuli within a category indiscriminable. This process would be analogous to filling in. On the other hand, as I argue, it is possible that categorization is simply finding out. That is, the goal of speech perception is categorization, and it is possible to find out which category best represents the speech event without necessarily modifying the sensory/perceptual representation of it. In terms of the FLMP, one evaluates, integrates, and makes a categorical decision if need be without necessarily modifying the sensory/perceptual representations of the speech event.

Filling in might also appear to be an attractive explanation of phenomenal experience of contradictory auditory and visual speech. When told to report what one hears, the visible speech biases one's experience relative to the unimodal case. Because it is auditory experience that one reports, it seems only natural to believe that the representation of the auditory speech has been changed—filled in—by the visual. Another interpretation, however, is that we do not have veridical access to the auditory representation. As Marcel (1983) has pointed out, we report interpretations—finding out—and not representations. Thus, one must be careful about equating phenomenal reports with representations.

As pointed out by N. McCarrell (personal communication, April, 1991), Dennett's argument is reminiscent of Gibson's (1969) argument for differentiation as opposed to enrichment. Gibson was primarily concerned with perceptual learning and argued that experience allows better differentiation among sensory/perceptual representations rather than modification of those representations. The issue of filling in versus finding out can be addressed independent of learning, however. At face value, finding out is much more compatible with the Gibsonian framework because it reduces the amount of processing that is assumed. However, a difficult point for the neo-Gibsonians is the apparently necessary admission that perceivers must at times go beyond the information given when they find out. For neo-Gibsonians, perhaps, finding out is too like inferential perception.

Categorical perception has been a popular assumption because it appears to place certain constraints on the speech perception process—constraints that make speech perception possible or easier. If the infant were limited to perceiving only the discrete categories of his or her language, then acquisition of that language would be easier. However, an ability to discriminate within-category differences can only hurt speech perception. We know that higher order sentential and lexical information contribute to speech perception. If categorical perception were the case, errors would be catastrophic because perceivers would access incorrect categories. Categorical perception would also make it difficult to integrate sentential and lexical information with the phonetic information. Continuous information is more naturally integrated with higher order sources of information (Massaro, 1987).

One of the impediments to resolving the controversy is the term *perception*. If perception simply refers to our reported experience, then we cannot deny categorical perception because we naturally attend to the different categories of language. If perception refers to the psychological processing, however, then it is clear that the processing system is not limited to categorical information. One possible reason why categorical perception has been viewed so positively is that scientists have misinterpreted the outcome for the processes leading up to the outcome.

Despite phenomenal experience and the three decades of misinterpreting the relation between the identification and discrimination of auditory speech, we must conclude that speech is perceived continuously, not categorically. Various work shows that visible and bimodal speech are also perceived continuously. This observation also seems to undermine current views of language acquisition that attribute discrete speech categories to the infant and child (Eimas, 1985; Gleitman & Wanner, 1982). Most important, the case for the modularity or specialization of speech is weakened considerably because of its reliance on the assumption of categorical perception. We are now faced with the bigger challenge of explaining how multiple continuous sources of information are evaluated and integrated to achieve a percept with continuous information.

Individual Variability

This prescription involves looking at individual differences and similarities. We might expect large individual differences in the influence of visible speech on bimodal speech perception. On the other hand, we might expect very little variability across individuals. In either case, the question of individual variability is of interest and should be addressed by models of the phenomenon. As students, we all learned the sins of averaging results across subjects. Group results can camouflage the nature of the individual results. However, it is fair to say that our science remains mostly one of averages rather than of individuals.

Individuals

It is well-known that individual differences exist, and our experimental investigations are aimed usually at reducing them as much as possible. In accuracy studies, for example, we often adjust the stimulus conditions to give relatively equal overall performance across individuals. There is nothing wrong with this procedure, but it may preclude discovery of important properties of the processes of interest. Individual differences can be meaningless or misleading, however, unless the investigator has available a good process model of the task. We all know that individuals differ but need to know how they differ; that is, individuals might simply differ with respect to the information they have, or they might differ in how they process the information. We must verify a process model of the task as much as possible to understand individual differences.

My theoretical and experimental strategy has focused on the analysis and prediction of individual subjects' results. In contrast to most research, this requires a large number of observations from each subject to test the quantitative models against the individuals' data.

The FLMP is ideal for locating the effects of individual variability. As described by Massaro (1987, 1989a), the model allows one to make an important distinction between information and information processing. Information corresponds to the outcome of evaluation: how much a given stimulus characteristic by itself supports the various alternatives. Information processing corresponds to the process of integration: how the various sources of information are combined. Individual perceivers might differ regarding either or both of these characteristics. Consider the second level along a synthetic speech continuum between /ba/ and /da/. It is not possible to predict how much this stimulus will support the alternative /ba/ for a given subject. Subjects have unique representations of speech categories given their unique speech histories. We can guess that the stimulus will be perceived as more /ba/-like than /da/-like, but we cannot quantify how much—even given the results of hundreds of other observers.

The FLMP makes a very strong prediction, however. Regardless of the amount of /ba/-ness from a given source of information, it will be combined with other sources of information as prescribed by the integration and decision operations. Thus, the model allows for individual differences at the level of evaluation but not in the processes of integration and decision. Thus, testing the FLMP against the results also tests whether individual differences can be located entirely at the evaluation stage of processing.

To test this strong prediction of the FLMP, we reanalyzed subjects from several of our early experiments in bimodal speech perception. A 9-step /ba/–/da/ auditory continuum was factorially combined with a visual /ba/, a visual /da/, or no-lip movements coming from the face of the speaker. The speech events were identified as /ba/ or /da/. Thirty-nine subjects were tested across three experiments. First, we asked whether the individual differences can be accounted for simply in terms of information. This means that the model should give a good fit to the results of all subjects, not just to a subset of the subjects. Second, to locate the individual differences in terms of information, we looked at the magnitude of the effects of the auditory and visual sources of information.

Figure 9 plots the distribution of *RMSD* values from the fit of the FLMP across the 39 subjects. As can be seen in Figure 9, the values appear to make up a fairly homogeneous distribution. There is no evidence that the model accounts for the results of only a subset of the population. To provide a better test, we contrasted the predictions of the

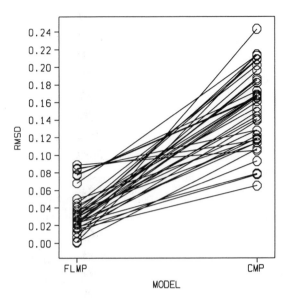

FIGURE 9   The root mean square derivation (*RMSD*) values from the fit of the fuzzy logical model of perception (FLMP; left distribution) and from the fit of the categorical model of perception (CMP; right distribution) for the 39 subjects. (The lines connect the fits of the two models for each subject.)

FLMP with those of the CMP. Figure 9 also plots the distribution of *RMSD* values from the fit of the CMP across the 39 subjects. The two distributions have little overlap, even though the figure is somewhat illusory in giving the appearance of more overlap than there actually is. Even the worst fitting FLMP subject was a better fit than for 36 of the 39 CMP subjects. Also shown in Figure 9, the FLMP provides a better description than does the CMP for each of the 39 subjects.

To assess the individual differences at the evaluation stage, the sizes of the visual and auditory effects were computed for each subject. A visual-effect size (*V*) for each subject was defined by the marginal difference between the probability of a /da/ or /ba/ response to a visual /da/ or a visual /ba/, respectively:

$$V = P(/da/|visual/da/) - P(/da/|visual/ba/). \tag{3.1}$$

This value varies between 0 and 1. An analogous measure was computed for the auditory effect *A* using the probability of a /da/ response to the first and ninth level along the auditory continuum. Figure 10 plots the size of the predicted visual effect as a function of the predicted auditory effect. As can be seen in Figure 10, there was impressive negative correlation ($r = -.925$) between these two effects. This result is expected from the FLMP integration algorithm in which the influence of one source of information is negatively correlated with the influence of another source of information. Figure 10 also illustrates the tremendous individual variability in the dominant source of information and the relative dominance of the dominant source. The goodness-of-fit of the FLMP for all subjects is all the more impressive given the large variability across subjects.

It is of interest whether the fit of the FLMP varies with the influence of the two sources of information. To assess this question, a correlation was computed between the *RMSD* and the visual range and between the *RMSD* and the auditory range. The correlations were relatively small ($r = .156$ and $.324$ for the visual and auditory ranges, respectively). Thus, the goodness-of-fit of the FLMP does not vary much with the magnitude of the influence of the audible and visible speech. This generalization of the model across individual variability enhances our faith in the model.

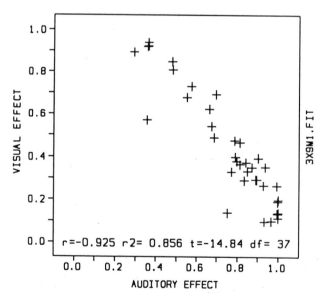

FIGURE 10 Scatterplot of the predicted visual effects as a function of the predicted auditory effect for the 39 subjects. (The ranges are computed from the parameter values of the fit of the fuzzy logical model of perception.)

Task Variability

This prescription addresses the extent to which the phenomenon of interest generalizes across task variability. Investigators should be concerned with whether their findings generalize across different variations of the experimental task. Evaluating changes in behavior as a function of variations within and between different tasks provides valuable information on several fronts. The study of performance in various tasks improves the chances of gaining insights into underlying mechanisms. We do not expect superficial results, such as whether an independent variable had a significant effect, to generalize across tasks. However, we do expect our theories to account for performance across variability in the task domain. Our understanding of psychological mechanisms is good to the extent that we can predict across different tasks.

Generalizing Across Domains of Inquiry

One of the most engaging issues of this decade has been modularity of mind (Fodor, 1983). This thesis makes the very strong prediction that mechanisms uncovered in one domain will not be adequate to describe performance in a different domain. Of course, this thesis is most directly tested by studying behavior as a function of domain variability.

Regarding speech perception by eye and ear, the question is to what extent similar processes occur in speech perception by means of other modalities. There is substantial evidence that the processes found in speech perception by ear and eye generalize to electrical stimulation of cochlear implants and tactile stimulation on the skin. Modularity of mind has been the center of much controversy, and the issue of the modularity of speech perception is equally relevant (Mattingly & Studdert-Kennedy, 1991). Do the processes uncovered in speech perception occur in other domains? Table 1 lists the different domains that have supported the processes assumed by the FLMP. As can be seen in the table, the FLMP has given a good description of various aspects of speech perception (Massaro, 1989b; Massaro & Cohen, 1990; Massaro, Cohen, & Thompson, 1988), letter and word recognition in reading (Massaro & Cohen, 1991), language processing (Massaro, 1987, chapter 9), object categorization (Oden, 1981), the visual perception of depth (Massaro, 1988), the localization of sound in space (Fisher, 1991), memory retrieval (Massaro, Weldon, & Kitzis, 1991), person impression (Massaro, 1987, chapter 9), and decision making (Massaro, 1990).

TABLE 1
Domains of Evidence for the Fuzzy Logical Model of Perception

Domain	Test situation
Speech perception	Acoustic features
	Phonological constraints
	Lexical constraints
	Syntactic constraints
	Semantic constraints
	Audible and visual speech
	Audible speech and gesture
	Audible speech and written letters
Reading	Letter features
	Orthographic constraints
	Lexical constraints
Language	Semantic and syntactic information
Categorization	Object classification
Visual perception	Cues to exocentric distance
Localization	Audible and visible stimuli
Memory retrieval	Letters and semantic cues
Social events	Person impression
Reasoning	Conjunction fallacy

Dynamics of Information Processing

The final prescription is to study the dynamics of information processing. This advice might seem superfluous at this time of heady dynamic modeling within the connectionist framework. It is fair to say, however, that most of the work involves learning input–output correspondences without consideration of the time course of processing a given event. In some recent work, we have contrasted the interactive activation model of word recognition with the FLMP. Although a revised form of the interactive activation model (McClelland, 1991) and the FLMP make similar asymptotic predictions, it is possible to distinguish between the models in terms of the dynamics of information processing.

Visual Information and Orthographic Context in Reading

In an experiment reported by Massaro (1979), a reader was asked to read lowercase letter strings with an ambiguous test letter between c and e. It was possible to gradually transform the c into an e by extending the horizontal bar. The interpretation of the ambiguous letter differed in the different letter strings. To the extent that the bar was long, there was good visual information for an e and poor visual information for a c. Now consider the letter presented as the first letter in the context -*oin* and the context -*dit*. Only c is orthographically admissible in the first context because the three consecutive vowels *eoi* violate English orthography. Only e is admissible in the second context because the initial cluster *cd* is an inadmissible English pattern. In this case, the context -*oin* favors c, whereas the context -*dit* favors e. The context -*tsa* and -*ast* can be considered to favor neither e nor c. The former remains an inadmissible context whether e or c is present, and the latter is orthographically admissible for both e and c. Similar contexts were constructed for the other three possible letter positions.

The experiment factorially combined six levels of visual information with these four levels of orthographic context, giving a total of 24 experimental conditions. The bar length of the letter took on six values from a prototypical c to a prototypical e. The test letter was presented at each of the four letter positions in each of the four context types. The test string was presented for a short duration, followed after a short interval by a masking stimulus composed of random letter features. Subjects were instructed to identify the test letter on the basis of what they saw. The results of the experimental test are shown in Figure 11. As can be seen in Figure 11, both the test letter and the context influenced performance in the expected direction. Furthermore, the effect of context was larger for the more ambiguous test letters along the stimulus continuum.

This study also evaluated context effects as a function of processing time controlled by backward masking. The test stimulus was presented for 30 ms. Four masking interstimulus intervals (5, 40, 95, or 210 ms) were tested at each of the other experimental conditions. The points in Figure 11 show the probability of an e response as a function of the bar length of the test letter and the four contexts at each of the four masking intervals. Each point represents data from 176 trials (16 observations from each of 11 subjects). As can be seen in the figure, performance was more chaotic at the short masking intervals. That is, less processing time led to less orderly behavior—as expected from research on the time course of perceptual processing. Even for

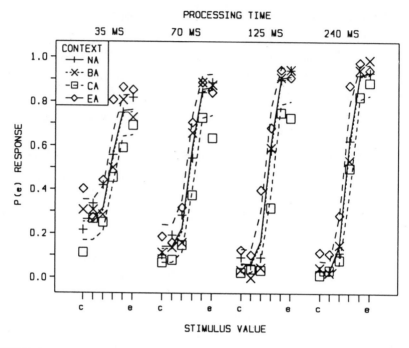

FIGURE 11   Observed (points) and predicted (lines) probability of *e* identification as a function of the bar length of the test letter, the orthographic context, and the processing interval between the onset of the test stimulus and the onset of the masking stimulus. (Adapted from Massara, 1979. Copyright 1979 by the American Psychological Association.)

unambiguous test letters, subjects did not make consistent identification judgments at short masking intervals. According to perceptual processing theory, there was not sufficient time for feature evaluation and integration to take place before the onset of the masking stimulus.

Both the test letter and the context influenced performance at all masking intervals. The effect of the test letter was attenuated at the short, relative to the long, processing time. That is, the identification functions covered a larger range across the *e–c* continuum, with increases in processing time. Context had a significant effect at all masking intervals. In fact, the context effect was larger for the unambiguous test letters at the short than at the longer masking intervals. This result followed naturally from the trade-off between stimulus information and context in the FLMP. Context had a smaller influence to the extent that the stimulus information was unambiguous. Figure 11 also gives the predictions of the FLMP (lines) along with the observed (points) data. The *RMSD* between the observed and predicted points was .0501.

These same results dictated the falsification of stochastic interactive activation (SIAC) models. A strong context in the FLMP will not override a relatively weak stimulus as it can in the SIAC models. Given the assumption of interactive activation, context can sometimes overwhelm stimulus information about the target as additional processing occurs. This prediction is contradicted by both phenomenological experience and experimental results. The more carefully one reads a word, the more likely one is to notice a misspelling. In experiments varying target information, context, and processing time, stimulus effects were larger to the extent that the processing time was substantial (Massaro & Cohen, 1991). These SIAC models could not simultaneously predict the observed stimulus and context effects with increasing processing time. Although the FLMP and SIAC models made similar predictions for asymptotic performance, we were able to discriminate between the models by attending to the dynamics of information processing.

Summary

This chapter has described the FLMP account of speech perception by eye and ear and has illustrated several prescriptions for psychological inquiry. The idea is that the information-processing framework can be broadened to make it much more valuable and general. The first prescription is that investigators should follow the principles of falsification and strong inference. Strong inference should be used in conjunction with specific models, precise experiments, and a fine-grained analysis of the results. A second prescription involves analyzing individual variability; a good theory accounts for performance across a wide range of individual differences. A third prescription consists of determining to what extent the processes uncovered in the task of interest generalize across different domains. Finally, the fourth prescription centers around the importance of accounting for the dynamics of information processing. These prescriptions were discussed within the context of the theoretical framework of the FLMP and its application to speech perception by ear and eye. I look forward to the next 25 years of our inquiry.

References

Anderson, J. R. (1990). *Cognitive psychology and its implications.* San Francisco: Freeman.

Bornstein, M. H. (1987). Perceptual categories in vision and audition. In S. Harnad (Ed.), *Categorical perception: The groundwork of cognition* (pp. 287–300). Cambridge, England: Cambridge University Press.

Chandler, J. P. (1969). Subroutine STEPIT—Finds local minima of a smooth function of several parameters. *Behavioral Science, 14,* 81–82.

Eimas, P. D. (1985, January). The perception of speech in early infancy. *Scientific American, 252,* 46–52.

Fisher, B. (1991). *Integration of visual and auditory information in perception of speech events.* Unpublished doctoral dissertation, University of California, Santa Cruz.

Flavell, J. H. (1985). *Cognitive development.* Englewood Cliffs, NJ: Prentice-Hall.

Fodor, J. A. (1983). *Modularity of mind.* Cambridge, MA: Bradford Books.

Gibson, E. J. (1969). *Principles of perceptual learning and development.* New York: Appleton-Century-Crofts.

Gleitman, L. R., & Wanner, E. (1982). Language acquisition: The state of the state of the art. In E. Wanner & L. R. Gleitman (Eds.), *Language acquisition: The state of the art* (pp. 3–48). Cambridge, England: Cambridge University Press.

Hintzman, D. L. (1991). Why are formal models useful in psychology? In W. E. Hockley & S. Lewandowsky (Eds.), *Relating theory and data: Essays on human memory in honor of Bennet B. Murdock* (pp. 39–56). Hillsdale, NJ: Erlbaum.

Jackendoff, R. (1988). Conceptual semantics. In M. Santambrogio & P. Violi (Eds.), *Meaning and mental representations* (pp. 81–97). Bloomington: Indiana University Press.

Jenkins, J. J. (1979). Four points to remember: A tetrahedral model of memory experiments. In L. S. Cermak & F. I. M. Craik (Eds.), *Levels of processing in human memory* (pp. 429–446). Hillsdale, NJ: Erlbaum.

Jenkins, J. J. (1980). Can we have a fruitful cognitive psychology? In H. E. Howe, Jr., & J. H. Flowers (Eds.), *Nebraska symposium on motivation* (pp. 211–238). Lincoln: University of Nebraska Press.

Kanevsky, D. (1989). A multiple source, or, is a striped apple more striped than a striped orange? *Behavioral and Brain Sciences, 12,* 767–769.

Kuhl, P. K. (1987). The special-mechanisms debate in speech research: Categorization tests on animals and infants. In S. Harnad (Ed.), *Categorical perception: The groundwork of cognition* (pp. 355–386). Cambridge, England: Cambridge University Press.

Kuhl, P. K. (1990). Towards a new theory of the development of speech perception. *Proceedings of 1990 International Conference on Spoken Language Processing, 2,* 745–748.

Liberman, A. M., Harris, K. S., Hoffman, H. S., & Griffith, B. C. (1957). The discrimination of speech sounds within and across phoneme boundaries. *Journal of Experimental Psychology, 54,* 358–368.

Luce, R. D. (1959). *Individual choice behavior.* New York: Wiley.

Marcel, A. J. (1983). Conscious and unconscious perception: An approach to the relations between phenomenal experience and perceptual processes. *Cognitive Psychology, 15,* 238–300.

Massaro, D. W. (1979). Letter information and orthographic context in word perception. *Journal of Experimental Psychology: Human Perception and Performance, 5,* 595–609.

Massaro, D. W. (1987). *Speech perception by ear and eye: A paradigm for psychological inquiry.* Hillsdale, NJ: Erlbaum.

Massaro, D. W. (1988). Ambiguity in perception and experimentation. *Journal of Experimental Psychology: General, 117,* 417–421.

Massaro, D. W. (1989a). Multiple book review of *Speech perception by ear and eye: A paradigm for psychological inquiry. Behavioral and Brain Sciences, 12,* 741–794.

Massaro, D. W. (1989b). Testing between the TRACE model and the fuzzy logical model of perception. *Cognitive Psychology, 21,* 398–421.

Massaro, D. W. (1990). *A pattern recognition account of decision making.* Paper presented at the meeting of the XXIV International Congress of Psychology, Sydney, Australia.

Massaro, D. W., & Cohen, M. M. (1983). Evaluation and integration of visual and auditory information in speech perception. *Journal of Experimental Psychology: Human Perception and Performance, 9,* 753–771.

Massaro, D. W., & Cohen, M. M. (1990). Perception of synthesized audible and visible speech. *Psychological Science, 1,* 55–63.

Massaro, D. W., & Cohen, M. M. (1991). Integration versus interactive activation: The joint influence of stimulus and context in perception. *Cognitive Psychology, 23,* 558–614.

Massaro, D. W., Cohen, M. M., & Thompson, L. A. (1988). Visible language in speech perception: Lipreading and reading. *Visible Language, 22,* 9–31.

Massaro, D. W., & Friedman, D. (1990). Models of integration given multiple sources of information. *Psychological Review, 97,* 225–252.

Massaro, D. W., & Oden, G. C. (1980). Speech perception: A framework for research and theory. In N. J. Lass (Ed.), *Speech and language: Advances in basic research and practice* (Vol. 3, pp. 129–165). San Diego, CA: Academic Press.

Massaro, D. W., Weldon, M. S., & Kitzis, S. N. (1991). The integration of orthographic and semantic information in memory retrieval. *Journal of Experimental Psychology: Learning, Memory, and Cognition, 17,* 277–287.

Mattingly, I. G., & Studdert-Kennedy, M. (1991). *Modularity and the motor theory of speech perception.* Hillsdale, NJ: Erlbaum.

McClelland, J. L. (1991). Stochastic interactive processes and the effect of context on perception. *Cognitive Psychology, 23,* 1–44.

McGurk, H., & MacDonald, J. (1976). Hearing lips and seeing voices. *Nature, 264,* 746–748.

Miller, G. A. (1981). *Language and speech.* San Francisco: Freeman.

Oden, G. C. (1981). A fuzzy propositional model of concept structure and use: A case study in object identification. In G. W. Lasker (Ed.), *Applied systems and cybernetics* (Vol. 6, pp. 2890–2897). Elmsford, NY: Pergamon Press.

Pastore, R. E. (1987). Categorical perception: Some psychophysical models. In S. Harnad (Ed.), *Categorical perception: The groundwork of cognition* (pp. 29–52). Cambridge, England: Cambridge University Press.

Platt, J. R. (1964). Strong inference. *Science, 146,* 347–353.

Popper, K. (1959). *The logic of scientific discovery*. New York: Basic Books.

Repp, B. H. (1984). Categorical perception: Issues, methods, findings. In N. J. Lass (Ed.), *Speech and language: Advances in basic research and practice* (Vol. 10, pp. 243–335.). San Diego, CA: Academic Press.

Selfridge, O. G. (1959). Pandemonium: A paradigm for learning. In *Mechanization of thought processes*. London: Her Majesty's Stationery Office.

Studdert-Kennedy, M., Liberman, A. M., Harris, K. S., & Cooper, F. S. (1970). Motor theory of speech perception: A reply to Lane's critical review. *Psychological Review, 77,* 234–249.

Werker, J. (1991). The ontogeny of speech perception. In I. G. Mattingly & M. Studdert-Kennedy (Eds.), *Modularity and the motor theory of speech perception* (pp. 91–109). Hillsdale, NJ: Erlbaum.

Zadeh, L. A. (1965). Fuzzy sets. *Information and Control, 8,* 338–353.

CHAPTER 4

Ecological Foundations of Cognition: Invariants of Perception and Action

M. T. Turvey

W hat is required to build a theory of cognition? What kinds of concepts are needed? What classes of empirical phenomena should lead the way? There is overwhelming consensus in contemporary science that theorizing on cognition means giving an account of mental processes and mental models. In my opinion, the search for mental mechanisms (of either the symbolic or subsymbolic kind) is overvalued. The challenges facing cognitive theory are considerably more profound, having to do with laws and principles formative of the functional order characterizing nature's ecological scale—the scale at which animals and their environments are defined. I believe that the major concepts needed to address cognition will not be found in the concepts provided by formal logics, computational languages, or network architectures. Rather, the kinds of concepts needed will be developed in the context of an emerging ecological physics and must include a physical notion of information that

Preparation of the manuscript and much of the research reported was supported, in part, by the National Science Foundation (Grants NSF 8720144, NSF 8811510, and NSF 9011013).

satisfies the conditions of information about, in the sense of specificity to, and a notion of intentionality suited to the task of particularizing very general principles. (Despite its frequent usage and overwhelming prominence, *information* in cognitive psychology is a dummy term, always left undefined and usually ascribed whatever qualities are convenient for the explanatory task at hand [der Heijden & Stebbins, 1990]. Intentions, goals, and plans are left at the level of symbol strings and representational formats, with no effort expended to explain their fit to the actual physical facts of controlled action.)

The types of phenomena that should lead the way must be drawn from perception in the service of action and from action in the service of perception. There are two major reasons for confidence in this choice. First, what is known by humans and other animals is grounded in perceiving and doing (Neisser, 1991). Second, the control of perception by action and the enhancement by exploratory action of the opportunities to perceive are so fluent, reliable, and widely manifest in living things that they must be underwritten by principles of the most basic and general kind (cf. Marr, 1977). Whatever the cognitive capability of interest, it can be expected that the laws and principles that make perceiving and acting possible play a central role in shaping the characteristics that define the given capability (e.g., Browman & Goldstein, 1990).

Theoretical Issues

A law-based perspective toward psychological matters raises many issues (e.g., Kugler, Shaw, Vincente, & Kinsella-Shaw, 1990; Kugler & Turvey, 1987; Turvey, Shaw, Reed, & Mace, 1981). I address three of the major ones here to set the stage for the experimental results on perception-action systems that comprise the larger part of this chapter.

Strategic Reductionism (or Level-Independent Physics)

Living systems are ordinary physical systems in the deep sense of conforming to the ordinary laws and principles governing energy transactions. At the same time, they are outstanding physical systems, extraordinary in their means of using the general laws and principles and exceptional in their exploitations of the particular invariant relations among properties that characterize nature's ecological scale.

If perception and action capabilities of living things are law based, as intimated by the preceding, then how should the implied reductionism be interpreted? The prospects for explaining perception and action capabilities through classical reductionism are slim and the effort to do so probably misguided. Classical reductionism is the substitution of the properties at one scale of nature—here, the scale at which perception and action are in evidence—by the properties at another, putatively more basic, scale. The principal (but generally unacceptable) idea of classical reductionism is that the taxonomy of physical types by which nature is described at its rock-bottom (e.g., quantum mechanical) scale is the taxonomy of physical types by which nature is to be described at any scale.

Contemporary science, however, provides more than one version of physical reductionism (Yates, 1987). The version that seems most suited to the task is based on the premise that there is a single set of strategies that applies, with equanimity, to each of nature's scales. These strategies produce, at any given scale, event regularities and morphological objects that are often unique to the scale. Many of these strategies have been identified and catalogued by physics; glimpses of others are seen in the rapidly growing study of self-organizing physical systems and the ubiquity of constrained randomness (e.g., Haken, 1977; Iberall & Soodak, 1987; Kugler & Turvey, 1987, 1988; Nicolis & Prigogine, 1989; Schöner & Kelso, 1988). Collectively, they provide a repertoire of methods by which nature, at any scale, can be investigated. A useful working premise, therefore, is that a strategic physics, applied systematically to perception–action capabilities, will deliver a parsimonious, principled account thoroughly consistent with the accounts given of phenomena investigated within the so-called hard natural sciences.

A commitment to addressing perception–action capabilities in terms of laws imposes particular demands (Turvey, 1990a). First, classical ideas in physics will have to be applied in novel ways, and some will have to be discarded. Second, strict determinism will have to be relinquished to embrace the novelty and diversity of perception–action capabilities. Third, evolutionary processes (i.e., historical, irreversible processes) will have to be comprehended much more deeply. Fourth, the notion of law will have to be widened (e.g., Reed, 1986) and the (outdated) criterion of universal scope relinquished (Turvey et al., 1981). Fifth, the essential localness of reference frames will have to be addressed so that an understanding of locally defined metrics and intrinsically defined coordinate systems can be developed systematically (Kugler & Turvey, 1987; Turvey, 1986). (In concrete terms, the challenge of the preceding is understanding the ability of each and every animal to perceive the surrounding layout in the scale of its body and action capabilities [J. J. Gibson, 1979].) And sixth, information and intentionality will have to be understood in physical terms. Of the above, the significance of clear understandings of information and intentionality is most readily appreciated by students of cognition.

The Challenge of Information

There is no physical theory of information. The received theory of information in physics is a phenomenological theory of such generality that it disregards the physical states of affairs defining informational interactions between a system and its surround (Bunge, 1977). Questions of the following kind rarely arise: What kinds of structures carry or contain information? What kinds of energy forms and energy quantities are involved? What are the physical conditions for generating and detecting information naturally? How is information connected to dynamics? A law-based account of perception and action will require a physical theory of information, and it seems that it will have to come from the study of perception and action capabilities themselves (Kugler & Turvey, 1987).

In physics and engineering, the concept of information is developed to address the communication and representation of physical situations. Shannon's now classical measure, for example, indicates the minimum equivalent number of binary steps by which a given representation may be selected from an ensemble of possible representations. Other measures speak to the informational requirements for constructing a representation (MacKay, 1969). These quantifications have limited bearing on the perceivings and actings of animals. The most generous reading is that the mathematical theory of information is a concept befitting perceivings and actings considered as discriminations (roughly, it addresses what something is not but might have been), and that is far from adequate. The perception of the properties of places, objects, events, and ongoing actions is more fundamental than the perception of the differences among them. Controlling and coordinating acts in ordinary, cluttered surroundings demand information in the sense of information about something, information specific to something; that is, information of a kind that permits the perception of something, as J. J. Gibson (1966, 1979) would put it. The point is that conceptions of information that address how to distinguish among and how to represent propertied things are inconsequential if they are not nested within a conception of information that addresses how there can be awareness of those propertied things in the first place.

J. J. Gibson's (1966, 1979) move is to relate the notion of information to lawful regularity. At the ecological scale, the systems of interest—living things—are immersed in energy distributions. Notable among these ambient energy distributions are those for which the mean energy content is extremely low relative to the energy associated with animals (e.g., optical distributions and distributions of volatile materials ambient to a path of observation traversed by a flying insect or a running mammal). The mass term can, therefore, be suppressed effectively in the descriptions of these energy distributions as they bear on the control and coordination of movement (Kugler & Turvey, 1987, 1988). The descriptions in the optical case, for example, are of the spatio-temporal structure (i.e., the adjacent and successive order) that is imposed on the ambient optical distributions by the layout of environmental surfaces (e.g., attached and detached objects, places, one's body, movements of one's body, surface displacements, deformations, collisions). Gibson's (1966, 1979) ecological conception of information is founded on the assertion that invariant relations exist between layout properties of general significance to the governing of activity (affordances) and macroscopic, noninertial properties of structured ambient (optical, mechanical, chemical) energy distributions. The latter, therefore, can specify the former.

The distinction between information about something and the something in question needs to be emphasized. Fields of diffusing volatile materials fill the air and are ambient to every animal. The sources of these odors are other animals and their products, plants and their products, and a few types of inorganic things. (For the most part, the minerals of the earth, the air, and the water are odorless.) The information carried by a diffusion field specifies its source but is not chemically identical with its source (J. J. Gibson, 1966). For example, the body odor of an individual animal is specific to its body but does not have the same chemical composition. Behind the explication of the information carried by fields of diffusing volatile materials is an ecological chemistry (J. J. Gibson, 1966). This chemistry expresses the fact that some vapors (and, in the case of tasting, some solutions) are informative about their sources without being chemically identical with them. Analogous tasks confront ecological optics (J. J. Gibson, 1961; Reed & Jones, 1982), ecological acoustics (J. J. Gibson, 1966; B. Shaw, McGowan, & Turvey, 1991), ecological mechanics (J. J. Gibson, 1966; Solomon, Turvey, & Burton, 1989a), and so on.

Also deserving of emphasis is the distinction between available information and detected information. Energy distributions ambient to a point of observations are structured in ways specific to the surface layout surrounding the point of observation and to the point of observation's position relative to those surroundings. They provide, therefore, opportunities for "being informed." These opportunities are what they are because the invariant relations between the properties of the surround and observation point and the properties of structured ambient energy distributions are what they are. These opportunities are not dependent on living things; they are simply available, and whether or not they are used by a living thing depends on its perceptual capacities, the activity it is engaged in, and other factors.

Intentions as Attractors

Intentions constrain dynamics and, in turn, are constrained by them in a subtle interplay in which intentions opportunistically exploit the invariant and variant dynamical qualities specific to a task (Bingham, 1988). The image cast by the experimental analysis of juggling, simple interlimb coordinations, effortful touch, table tennis, and other data presented in this chapter is of intentions (goals, plans, schemata) superimposed on general laws and principles to yield the facts of movement coordination. The perceptual control of action and the enhancement of perception by exploratory activity are specialized or particularized by initial conditions and constraints that stem largely from what a person intends. From the perspective of attempting an understanding of perception and action in dynamical terms, how might intention be defined so as to satisfy dynamical requirements and, importantly, to motivate experimental analyses? One suggestion is to regard an intentional constraint as an attractor (Kugler, Shaw, Vincente, & Kinsella-Shaw, 1990; Shaw & Kinsella-Shaw, 1988; Turvey, Saltzman, & Schmidt, 1991). The relation between an attractor and the dynamics to which it refers is lawful, rather than merely definitional or associative; an attractor is far less detailed than its related dynamics. The latter qualities are so because an attractor defines a system's asymptotic dynamics and does so in the form of a low-dimensional equation set derived from the higher dimensional equation set describing the original system (e.g., Thompson & Stewart, 1986). A key idea, with significant implications for the experimental study of the intentional control of perception–action cycles, is that intentions can be defined as attractors in the same space of collective variables as that in which the intrinsic dynamics of perception–action cycles are defined (Scholz & Kelso, 1990; Schöner & Kelso, 1989).

Gibson's Ecological Approach to Perceiving

Let me collect the major points above in the context that was their inspiration, namely, the approach to perception developed by J. J. Gibson (1966, 1979; Reed & Jones, 1982). This approach dismisses dualism and emphasizes the mutuality of an animal and its environment. In this approach, perceiving is defined as the means by which an animal maintains contact with its environment. It is a phenomenon to be understood in terms of lawful regularities and symmetry principles defined at the ecological scale of animals and environments, rather than in terms of mental states or formal languages of representation and computation (e.g., Turvey, 1990a; Turvey et al., 1981). The essentials of the approach can be expressed succinctly: Information is specific to the environment (comprising surface layouts, objects, and events) and to self-movements; perception is specific to information. Hence, perception is specific to the environment (extero-perception) and to self-movements (proprio-perception and exproprio-perception [Lee, 1978]).

The ecological approach advanced by J. J. Gibson (1979) is a programmatic analysis of (a) the nature of information, (b) the basis of perception, and (c) the development of perception. With respect to (a), the ecological approach attempt to identify the specificity between the structured energy distributions available to a perceptual system and the environmental and movement properties causally responsible for that structure. As noted above, this specificity is what is meant by information in the ecological approach. With respect to (b), the ecological approach asserts the directness of perception in the sense that the specificity of perception to information dispenses with any intervening special process, such as inference or recourse to templates. Integral to (b) is a hypothesis that imposes significant constraints on conducting research: For every property perceived, there is a property of the structured energy distribution to which the perceived property maps uniquely. This generalized hypothesis of information-perception specificity directs investigation to the uncovering of one-to-one mappings between information and perception. A particular perception results only if a particular informative structure is detected. At a deeper level, the challenge of (b) is the development of theory and research directed at understanding how specificity is preserved over the components of an animal–environment system and the perception–action cycles that it manifests. (In cases of perceiving adjacent surfaces by active touch, for example, the aforementioned components would include properties of surface layout, patternings of mechanical energy, and the states of muscular, connective, and neural tissues.)

With respect to (c), improvement in perceiving in any given situation follows from the discovery of, and attunement to, information. The specificities in any given situation—the lawful regularities between aspects of surface layout or self-movement and macroscopic properties of structured energy distributions—vary from embracing more than or less than the property of interest to the property of interest only. The improvement is gradual (to a greater or lesser degree) because the perceiver, in order to improve, must come to attend to the exact specificity rather than to the narrower or broader specificity. That is, with respect to learning to perceive an environmental property, the perceiver progresses from under- and over-differentiating the ambient energy distribution, differentiating it precisely (E. J. Gibson & J. J. Gibson, 1972; J. J. Gibson & E. J. Gibson, 1955).

Experimental Observations

In what follows, I describe several kinds of experimental results on perception and action capabilities motivated by the issues and ideas sketched above and intended, ideally, to provide insight into their significance for the development of a general theory of cognition.

Knowing by Touching

Most theorizing on perception is based on vision, with audition playing a subsidiary role. Hardly any theories of perception are constructed with touch in mind. From an evolutionary standpoint, this state of affairs is anomalous: Touching is older than either looking or listening. The most primitive creatures feel objects and explore surfaces with parts of their bodies; seeing and hearing are capabilities of the more recently evolved species. Nevertheless, active exploratory touch has, until recently, been the subject of relatively little study for several reasons (catalogued by Neisser, 1976): No specialized organ, neural activity is widespread; no obvious stimulus, tissue deformation patterns resist quantification by standard means (Boring, 1942; J. J. Gibson, 1966); there is no obvious separation between stimulus and response and no obvious way to impose active touch on a subject.

I focus here on effortful or dynamic touch. As will become evident, this form of touch provides rich opportunities to broach the issue of knowing by touching in general physical terms. It promises to redress the imbalance between touch and vision as sources of theories about how animals can know about their surroundings.

Invariants of Rigid Body Motion Specifying Properties of Hand-Held Objects

The haptic subsystem of effortful or dynamic touching refers to situations in which muscular effort and deformation of muscles and tendons is particularly involved in perceiving the properties of objects and adjacent surface layout (J. J. Gibson, 1966). When a rod is held firmly at one end and wielded (i.e., shaken, twisted, whipped back and forth, and so on), the awareness one has of properties of the rod's dimensions is based on effortful or dynamic touch. Investigations of the perception of a variety of object properties on the basis of wielding (see Turvey, Solomon, & Burton, 1989, for a review) have shown a consistent dependence on the object's pattern of different resistances to rotational acceleration in different directions—a pattern that is quantified by the inertia tensor $\mathbf{I}$. In the 3×3 matrix representation of $\mathbf{I}$, the resistances to rotational acceleration about the three axes are quantified by the diagonal terms I_{xx}, I_{yy}, and I_{zz} (moments of inertia), and the resistances to rotational acceleration in directions perpendicular to the axial rotations are quantified by the off-diagonal terms I_{xy}, I_{yx}, I_{xz}, I_{zx}, I_{yz}, and I_{zy} (products of inertia). I is a symmetric tensor; accordingly, $I_{xy} = I_{yx}$, $I_{xz} = I_{zx}$, and $I_{yz} = I_{zy}$. For any object, a coordinate system can be defined in which off-diagonals disappear, leaving only diagonal terms. The diagonal terms in this representation of the object's rotational inertia are the principal moments or eigenvalues (I_{xx}^*, I_{yy}^*, I_{zz}^*), and the coordinates with respect to which they are defined are the principal directions or eigenvectors. Perceived length of a rod or a rod segment is a function of the rod's or rod segment's moments of inertia and possibly of its eigenvalues (Fitzpatrick, Carello, & Turvey, 1990; Solomon & Turvey, 1988; Solomon, Turvey, & Burton, 1989a, 1989b). Perceived orientation of a branch perpendicular to the stem of a rod is specific to the eigenvector of the inertia tensor in the direction of the branch (Pagano, Turvey, & Burton, 1990; Turvey, Burton, Pagano, Solomon, & Runeson, in press). Perceived shape can be expressed as a function of the ratio of the maximum to the minimum eigenvalues (Burton, Turvey, & Solomon, 1990; Turvey et al., 1989).

The haptic subsystem of effortful touch is a system for sampling the structure of mechanical energy distributions and extracting its invariants. J. J. Gibson (1966, 1979) called the activity of getting information from ambient structured arrays *information pickup* and noted that it involved orienting, exploring, adjusting, optimizing, resonating, extracting, and equilibrating. These physical metaphors contrast sharply with the metaphors of inferring, hypothesis testing, constructing, conceptualizing, and so on that tend to dominate most interpretations of cognition. In an early formulation of the notion of pickup, J. J. Gibson (1966) wrote,

> If the invariants of this structure can be registered by a perceptual system, the constants of neural input will correspond to the constants of stimulus energy, although the one will not copy the other. . . . The brain is relieved of the necessity of constructing such information by *any* process—innate rational powers (theoretical nativism), the storehouse of memory (empiricism), or form-fields (Gestalt theory). . . . Instead of postulating that the brain constructs information from the output of a sensory nerve, we can suppose that the centers of the nervous system, including the brain, resonate to information. (p. 267)

Terms such as *resonance, tuning, equilibration, invariants,* and the like are terms that imply laws. Can the law-based perspective implicated in the notion of pickup be developed? Regarding the kinds of data identified above, a description of effortful or dynamic touch has been given as a particular embodiment of particular lawful regularities suitably harnessed by the person's intentions. Solomon has advanced the idea that the variables defining the haptic subsystem with respect to the goal of perceiving rod extent can be identified in the form of operator equations, where the operators are taken to be natural laws (Solomon, 1988; Solomon & Turvey, 1988; Solomon, Turvey, & Burton, 1989a, 1989b). A brief overview of this enterprise follows.

Let wielding take place through motions of the hand. Let a vector quantity $\mathbf{r}$ represent the hand–rod rigid body system. The matrix $\mathbf{A}$, then, represents an operator such that $\mathbf{Ar} = \mathbf{y}'''$ is a description of rigid body motion about a fixed axis in the wrist. Now, let a vector quantity $\mathbf{h}$ represent the haptic subsystem, a functional organ comprising mobile, mechanoreceptive tissues. The effect of the rigid body motion, expressed as $\mathbf{AR} = \mathbf{y}'''$, is a deformation of the haptic subsystem. The resultant deformable body motion is described by the operator equation $\mathbf{Dh} = \mathbf{y}''$. Now, assume an invariant property of the tissue deformation $\mathbf{y}''$ that is specific to the particular object property on which the perception of object length is based. This assumption can be expressed as the claim that there exists an operator $\mathbf{Q}$ such that when it acts or operates on $\mathbf{Dh}$, it yields the transform $\mathbf{y}'$, where $\mathbf{y}'$ is an invariant of this deformable body motion specific to the object property on which the perception of object length is based: $\mathbf{QDh} = \mathbf{y}'$. $\mathbf{y}'$ is not the ultimate measurement of the haptic perceptual instrument; that is, it is not the locations reachable by the hand-held rod. Consequently, to complete the description, a further operator is needed. This operator $\mathbf{L}$ must render $\mathbf{y}'$ as a location in a coordinate system centered at the subject. That is, $\mathbf{LQDh} = \mathbf{y}$, where $\mathbf{y}$ is the location of the distal tip of the hand-held rod.

The operators $\mathbf{A}$, $\mathbf{D}$, $\mathbf{Q}$, and $\mathbf{L}$ are, in principle, embodiments of physical laws. Thus, note that $\mathbf{A}$ is the inertia tensor, $\mathbf{D}$ is the strain tensor or rate of strain tensor, and $\mathbf{Q}$ is functionally equivalent to a nonsingular matrix that diagonalizes simultaneously the symmetric inertia and strain tensors. These operators connect the explanatory activity of the haptic subsystem, the rigid body motions produced by that activity, the tissue deformations that they in turn induce, and the property of the environment that the subject intends to perceive. Collectively, they (a) define the haptic perceptual instrument that "measures" the extent of a hand-held object and (b) preserve specificity over the various components of the perceiving–acting cycle. The central idea is that, given the operators, a single-valued, determinate mapping is guaranteed between a hand-held object's resistance to rotational acceleration and the perception of its length. Ideally, the operator formulation of information pickup can be pursued for the other haptic subsystem capabilities noted above. In each case, further experimentation and theoretical work will be required to establish the relevant operators and the laws thereby embodied.

Invariant Basis for Perceiving Surface Separation by Probing

A crucial aspect of the information-perception specificity hypothesis is that one should be prepared to discover new quantities characterizing energy distributions, quantities to which perceiving proves to be specific. The point is well made by experiments on haptic probing.

I return to the wielding of a given object to identify more explicitly the approach to be taken toward effortful touch in its many manifestations. The state of the wielded object at any given moment is defined by its displacement, x, and its rate of change of displacement of velocity, v. Muscular forces act on this system to bring about new states, with each new state expressible by a particular pair of x and v values. The rate of change of state as a function of force is expressed, of course, by Newton's third law. Thus, given a state (x, v), the next state is $(x + v\mathrm{d}t, v + F\mathrm{d}t)$, where the force F is given by $F = F(x, v, t)$. The set of state transitions defines the trajectory or behavior of the object. It is expected that both within an instance and across instances of wielding to perceive a given property, there will be considerable variability in the object's behavior.

An important feature of the standard mechanical construal expressed in the preceding is the division of system and environment; the system is characterized by states (x_i, v_i); the environment is not, and once a system has been defined, everything remaining defines its environment. Forces are part of the environment. It is important to note that the function defined above for force implicitly includes a number of constants or parameters (independent of states and time). These express the specific way in which a system is coupled to the forces imposed on it by its environment. It is the parameters (e.g., rotational inertia, mass, coefficient of elasticity, coefficient of friction) that confer on a system its specific identity independent of whatever radical changes occur in the system's states (Rosen, 1988). In attempting to perceive the spatial features of an object by wielding about axes in the wrist, the dynamical system is object-with-fixed-rotation point. As observed in the preceding subsection, the parameter $\mathbf{I}$ couples the torques $\mathbf{N}$ to the angular motions, $\mathbf{N} = \mathbf{I}d\omega/dt$, where ω is angular velocity. To reiterate, research has shown that the perceptions of length, orientation, and shape are a function of $\mathbf{I}$. The implication is that effortful touch is attuned to the invariant parameters of the object's dynamics rather than to the varying states and torques.

If one were to study the haptic capacity for perceiving surface layout by probing, then the strategy would seem to be as follows: (a) define the dynamical system, (b) identify the parameters that couple the (muscular and other) forces impressed on the system to the system's states, (c) determine, for the given property of the surface layout, the parameter or parameters that constrain fully the perception, and (d) provide a reasoned basis for the relation between the pertinent parameter(s) and the perception. With respect to (c), it would be important to keep open the possibility that the parameter in question is of a novel kind in the sense that it may not yet be identified within conventional physics. Party for convenience, but also because of the potential for linking research on the haptic and movement systems, the relevant parameters might be referred to as *order parameters*. In the study of coordinated movements discussed below, the phase relation between limbs is classified as an order parameter (e.g., Haken, Kelso, & Bunz, 1985; Schmidt, Carello, & Turvey, 1990) in the sense that it is a collective variable that captures the spatio-temporal organization of the component subsystems and changes more slowly than do the variables characterizing the states of the component subsystems (e.g., velocity, amplitude). Regarding the haptic perceptual system, one can expect to identify single quantities that capture the unchanging spatial-temporal structure of a probing situation. An example comes from experiments on the ability to perceive the magnitude of surface separation by striking the surfaces' interiors with a hand-held rod through essentially horizontal motions (Barac-Cikoja & Turvey, 1991).

The methodology is depicted in Figure 1 (left panel). The variables manipulated were aperture size, magnitude of angular displacement Θ (with the rotation point O in the wrist always on the bisector of the angle), distance b of the point of contact with the surfaces from the axis of rotation, hand-rod mass m, location of the hand rod's center of mass a, and moment of inertia I_{yy} of the hand rod about O. (Thinking of a rod parallel to the ground, the z axis is its longitudinal axis, the y axis is vertical and perpendicular to z, and the x axis is horizontal and perpendicular to z.) Analysis of the patterning of forces resulting from exploratory striking revealed a collective quantity $\lambda = \sin(\Theta/2) [1 - (2a/b) + (ma^2/I_{yy})]$ that was—for a given rod, aperture, and distance—invariant over muscular forces and resultant torques. Haptic perception of aperture size was not unique to aperture size but varied with distance, angle, and probe properties (Figure 1 [center panel]). It was, however, specific to λ, which predicted successfully the interdependent effects of angular displacement, distance of surfaces, and the mechanical properties of the implement as shown in Figure 1 (right panel).

The haptic probing situation depicted in Figure 1 (left panel) limits exploration to motions about a fixed point in the wrist. It is obviously not the most general of circumstances. Nonetheless, the perceptions obtained under these conditions are invariantly related to the surface layout relative to the fixed point and to the qualities of the probe.

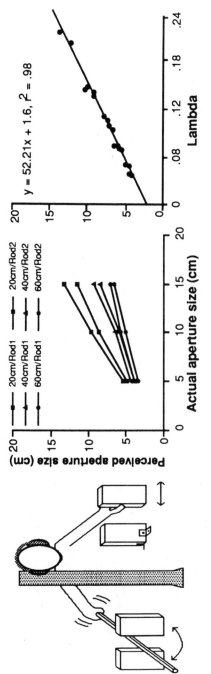

FIGURE 1 Left panel: Haptic exploration of an aperture by means of a hand-held probe. Center panel: Perceived aperture size as a function of actual aperture size, length of probe, and moment of inertia of probe (Rod 1 < Rod 2). Right panel: Perceived aperture size as a function of λ. (From Barac-Cikoja & Turvey, 1991. Copyright 1991 by the American Psychological Association. Reprinted by permission.)

The mapping depicted in Figure 1 (right panel), together with the mappings identified in the discussion of perceiving by wielding, might be indicative of a very general tendency on the part of the haptic system. If λ^* is the tissue deformation invariant corresponding to λ, then it appears that, under the intention of perceiving aperture size, the haptic subsystem resonates to λ^*. Eigenvalues of dynamical systems define geodesics and minima (e.g., Strang, 1986), and we can suppose that λ^* does likewise. The haptic system's sensitivity to invariants may be continuous, therefore, with the very general propensity of physical systems to orient toward dynamics of minimum energy.

Knowing That and Knowing How in Locomotion

Locomotory activity is fundamental. Here I consider the possibility of a general dynamic governing the disposition in quadruped to switch at higher speeds from alternate gaits (i.e., limbs of the same girdle moving together in opposite directions) to symmetric gaits (i.e., limbs of the same girdle moving together in the same direction). Surprisingly, the evidence is found in studies with humans coordinating upper or lower limbs in a variety of situations.

If the organization of the limbs during locomotion is governed by general principles (Schöner, Jiang, & Kelso, 1990; Turvey, Schmidt, Rosenblum, & Kugler, 1988), then one might suppose that the perceptual basis for the control of such organization is also lawfully grounded. Vision plays a dominant role in the steering of locomotion, and from a law-based perspective, it does so because optical information in J. J. Gibson's specificational sense is richly available. I begin with an important example of the optical support for locomotory activity and then turn to the issue of "gait" transitions.

Invariant Optical Specification of Impact (Hard or Soft)

During locomotion, the optical structure available to the eyes undergoes transformations. This transforming optical structure has been referred to as the optic flow field (J. J. Gibson, 1966, 1979; Koenderink, 1986). For a point of observation approaching a surface, an optical solid angle Ω can be defined that has the surface as its base and the point of observation as its apex. The inverse of the relative rate of expansion of Ω, $[(1/\Omega)d\Omega/dt]^{-1}$, defines a variable τ that is specific to the time elapsing before contact with the surface will be made given the current approach velocity $\dot{x}$. Mathematical analysis (Lee, 1976, 1980) suggests that the dimensionless quantity $\dot{\tau}$ has a critical value with implications for controlling activity. If $\dot{\tau} \geq -0.5$, then the upcoming contact with a substantial surface will involve no momentum exchange; that is, the contact will be "soft." If, to the contrary, $\dot{\tau} < -0.5$, then the upcoming contact will involve momentum exchange; that is, the collision will be "hard" or violent. To see how the critical number of -0.5 is derived mathematically, consider a bird moving toward a branch with a kinetic energy of $m\dot{x}^2/2$. To contact the branch gently, the bird must provide a decelerative force F over the distance x, such that the kinetic energy is zero by the time contact is made. A measure of the appropriateness of F at any point is whether or not $Fx \geq m\dot{x}^2/2$, that is, whether $x \ddot{x}/\dot{x}^2 \geq 0.5$. The magnitude of $x/\dot{x}$ is the time to contact specified by the optical variable τ . Differentiating the expression $x/\dot{x} = \tau$ with respect to time gives $x \ddot{x}/\dot{x}^2 = 1 + \dot{\tau}$. Substituting $x \ddot{x}/\dot{x}^2 \geq 0.5$ yields $\dot{\tau} \geq -0.5$. Experiments have demonstrated the ability of human observers to perceive the harshness of simulated collisions as a function of $\dot{\tau}$ (Kim, Turvey, & Carello, in press). The importance of $\dot{\tau}$ is that it provides a lawful optical basis for determining the adequacy of forces for an intended contact. Highly mobile and reasonably large ($>.001$ kg) animals must locomote in object-cluttered surrounds and must keep their momentum exchanges with those objects within particular limits to avoid internal fracture. As a rule of thumb, irreversible damage would be done to a mammal, whatever species and whatever size, if the velocities before and after contact differed by 7.62 m/s or more (Kornhauser, 1964). It might be hypothesized, therefore, that the evolution of locomotory capability is tightly constrained by the requirement of sensitivity to $\dot{\tau}$.

Invariant Dynamic for Spontaneous Transitions in Interlimb Coordination

Characteristic of locomotion in horses, dogs, cats, and the like is the presence of relatively sharp transitions between one gait and another as the speed of locomotion increases. An appealing idea is that gait transitions, and perhaps rapid spontaneous shifts in movement organizations more generally, are analogous to the simplest form of self-organization known in physics, namely, the phase transition (Kugler, Kelso, & Turvey, 1980, 1982).

The phase relation Φ between limbs is classified as an order parameter (e.g., Haken et al., 1985; Schmidt et al., 1990). Repeating the definition given above, it is a collective variable that captures the spatio-temporal organization of the component subsystems and changes more slowly than the variables characterizing the states of the component subsystems (e.g., velocity, amplitude). The common frequency of the limbs, $\omega_{coupled}$, is classified as a control parameter—a variable that is held constant during a given "dynamical run," is changed across dynamical runs, and is associated with changes (bifurcations) in the order parameter at particular critical values. If the change in interlimb coordination is a phase transition of the kind typifying nonequilibrium systems, then the phase relation quantity must exhibit the following properties: modality, meaning that the quantity has two or more distinct values in which it may occur; inaccessibility, meaning that values outside of the distinct states cannot be maintained reliably; sudden jumps, meaning that a slow change in the control parameter may lead to a relatively rapid change in the order parameter; hysteresis, meaning that a sudden jump and its reverse do not occur at the same values of the control parameter; critical slowing down, meaning that the time taken by the order parameter to return to its value before a perturbation increases as the transition point is approached; and critical fluctuations, meaning that the variance in the order parameter may become large as the transition point is approached.

The preceding criteria have been observed in experiments in which a person is required to oscillate the two index fingers (or two hands) at a common frequency (Kelso, Scholz, & Schöner, 1986; Scholz, Kelso, & Schöner, 1987) varied by a metronome that the person tracks. Results show that there are only two steady states: in phase and antiphase. With increasing frequency, antiphase switches rapidly to in phase. In phase, however, does not switch to antiphase, and the antiphase to in-phase transition is not reversed by a reduction in frequency (that is, there is hysteresis). Most significant, the order parameter exhibits critical slowing down and critical fluctuations. Recently, investigations have been conducted on the spontaneous jumps in coordination when two limbs are connected optically between two people rather than anatomically within a person. In these experiments (Schmidt et al., 1990), two seated people each oscillated a leg with the goal of coordinating the two legs out of phase or in phase as the frequency of the movement was increased. To satisfy the goal, the two people watched each other closely. As with the within-person case, the between-person case exhibited a sudden behavioral transition from out of phase to in phase, but not vice versa; it showed divergence, hysteresis, and critical fluctuations (critical slowing down was not investigated). If the two people began their movements out of phase and increased limb frequency simultaneously at the same rate without watching each other, then no transition occurred. The phase transition depended on looking.

Phase transitions in visually coordinated movements are not restricted to situations in which both oscillators are biological with a bilateral coupling between them. Experiments by Wimmers, Beek, and van Wieringen (in press) showed that the phenomenon can also be induced in subjects who are required to oscillate the lower arm out of phase with a dot moving at increasing frequency back and forth on an oscilloscope. In this situation also, an abrupt jump occurred from out of phase to in phase, but a jump from in phase to out of phase could not be induced (either by means of a reduction in frequency or with in phase as the initial condition). The observed jump qualified as a phase transition in exhibiting the requisite criteria of divergence, hysteresis, critical fluctuations, and critical slowing down. Further experiments revealed the importance of the orientation of the tracking signal relative to the orientation of the movement. If the two orientations were exactly orthogonal, then no phase transitions occurred because in this special case, the difference between in phase and out of phase was meaningless. A deviation of 5° in the orientation of the scope signal from orthogonality was sufficient to reintroduce the phase transition from out of phase to in phase.

The three cases of phase transition differ in many ways, most notably in the populations of neurons involved (the nervous systems of two people vs. the nervous system of one person), the perceptual systems involved (the visual perceptual system in between-persons coordination vs. the haptic perceptual system in within-person coordination), and the direction of the coupling (bilateral in the within-person and between-persons case and unilateral in the person–environment case). That these differences did not affect the major qualitative features of the phase transition phenomenon suggests the possibility of an order parameter dynamics that applies invariantly across the three kinds of neural, perceptual, and actuator settings because, presumably, the interactions in these settings are only superficially different. The within-person, between-persons, and person–environment cases involve the same observable quantities related dynamically in the same way. As such, the same dynamics can be used to model the differential stability of the within-person and between-persons coordination modes and the phase transition between them, whereas the inherent asymmetry of the person–environment case requires minor adjustments in the coupling function to preserve the same global dynamics.

Knowing How to Coordinate the Limbs

Behind the research reported in the preceding section is a physical (dynamical) perspective that interprets biological movement systems as self-organizing systems (e.g., Beek, 1989a; Haken & Wunderlin, 1990; Kugler, Kelso, & Turvey, 1980, 1982; Kugler & Turvey, 1987; Schöner & Kelso, 1988; Turvey, 1990a, 1990b). This perspective leads to the expectation that macroscopic organizations (e.g., coordination modes or patterns) can be assembled spontaneously from the many microscopic degrees of freedom when control parameters, unspecific to the resultant organization, are changed. It also leads to the expectation that amplification of intrinsic nonlinearities, by scaling of control parameters or other means, will form stable and reproducible spectra of coordination modes. And it leads to the expectation that perception–action systems, although they are ordinary physical systems (in the sense of conforming to physical laws and principles), can achieve extraordinary accomplishments through the smart, special-purpose exploitation of the regularities (symmetries) inherent in behavioral tasks. This perspective is elaborated by the research reported in the following sections.

Invariant Modes of Coordination: Farey Tree Principles

Much research has been conducted on polyrhythmic behavior, and there have been efforts to explain the outcomes in terms of local models appealing to specific internal representations (motor programs; e.g., Deutsch, 1983). The hypothesis to be pursued from the perspective discussed above is that these outcomes comport with mechanisms of a very general nature. The idea is that when polyrhythmic behavior or mode locking is unattainable, or attainable briefly but not sustainable, the observed coordination pattern remains understandable in terms of general principles of mode attraction (deGuzman & Kelso, in press; Peper, Beek, & van Wierengen, in press).

Several qualitative features of the mode-locking structure of driven nonlinear oscillators can be universally described with the aid of the so-called Farey sum (Gonzalez & Piro, 1985). Let $W = K/L$ be the winding number (for K oscillations of one oscillator; the other oscillator completes L oscillations), and let this number be a rational number. Then, Farey summation $\oplus$ is defined as: $W_1 \oplus W_2 = (K_1 + K_2)/(L_1 + L_2)$. Two winding numbers that obey the relation $|K_i L_j - K_j L_i| = 1$ are called *unimodular* or *mod 1 numbers* and are said to be adjacent; their Farey sum is called their *mediant.* Given the preceding, all the rational numbers between 0 and 1 (and, synonymously, all possible phase-locked regions) can be organized hierarchically into a tree in the following manner: Start with the parents 0/1 and 1/1 and form successive layers of mediants. The first level of the tree is defined as $1/2 = 0/1 \oplus 1/1$; the second level is given by $1/3 = 0/1 \oplus 1/2, 2/3 = 1/2 \oplus 1/1$, and so on. The Farey tree up to Level 4 is shown in Figure 2. Its branching structure summarizes all the possible mode locks that complex dynamical systems may attain and their possible bifurcation routes.

To aid in appreciating the Farey tree as a representation of mode-locking phenomena, consider a circle map—an iteration of a simple equation that takes one point Θ_n on the circumference of a circle to a second point Θ_{n+1} (with $0 \leq \Theta < 1$). A popular version is $\Theta_{n+1} = \Theta_n + [(K/2\pi)\sin 2\pi\Theta_n)] + \Omega$ where K represents the amplitude of the periodic forcing or coupling, Ω represents (as before) the ratio of uncoupled frequencies, and the sinusoidal term represents the effect of the forcing. In the space of the control parameters K and Ω, the mode-locking regions or "Arnold tongues" (given by

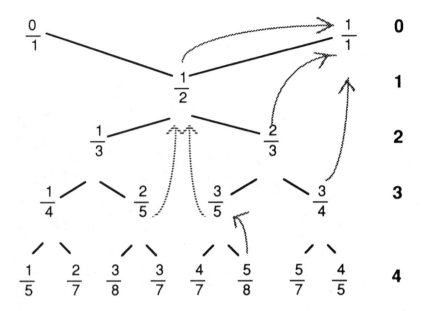

FIGURE 2   Farey tree. (Arrows indicate mod 1 transitions.)

recurring Θ values) are distinct when $K < 1$, with one region for each rational value of Ω (see Figure 3). When forcing is weak to moderate $(K < 1)$, there are distinct regions of stable entrainment or frequency- and phase-locking, with quasiperiodicity found in the regions outside the tongues. Of particular importance to the Farey tree representation are the facts that (a) the mode-locked regions differ in width below $K < 1$, and (b) narrower regions are interspersed with wider regions along the Ω axis. The widest mode-locked regions (1:1, 1:2, 2:3, 1:3, and so on) are the most stable and the most attractive. These regions correspond to the higher Farey levels. With little noise in a system of coupled oscillators, less stable mode-locked states can be maintained; with significant noise, how-ever, the system is likely to be propelled into a neighboring, more stable region (e.g., 3:4 to 2:3). Thus, Peper et al. (in press) found that with increasing frequency, people execut-ing well-learned 2:5 and 3:5 polyrhythmic coordination patterns made transitions into mode locks with smaller integer ratios.

Ideally, to probe thoroughly the Farey tree as a constraint on simple rhythmic and polyrhythmic coordination patterns, one needs a method so simple that any person, expe-rienced or not, can achieve any integer ratio (see Kelso & DeGuzman, 1988). To this end, experiments have been conducted with a procedure in which the subject swings a

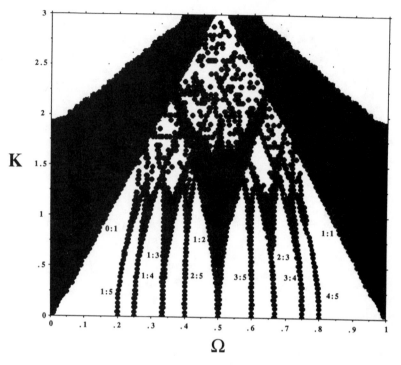

FIGURE 3   Mode-locking regions (Arnold's tongue) as generated by the circle map. (K = amplitude of the periodic forcing or coupling; Ω = ratio of uncoupled frequencies. Above $K = 1$, there is resonance overlap or chaos. From Schmidt, Beek, Treffner, & Turvey, 1991. Copyright 1991 by the American Psychological Association. Reprinted by permission.)

pendulum in his or her right hand at the most comfortable frequency (i.e., close to its resonance as a strictly gravitational pendulum), and a metronome is then set at a frequency that forms a particular integer ratio with the pendular rhythm. The subject tracks the metronome with a drumminglike motion executed with a small, light stick held in the left hand. It is emphasized to the subject that he or she must attend to and track the metronome as closely as possible and at the same time keep the pendulum oscillating comfortably. As a consequence, the two limbs can exhibit a coordinated pattern such as 4:5, 3:4, and so on without the subject being overly stressed and without lengthy (and often unsuccessful) learning. Averaged across trials and subjects, actual ratios (those achieved by the subject) matched expected ratios (those set by the experimenter, which were 1:2, 2:3, 2:5, 3:5, 3:4, 4:7, 5:8, and 4:5; Treffner & Turvey, 1990). Within the individual subject data, however, there were a large number of transitions from the expected ratio to other ratios. Most typically, a subject would change the frequency of the pendulum (unknowingly) to stabilize the interlimb coordination at the largest neighboring resonance. That is, the transitions were mostly mod 1 transitions upward (e.g., 5:8 to 3:5, 2:5 to 1:2, 2:3 to 1:1). It would seem that the stability conditions prescribed by the theory of mode locking are selective of the coordination patterns that can be maintained over the limbs and limb segments.

An Invariant Strategy for Achieving a Balance of Order and Variability: 1|f Scaling

Interlimb coordinations, as modes of a system of many degrees of freedom at many levels, may benefit from a principle of self-similar fluctuations over multiple time scales. This fractal principle provides an optimal balance of order and variability (West & Shlesinger, 1990).

Interlimb frequency locking in a 1:1 pattern involves several subtasks; for example, sequential contractions of the flexors and extensors of one limb and sequential contractions of the flexors and extensors of the other limb. Insofar as these latter subtasks are nested within the 1:1 limb pattern, their frequencies are higher. At finer grains one can expect to identify more and more subtasks operating at even shorter time scales. One can also expect subtasks the time scales of which are longer than those of the interlimb coordination; for example, a capillary red blood cell flow acting as an oxygen choke limiting the rate of local oxidation in muscle tissue at about .01 Hz (Iberall, 1969). For complex systems, a spectral plot shows how the energy of a process is distributed across different kinds of activities at different time scales (Bloch et al., 1971; Iberall, 1977, 1978; Iberall, Soodak, & Hassler, 1978). A prominent observation for such systems is that the power at a given frequency is a function of the inverse of the frequency; that is, the spectrum can be characterized by a relation that scales the magnitude of activity to $1/f^{\delta}$, where f is frequency and δ is a scaling factor. These spectra are called *inverse power law spectra* and have been reported for a number of biological processes (e.g., Goldberger, Bhargava, West, & Mandell, 1985; Goldberger, Kobalter, & Bhargava, 1986; Koboyashi & Musha, 1982). A spectrum that scales power to $1/f^{0}$ is a flat spectrum of white noise. It represents a random organization of subtasks; fluctuations at any moment are independent of fluctuations at any other moment. Brownian noise, with its frequency spectrum defined by the term $1/f^{2}$, has fluctuations (subtasks) that are strongly correlated. The $1/f$ spectrum ($\delta = 1$) represents a state of organization such that the power at each frequency is proportional to the inverse of the frequency (power $\propto \tau$). Because power is not localized but distributed across the entire spectrum, fluctuations at any one time scale are only loosely correlated with those of any other time scale. This linear distribution of energy with $1/f$ makes the system adaptive; a perturbation to a process at one time scale will not adversely affect the system's global integrity (West & Shlesinger, 1990).

Schmidt, Beek, Treffner, and Turvey (1991) examined the spectrum for frequency-locked limbs. Specifically, they addressed the question of how the human movement system meets the challenge of competing frequencies; that is, how does the ratio of uncoupled frequencies Ω affect the organization of the rhythmic subtasks producing 1:1 interlimb coordination? They manipulated Ω by means of pendulums held and swung in each hand, with the pendulums equal or different in dimensions. The spectra of the order parameter (relative phase between the hand-held pendulum motions) obeyed inverse power law behavior, with δ in the neighborhood of 2 but lessening in the direction of 1 as Ω deviated more from 1. The total power, which increased with deviations from $\Omega = 1$, was concentrated at spectral peaks that were integer multiples of $\omega_{coupled}$. Old spectral peaks grew in magnitude and new peaks, at higher integer multiples, were added as the frequency competition amplified. Importantly, 1:1 frequency locking in the mean was achieved for all Ω. What was seen, therefore, was how the subtasks reacted systematically to Ω, producing varied forms of time-varying (relative) coordinations to yield a single form of 1:1 frequency locking in the mean (viz., the one intended). The direction of change in δ toward 1 suggests that the subtask reaction to increasing frequency competition amounts to a systematic equalizing of activity per time scale. The implication is that, to sustain the 1:1 frequency locking in the mean in the face of strong frequency competition, the movement system assembles coordinations on a fractal plan.

Knowing How to Juggle and How to Play Table Tennis

Recognizing the essential role of dynamics in interlimb rhythmic coordinations leads to a particular strategy for understanding the learning of skilled behavior. The strategy begins, ideally, with the identification of the dynamical laws and resultants regularities at work within the skill, a step that is undertaken preferably by the empirical and theoretical study of the skill as performed most proficiently. Once available, these laws and regularities provide, in principle, a frame of reference within which the process of learning can be interpreted. Ideally, the interpretations should be couched in a language that relates closely to the dynamics. For a general theory of how a person comes to know a skill, and the form taken by that knowledge, the dynamical strategy just outlined is not without significance. Learning to juggle has been described as debugging (Minsky & Pappert, 1972), constructing a program (Austin, 1976), and discerning a grammar (Norman, 1976). Efforts to address juggling in terms of forming cognitive representations are compromised by the absence of answers to the questions, What determines the content of the representations? What is their origin? What principles govern their changes? As abstract control structures for the skill of juggling, proposed cognitive representations are prone to be arbitrary and fictitious without a well-established linkage to the physical principles and information kinds that make the skill possible. From a perspective that emphasizes dynamics and information in J. J. Gibson's (1966, 1979) specificational sense more so than representations, the ultimate challenge is an account of skill learning that provides the lawful underpinnings of the evolving control structure, thereby motivating its content and rationalizing its origin (Beek, 1989a; Schmidt, Treffner, Shaw, & Turvey, in press).

Invariants in the Temporal Structure of Cascade Juggling

In the cascade juggling of an odd number of balls in a figure-eight pattern, what must the juggler do to ensure smooth juggling without the balls colliding? The answer is likely to be found primarily in the relation among the various time quantities having to do with the hand movements and the motions of the balls in flight. A hand loop is made up of two distinguishable times. One time is the duration in which the hand carries a ball; the other time is the duration in which the ball is in flight. Regardless of the exact values of these durations, to juggle in cascade fashion (or any other recurrent pattern that does not allow two balls in the same hand at any one time), the total of flight time and hand-loaded time per ball in a complete cycle must equal the total of hand-unloaded time and hand-loaded time per hand in a complete cycle. In other words, the ratio of the basic period of the balls to the basic period of the hand equals the ratio of the number of balls to the number of hands. This timing constraint was first identified by Shannon (Horgan, 1990; Raibert, 1986). It applies beyond cascade juggle to all versions (e.g., reversed cascade, fountain, shower) and may, therefore, be considered a universal field equation for juggling (Horgan, 1990). It captures what must remain invariant over the variations introduced by object mass, object shape, posture, speed, actuator forces, limb directions, and so on and whether or not the juggler is a person or a machine.

For the theory of perception–action systems, the equation's significance lies in its universality and the precision with which it is formulated. Newell (1986) has emphasized the need to consider environmental, organismic, and task constraints on coordination; optimal coordinations are said to be fixed by the interaction among them. What Shannon's equation makes clear is that task constraints are potentially definable independent of the particular environmental setting and the specific individual animal. The intimation that all tasks (all coordinations) are, in general, like that of juggling (i.e., typically invariant over environmental and organismic variations) can be developed empirically only to the extent that their constraint structures can be expressed with mathematical precision. In general, the precise mathematical formulation of the constraints characterizing skilled acts is in its infancy and awaiting the emergence of more appropriate analytic tools. In the meantime, however, the study of the precisely formulated juggling task can lay the groundwork for a broader appreciation of the formative role of task constraints in assembling coordinations.

How do the distinguished component times relate to one another within Shannon's equation? In how many different ways can the juggler completely fill the total loop time of the hands and the total loop time of the balls with component times? Looking just at the hands, one can imagine that the "temporal tiling problem" reduces for the juggler to the problem of how long to hold onto a ball during a cycle of the hand. That is, what proportion of the hand's cycle time is to be taken up by holding or carrying a ball? (Clearly, this is an important measure because it determines the mean number of balls in the air over time and, thus, the visual quality of the juggle.) Experiments conducted on expert jugglers revealed that, across eight different jugglers (two of whom were professionals), the ratios of time holding the ball to a hand's cycle time varied from 0.54 to 0.86 (mean = 0.70) when the number of balls was three and the instructions were to juggle at a high, preferred, and low frequency of juggling (Beek, 1989b). With five balls, however, the proportion of the hand's cycle time taken up by holding or carrying the ball to total loop time was always close to but not exactly 3:4 (range = 0.71–0.79; mean = 0.75), whereas the three jugglers who could cascade juggle seven balls approached the ratio of 3:4 even more closely (Beek & Turvey, in press). Apparently, all cascade jugglers essentially tiled according to the same blueprint of ¾ of total cycle time. For the task of cascade juggling, a 3:4 ratio may be regarded as identifying an Arnold tongue (see Figure 3), and a wave modulation measure may be developed for the degree of quasi-periodicity or deviation from the Arnold tongue. The plot of the actual ratios against this measure was slightly quadratic for the three-ball juggling and linear for the five-ball juggling, with the values for the eight jugglers at the three rates distributed on either side of the 3:4 ratio coinciding with zero deviation. The average deviations or quasi-periodicities were smallest for the professional jugglers.

Juggling, apparently, does not entail perfect mode or frequency locking. In fact, one might argue that imperfect mode locking is both inevitable and desirable. The circle map teaches us that if forcing is weak, then continued residence in an Arnold tongue demands precision with respect to forcing magnitude and forcing frequency (or their analogies) from cycle to cycle. Exact reproduction of parameters, however, is not characteristic of biological movement systems. Moreover, parameter flexibility, rather than rigid mode locking, is required to juggle adaptively and with flair. It remains true, nonetheless, that juggling success depends on a stable coordination, especially as task constraints become more severe, such as in juggling more than three balls. The variability–stability dualism is resolved by the juggler operating close to, but not in, an Arnold tongue, and as we have seen, the more skilled the juggler, the closer to an Arnold tongue—to true mode locking—he or she gets. These skilled jugglers have acquired the stability and reproducibility of performance that enables them to keep five or seven balls going.

Why should the ratio of the time a ball is held to the total loop time of the hand hover in the vicinity of 3:4? It has been suggested that it does so because the most generic partitioning principle of time in juggling proves to be one in which the flight time of the balls is tiled in units of time loaded minus time unloaded—a "hidden" unit of time produced by the inequality of hand-loaded time and hand-unloaded time in a hand loop. One may think of this hidden unit of time as "a gap of time being thrown into the flights of the balls at each toss." Intriguingly, if the fall time of a ball (which halves the flight time) is covered exactly with the mean number of balls in the air multiplied by this hidden unit of time, then the ratio of hand-holding time to total hand-loop time is 3:4, regardless of the frequency of juggling, the number of balls juggled, or the number of hands that juggle (hence, "most generic"). In a sense, knowing this partitioning is equivalent to knowing the symmetry solution of cascade juggling.

Invariant Organization of a Rapid Interceptive Skill

Consider a table tennis player returning a serve with the intent of having the ball strike the table top within a circularly bounded region of 55-cm diameter at 2.5-m distance. The situation described was investigated experimentally by Bootsma and van Wierengen (1990) with several world-class players. Striking the ball occurs at high velocity, approximately 800°/s. The controlled variable is the direction of travel of the bat at the moment of bat/ball contact. Given that the bat is changing direction rapidly near the moment of contact, due to the bat's high velocity on a curved trajectory, substantial space–time constraints must be satisfied for successful contact. Bootsma and van Wierengen's analysis revealed that balls were contacted with the bats' direction of travel not varying more than 6° around the line through the center of the target area. Moreover, for expert subjects, the accuracy of timing was computed to be of the order of 2–4 ms (as given by the standard deviation of direction divided by the mean of the directional velocity).

Because of the nature of the experimental arrangement, Bootsma and van Wierengen (1990) were able to observe the variability in performance over trials in which the conditions from trial to trial were held constant (speed and direction of the served ball was mechanically controlled). A careful analysis of the data revealed two major observations. First, the sooner the drive was initiated (a larger value of τ, the optic variable specifying time to contact), the smaller were the mean velocity and acceleration; the later the drive was initiated (smaller τ), the larger were the mean velocity and acceleration. Second, significant negative correlations were found in the first half of the drive and in the second half of the drive when the first half was partialled out, suggesting that the act was amended during execution. A major conclusion from these observations is that the skilled playing of table tennis entails a synergy of perception variables (e.g., τ) and action variables (e.g., bat acceleration). Motor equivalence in table tennis—varieties of movement patterns satisfying the same goal—is a feature of the perception–action cycle and not of motor processes alone. To know how to play table tennis well is to know how to co-organize information detection and performatory activity as one.

Summary: In Search of Cognition's Holonomic Foundations

The machine (or artifactual) perspective and the dynamics (or natural) perspective have long been recognized as contrasting orientations to psychological phenomena (Köhler, 1947). Thinking of biological processes in machine terms focuses attention on how matter is configured in particular ways (e.g., the parts and linkages of a combustion engine) to bring about directed motions; thinking of biological processes in dynamical terms focuses attention on the laws of motion and change. In advocating the invariance postulate of evolution (Köhler, 1969)—that animate matter is continuous with inanimate matter and, therefore, has to be understood on the same grounds—the Gestaltists made clear their stand in favor of the dynamics perspective. As they took pains to note, their position was neither that of the empiricist nor that of the nativist (it makes no sense to say that abiding by the laws of nature is an inherited trait). By their reading, both of the traditional schools adopted the machine perspective, seeking explanations of the order and regularity in perception and action in terms of constraints realized in the architecture of the nervous system. The empiricist saw these constraints established over the life span of the individual. The nativists (in neo-Darwinian garb) saw these constraints established over the time scale of evolution. The Gestaltists did not deny that learning and evolution affected the compositions of nervous systems, nor did they deny that learning and evolution were important; what they did deny was the primacy in explanation ascribed to the constraints wrought by learning and evolution. For them, primacy in explanation had to be given to dynamics because it was the laws of motion and change that were fundamentally responsible for the patternings in nature, wherever and whenever they were observed.

Despite their tremendous respect for laws and principles, Gestalt theorists were, in my view, limited and misguided in their application of the dynamics perspective (Shaw & Turvey, 1981). They focused on how laws and principles might configure brain states to achieve perceptually the order that, they believed, was not present in light, airborne or volatile materials, sound, and so on. They did not inquire into the laws and principles of ecological optics, ecological chemistry, ecological acoustics, and so forth; they did not see, as J. J. Gibson did, the need for law-based, mutually compatible theories of environment, energy distributions, and biology (Mace, 1977). They were not interested in building a realist theory of knowing. These criticisms aside, it remains the case that the Gestalt theorists' advocacy of dynamics over the machine perspective was a major contribution. It can be elaborated further.

Physics distinguishes two classes of constraints, the holonomic and the nonholonomic. A significant distinction between the two is that, whereas nonholonomic constraints require a physical embodiment, holonomic constraints do not. Nonholonomic constraints relate to the machine perspective; holonomic constraints relate to the dynamics perspective. When one thinks of coordination patterns as being achieved by means of motor programs, for example, one is usually thinking in terms of nonholonomic constraints in the sense that a program must occupy some material degrees of freedom. One can see intuitively that some cells at some level must be preoccupied with the task of representing the details of the program. In contrast, when one thinks of coordinations shaped by dynamics, one is usually thinking in terms of holonomic constraints (Kugler, Turvey, Schmidt, & Rosenblum, 1990). The phase-transition, mode-locking, and $1/f$ principles are exemplary of such constraints, as are the eigenvalues of the inertia and deformation tensors and the optical invariants τ and $d\tau/dt$. They constrain perception and action but do so without occupying any material degrees of freedom. At no level of nervous function or biomechanical activity in 1:1 interlimb rhythmic coordination, locomoting, juggling, playing table tennis, and so on should one expect to find components occupied with the task of representing the specifications of these invariants. In a word, the constraints on behavior provided holonomically come for "free."

The holonomic versus nonholonomic distinction is an important contrast in the contemporary effort to build an account of the "knowings" of animals and humans. In largest part, the modern study of cognition is directed at nonholonomic constraints. Analyses tend to focus on symbolic representations, perceptual algorithms, connection matrices, motor programs, schemata, templates, and so on as the causal bases for the phenomena of interest. All of the foregoing are structures or processes that require material embodiment. They are usually modeled on a computer, and the concerns they invoke about the amount of space needed to accommodate them clearly bespeak their nonholonomic nature.

In this chapter, I have focused on theory and research directed at holonomic constraints. The question posed repeatedly has been, What kind of holonomy is at work in this perception–action situation? From my vantage point, this question deserves serious consideration for at least two reasons. First, nonholonomic constraints have meaning only in the context of the holonomy that they harness (Pattee, 1968, 1971); consequently, nonholonomic constraints proposed without an understanding of the lawful regularities are prone to be arbitrary (as suggested in the discussion above of skill learning). Second, in pursuing the aforementioned question, one responds to the general charge of J. J. Gibson's (1979) ecological approach, which I read as, Identify the holonomic constraints that make the everyday epistemic achievements of living things possible.

References

Austin, H. A. (1976). *A computational theory of physical skill.* Unpublished doctoral dissertation, Department of Electrical Engineering and Computer Science, MIT, Cambridge, MA.

Barac-Cikoja, D., & Turvey, M. T. (1991). Perceiving aperture size by striking. *Journal of Experimental Psychology: Human Perception and Performance, 17,* 330–346.

Beek, P. J. (1989a). *Juggling dynamics.* Amsterdam: Free University Press.

Beek, P. J. (1989b). Timing and phase-locking in cascade juggling. *Ecological Psychology, 1,* 55–96.

Beek, P. J., & Turvey, M. T. (in press). Temporal patterning in cascade juggling. *Journal of Experimental Psychology: Human Perception and Performance.*

Bingham, G. P. (1988). Task-specific devices and the perceptual bottleneck. *Human Movement Science, 7,* 225–264.

Bloch, E. S., Cardon, S., Iberall, A., Jacobowitz, D., Kornacker, K., Lipetz, L., McCulloch, W., Urquhart, J., Weinberg, M., & Yates, F. (1971). Introduction to a biological systems science (*NASA CR-1720*). Springfield, VA: National Technical Information Service.

Boring, E. (1942). *Sensation and perception in the history of experimental psychology.* New York: Appleton-Century-Crofts.

Bootsma, R., & van Wierengen, P. (1990). The timing of rapid interceptive actions. *Journal of Experimental Psychology: Human Perception and Performance, 16,* 21–29.

Browman, C. P., & Goldstein, L. (1990). Representation and reality: Physical systems and phonological structure. *Journal of Phonetics, 18,* 411–424.

Bunge, M. (1977). *Treatise on basic philosophy: Vol. 3. Ontology 1: The furniture of the earth.* Boston: Reidel.

Burton, G., Turvey, M. T., & Solomon, H. Y. (1990). Can shape be perceived by dynamic touch? *Perception and Psychophysics, 48,* 477–487.

deGuzman, C. G., & Kelso, J. A. S. (1991). Multifrequency behavioral patterns and the phase attractive circle map. *Biological Cybernetics, 64,* 485–495.

der Heijden, A. H. C., & Stebbins, S. (1990). The information processing approach. *Psychological Research, 52,* 197–206.

Deutsch, D. (1983). The generation of two isochronous sequences in parallel. *Perception and Psychophysics, 34,* 331–337.

Fitzpatrick, P., Carello, C., & Turvey, M. T. (1990, October). *Maximum and minimum rotational moments affect the perception of length by effortful touch.* Presented at the meeting of the International Society for Ecological Psychology, Hartford, CT.

Gibson, E. J., & Gibson, J. J. (1972, June 23). The senses as information-seeking systems. *The London Times Literary Supplement,* 711–712.

Gibson, J. J. (1961). Ecological optics. *Vision Research, 1,* 253–262.

Gibson, J. J. (1966). *The senses considered as perceptual systems.* Boston: Houghton Mifflin.

Gibson, J. J. (1979). *The ecological approach to visual perception.* Boston: Houghton Mifflin.

Gibson, J. J., & Gibson, E. J. (1955). Perceptual learning: Differentiation or enrichment? *Psychological Research, 62,* 32–41.

Goldberger, A. L., Bhargava, V., West, B. J., & Mandell, A. J. (1985). On a mechanism of cardiac electrical stability: The fractal hypothesis. *Biophysics Journal, 48,* 525–528.

Goldberger, A. L., Kobalter, K., & Bhargava, V. (1986). 1/f-like scaling in neutrophil dynamics: Implications for hematologic monitoring. *IEEE Transactions on Biomedical Engineering, 33,* 874–876.

Gonzalez, D. L., & Piro, O. (1985). Symmetric kicked self-oscillators: Iterated maps, strange attractors, and symmetry of the phase locking Farey hierarchy. *Physical Review Letters, 55,* 17–20.

Haken, H. (1977). *Synergetics: An introduction.* Berlin: Springer Verlag.

Haken, H., Kelso, J. A. S., & Bunz, H. (1985). A theoretical model of phase transitions in human hand movements. *Biological Cybernetics, 51,* 347–356.

Haken, H., & Wunderlin, A. (1990). Synergetics and its paradigm of self-organization in biological systems. In H. T. A. Whiting, O. G. Meijer, & P. C. W. van Wieringin (Eds.), *The natural-physical approach to movement control* (pp. 1–36). Amsterdam: VU University Press.

Horgan, J. (1990). Profile: Claude Shannon. *Scientific American, 262,* 22–24.

Iberall, A. S. (1969). A personal overview, and new thoughts in biocontrol. In C. Waddington (Ed.), *Towards a theoretical biology: Vol. 2. Sketches* (pp. 166–178). Chicago: Aldine.

Iberall, A. S. (1977). A field and circuit thermodynamics for integrative physiology: I. Introduction to the general notions. *American Journal of Physiology, 233*, R171–R180.

Iberall, A. S. (1978). A field and circuit thermodynamics for integrative physiology: III. Keeping the books—A general experimental method. *American Journal of Physiology, 234*, R85–R97.

Iberall, A., & Soodak, H. (1987). A physics for complex systems. In F. E. Yates (Ed.), *Self-organizing systems: The emergence of order* (pp. 499–520). New York: Plenum Press.

Iberall, A. S., Soodak, H., & Hassler, F. (1978). A field circuit thermodynamics for integrative physiology: II. Power and communicational spectroscopy in biology. *American Journal of Physiology, 234*, R3–R19.

Kelso, J. A. S., & DeGuzman, G. (1988). Order in time: How cooperation between the hands informs the design of the brain. In H. Haken (Ed.), *Neural and synergetic computers* (pp. 180–196). Berlin: Springer-Verlag.

Kelso, J. A. S., Scholz, J. P., & Schöner, G. (1986). Nonequilibrium phase transitions in coordinated biological motion: Critical fluctuations. *Physics Letters, 118*, 279–284.

Kim, N.-G., Turvey, M. T., & Carello, C. (in press). Optical information about the severity of upcoming contacts. *Journal of Experimental Psychology: Human Perception and Performance.*

Koenderink, J. J. (1986). Optic flow. *Vision Research, 26*, 161–180.

Koboyashi, M., & Musha, T. (1982). 1/f fluctuation of heartbeat period. *IEEE Transaction on Biomedical Engineering, 29*, 456–457.

Köhler, W. (1947). *Gestalt psychology.* New York: Liverwright.

Köhler, W. (1969). *The task of Gestalt psychology.* Princeton, NJ: Princeton University Press.

Kornhauser, M. (1964). *Structural effects of impact.* Baltimore: Spartan Books.

Kugler, P. N., Kelso, J. A. S., & Turvey, M. T. (1980). On the concept of coordinative structures as dissipative structures: I. Theoretical lines of convergence. In G. E. Stelmach & J. Requin (Eds.), *Tutorials in motor behavior* (pp. 3–47). New York: North Holland.

Kugler, P. N., Kelso, J. A. S., & Turvey, M. T. (1982). On the control and coordination of naturally developing systems. In J. A. S. Kelso & J. E. Clark (Eds.), *The development of movement control and coordination* (pp. 5–78). New York: Wiley.

Kugler, P. N., Shaw, R. E., Vincente, K. J., & Kinsella-Shaw, J. (1990). Inquiry into intentional systems: 1. Issues in ecological physics. *Psychological Research, 52*, 98–121.

Kugler, P. N., & Turvey, M. T. (1987). *Information, natural law, and the self-assembly of rhythmic movement.* Hillsdale, NJ: Erlbaum.

Kugler, P. N., & Turvey, M. T. (1988). Self organization, flow fields, and information. *Human Movement Science, 7*, 97–129.

Kugler, P. N., Turvey, M. T., Schmidt, R. C., & Rosenblum, L. (1990). Investigating a nonconservative invariant of motion in coordinated rhythmic movements. *Ecological Psychology, 2*, 151–189.

Lee, D. N. (1976). A theory of the visual control of breaking based on information about time to collision. *Perception, 5*, 437–459.

Lee, D. N. (1978). The functions of vision. In *Modes of perceiving and processing information* (pp. 159–170). Hillsdale, NJ: Erlbaum.

Lee, D. N. (1980). The optic flow field: The foundation of vision. *Philosophical Transactions of the Royal Society of London, B 290*, 169–179.

Mace, W. M. (1977). Gibson's strategy for perceiving: Ask not what's inside your head but what your head's inside of. In R. E. Shaw & J. Bransford (Eds.), *Perceiving, acting and knowing* (pp. 43–66). Hillsdale, NJ: Erlbaum.

MacKay, D. M. (1969). *Information, mechanism, and meaning.* Cambridge, MA: MIT Press.

Marr, D. (1977). Artificial intelligence: A personal view. *Artificial Intelligence, 9*, 37–48.

Minsky, M., & Pappert, S. (1972). *Perceptrons.* Cambridge, MA: MIT Press.

Neisser, U. (1976). *Cognition and reality.* San Francisco: Freeman.

Neisser, U. (1991, November). *Without perception, there is no knowledge: Implications for artificial intelligence.* (Emory Cognition Project Report No. 22). Atlanta, GA: Department of Psychology, Emory University.

Newell, K. (1986). Constraints on the development of coordination. In M. G. Wade & H. T. A. Whiting (Eds.), *Motor development in children: Aspects of control and coordination* (pp. 341–360). Dordrecht, The Netherlands: Martinus Nijhoff.

Nicolis, G., & Prigogine, I. (1989). *Exploring complexity.* San Francisco: Freeman.

Norman, D. A. (1976). *Memory and attention.* New York: Wiley.

Pagano, C., Turvey, M. T., & Burton, G. (1990). Invariant principal directions underly haptically perceiving the orientation of hand-held objects. *Perceiving–Acting Workshop Review, 5*, 24–28. (Technical report of the Center for the Ecological Study of Perception and Action, University of Connecticut, Storrs, CT.)

Pattee, H. (1968). The physical basis of coding and reliability in biological evolution. In C. H. Waddington (Ed.), *Towards a theoretical biology* (Vol. 1, pp. 69–93). Chicago: Aldine.

Pattee, H. (1971). Physical theories of biological coordination. *Quarterly Review of Biophysics, 4*, 255–276.

Peper, C. E., Beek, P., & van Wierengen, P. C. W. (in press). Bifurcations in polyrhythmic tapping: In search of Farey principles. In J. Requin & G. E. Stelmach (Eds.), *Tutorials in motor neuroscience.* Amsterdam: North Holland.

Raibert, M. (1986). *Legged robots that balance.* Cambridge, MA: MIT Press.

Reed, E. S. (1986). An ecological approach to the evolution of behavior. In T. D. Johnston & A. T. Pietrewicz (Eds.), *Issues in the ecological study of learning* (pp. 357–383). Hillsdale, NJ: Erlbaum.

Reed, E., & Jones, R. (1982). *Reasons for realism: Selected essays of James J. Gibson.* Hillsdale, NJ: Erlbaum.

Rosen, R. (1988). Similarity and dissimilarity: A partial overview. *Human Movement Science, 7*, 131–154.

Schmidt, R. C., Beek, P., Treffner, P., & Turvey, M. T. (1991). Dynamical substructure of coordinated rhythmic movements. *Journal of Experimental Psychology: Human Perception and Performance, 17*, 635–651.

Schmidt, R. C., Carello, C., & Turvey, M. T. (1990). Phase transitions and critical fluctuations in the visual coordination of rhythmic movements between people. *Journal of Experimental Psychology: Human Perception and Performance, 16*, 227–247.

Schmidt, R. C., Treffner, P., Shaw, B., & Turvey, M. T. (in press). Dynamical aspects of learning an interlimb coordination pattern. *Journal of Motor Behavior.*

Scholz, J., & Kelso, J. A. S. (1990). Intentional switching between patterns of bimanual coordination depends on the intrinsic dynamics of the patterns. *Journal of Motor Behavior, 22,* 98–124.

Scholz, J. P., Kelso, J. A. S., & Schöner, G. (1987). Nonequilibrium phase transitions in coordinated biological motion: Critical slowing down and switching time. *Physics Letters, 123,* 390–394.

Schöner, G., Jiang, W., & Kelso, J. A. S. (1990). A synergetic theory of quadupedal gaits and gait transitions. *Journal of Theoretical Biology, 142,* 359–391.

Schöner, G., & Kelso, J. A. S. (1988). Dynamic pattern generation in behavioral and neural systems. *Science, 239,* 1513–1520.

Schöner, G., & Kelso, J. A. S. (1989). A dynamic pattern theory of behavioral change. *Journal of Theoretical Biology, 135,* 501–524.

Shaw, B., McGowan, R., & Turvey, M. T. (1991). An acoustic variable specifying time-to-contact. *Ecological Psychology, 3,* 253–261.

Shaw, R. E., & Kinsella-Shaw, J. (1988). Ecological mechanics: A physical geometry for intentional constraints. *Human Movement Science, 7,* 155–200.

Shaw, R. E., & Turvey, M. T. (1981). Coalitions as models for ecosystems: A realist perspective on perceptual organization. In M. Kubovy & J. Pomerantz (Eds.), *Perceptual organization* (pp. 343–416). Hillsdale, NJ: Erlbaum.

Solomon, H. Y. (1988). Movement produced invariants in haptic explorations: An example of a self-organizing, information driven, intentional system. *Human Movement Science, 7,* 201–224.

Solomon, H. Y., & Turvey, M. T. (1988). Haptically perceiving the distances reachable with hand-held objects. *Journal of Experimental Psychology: Human Perception and Performance, 14,* 404–427.

Solomon, H. Y., Turvey, M. T., & Burton, G. (1989a). Gravitational and muscular variables in perceiving extent by wielding. *Ecological Psychology, 1,* 265–300.

Solomon, H. Y., Turvey, M. T., & Burton, G. (1989b). Perceiving the extents of rods by wielding: Haptic diagonalization and decomposition of the inertia tensor. *Journal of Experimental Psychology: Human Perception and Performance, 15,* 58–68.

Strang, G. (1986). *Introduction to applied mechanics.* Wellesley, MA: Wellesley Cambridge Press.

Thompson, J. M. T., & Stewart, H. B. (1986). *Nonlinear dynamics and chaos.* New York: Wiley.

Treffner, P., & Turvey, M. T. (1990, May). *Doing what comes naturally: Resonance constraints on rhythmic movement.* Paper presented at the meeting of the International Society for Ecological Psychology, Champaign, IL.

Turvey, M. T. (1986). Intentionality: A problem of multiple reference frames, specificational information, and extraordinary boundary conditions on natural law. *Behavioral and Brain Sciences, 9,* 153–155.

Turvey, M. T. (1990a). The challenge of a physical account: A personal view. In H. T. A. Whiting, O. G. Meijer, & P. C. W. van Wieringin (Eds.), *The natural-physical approach to movement control* (pp. 57–93). Amsterdam: VU University Press.

Turvey, M. T. (1990b). Coordination. *American Psychologist, 45,* 938–953.

Turvey, M. T., Burton, G., Pagano, C., Solomon, H. Y., & Runeson, S. (in press). Role of the inertia tensor in perceiving object orientation by effortful touch. *Journal of Experimental Psychology: Human Perception and Performance.*

Turvey, M. T., Saltzman, E., & Schmidt, R. C. (1991). Dynamics and task-specific coordinations. In N. I. Badler, B. A. Barsky, & D. Zeltzer (Eds.), *Making them move: Mechanics, control, and animation of articulated figures* (pp. 157–170). San Mateo, CA: Morgan Kaufmann.

Turvey, M. T., Schmidt, R. C., Rosenblum, L., & Kugler, P. N. (1988). On the time allometry of coordinated rhythmic movements. *Journal of Theoretical Biology, 130,* 285–325.

Turvey, M. T., Shaw, R. E., Reed, E., & Mace, W. (1981). Ecological laws of perceiving and acting: In reply to Fodor and Pylyshyn (1981). *Cognition, 9,* 237–304.

Turvey, M. T., Solomon, H. Y., & Burton, G. (1989). An ecological analysis of knowing by wielding. *Journal of the Experimental Analysis of Behavior, 52,* 387–407.

West, B. J., & Shlesinger, M. F. (1990). The noise in natural phenomena. *American Scientist, 78,* 40–45.

Wimmers, R. H., Beek, P. J., & van Wieringen, P. C. W. (in press). Phase transitions in rhythmic movements: A case of unilateral coupling. *Human Movement Science.*

Yates, F. E. (1987). *Self-organizing systems: The emergence of order.* New York: Plenum Press.

PART TWO

Aspects of Thinking

CHAPTER 5

Alternative Representations for Cognition: Search and Reasoning

Herbert A. Simon

I n the first edition of his *Experimental Psychology*, Woodworth (1938) devoted two chapters to complex cognitive processes: one to problem solving, the other to reasoning. The two chapters dealt with almost wholly distinct cognitive tasks, and the explanations proposed for the phenomena were almost entirely unrelated.

It is instructive to read what Woodworth (1938) himself, at the beginning of the first of these chapters, said about the division,

> Two chapters will not be too many for the large topic of thinking, and we may make the division according to the historical sources of two streams of experimentation, which do indeed merge in the more recent work. [I will subsequently question whether they really have merged.] One stream arose in the study of animal behavior and went on to human problem solving; the other started with human thinking of the more verbal sort.

The chapter on problem solving took its form primarily from Thorndike's puzzle box for cats: In this view, problem solving is trial-and-error search, with some degree of selectivity. The chapter on reasoning took its form principally from the logic of the syllogism and the notion that human everyday reasoning has (should have?) something to do with deductive logic. Inductive reasoning (in concept formation) is also dealt with in this chapter.

Woodworth's book was published in 1938, at roughly the midpoint in the history of modern experimental psychology, about a half century after Wundt, Ebbinghaus, and the other fathers of psychology began their research. Now, although another half century has passed, a widely used contemporary text on cognition, Anderson's (1990) *Cognitive Psychology* retains the same division of chapters as did Woodworth: Chapter 8 is devoted to problem solving and chapter 10 to reasoning. (They are separated by chapter 9, on the development of expertise.)

I do not wish to imply that there has been no progress in the psychology of thinking since 1938 or that Anderson's (1990) book fails to reflect the progress that has occurred. On the contrary, at least three quarters of the empirical work discussed by Anderson in his chapter on problem solving was not available to Woodworth in 1938, and the underlying theoretical framework, information processing theory, has only appeared in the past quarter century or so. Trial-and-error search as the basis for solving problems has been elaborated into much more sophisticated search, making use of both general and task-dependent heuristics to achieve selectivity and avoid exponential explosion.

Anderson's chapter 10, on reasoning, documents less drastic change. The first half of the chapter still has its roots firmly fixed in deductive logic and the syllogism, with some nods toward the role that heuristics might play in reasoning (especially in causing errors of reasoning). There is an information-processing flavor to the explanations of phenomena, and the normative concerns of logic are carefully distinguished from the descriptive and explanatory concerns of psychology. Nevertheless, the syllogism and the verbal proposition are the centerpieces of this chapter's treatment of deductive reasoning.

The last half of chapter 10 introduces inductive reasoning, as applied especially to concept formation. Here, although Anderson keeps information processing in view, the conceptual framework draws heavily on inductive logic, including the use of Bayes's theorem as a norm for inductive reasoning. There is a minimum of overlap between the literatures cited at the conclusions of chapters 8 and 10.

Sources of Diversity

Outstanding textbooks such as Woodworth's (1938) and Anderson's (1990) reflect the state-of-the-art at the time they were published. What we learn from these two books, written nearly half a century apart, is that the study of the "higher mental processes" in psychology has had, through all this time, two main strands (or even three, if we count induction separately) and that there has been very little sharing of experimental tasks or conceptual frameworks, and even little communication between the scientists pursuing these disparate paths. The same conclusion can be reached by studying citations in these bodies of literature: There is a minimum of cross-referencing between the problem-solving, reasoning, and induction research.

Sociological and Disciplinary Roots

An inquiry into the causes of the isolation of these intellectual traditions from each other brings us to the sociological or disciplinary structure of contemporary cognitive science, the meeting place of researchers who wish to understand intelligence of both natural and artificial kinds (Simon & Kaplan, 1989). Cognitive scientists have been drawn in substantial numbers from psychology, artificial intelligence in computer science, linguistics, and philosophy (especially epistemology). Others have come from cultural anthropology, and it is probably only a matter of time before we will see numerous immigrants from literary criticism (especially the currently popular hermeneutics), decision theory, and elsewhere (Simon & Kaplan, 1989).

Each of these contributory disciplines has its own departments, curricula, and journals, whereby it reproduces itself and reinforces the cultural ties of its members. Cognitive science, today an interdiscipline rather than a discipline, may broaden viewpoints and provide glimpses of foreign lands, but it does not yet strongly challenge the traditional disciplinary affiliations.

Psychological research and theorizing about problem solving has its primary roots in experimental psychology, both behaviorist and Gestalt, and in artificial intelligence. (The latter, in turn, has borrowed heavily from psychology and from the theory of chess playing for its approach to problem solving.) Research and theorizing about deductive reasoning has its roots in logic and linguistics. Research and theorizing about inductive reasoning has its roots in logic and statistical decision theory. In all three cases, the roots go back to times when these disciplines, including psychology, were just beginning to emerge from more general philosophical and humanistic studies.

But language and logic on the one side and heuristic search on the other do not exhaust the separate strands that make up the contemporary psychology of thinking. One also must look at research on perception and memory, both of which share an extremely fuzzy borderland with cognition. Chapters 3 and 4, for example, of Anderson's (1990) cognition textbook are devoted explicitly to attention and perception. His chapter 6, on memory, discusses, among other topics, the process of recognition.

The Competing Metaphors

How do these differences in origins of the several strands of cognitive science account for differences in the theories that emerge from them? Behind each strand of research is a metaphor, and different metaphors propose different research tasks and different interpretations of the research findings. A metaphor for a problem domain is, in fact, a representation of that domain, a particular way of formulating one's thoughts about it. Adopting a metaphor, or changing from one to another, can have major consequences for theory and research.

I would like to describe some of these metaphors and their consequences.

My account will emphasize language and logic, on the one hand, and heuristic search through a maze, on the other. But it will also include the metaphor of seeing that has been prominent in research on perception and the metaphor of recognizing that provides an account of the phenomena of intuition and insight. In fact, I will begin the discussion with the metaphor of seeing so as to cast loose our thinking from its customary moorings and to inspect reasoning from an unorthodox viewpoint.

Reasoning by Seeing

The term *reasoning* has been co-opted by logicians, experimental psychologists, and perhaps others to refer almost exclusively to deductive and inductive inference. To understand the processes of human cognition, we must learn to use the term much more broadly—essentially, as coextensive with thinking. Reasoning must extend to all processes that derive new information from the information that is explicitly given. There is a great deal of thinking that does not fit the formalisms of logic. For example, we ordinarily regard the use of analogy and metaphor as thinking, but these processes do not fall within the logicians' paradigms for reasoning.

Consider an example even more remote from logic. Visualize a rectangle in the vertical plane that is twice as wide as it is high. Now, drop a vertical line from the midpoint of the upper edge to the midpoint of the lower edge. Then draw a diagonal from the northwest corner of the rectangle to the southeast corner. Does this diagonal intersect the first vertical line?

Almost everyone will agree that it does. But how does one know? Does one prove it using the axioms of Euclidean geometry or an algebraic calculation based on analytic geometry? Probably not. One most likely just "saw" it (Simon, 1972, 1978).

Reasoning needs to be defined broadly enough to encompass inferences like this one. The mind represents information in various ways, in this case, in the form of a mental picture. (By *mental picture*, I mean whatever representation of the rectangle permitted an inference that the diagonal and vertical lines intersected.) We have available certain processes, or operators—some of them conscious, some not—for operating on and drawing conclusions from this information. In the case at hand, the subconscious operator applied is one called *seeing*. It is available for extracting information from both external visible displays and pictures in the "mind's eye."

Inferring something because you can see it in your mind's eye, or even on a piece of paper, is not always a reliable process. In either case, there are severe limits on the resolution of the picture and the accuracy of the information-extracting processes. Consider the following example: We imagine a square with 1-cm sides. Around the northwest corner of the square as center, we draw (in imagination) a circle with radius equal to the side of the square. Around the southeast corner, we draw a second circle with radius the length of half the side. Do the two circles intersect? Can you see the intersection or the lack of one? How certain are you of your answer? A fairly simple calculation, which I leave to you, will convince you that the two circles do indeed intersect. But if the calculation convinces you, remember that it is a calculation and not a "seeing." What are the limits of what can be seen in a simple geometric figure?

These brief demonstrations show that we draw many inferences implicitly, by seeing them, and that this ability is defined and limited by quite specific characteristics of the sensory and perceptual systems. It has nothing to do, in any obvious way, with the processes that logicians prescribe for valid reasoning. I turn next to inferences that we draw with greater deliberation and awareness and that do follow, at least to some extent, the logicians' procedures.

Formal Reasoning, Natural Language

Logics are languages. Logics follow strict formalisms that are rather different from those of natural languages, but they are languages nonetheless. The fundamental representational device of logics and natural languages is the sentence, the meaning of which is given by a proposition. If logics or languages are the vehicles of thought, then the symbolic media for thought are sentential structures, and thinking is a process of fashioning new sentences from old.

Logics developed as sets of normative rules for correctness of thinking, but they were often regarded as approximate descriptions of actual thinking and, hence, as the appropriate representations for modeling cognitive processes. Since logics are languages, it is not surprising that there has been a close affinity between logicians' and linguists' approaches to cognitive science.

The notion that language provides the suitable representation for modeling thinking has been further reinforced by the view, held by Chomsky (1965) and others, that language is a unique and inborn human capability that can be analyzed more or less independently of other components of the human mind. Although I cannot examine that claim within the limits of this chapter, I believe it to be false and that the commonalities in all human language are due not to the existence of a special language faculty but to the fact that human memories are organizations of symbolic list structures that can be used to represent sentences, images of visual perceptions, and perhaps other forms of semantic meaning. The general properties of language are the properties one would expect if information were stored in memories organized as list structures (Simon & Siklóssy, 1972).

A more or less justified claim often made for reasoning that uses the strict rules of formal logic is that such reasoning is perfectly reliable. A modern system of formal logic provides a small set of axioms and an even smaller set of processes (inference rules) for deriving new expressions from the axioms. In *Principia Mathematica* (Whitehead & Russell, 1925), for example, there are about half a dozen axioms and only two inference rules, *modus ponens* and substitution.[1] Every derivation consists of a sequence of easily checked steps given that the terminal expression in each step must be derivable, by application of one of the two rules of inference, from previously derived axioms or theorems.

In spite of the reliability that should be obtainable in this way, logic suffers from grave problems that begin at the very foundations. First, there are the Gödel theorems, which guarantee, for an even moderately rich system of logic, that if the logic is consistent (and who would want an inconsistent logic?), it is incomplete; there are true statements expressible in the language of the logic that are not provable in that language.

---

[1] *To shorten their proofs, Whitehead and Russell (1925) do subsequently introduce two or three other inference rules that cannot be justified on the basis of these two, but nonetheless, because they were concerned with validation and not discovery, they emphasized economy of inference.*

Moreover, as distinguished logicians such as Frege, Russell, and Quine have at one time or another discovered, a contradiction may lurk in even the most carefully crafted system of logic.

However, logic suffers from even graver difficulties than the possible presence of contradictions and the certain presence of incompleteness. Because it restricts itself to a small number of inference rules, it proceeds by tiny steps and hence takes almost forever to get anywhere. Almost no serious mathematics is done using the strict rules of mathematical logic. Working mathematicians take giant steps from already-proven expressions to new consequences. In part, they achieve this by converting theorems into new inference rules, permitting much larger steps from one theorem to another. In part, mathematicians achieve this by introducing heuristic inference rules the validity of which is not guaranteed in all cases but usually can be relied on.

Mathematicians take these shortcuts with a certain measure of confidence that anyone skilled in the art, given time and patience, can fill in the numerous missing intermediate steps. Sometimes they are wrong (witness the recent failed claim by a very competent professional mathematician of a proof for Fermat's last theorem) and have to patch up their proofs by restricting the claims of their theorems or by other means. If they are good mathematicians and not too adventuresome, their proofs are right more often than not but are not absolutely certain.

Only a small fraction of the inferences people make, even when those people are mathematicians, are achieved by processes that look like the ones described in logic textbooks. The remaining inferences use processes having quite different characteristics—processes of heuristic search and of recognition and imaging or seeing. But if thought processes are not all like the processes of logic, the underlying representational structures may also be quite different from assemblages of sentences. I next consider the ways in which heuristic thinking differs from the reasoning of formal logic.

Heuristic Reasoning

It would appear that mathematicians reason just like other people. They are not a separate subspecies of the human race. They acquire, in the course of their training and experience, a rich set of inference operators that allow them, with a certain degree of assurance, to proceed from a description of a state of affairs to inferences about it that are implied but are not explicitly stated in the description. Their inference processes provide a tolerable level of reliability in their reasoning, but not certainty. In return for taking the risk of being mistaken, mathematicians are rewarded by being able to reason far more powerfully and rapidly than if they stuck to the strict inference rules of logic. The prudent among them, and among those of us who are not mathematicians, often divide the reasoning process into two parts, a discovery part and a verification part. First, we rely on quite powerful but somewhat unreliable inference operators, so-called heuristic processes, to discover new conclusions. Then, before we announce our new truths or act on them, we subject them to careful scrutiny, using more microscopic and reliable inference rules to test the doubtful steps. In the common practice of reasoning, these discovery and verification steps are intermingled given that we may alternate between them at all stages of our thinking.

If absolute reliability is not essential, we can use even more powerful, but less reliable, heuristic rules and be quite relaxed about verification. We may be obliged to do so when we have to act in real time: Need we verify in a strictly logical way that an automobile is about to run us over? Or we may prefer to use unreliable but powerful procedures if mistakes can be repaired or are not irrevocable. Then we leave verification to Nature, who will ultimately tell us if we were in error.

Thus, human reasoning cannot be identified with the processes prescribed in books on formal logic. Reasoning is much less preoccupied with absolute reliability than is logic and is much concerned with the availability of inference operators that are powerful, if sometimes fallible. Let me be more specific about how heuristic search deviates from logic with respect both to its processes and its representations.

Thinking Is Not Tautological

One characteristic of logic on which I have not focused is that formal logic is generally supposed to be tautological; that is, the conclusions of an argument in formal logic should not place any restrictions on the range of possible worlds that are not imposed by the axioms. If the premises admit unicorns, then the conclusions must not exclude them. It is because of this tautological or analytic character of the inference rules of a proper logic that one can have confidence in the conclusion of a chain of reasoning without feeling the need to check it by empirical observation or experiment. If one does make empirical tests and the tests fail, one does not blame the inference rules but blames the axioms.

We do not question the structure of the syllogism, *All men are mortal. Socrates is a man. Therefore, Socrates is mortal.* If we find that Socrates is still alive today, we conclude either that his death will occur at some future date or that the major or minor premises of the syllogism are in error. The rule of *modus ponens* is irreproachably analytic and cannot be invalidated by empirical evidence.

But do people follow this principle in their everyday reasoning? Imagine a weight hanging from one end of a rope thrown over a pulley and a second weight hanging from the other end of the rope. Both weights are stationary, and the pulley looks quite new and not rusted. We notice that the weight attached to the left end of the rope is 10 kg and conclude that the weight attached to the right end is also 10 kg. Perhaps we reasoned to this conclusion using only analytic inference rules. Perhaps all of the knowledge of the laws of physics was stored in axioms. It would be an interesting (but exceedingly tedious) exercise to construct a proof along these lines, using only *modus ponens* and substitution as rules of inference. The alternative is to include laws of physics, not just among the axioms but among the inference rules as well. One can write the rules in the form of productions, C → A, which reads *Whenever the conditions C are satisfied, execute the actions A.* In the present example, the production might take the form, *If a weight is hanging from the rope on one side of a pulley wheel and another weight is hanging on the other side, and if the pulley is frictionless, and if the weights are motionless, and if the weight on one side has a known value →* assign the same value to the weight on the other side.

Of course you pay a price for this law of inference. It will lead you to correct conclusions only in a world governed by Newton's laws of motion (and only in a world in which one can detect reliably whether a pulley is frictionless). If the conclusion, subjected to other tests, turns out to be false, it may be the inference rule that is at fault, not the other assumptions.

Thus, contrary to the prescriptions of formal logic, human inference does not restrict itself to a small number of inference rules, embedding all other assumptions in axioms. On the contrary, everyday reasoning makes use of large numbers of inference rules, and these inference rules, far from being tautological, encompass a great deal of empirical knowledge (correct or incorrect, general or contingent) of the world. It is the power of these numerous contingent inference rules that enables people to deal in real time with the complex real world.

Nonsentential Representations

Proceeding in the way just described constitutes more than merely assuming Newton's laws of motion or even embodying them in inference rules; it provides powerful means of making inferences that would otherwise be very difficult to make. Suppose, for example, that the pulley problem is presented to us as a diagram in a physics book or that it is presented in words, but we form our own mental diagram. (There is a great deal of empirical evidence that people, especially people who are good at solving physics problems, frequently do this.) Then, if we happen to have acquired a production, like the one described in the previous section, corresponding to Newton's third law, we will be able to reason about the pulley.

Although it is well-known that many problem solvers form internal representations of the sort called *diagrams,* it is not at all known what kinds of symbol structures represent such diagrams or how different such symbol structures are from assemblages of sentences. Larkin and Simon (1987) have proposed one kind of internal representation for diagrams (not unlike one proposed earlier by Baylor, 1971, and still earlier by Simon & Barenfeld, 1969, for modeling chess perception and other cognitive tasks). It is possible that different representations (more closely resembling rasters of pixels) would be required to model some of the tasks described in the earlier section of this chapter on seeing or some of the tasks used in Kosslyn's (1980) experimental work.

Corresponding to the inference rules in a system of logic are the productions in a heuristic search system using diagrams. The productions are evoked whenever the cues are present in the diagram that match their conditions. In the example of a pulley system, when a pulley presents itself satisfying the conditions of the production or an external or mental diagram of one, we will notice it and notice that the conditions are satisfied. The corresponding actions will be evoked from our memory, and we will take the action—in this case, reach a conclusion about the unknown weight.

Mental Models

The symbolic representations I have been calling *diagrams* are essentially identical to those that have been christened *mental models* (Johnson-Laird, 1983). When diagrams, or mental models, are used in solving problems, the operators may progressively change the representation of the current situation to simulate the history of the system described by the diagram. For example, in modeling a problem like the well-known missionaries and cannibals puzzle, one set of symbols is used to represent the missionaries, cannibals, and boat on one bank of the river, and another set represents those on the other bank. A move operator removes one or more symbols from one of these sets and adds them to the other, thereby representing the effect of a boat trip across the river (Newell & Simon, 1972, pp. 854–857; Reed & Simon, 1976).

Mental models have also been used recently by researchers from the linguistics–logic branch of cognitive science who are apparently oblivious to such models' extensive use for the past 35 years by researchers from the heuristic–search branch (Johnson-Laird, 1983). This convergence, however accidental, is a very good omen of better future communication and convergence of conceptualization between the two branches.

Problem Solving by Recognition

Experiences with geometry or logic, or with mathematics generally, may lead one to think of reasoning as a process of constructing long chains of steps that lead from premises to conclusions. In everyday life, reasoning is seldom quite like that. In any specific situation within a given task, only a few productions are likely to be evoked at any moment.

Reasoning Chains

Human attention at any given time focuses on only a very restricted set of stimulus features, visible or audible, in the external environment or recovered from memory and held temporarily in short-term memory. It is this limited set of stimuli that are noticed and held in attention, that must supply the cues that evoke productions—the conditions that must be satisfied. The evokable productions may be further restricted to those that are relevant to the goal at hand because one of the conditions on which a production depends may be a goal symbol held in short-term memory. In the absence of that symbol, the production will not be evoked.

Consider the productions used by someone with the requisite skills to solve a simple algebra equation. Memory holds the goal of solving the equation. If a constant term is noticed to the left of the equality sign, a production is evoked that subtracts the term from both sides of the equation. If a term in the variable is noticed to the right of the equality sign, a second production is evoked that subtracts that term from both sides of the equation. If the variable term on the left of the equality sign has a coefficient other than unity, a third production divides all terms in the equation by that coefficient. All else that remains to solving such an equation is collecting the terms. What is required is that the three productions described be available, that they be evoked by the cues on the paper and in memory, and that they not be interfered with by a lot of other irrelevant productions evoked at the same time. The latter obstruction is prevented by the narrow span of attention and the presence of appropriate goal symbols among the conditions of the productions.

It should be noted especially that the action of each production creates a new situation that makes appropriate and evokes the action of the next production. The chaining is accomplished by the continually changing problem situation that evokes the appropriate chain of productions. The productions do not have to be strung together in memory. The situation evokes them at the proper time.

In those frequent cases in everyday experience in which attention is directed primarily to the external environment, the cues in this constantly changing scene, which are constantly modified by the actions of the system, provide the triggers for evoking the successive productions. This is the simple essence of the currently popular ideas of situated action and situated learning. Simon (1975) has described such a perceptual strategy for solving the Tower of Hanoi puzzle by situated action and has contrasted it with strategies that rely on internal plans held in memory. The solution to the pulley problem using a written diagram, described in Larkin and Simon (1987), provides another clear example of a production system carrying out situated action.

Expert Systems

The production system schemes I have described also provide the backbone for most of the reasoning systems that are called *expert systems*. A medical diagnostic system, for example, responds to symptoms by hypothesizing disease entities. The presence of such hypotheses evokes other productions that propose additional tests to discriminate among alternatives. After a diagnosis has been accepted, yet other productions will supply a Latin name for the disease entity, will make a prognosis, will propose treatment, and so on.

The result may be logical enough, but there is little about the process that resembles the long chains of steps that characterize formal logical inference. At each successive moment, the system simply does what the situation calls for, or even more accurately, what it is reminded of by the situation. The central process such a system uses is the process of recognition, in which cues permit the recognition of familiar situations or objects and thereby gain access to the information about them that is stored in memory.

Each production can, of course, be formally regarded as an inference rule. If we tried to state just what the inference is, we would have to say something like, "The situation satisfying conditions C implies that it would be a good idea to take the actions A." In the pulley example, it being known (and noticed) that the force on the left end of the rope over the pulley is F, it is a good idea to assign the force F to the right end of the rope as well. The implication is a very conditional one, requiring both that our goal is to find the forces in the pulley system and that the system is governed by Newton's laws. If either condition is not satisfied, the production is inappropriate, and we would hope that it would not be evoked.

A crucial difference between productions and more familiar rules of inference is that the former are mandatory (they are to be executed whenever their conditions are satisfied), whereas the latter are permissive (they may be executed at any time, but it is nowhere specified under what circumstances they ought to be executed). Rules of logic do not, in themselves, prescribe behavior; they must be augmented by a control structure. A production system combines both functions.

Recognition and Intuition

The recognition system provided by productions gives us a straightforward explanation of the phenomena of intuitive thinking and insight. It often happens that when a problem is presented to someone, an immediate answer is returned, frequently a correct one. Often, the respondent is unable to explain how the answer was arrived at and ascribes it to intuition (or even insight or inspiration). Such performances may be startling, especially if the problem seems hard. Usually, examination of the responses reveals that the respondent is experienced in the domain of the problem and was simply "reminded" of the answer (i.e., it was retrieved by an act of recognition, the question constituting a cue that evoked one or more appropriate productions). As Pasteur once put it, "Chance favors the prepared mind."

Thus, production systems appear to provide a wholly satisfactory mechanism for explaining intuition and insight, and we need no longer regard these phenomena as mysterious or as produced by mechanisms at all different from those implicated in other thought phenomena.

Necessity and Sufficiency

In formal logic and mathematics, we pay a great deal of attention to whether premises are necessary or sufficient for conclusions. Insufficiency is, of course, the mortal sin because it means that conclusions need not hold under all conditions. Lack of necessity is only a venal sin, an unesthetic redundancy that makes the conclusion fall short of the greatest generality it could achieve.

Everyday reasoning is moderately concerned with sufficiency but seldom with necessity. Even in the matter of sufficiency, people are usually very pragmatic. Fischer and

Morch (1988) have provided the following example, which comes from a computer software system that helps architects design kitchens. When the system examines a particular design in which the kitchen sink does not face a window, it critiques the design, reporting to the architect that the placement is undesirable. When the architect asks why, it replies, "The water pipes are usually installed with the expectation that the sink will be at the window, and are more accessible there. More important, the housewife [*sic*] spends a good deal of time at the sink, and finds it pleasanter to have a view from a window than to face a wall" (p. 180). These are only two considerations of many that must go into a kitchen design. In particular, they do not take into consideration the conflicting requirements of other fixtures and the problem of tradeoffs among them. Yet, they serve as reasons for placing the sink in a particular place, and it is precisely fragmentary reasons of this kind that people use in everyday life to justify most of their actions. We tend to accumulate reasons, no subset of which is wholly necessary, but we neglect many interactions, so that our reasons are almost never sufficient.

A principal reason why such an unrigorous procedure is satisfactory is that people are in constant interaction with the environment. We take a step, notice new conditions and constraints that our reasoning ignored and adjust our next step accordingly. In designing, we record our tentative design decisions in a drawing, and the drawing reveals interactions that were ignored in our premises. If these interactions are important, we convert them into new constraints (new reasons) and modify the design to take account of them. Here again, is situated action arising from the operation of a production system.

We human beings, except when using the formal tools of algebra (preferably with the help of a large computer) are not at all good at handling simultaneous equations. We solve them by successive approximations, finding an answer that seems to fit a small subset of the equations and then modifying it to fit others. One of the skills that the professional designer acquires in any domain is discernment of which constraints to satisfy first so that the plan can be carried to completion with a minimum of revision.

Qualitative Reasoning

I now turn from reasoning in general to qualitative reasoning. Roughly speaking, reasoning is qualitative when it leads to conclusions that do not specify how much. Driving an automobile uses a production that can be paraphrased, If one presses down on the accelerator, the car will go faster. Leaving aside details, such as why we speak of the accelerator as determining velocity and not acceleration, what can we do with such a vague inference? What we can do with it is regulate the speed of our car by pressing on the pedal if the car is going too slow and easing up if it is going too fast. We need no numbers, just a calculus of more, less, and equals—an ordinal calculus.

In the field of artificial intelligence, there has been a rash of proposals during the past decade for schemes capable of doing qualitative, ordinal reasoning about complex systems (Weld & de Kleer, 1990). A formal theory providing solid foundations for such schemes has, in fact, existed for more than 50 years, having been developed by the economists Griffith Evans (1930) and Paul Samuelson (1947) for use in economic reasoning. In somewhat less explicit form, it was used even earlier in such domains of physics as mechanics and thermodynamics. In particular, it supported a form of analysis often called *comparative statics*.

A great deal of everyday thinking takes the form of qualitative reasoning. It is the exception, rather than the rule, that people reason in terms of numbers or exact quantities of any kind. Even when we wish a numerical answer, we may first sketch out our analysis in qualitative terms or check a quantitative result qualitatively to see whether it "makes sense." In what follows, I show, primarily by means of examples, how qualitative reasoning works in order to demonstrate its robustness when the variables are subjected to arbitrary monotonic transformations, to relate it to simple principles of the calculus and simple results in differential equations, and finally, to relate it to reasoning about diagrams and their corresponding mental pictures.

Comparative Statics

A great many reasoning problems have the following general form: A system is in equilibrium or in some sort of steady state. The exact position of equilibrium depends on some system parameters, which may be regarded as exogenous variables, the values of which are determined by mechanisms independent of the system itself. If the value of one or more system parameters is changed (e.g., increased), after the disturbance, the system settles into a new equilibrium. One would wish to infer how various system variables will change from the original equilibrium to the new equilibrium and whether they will increase or decrease or remain constant.

Often, questions like this can be answered even if one does not know the numerical values of the variables in the system or the parameters but knows only their signs in purely qualitative terms. Consider a simple example from classical price theory in economics. (I am indebted to H. Tabachneck, personal communication, for this example.) The quantity of a good that suppliers will offer varies with the price, larger quantities being offered at higher prices. The quantity of the same good that buyers will purchase also varies with the price, smaller quantities being purchased at higher prices. At the equilibrium price, the quantity supplied equals the quantity demanded. Suppose that a tax is levied on the good. The cost of producing it will increase by a corresponding amount, and the price at which any specified quantity of the good will be offered by the suppliers will increase by the same amount. (In a graph with price as the vertical axis, the entire supply curve—the schedule showing the prices at which different quantities will be offered—will be displaced upward by the tax.) The amount that buyers will purchase at any given price will remain unchanged.

Presented with these assumptions, it is not too difficult to conclude that the new equilibrium price (the price at which the quantity offered will equal the quantity demanded) will be higher than the previous price and that the quantity exchanged at the new price will be smaller than the quantity exchanged in the previous equilibrium. One way to carry out the reasoning is to argue that suppliers will demand a higher price for the quantity that has previously been exchanged, but fewer purchases will be made at this higher price. The reduction in demand will, in turn, push the price downward, and therefore the net increase in price will be somewhat less than the amount of the tax. There is a notable gap in this reasoning: Will the process actually converge to a new equilibrium? Perhaps the reduction in demand caused by the higher price will be so great as to carry the price lower than in the previous equilibrium. This price change may, in turn, produce a new reduction in the quantity offered by sellers, and so on. In fact, we often carry out such qualitative reasoning without worrying about possible nonconvergence. To deal with that problem requires a more sophisticated form of qualitative reasoning, which I will address later.

However, the general process I describe of propagating initial effects through the system of variables is familiar enough. It can easily be represented by a simple production system. A set of variables is connected by a system of mechanisms. One can consider a change in one of the mechanisms (e.g., in a parameter or an exogenous variable) and propagate that change through the variables by means of the mechanisms that connect them. For example, an increase in rainfall increases the wheat crop, which increases the amount of wheat offered on the market, which reduces the equilibrium price at which wheat is sold. Hence, one can confidently conclude that good growing weather will reduce the price of wheat. This particular example is simpler than the previous one because it omits any subsequent feedback from the market price to the quantity that is supplied (the latter being supposed to be determined by the weather). Propagation of the effect is straightforward and does not raise any question of convergence or stability. Notice that the reasoning also depends on a *ceteris paribus* assumption that only one parameter or exogenous variable has changed, the others remaining constant.

Monotonic Transformations

Since the kind of reasoning I have illustrated depends only on relations of greater than or less than and not on cardinal quantities, it remains valid even if we stretch or contract the scales on which we measure the variables, so long as the distortions are monotonic. For price in the economic example, we can substitute any other variable that is a positive monotonic function of price and for quantity, an arbitrary positive monotonic function of quantity. The reasoning will be unchanged so long as the ordering of corresponding values of the variables is unchanged: The greater value will remain the greater, and the smaller the smaller.

There is no difficulty in constructing a formal mathematics of ordinal variables, or what amounts to the same thing, of relations that are invariant under monotonic transformations. What is more important is that human beings can make the inferences implied by this mathematics quite readily, at least in simple cases. By simple cases I mean situations in which an effect can be propagated linearly through the system without interactions among different paths of propagation.

Even if the signs of all the connections are known, the possibility of drawing unequivocal inferences disappears quite rapidly in the presence of interactions. The reason is fairly obvious. Along one path of propagation, the effect of a change in parameter on a system variable may be positive and along another path, the effect on the same variable may be negative. The net effect, the sum of the positive and negative effects, is not invariant under monotonic transformations of the variables. To draw definite conclusions under these circumstances, more information about the variables (i.e., information on their cardinal values) is required. Not surprisingly, people do not reason very well in the presence of such interactions, which require them, in effect, to solve simultaneous equations.

Qualitative Treatment of Differential Equations

The problem of convergence that I have raised above can sometimes be dealt with if we know something about the dynamics of the system with which we are dealing. The equations of a system in equilibrium can be "dynamicized" by displacing the dependent variable of each equation to the right-hand side and replacing it by its time derivative. That is, starting with $y = ax$, one would write $0 = ax - y$ and then $dy/dt = ax - y$. The equilibrium of the system of differential equations constructed in this way is simply the original set of algebraic equations.

Of course, we should not write down these dynamic relations arbitrarily. Each equation is a causal assertion about the mechanism that determines the rate of change of the corresponding dependent variable (the one whose derivative appears). The system consisting of $0 = ax - by$ and $0 = cx - dy$ can be dynamicized in two ways depending on which equation we choose to represent the mechanism regulating x and which to represent the mechanism regulating y. Which is the correct representation is not a matter of fiat but a substantive question about how the system under consideration actually works—what its causal mechanisms are.

Dynamicizing a system of static equations provides new information about the system and new abilities to draw conclusions about its comparative statics because we can now solve the differential equations, obtaining their roots as functions of the system parameters. But these functions determine whether the roots correspond to a stable or an unstable equilibrium. If we assume stability, then we obtain new conditions on the parameters, which give us additional information about the net changes that will be produced.

Returning to the earlier example of the demand and supply relations, we now replace the supply function with a differential equation determining the rate of change in the quantity supplied as a function of the difference between the supply price for that quantity and the market price. The second differential equation determines the rate of change in the price as a function of the difference between the quantities supplied and demanded, respectively, at the current market price. In the new dynamic system, requiring stability constrains the system parameters so as to guarantee convergence of price and quantity adjustments and determines the directions of the changes of price and quantity produced by a change in a parameter or exogenous variable. If one dynamicizes the system in other ways, the stability conditions will of course be different.

It can be shown that the stability conditions are invariant under monotonic transformations of the variables. Hence, stability depends on relations of greater than and less than among variables, and not on the cardinal properties of the individual variables.

Qualitative Reasoning With Diagrams

All of these modes of ordinal reasoning, in both the static and dynamic cases, can be carried out with productions either by reference to an actual diagram on paper or one visualized in the "mind's eye." Hence, when we see people reasoning ordinally, we cannot be sure whether they are operating with propositions or by visualization.

In analytic geometry, we all learned to convert equations into geometrical curves or surfaces and geometrical figures into the equations of their boundaries. Thus, the example given earlier of the effect of a tax on equilibrium price and quantity of a commodity can be represented by two curves: a supply function and a demand function, both on a plane with price and quantity as the axes. The equilibrium point is the intersection of the two curves, and the effect of the tax is represented by a parallel displacement of the supply curve, producing a new intersection. The conclusions reached earlier by "propagation" can be reached simply by observing the properties of the diagram, that is, the relative positions of the intersections before and after displacement.

To handle diagramatically the questions of convergence and stability requires a more complex diagram. In the dynamicized static system, the differential equations determine possible paths of the system in the price–quantity plane. Such a path is uniquely determined for each initial point, and the paths cannot cross (since the system cannot proceed along two different paths from the same state). The collectivity of such paths is called the *direction field* for the system, and from the direction field, one can infer how the system will move from any starting point—specifically, whether it will move to an equilibrium.

Consider again the example of the commodity market. The static equations for the demand and supply curves correspond to the states in which the price and the quantity, respectively, are in equilibrium and therefore where $dp/dt = 0$ and $dq/dt = 0$, respectively. Hence, the paths will be horizontal where they cross the former curve and vertical where they cross the latter. It can be seen that if the supply curve is steeper than the demand curve (demand more elastic than supply), the path will converge to the (stable) equilibrium point at the intersection of the supply and demand curves. If the supply is more elastic, the paths will diverge from the (unstable) equilibrium.

A little further consideration shows that these properties are invariant under stretching or contraction of the two axes—under monotonic transformation of the variables. Hence, the diagrammatic analysis exactly parallels the algebraic analysis in terms of ordinal variables.

Conclusion

This brings us full circle to the topic of visualization and the role of the mind's eye and of external visual displays in human thinking. I have tried to survey some of the main tools and processes that seem to be implicated in everyday reasoning—the kind that carries us through the day, dealing with problems as they arise.

The thinking I have described does not look at all like formal logic and only a little like mathematics. It makes use of a great multitude of inference rules, which are not tautological rules of logic but incorporate much real-world knowledge. Such thinking appears to be remarkably unconcerned with questions of sufficiency and necessity. It proceeds in the simpler cases by executing sequences of productions that propagate information by means of a succession of inferences. In more complex cases, it undertakes heuristic search, using its powerful operators to explore selectively but rapidly.

When it deals with quantities, as it often must, it usually handles their ordinal rather than cardinal properties. It makes great use of diagrammatic representations, or mental diagrams in the mind's eye, which allow it to simulate the processes of the situations it is modeling. To compensate for its severe limitations in handling simultaneous relations, it proceeds by successive approximations and halts when it has satisfied the relations.

We have now had enough experience in building expert systems for human professional-level tasks to know that these systems require mainly sizable knowledge bases in which knowledge is accessed by the execution of productions triggered by cues in the problem situation, aided by modest inference capabilities in the form of heuristic search processes. Knowledge plus recognition provide the backbone of such systems.

The knowledge on which inference rules operate may be stored in memory in a variety of ways, including propositional structures but also including structures that are better viewed as mental images. Perhaps there are others as well. By the standards of formal logic, it is an unsystematic, jerry-built structure. But it gets us through the day.

References

Anderson, J. R. (1990). *Cognitive psychology* (3rd ed.). San Francisco: Freeman.

Baylor, G. W. (1971). Program and protocol analysis on a mental imagery task. *Proceedings of the Second International Joint Conference on Artificial Intelligence* (pp. 218–227). London: British Computer Society.

Chomsky, N. (1965). *Aspects of the theory of syntax.* Cambridge, MA: MIT Press.

Evans, G. C. (1930). *Mathematical introduction to economics.* New York: McGraw-Hill.

Fischer, G., & Morch, A. (1988). CRACK: A critiquing approach to cooperative kitchen design. *Proceedings of the International Conference on Intelligent Tutoring Systems* (pp. 176–185). Montreal, Canada.

Johnson-Laird, P. M. (1983). *Mental models.* Cambridge, MA: Harvard University Press.

Kosslyn, S. M. (1980). *Image and mind.* Cambridge, MA: Harvard University Press.

Larkin, J. H., & Simon, H. A. (1987). Why a diagram is (sometimes) worth 10,000 words. *Cognitive Science, 11,* 65–99.

Newell, A., & Simon, H. A. (1972). *Human problem solving.* Englewood Cliffs, NJ: Prentice-Hall.

Reed, S. K., & Simon, H. A. (1976). Modeling strategy shifts in a problem solving task. *Cognitive Psychology, 8,* 86–97.

Samuelson, P. A. (1947). *Foundations of economic analysis.* Cambridge, MA: Harvard University Press.

Simon, H. A. (1972). What is visual imagery? In L. W. Gregg (Ed.), *Cognition in learning and memory* (pp. 183–204). New York: Wiley.

Simon, H. A. (1975). Functional equivalents of problem solving skills. *Cognitive Psychology, 7,* 268–288.

Simon, H. A. (1978). On the forms of mental representation. In C. Wade Savage (Ed.), *Perception and cognition* (pp. 3–18). Minneapolis: University of Minnesota Press.

Simon, H. A., & Barenfeld, M. (1969). Information processing analysis of perceptual processes in problem solving. *Psychological Review, 76,* 473–483.

Simon, H. A., & Kaplan, C. (1989). Foundations of cognitive science. In M. I. Posner (Ed.), *Foundations of cognitive science* (pp. 1–48). Cambridge, MA: MIT Press.

Simon, H. A., & Siklóssy, L. (1972). *Representation and meaning.* Englewood Cliffs, NJ: Prentice-Hall.

Weld, D. S., & de Kleer, J. (1990). *Readings in qualitative reasoning about physical systems.* San Mateo, CA: Morgan Kaufman.

Whitehead, A. N., & Russell, B. (1925). *Principia mathematica* (2nd ed.). Cambridge, England: Cambridge University Press.

Woodworth, R. S. (1938). *Experimental psychology.* New York: Holt.

CHAPTER 6

A Cognitive Architecture for Comprehension

Walter Kintsch

Cognitive Architectures

Functional Relations, Miniature Models, and Cognitive Architectures

Fifty years ago, it was the acknowledged goal of leading psychologists to develop and test empirically unified theories that would account for all or most aspects of behavior. These global theories went out of fashion in psychology in the 1950s, shortly before the advent of cognitive psychology. The reason for the failure of such grandiose projects as Hull's (1943) principles of behavior are manifold and well-known. In response, psychologists retreated to a cautious functionalism or to the piecemeal construction and evaluation of miniature models. Cognitive psychology grew up with a surplus of models but without a coherent theory.

The preparation of this chapter was supported by Grant MH-15872 from the National Institute of Mental Health, which also has supported the research discussed here. Additional research support is acknowledged from the National Science Foundation, Grant IRI-8722792, and the Army Research Institute, Project MDA903-86-C0143. I thank Peter Polson for stimulating discussions of the methodological questions raised here and Eileen Kintsch for her comments.

Lately, there have been signs of a resurging interest in global theories. The limitations of the alternative strategy of extracting knowledge from nature experiment by experiment and model by model have become apparent, and a fair amount of consensus has formed as to the significant facts regarding cognition that need explaining. As a consequence, several researchers have attempted to develop a unified theory of cognition, especially Anderson (1983) with his work on the ACT* family of models and Newell (1990) with his SOAR project. These researchers have argued eloquently in favor of global approaches using arguments that I fully embraced but will not repeat. Instead, I will sketch an alternative cognitive architecture for comprehension and then focus on the problems presented by the empirical evaluation of this architecture. I focus on these problems not because SOAR and ACT* have neglected them but to generate more public discussion of the questions and methodological issues involved. What was done in testing SOAR and ACT*—or for that matter, the construction-integration theory sketched below—is by no means unreasonable or inadequate. But there is neither a standard, proven methodology to fall back on nor are psychologists sufficiently familiar with the serious problems arising from the empirical evaluation of global theories in cognitive science.

The Domain of Comprehension

One way to characterize cognition is as a continuum of processes ranging from perception to problem solving or possibly as a dichotomy. One would not say that perception *is* problem solving, although in certain impasse situations perception clearly can involve conscious and deliberate problem solving. Neither would one say that problem solving *is* perception, although sometimes one surely "sees" the solution to a problem.

Comprehension is located somewhere along that continuum between perception and problem solving. It is rarely equated with perception, mostly because perceptual researchers are usually concerned with more elementary processes, content to leave the complexities of comprehension to others (e.g., in the study of reading). In contrast, comprehension processes are frequently subsumed under problem solving. In the introduction section of almost every paper on text understanding it is either explicitly asserted or implied that comprehension *is* problem solving.

I argue that comprehension is a domain *sui generis* and that it is indeed useful to consider much of what we have regarded as problem solving from the perspective of comprehension. The construction–integration (CI) model I discuss is an architecture for comprehension and represents an attempt to account for a broad range of phenomena that we label *comprehension* in everyday language. Success in this enterprise would demonstrate that it is useful to separate comprehension processes from perception, on the one hand, and from problem solving, on the other. However, I do not claim that all problem solving can be viewed as comprehension. SOAR conceptualizes all cognitive tasks, including sentence comprehension, as searches in problem spaces and hence is intended as a general architecture for cognition. The CI model has a more restricted scope in that even if its account of comprehension were entirely successful, there still would be a need for a theory of problem solving proper, complementing but not subsuming the comprehension theory.

I do not intend to discuss the question of whether cognitive architectures are possible, but anyone who proposes another cognitive architecture must at least take some position on this by no means trivial question. In a recent and very clear presentation of the issues involved, Anderson (1990) answered this question essentially in the negative, and I cannot fault his arguments. But they trouble me very little in my work as a cognitive scientist. If we want to know the absolute truth about what is out there in the world, or in our heads, there are, indeed, reasons to be pessimistic, as Anderson has argued. I, however, prefer to take a lighter view of the scientific enterprise: The goal is not to find out the real truth about how the mind works but to find useful descriptions thereof. What we know about cognition may never offer enough constraints to determine the one and only cognitive architecture, but if we are willing to live with approximations, distinguishing between a good, broad, elegant, and internally consistent theory with detailed empirical support and a poor one is by no means hopeless. It is not a trivial task, however, and the problems involved are what I discuss in this chapter.

Empirically Evaluating Cognitive Architectures

There are quite a few things about evaluation that psychologists do know. For instance, suppose one is interested in a question such as, What are the effects of Factors A and B on Behaviors X and Y in Circumstances F and G for Populations P and Q? One might know how to design the right experiment, when to reject the null hypotheses, and even calculate the power of one's tests if necessary. If that is the game one wants to play, the statistics books tell us how.

A few troubling questions arise, however, when the "scientific game" takes on a slightly different form. With the rise of mathematical psychology in the 1950s and 1960s, what psychologists were interested in often could not be answered with questions such as the one just posed. What they really wanted to know was, Does my model fit the data well enough, or do I need to look for another one? Much thought has gone into this problem, but to this day the answers are not totally satisfying. It is somehow not right that the better one's data are, the more likely a goodness-of-fit test will reject one's model, even though there are ways to get around that problem and the admonition to modelers not to test a theory in isolation but to test it against some equally well-specified alternative theory goes largely unheeded.

My purpose here is not to review or discuss the many problems that are connected with the empirical evaluation of models. Instead, I want to tackle a much larger problem, that so far has not received enough public discussion. The question is how to evaluate empirically a cognitive architecture. In general terms the answer is obvious: It must involve some sort of convergence of evidence. Many specific models must be developed using that architecture, and eventually the success or failure of that enterprise will become clear.

Behind this facile generalization lurk a number of serious problems. Do we have methods to tell how well or poorly the evidence is converging? Where does the architecture end and a model start? When a does model not work, and when does that count as a failure of the architecture rather than just as a poor instantiation? Are we free to estimate ever new parameter values in each new situation? How many parameters is too much? It is questions like these that I will illustrate with reference to a cognitive architecture for comprehensive processes.

The Construction–Integration Theory

When I first became interested in the area of comprehension (Kintsch 1970, 1972, 1974), it was widely felt that comprehension processes were too complex to be analyzed except for simple, brief, isolated sentences. In contrast, it appeared to me that single sentences present the most difficult problems of analysis (e.g., because of their ambiguity), whereas sentences within a discourse or other context offered a much more promising target. Thus, in the CI theory, comprehension is defined only in terms of the discourse or situation as a whole. The theory has no better notion of how to interpret *They are flying planes* than did ordinary subjects in experiments.

The representations generated by the CI theory as a result of comprehension processes are wholistic structures. An associative network of elements (e.g., propositions, concepts) is constructed to represent the meaning of a discourse or situation as a whole, but at the same time, the elements derive part of their meaning from the structure in which they are embedded. The final network is based on principles of constraint satisfaction: The elements of the network affect each other positively or negatively until a balanced state is achieved in which the positively interrelated core of the network dominates and outliers are rejected.

The CI theory is an interactive theory in that comprehension always involves the interaction of an outside input, typically a text, with the goals and knowledge of the comprehender. Figure 1 provides a sketch of these interaction processes. The CI theory is concerned with only some of the processes indicated in this figure. In particular, the theory neglects the perceptual aspects of reading a text (or listening), as well as the question of how the semantic representation of a text is constructed. It typically starts not with a text proper but with a hand-coded propositional representation of the text. It accepts the text elements as given and asks how these elements are combined to form larger wholes. (Perhaps within a few years one of the systems that is currently being developed to parse texts can be used as a front end to CI models.)

The processes that the theory focuses on are how the text propositions activate knowledge and how an integrated representation of text and knowledge is achieved. The basic assumption here is that knowledge is activated by means of local, associative processes, without the benefit of guidance from such control structures as frames and schemata. Thus, contextually relevant as well as irrelevant knowledge is activated,

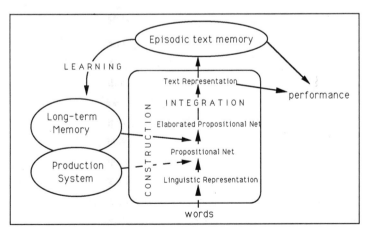

Figure 1   Components of the construction–integration model.

necessitating a constraint satisfaction process—the integration process—to reject the contextually irrelevant or contradictory material. The result of these processes is a text representation, which can be the basis for action. This representation is stored in episodic text memory, which is involved in such experimental tasks as recall and summarization. Finally, the CI theory is concerned with how comprehending a text alters the comprehender's knowledge base or long-term memory, that is, with learning proper (as distinguished from, e.g., text recall).

The label *construction–integration theory* reflects the central assumption about the nature of the reader–text interaction in comprehension: Knowledge activation is locally guided and is therefore crude and imprecise, but a contextual integration process in the connectionist manner can nevertheless yield a coherent text representation. The CI theory is, therefore, a hybrid theory. Its construction component is rule based and symbolic, but the integration process uses a connectionist approach.

In what follows, I briefly sketch the various assumptions and components of the theory in general terms. The first attempt to construct a psychological process model of discourse comprehension was made by Kintsch and van Dijk (1978). The present version of CI theory still retains the essential features of this model but has become greatly elaborated and refined, principally in van Dijk and Kintsch's (1983) later work. The construction-integration mechanism for knowledge activation and inferencing was added to that basic processing model later by Kintsch (1988).

Textual Construction Processes

A computationally viable, general parser that would take any English text and derive a propositional representation thereof is not available. Domain-specific or otherwise limited parsers are easier to construct but are of little value for the present work because the experiments and studies researchers want to account for involve all kinds and types of texts. Instead, it is expedient to code texts by hand according to some consistent criteria. Depending on the goals of one's analyses, this coding may be fine grained (e.g., Turner, 1987), less detailed (e.g., Bovair & Kieras, 1985), or even quite crude (e.g., Kintsch & Vipond, 1979). The general characteristics of a parser within the CI framework, and the knowledge base needed to support it, have been discussed by Kintsch (1985). Given a sentence such as *Mary gives John a book* and the template GIVE[PERSON-1, PERSON-2, OBJECT] in the knowledge base, the text proposition GIVE[MARY, JOHN, BOOK] is constructed.

Two points need to be emphasized. First, a parser for a CI model does not have to be perfect. If it constructs some inappropriate forms in addition to the right ones, the context will usually be constraining enough to suppress the wrong ones. For instance, if the proposition KNOW[LINGUIST, SOLUTION, OF-PROBLEM] is constructed for the sentence *The linguist knew the solution of the problem would not be easy*, no damage is done. Once the right proposition is constructed, it will suppress the wrong form because it satisfies the constraints of the sentence as a whole better than the initial attempt (Kintsch, 1988). Thus, the same connectionist mechanism that allows one to select the contextually appropriate knowledge from all the knowledge that has been activated can be used to simplify parsing.

Another important point about textual constructions is that not only the propositions that correspond directly to the words of the text need to be constructed but also the macropropositions that are not always explicitly expressed in the text. If a macroproposition is expressed explicitly, it must be recognized as such and tagged appropriately in the network. If it is not (e.g., if a generalization or construction rule must be applied to generate it), the macroproposition must nevertheless be incorporated into the text representation. Although there are rules for this—the macrorules of van Dijk (1980)—these rules are not implemented at present in an actual computational system. Thus, the whole process of textual construction requires hand coding.

Moreover, comprehension processes are not complete with the formation of certain concepts and propositions. It is also necessary to determine their relations. This is complicated by the fact that it is not possible to maintain in working memory all the propositions of a (long) text. Texts are read roughly one sentence at a time (sentence groups if the sentences are very short or phrases if a sentence is too long). If only a single text unit can be processed in working memory at any one time, how is it possible to construct a coherent representation of the whole text? The CI theory assumes that as a reader moves from one text unit to the next, not all of the material in working memory is deactivated (i.e., consigned to secondary memory as distinguished from primary memory in the Jamesian sense); rather, a small number of propositions (with estimates ranging from one to four, with a mode of two) from the just-finished processing cycle is retained in the foucs of attention and reprocessed together with the material from the next processing cycle. If all works out well, these buffered propositions form a link between the previous text and the new input. It is, of course, very important to select those propositions that are most likely to serve as bridges from one cycle to the next. In general, the more important a proposition, the more likely it is to serve this bridging function. In the CI theory, the activation value of each proposition provides an index of importance (as I will explain), and hence it is assumed that the two (or so) most highly activated propositions in each cycle will be retained in a buffer for further processing. These usually include a macroproposition or other central proposition, because, as I will show, it is the connectedness of a proposition that determines its eventual level of activation. The CI theory thus generates a text representation in which not all potential connections among the propositions of a text are realized. Only if two propositions are processed together in working memory is their relation encoded in the text representation.

Thus, a researcher analyzing a text, or a reader with the right kind of motivation and adequate time and resources, may detect many more relations in a text than are encoded on-line during normal reading. For example, a graph of the causal relations among the elements of a story (Trabasso & van den Broek, 1985) includes many links that are not actually realized by someone listening to the story or reading it fluently (Fletcher, Hummel, & Marsolek, 1990). This has important implications for questions concerning the structure of a text. Is it some property of the text or of the mental representation created by the reader? The CI model provides a mechanism to specify precisely the structure generated, depending on the nature of the reader–text interaction. Thus, the "normal" reader with a buffer size of two generates a different structure than someone who skims the text with a buffer containing only a single proposition; the analytic reader who goes over the text repeatedly and studies it carefully generates yet a different structure. In all cases, however, the properties of the text set boundary conditions. That the structure of a text is jointly determined by what is on the page and what the reader does with it is not a novel view (e.g., Rosenblatt, 1978); however, the CI model goes beyond other proponents of this view in providing a precise computational mechanism to describe the nature and results of this interaction.

There is, of course, no guarantee that the process of linking consecutive text units by means of a small buffer, as described above, will be successful. In that case, the careful reader can either attempt to retrieve from secondary memory a proposition that does provide a link with the current text unit or attempt to infer a proposition that has the same effect. It has been shown repeatedly that these processes are resource demanding and interrupt the smooth course of comprehension (Kintsch & Vipond, 1979; Miller & Kintsch, 1980; O'Brien, 1987). Alternatively, of course, the reader may decide to just continue. Local difficulties can sometimes be repaired later, but frequently the result will be an incoherent text representation, with corresponding gaps when the reader later attempts to recall or summarize the text.

Texts permit, and often demand, analyses at more than one level. There are the linguistic relations among the words and phrases that make up the text. There are the semantic relations among the corresponding propositions of the textbase, which are by no means identical with the former. The mental representation of a text that is formed during comprehension also includes a very important third level of relations, the level of the situation model, because comprehension typically involves the formation of a mental model of the situation described by the text. All three levels of representation have been shown to be important psychologically (Fletcher & Chrysler, 1990), but they are not always equally important. In some cases when texts are constructed from simple sentences of the same syntactic form, the memory for the actual words used may be totally absent (Bransford & Franks, 1971), whereas in other cases readers may be unable to form situation models (Bransford & Johnson, 1972). Furthermore, surface, textbase, and situational relations are by no means the only ones that may play a significant role in comprehension. When reading, poetry, rhyme, verse measure, and alliteration may dominate semantic factors (Kintsch, in press), whereas for understanding word algebra problems, the formal algebraic relations implied by the text (the "problem model") are indispensable (Kintsch & Greeno, 1985).

Knowledge-Based Constructions

Text representations always contain two components: what the reader constructs from the text itself, as described above, and the knowledge that the reader brings to the text. There is almost no limit to the latter. Textual analysis for certain texts (e.g., by a whole culture rather than by a single reader) can go on forever. The strategic, deliberate processes involved in such analyses are beyond the scope of the CI theory and would fall within the domain of a theory of problem solving. Subjects who are asked to give think-aloud protocols while reading typically read aloud for a while the text they are given but then interrupt themselves (e.g., when they encounter a comprehension breakdown) and comment on what they are doing. They are problem solving at this point, making inferences, retrieving appropriate knowledge, and so on. But even when they are just reading aloud, having nothing to say beyond what they are reading, they are activating knowledge, producing low-level inferences. It is this automatic, unreflective, nonstrategic kind of knowledge activation with which the CI theory is concerned.

Knowledge is represented in the CI theory as an associative net. The nodes of this network are propositions (or concepts, which can be considered a special type of proposition). Propositions have arguments, numbering between one and some small number, and a relational term. The arguments of a proposition may be other propositions. Thus, complex structures may be created through propositional embedding. The associative links in the knowledge net vary in strength. No distinction is made between episodic and semantic memory. That is, the knowledge net, also referred to as *long-term memory*, contains both general knowledge as well as particular experiences associated with specific contexts.

Knowledge activation according to the CI theory is local, associative, and without the guidance and control of a schema. Each proposition constructed from the textual input retrieves a few propositions from its long-term memory neighborhood (in actual simulations the number has usually been two). The probability of retrieval depends on the strength of the associative links between propositions. Hence, for the most part, long-term memory propositions highly associated to the text propositions will be activated by this process and incorporated into the text representation under construction. The local associates of single text propositions are of course not necessarily relevant in the context of the text as a whole.

The goals of the reader play a particular role in knowledge activation in that they are responsible for the activation of knowledge, including procedural knowledge, related to these goals. Thus, knowledge about arithmetic is included in the text representation under construction when a reader tries to solve a word arithmetic problem (Kintsch, 1988); procedural knowledge (how to do simple, basic operations) about the computer system becomes available when subjects try to understand instructions to perform routine computing tasks (Mannes & Kintsch, 1991); both procedural and declarative knowledge about the UNIX operating system is included in the text representation when subjects are given instructions to plan and execute command sequences on the UNIX system (Doane, Kintsch, & Polson, 1989). Of course, when trying to solve a particular arithmetic problem or perform a particular action, most of the knowledge about the respective domain is not needed. What needs to be explained is how the comprehender manages to selectively activate those portions of his or her knowledge that are in fact goal relevant.

Thus, at this point, the text representation generated (the "elaborated" representation in Figure 1) contains many irrelevant items (e.g., procedures not needed for the task at hand) as well as contradictory items (e.g., alternative arithmetic hypotheses). The integration process described below is needed to sort the wheat from the chaff.

Integration

The elaborated text representation following both the text- and knowledge-based construction processes contains (a) a set of propositions constructed from the text, (b) a few associates of each text proposition retrieved from long-term memory depending on the strength of the association, and (c) specific goals associating both procedural and declarative knowledge. All elements are represented as propositions and are added to the network under construction. Many of the propositions that are added through (b) and (c) are contextually irrelevant, however (e.g., local associates that do not fit into the overall context, procedures and knowledge unrelated to the specifics of the text).

The elaborated text representation is a richly interrelated network of propositions. The relations among the propositions may be based on sharing of the same referent ("argument repetition") or on more specific semantic connections such as causality. Relations may vary in strength (e.g., causal relations were weighted more heavily than were argument repetition by Mannes and Kintsch, 1991) and are not always positive (e.g., the mutually exclusive hypotheses that a certain set of "6 red marbles" is a WHOLE-SET and a PART-SET are connected by an inhibitory link, Kintsch, 1988). Not all of these links are symmetric (e.g., the procedure *edit-file* inhibits the procedure *delete-file*, which would destroy a precondition of editing a file, but not vice versa; Mannes & Kintsch, 1991). The matrix that specifies all the links in the elaborated text representation is called the *coherence matrix*.

Initially, all text propositions are given a weight of 1, and all knowledge-based propositions are given a weight of 0. A spreading activation process is then used to let this network find a stable state. What normally happens for a well-behaved network corresponding to a reasonable input text is that clusters of highly interconnected propositions attract most of the activation in the network, thus deactivating sparsely interconnected portions of the network as well as nodes with negative links. Mathematically, this corresponds to multiplying the initial activation vector with the coherence matrix and repeating this operation until the pattern of activation stabilizes. It is necessary, however, to normalize the activation after each multiplication operation to keep it from growing out of bounds. This is done by setting all negative activation values to 0 and dividing all activation values by the maximum activation value, so that the highest activation will always have a value of 1.[1]

In theory, as each proposition is constructed, it is integrated as described above into the growing network. In most simulations, however, all propositions corresponding

---

[1]A different normalization procedure was used in Kintsch (1988), as has been in most other published work, in which the total sum of activations was restricted to 1. This procedure introduced a dependence between activation values and the total number of propositions in the network. The present procedure avoids this difficulty.

to a single input cycle are constructed first and then integrated simultaneously. This computational simplification is innocuous if one is interested only in the final outcome of the process. It is important to realize, however, that this is only a simplification and that for certain purposes more detailed computations must be performed (e.g., to obtain the speed-accuracy trade-off functions in Kintsch, Welsch, Schmalhofer, & Zimny, 1990, or for some of the on-line priming experiments studied in Kintsch & Welsch 1991).

Episodic Text Memory

The integration process is performed on what amounts to a single input cycle in the Kintsch and van Dijk (1978) model. Its outcome represents the content of working memory at the end of a cycle. As the process shifts to the next cycle, two things happen. First, the whole structure that has been generated is deleted from working memory and stored in secondary memory as an episodic text representation. Second, the most highly activated propositions remain activated in working memory during the processing of the next input sequence. Another way of saying this is that at the end of a cycle, the focus of attention shifts to the new input, except for the most important propositions of the previous cycle, which continue to be attended to.

Episodic text memory consists of the accumulated results of each processing cycle (Kintsch & Welsch, 1991). For each processing cycle, there is a coherence matrix, summarizing the interrelations among all the elements constructed during that cycle. The outcome of comprehension modifies this coherence matrix in that the element c_{ij}—the relation between two nodes i and j in the network—is adjusted by the final action values a_i and a_j of the elements i and j so that the corresponding element in the episodic text representation becomes $e_{ij} = c_{ij} \times a_i \times a_j$. Thus, if the activation value of either element is 0 after the integration process, it is deleted from episodic text memory.

Learning in the CI model is defined in terms of the effects that the episodic text memory has on the long-term memory network (see Figure 1). Exactly how this is to be conceptualized is still under investigation. One possibility is that the episodic memory network is simply merged with the long-term memory network (maybe with some decay factor). Another possibility is that the links in the long-term memory net are updated with information from episodic memory, so that if the two nodes a and b exist in both the long-term memory net and in episodic memory with strengths values of l_{ab} and e_{ab}, respectively, their updated long-term memory strength will be $l_{ab} + k \times e_{ab}$, where k is a decay factor (Ferstl, 1991).

Applications of the CI Theory

Kintsch (1988) discussed word identification in a discourse context as well as a context of solving and understanding word arithmetic problems in terms of the CI theory. Kintsch et al. (1990) applied the theory to account for data from experiments on sentence recognition. Kintsch (in press) briefly explored approaches to poetic language. Two articles (Kintsch, 1991; Kintsch & Welsch, 1991) followed the strategy of taking well-known, classical results from the memory literature and simulating them with a CI model to explore whether the general theory was sufficiently rich to allow derivivation of adequate models for these phenomena (for which the theory was not specifically developed) without having to resort to ad hoc assumptions. The general theoretical framework, plus the task constraints inherent in the experiments analyzed, were shown to be sufficient to account for the role of syntactic signals in a text indicating discourse relevance, an analysis of the role played by causal relations in story understanding, and some priming results in a discourse context.

Finally, the theory was extended to texts requiring some specific action by the reader, following up the work of Kintsch and Greeno (1985) on word arithmetic problems. Mannes and Kintsch (1991) developed a model of how people understand instructions to perform routine computing tasks. The texts here are very brief—one or at most two sentences—but the amount of knowledge that needed to be activated (in just the right kind of sequence) to understand what one was supposed to do was relatively large. For instance, if I read in a mail message a request to send someone a particular paragraph from a paper I have on a file, I must exit the mail system, find the file, enter the editor, copy the paragraph, paste the paragraph into another buffer, and exit the editor before I can send anything. The simulation does all this planning by means of the comprehension mechanisms it has, as described above, as part of understanding the message, just like expert subjects who quickly grasp what they need to do without conscious, deliberate problem solving. Doane et al. (1989) worked out a similar model for the domain of UNIX commands, where the texts are even briefer and the required actions more complex. Readers of a story or a newspaper article cannot avoid some inferencing to connect and organize the text they are given, but in Doane et al., a very brief text was the stimulus for long and complex chains of inferences. The mechanisms the model uses were the same in both cases.

My purpose here is not to describe these applications of the theory in detail, however, but to point to some difficulties that have arisen in the empirical evaluation of these models.

Can an Architecture Be Evaluated?

Within the domain of text comprehension (an admittedly fuzzy domain), one ought to be able to derive a simulation model for every experimental task, given an adequate analysis of the goals and task constraints involved. But even for the few cases in which this has been tried, it is not always obvious when and on what grounds one should declare a success or admit a failure. Of the numerous issues that could be raised, I will concentrate on three areas in which I have encountered serious problems.

Complexity and Completeness

Although the CI theory is complex, not all features of the theory play a decisive role in every situation. For instance, the pre-1988 version of the theory did not deal with knowledge activation at all but nevertheless accounted successfully for quite a number of experimental phenomena, such as the levels effect in recall (more important propositions are recalled better than subordinate, less important propositions). Summarization, bridging inferences, and reading difficulties also could be simulated because these results depended primarily on the assumptions of the theory about processing cycles and the short-term memory buffer (Kintsch & van Dijk, 1978) rather than on knowledge activation. One can obtain good predictions for reproductive recall that way, for example, as long as one is willing to neglect reconstructive processes.

In fact, no single application of the CI theory mentioned above uses all features of the theory. In the study of sentence recognition, the integration process plays a central role, but neither the cyclical nature of processing nor knowledge activation does. Thus, the study of sentence recognition reported by Kintsch et al. (1990) totally neglected knowledge activation. This study dealt only with text propositions, and the coherence matrix was integrated over the whole text instead of sentence by sentence. Computationally, these shortcuts provide significant simplifications and hardly affect the outcome at all. The crucial factor for sentence recognition is that memory representations at three levels of analysis must be considered: the surface structure for the actual words and phrases used in the sentences, the meaning of the sentences (i.e., the textbase), and the model of the situation constructed by the reader from the text. A main result of the study was the demonstration that surface memory decayed quickly and completely under the experimental conditions used, the textbase decayed less rapidly and incompletely, and situation memory did not decay at all within the 4-day period studied. Another study in which the focus is on different levels of representation is that of Kintsch (in press). The children's counting rhyme analyzed had no situation model and had a degenerate textbase, but it had rich word-level relations based not only on syntax but also on rhyme, alliteration, and other poetic constraints.

In contrast, with some tasks, the distinction between levels of representation can often be disregarded entirely without substantially affecting the model computations. When dealing with brief texts out of context, as is frequently the case in psycholinguistic experiments, there is often no situation model distinct from the textbase, and, unless on-line tests are involved, surface memory is weak relative to memory for meaning and can be ignored without too much distortion. This has been the case in most of the applications of the CI theory mentioned above (e.g., Kintsch, 1991; Kintsch & Welsch, 1991; Mannes & Kintsch, 1991).

A similar picture emerges when one considers the knowledge activation component of the CI theory. It is the core of the Mannes and Kintsch (1991) model of understanding instructions for performing routine computing tasks. In this model, the text (the instruction) selectively activates those action plans that are needed to achieve whatever end re-sult the instructions specify. That is, the text operates on the knowledge, both declarative and procedural, about how the computer system works. The fact that each text proposi-tion also activates some associatively related propositions from long-term memory, on the other hand, plays a negligible role initially. However, once the system has performed a few tasks and remembers what it has done, this previously insignificant, superfluous mechanism assumes a dominant role. At this point, the text propositions associatively re-trieve the memory for previous cases, which in turn will influence the planning process in important ways. On the other hand, the work on understanding UNIX commands (Doane et al., 1989) does not include a memory for cases; hence, the whole associative knowl-edge retrieval component plays such a minor role that it has been dispensed with alto-gether in simulation.

Indeed, researchers have neglected knowledge activation in many applications of the model or have used it selectively. Knowledge activation plays no significant role in the work on syntactic signals of discourse relevance and the importance of causal rela-tions for story understanding in which researchers are basically concerned with reproduc-tive recall and summarization. In the analyses of some of the priming data reported in the literature, researchers have considered knowledge activation only insofar as it is directly relevant to the experiment. Thus, in accounting for the results of McKoon and Ratcliff (1980) that after reading a story about painting a tomato, the sentence *Tomatoes are red* is primed more strongly than the sentence *Tomatoes are round*, the association of *tomato* to *red* is of crucial importance. Hence, this association is incorporated into the simulation but not other associations to *tomato* or to the other words in the text.

My point is that none of the models that have been developed and tested within the construction–integration architecture have incorporated all the features of the theory. Different parts of the theory are tested in different simulations.

Quantitative Versus Qualitative Predictions

It is not clear how many free parameters the CI theory, or models developed from it, has especially given the partial testing strategy just discussed. There are, at any rate, so many that producing precise quantitative fits to some data set could be considered a meaningless exercise. In recent work, I have therefore chosen to forego quantitative fits and concentrate on the qualitative predictions the model makes. Thus, instead of estimating parameters, I have either used estimates from previous studies (the size of the short-term memory buffer is either 1 or 2) or reasonable but arbitrary values. For instance, in most recent work (Kintsch, in press; Kintsch & Welsch, 1991; Otero, 1990; P. Schwanenflugel, personal communication, 1991), all links were either 1 or 0; whenever special emphasis was needed (e.g., to designate macrorelevance), a value of 2 was used. These guesses seem to be the weakest, most minimal assumptions that could have been made. There is no way that they would fit precisely a disparate set of experiments. However, I find it more reassuring that a wide variety of different results are in qualitative agreement with models that are thus constrained than if nice quantitative fits to these data were produced with an ever-changing parameter set.

The drawbacks of qualitative predictions are obvious. There is no statistical evaluation, and there is room for disagreement. What looks like a good qualitative fit to one person may seem far off the data to another (e.g., the data and predictions for speed-accuracy trade-off effects in sentence recognition, Figures 8–9 and 12–13, respectively, in Kintsch et al., 1990).

Simulation of Examples

A mathematical model typically allows one to derive predictions for the expected value of some statistic, which then can be compared with the average data from a group of subjects. In contrast, in all the simulations mentioned above, only one (or at most a few) examples were analyzed and the results compared (qualitatively) with data averaged over subjects and items. Typically, the example that is simulated is the one used by the original experimenter to introduce and discuss his or her data. This is no doubt a very questionable procedure. Its success rests on the typicality of the example chosen for simulation, but even a typical example is not the same as data averaged over items as well as subjects.

However, questions can be raised about mathematical models in this respect, too. They typically yield predictions for the so-called ideal subject, and individual differences are neglected. Furthermore, the variability among items in these models is treated as noise, not as real differences between items. Mean predictions are obtained because assumptions such as normal variability are built into the theory. But variability among items (or, for that matter, among subjects) is not simply error variance; it reflects real differences. One text has different properties than the next. The present approach has a potential advantage in this respect: It allows one to deal with these differences explicitly.

Researchers using words or nonsense syllables as stimuli in their experiments have their materials well normed and are able to randomly sample items from a specified pool. Hence, they can validly generalize their results to that pool. Researchers using sentences or texts do not have this option. We all know that nothing determines the success of an experiment as much as the careful construction of the materials. What one strives for is comparability among texts or sentences: They have to be different, but ideally they should all be the same in some sense, be equally typical of some prototype one has in mind. This ideal, of course, cannot be achieved, and there will always be real differences among the texts used in an experiment. Differences between texts are random only in the sense that one sometimes cannot pinpoint them. Often it is quite obvious, after the fact, why something strange happened with a particular text. As an author, when discussing one's methods and results, one usually chooses a typical, "well-behaved" text for purposes of illustration. That is the example we usually use for our simulations. One should also note that it is always possible to construct examples in such a way that the outcome will be highly atypical, both in the experiment and in the simulation. Thus, the fact that the theory will yield weird predictions in some cases is not necessarily a fault of the theory because deviant experimental outcomes are equally possible.

Ideally, of course, one would simulate not one typical example but all the texts used in an experiment and would thus be able to compare averaged predictions with averaged data, as well as predictions for specific texts with their specific outcomes. The reason this has not been done is that the computations involved are labor intensive. Researchers are only now beginning to write more efficient programs that allow such an approach. Indeed, in a recent study of priming effects in discourse, Schwanenflugel (personal communication, 1991) took this approach and simulated not merely a typical example but all 20 texts used in her experiment. The results were encouraging: The qualitative (ordinal) predictions were the same for all 20 texts, mirroring the pattern of the data.

Conclusions

In this chapter, I have attempted, first, to sketch an architecture for comprehension and, second, to discuss some problems encountered in the empirical evaluation of this architecture. I have been less concerned with the details of the theory, primarily wishing to argue that carving out a separate domain for comprehension processes between perception and problem solving is a useful way of dividing up the field of cognition. Comprehension processes, according to the CI theory, are associative, based on weak rules rather than sophisticated control structures, and are best modeled as a hybrid system, combining features of symbolic systems with those of a localist connectionist network.

I have focused on three questions concerning the empirical evaluation of the proposed architecture. The solution to the problem of simulating examples seems quite straightforward: Simulating prototypical examples and then comparing the results of the simulation with data averaged over many examples as well as subjects is at best a permissible shortcut in cases in which no more than an informal treatment is required. Otherwise, one can make simulations more efficient by doing as Schwanenflugel (personal communication, 1991) did: Get predictions for all texts used in an experiment, and explicitly consider "individual differences" among the texts. In this way, what is now a weakness of the approach can be turned into a real strength.

The answer to the parameter estimation problem is perhaps not as obvious, but a good case can be made for continuing the present practice of aiming for qualitative fits rather than quantitative fits based on extensive, experiment-specific parameter estimations. Robust qualitative correspondences seem more convincing than precise fits based on delicate adjustments of many parameters.

Finally, I also think that there are satisfactory answers to the issue of piecemeal testing. Newell (1990) has pointed out the significance of the time scale of cognitive processes. In the millisecond range, one deals primarily with automatic processes that reflect properties of the architecture quite directly. As one moves to behaviors such as summarizing a story or understanding and solving a word arithmetic problem, strategic elements gain more and more significance, and one moves further and further away from the cognitive architecture proper. Thus, the simulation of knowledge activation in the planning of routine computing tasks depends most strongly on the knowledge analysis. Given the same knowledge, other planners using some form of backward chaining are certainly capable of simulating these protocols. If the Mannes and Kintsch (1991) simulations were the only achievement of the CI theory, it would be of little interest because other researchers committed to different views of planning could rightfully ask why they should prefer that account to their own. The Mannes and Kintsch simulation of planning is important because it shows that planning could be done within the same cognitive architecture that was also used in a wide variety of other tasks, from word identification and priming in discourse, to sentence recognition, story recall, and summarization, and all the way to algebra word problem solving. The only thing these applications of the CI theory have in common is the basic cognitive architecture because goals and task constraints vary widely. For each of these applications taken separately, one could easily devise some alternative theoretical explanation. The CI model is interesting because it ranges over all these comprehension tasks. Newell (1990) has made this argument before for SOAR, but it applies equally to other general theories of cognition, or semigeneral ones like the CI theory.

The piecemeal testing strategy is a consequence of applying an architecture to a broad range of cognitive phenomena. Each specific cognitive task engages only a portion of the cognitive capabilities people have. Hence, different components of the theory will have to be involved in the simulation of different tasks. The theory in this respect does no more than reflect the realities of cognition. Thus, it does not appear that the methodological problems I have detected in my work on the CI theory are too damaging. They are certainly worth worrying about and worth a public discussion, however, because if the future of psychology belongs to general theories, then more than the CI theory alone is at issue.

References

Anderson, J. R. (1983). *The architecture of cognition.* Cambridge, MA: Harvard University Press.

Anderson, J. R. (1990). *The adaptive character of thought.* Hillsdale, NJ: Erlbaum.

Bovair, S., & Kieras, D. E. (1985). A guide to propositional analysis for research on technical prose. In B. K. Britten & J. B. Black (Eds.), *Understanding repository text* (pp. 315–362). Hillsdale, NJ: Erlbaum.

Bransford, J. D., & Franks, J. J. (1971). The abstraction of linguistic ideas. *Cognitive Psychology, 2,* 331–350.

Bransford, J. D., & Johnson, M. K. (1972). Contextual prerequisites for understanding: Some investigations of comprehension and recall. *Journal of Verbal Learning and Verbal Behavior, 11*, 717–726.

Doane, S. M., Kintsch, W., & Polson, P. G. (1989). Action planning: Producing UNIX commands. *11th Annual Conference of the Cognitive Science Society* (pp. 458–465). Hillsdale, NJ: Erlbaum.

Ferstl, E. C. (1991). *Changes in the knowledge structure after reading a text.* Unpublished master's thesis, University of Colorado.

Fletcher, C. R., & Chrysler, S. T. (1990). Surface forms, textbases, and situation models: Recognition memory for three types of textual information. *Discourse Processes, 13*, 175–190.

Fletcher, C. R., Hummel, J. E., & Marsolek, C. J. (1990). Causality and the allocation of attention during comprehension. *Journal of Experimental Psychology: Learning, Memory, and Cognition, 16*, 233–240.

Hull, C. L. (1943). *Principles of behavior.* New York: Appleton-Century-Crofts.

Kintsch, W. (1970). Models for free recall and recognition. In D. A. Norman (Ed.), *Models of human memory* (pp. 333–374). San Diego, CA: Academic Press.

Kintsch, W. (1972). Notes on the structure of semantic memory. In E. Tulving & W. Donaldson (Eds.), *Organization and memory* (pp. 247–308). San Diego, CA: Academic Press.

Kintsch, W. (1974). *The representation of meaning in memory.* Hillsdale, NJ: Erlbaum.

Kintsch, W. (1985). Text processing: A psychological model. In T. A. van Dijk (Ed.), *Handbook of discourse analysis* (pp. 231–244). San Diego, CA: Academic Press.

Kintsch, W. (1988). The use of knowledge in discourse processing: A construction-integration model. *Psychological Review, 95*, 163–182.

Kintsch, W. (1991). How readers construct situation models for stories: The role of syntactic cues and causal inferences. In A. F. Healy, S. M. Kosslyn, & R. M. Shiffrin (Eds.), *From learning processes to cognitive processes: Essays in honor of William K. Estes* (Vol. 2, pp. 261–278). Hillsdale, NJ: Erlbaum.

Kintsch, W. (in press). Kognitionspsychologische modelle des textverstehens: Literarische texte. In K. Reusser & M. Reusser (Eds.), *Verstehen lernen—Verstehen lehren.* Bern, Federal Republic of Germany: Hans Huber.

Kintsch, W., & Greeno, J. G. (1985). Understanding and solving word arithmetic problems. *Psychological Review, 92*, 109–129.

Kintsch, W., & van Dijk, T. A. (1978). Towards a model of text comprehension and production. *Psychological Review, 85*, 363–394.

Kintsch, W., & Vipond, D. (1979). Reading comprehension and readability in educational practice and psychological theory. In L. G. Nilsson (Ed.), *Perspectives of memory research* (pp. 325–366). Hillsdale, NJ: Erlbaum.

Kintsch, W., & Welsch, D. (1991). The construction–integration model: A framework for studying memory for text. In W. E. Hockley & S. Lewandowsky (Eds.), *Relating theory and data: Essays on human memory in honor of Bennet B. Murdock* (pp. 367–385). Hillsdale, NJ: Erlbaum.

Kintsch, W., Welsch, D., Schmalhofer, F., & Zimny, S. (1990). Sentence memory: A theoretical analysis. *Journal of Memory and Language, 29*, 133–159.

Mannes, S. M., & Kintsch, W. (1991). Planning routine computing tasks: Understanding what to do. *Cognitive Science, 15*, 305–342.

McKoon, G., & Ratcliff, R. (1980). Priming in item recognition: The organization of propositions in memory for text. *Journal of Verbal Learning and Verbal Behavior, 19,* 369–386.

Miller, J. R., & Kintsch, W. (1980). Readability and recall for short passages: A theoretical analysis. *Journal of Experimental Psychology: Human Learning and Memory, 6,* 335–354.

Newell, A. (1990). *Unified theories of cognition.* Cambridge, MA: Harvard University Press.

O'Brien, E. J. (1987). Antecedent search processes and the structure of text. *Journal of Experimental Psychology: Learning, Memory, and Cognition, 13,* 278–290.

Otero, J. (1990). *Failures in monitoring text comprehension: An explanation in terms of the construction-integration model* (Tech. Rep. No. 90-17). Boulder, CO: Institute of Cognitive Science.

Rosenblatt, L. M. (1978). *The reader, the text, the poem.* Carbondale: Southern Illinois University Press.

Trabasso, T., & van den Broek, P. (1985). Causal thinking and the representation of narrative events. *Journal of Memory and Language, 24,* 612–630.

Turner, A. A. (1987). *The propositional analysis system: Version 1.0* (Tech. Rep. No. 87-2). Boulder, CO: Institute of Cognitive Science.

van Dijk, T. A. (1980). *Macrostructures.* The Netherlands, The Hague: Mouton.

van Dijk, T. A., & Kintsch, W. (1983). *Strategies of discourse comprehension.* San Diego, CA: Academic Press.

CHAPTER 7

Theories, Constraints, and Cognition

Douglas L. Medin and David M. Thau

O n glancing at the Table of Contents and leafing through the chapters of this volume, readers will quickly realize that there exists a diversity of approaches to research in psychology, each offering a distinct perspective. We view this pluralism as healthy, and our goal is to add to it another exemplar. In this chapter, we describe four highly interrelated factors or strategies that have influenced our research in the study of concepts and classification learning: (a) ecological sensitivity, (b) functions, (c) constraints, and (d) formal models and theories. We also outline some interrelations among these influences using examples drawn from the area of categorization. Finally, contrary to our exemplar theorist natures, we conclude with an abstracted version of the methodology we would like to embrace.

It is important to note that the four factors we discuss act in a highly parallel fashion and that, to a certain extent, some act as checks and balances for others. Before discussing the interrelations among these factors, however, it is important to describe our particular bias on each factor considered individually.

This research was supported by National Science Foundation Grants BNS 89-18701 and BNS 89-18700. Edward Smith, Larry Barsalou, Edward Wisniewski, Woo-Kyoung Ahn, Frances Kuo, and Colleen Seifert provided guidance on this chapter.

Ecological Sensitivity

Ecological Validity

We disagree with two extreme opinions concerning the role of ecological validity in psychology: (a) that nonnaturalistic experiments are flawed by their very nature and (b) that ecological validity should not even be a concern.

The first opinion is that if one wants to understand cognitive processes that operate in realistic, everyday situations, one should only conduct experiments that reflect the complexity of these situations. A problem with this argument is that the conclusion does not follow logically from the premise. Whatever ecological validity is, it cannot be equated with arguing against well-controlled experiments. We have never heard the claim that two confounded variables must ever more remain so because they happen to be correlated in realistic situations.

We also disagree with the premise of the argument. We do not think that our research agenda should be limited to the sort of practical questions that a layperson might find interesting. The most challenging questions about the mind typically involve processes that are so natural that we tend to take them for granted. For example, perception does not seem to be a problem because it does not occur to us to ask how a two-dimensional retinal projection gets converted into the experience of a three-dimensional world. Subjectively, the world is there and we see it, so there is nothing to be explained. Nor does it occur to us to ask just how we bring syntactic and pragmatic knowledge to bear on comprehending a sentence. People speak, and we understand them. We also know how children learn language—they imitate their parents. The mysteries arise only when we take a closer look, and our natural experience does not prompt us to do so. It is the different or unusual that catches our attention; shared cognitive abilities tend to be taken for granted.

The argument on the other side of the issue is that people have not evolved specialized cognitive modules that lead them to behave unusually in laboratory experiments. Therefore, artificiality is not a problem. Although we agree that introductory psychology has not yet been taught long enough for the natural selection of special-purpose survival strategies to take place, we think this position misses certain points.

First, any experimental situation will reveal some aspects of behavior and cognition and conceal others. For example, although one can learn something about schedules of reinforcement by putting pigeons in a Skinner box, this will not provide any information about how pigeons navigate. So, for openers, one needs to pay some attention to the world to determine which capabilities are in need of explanation.

Another important point is that ignoring real-world contexts increases the risk of failing to capture relevant information in analyses and at the risk of solving nonexistent problems. James J. Gibson argued that the view that we construct percepts by combining low-level sensory cues was a misguided consequence of elementaristic, impoverished psychological experiments (Gibson, 1979). Gibson's research program focused on an analysis of the information available in the environment, which he suggested was much more rich than people had assumed. By our reading, Gibson argued that inadequate analyses of the information available to the perceptual system may lead one to posit all sorts of complex computations to derive information that is actually already available. No analysis of perceptual processes can get very far without taking seriously the environment and the information it affords. Researchers in the area of artificial intelligence (AI), such as David Marr, were heavily influenced by Gibson's work, precisely because it addressed broad, computational-level questions (we use *computational* in Marr's, 1982, general sense, which is more abstract than its typical use in, for example, computational vision).

The Ecological and the Artificial

Although ecological sensitivity is important, it is clear that organisms are not driven by their environment alone. Because they have evolved along unique paths, different organisms will react differently to the same situation. Even at the level of sensory systems, some species are endowed with capabilities that others lack. Given that organisms have evolved mechanisms that process information from their environment, we must be concerned both with information in the environment and about the internal mechanisms that play a role in any given behavior.

Unfortunately, because organisms have evolved to cope with their environments, it is often difficult to determine whether an organism's behavior is due to cues in the environment or to some internal mechanism. It is in making this discrimination that the role of artificial situations becomes important. In our view, Shepard's (1984) evolutionary perspective on ecological constraints provides a clear example of this concern.

First of all, Shepard (1984) agreed with Gibson (1979) that organisms actively explore and manipulate their environment. He further argued that this exploration is not random but rather is guided by internal schemata. These schemata allow organisms to notice and anticipate vitally important events under conditions of impoverished information or time constraints.

The general notion is that organisms are attuned to their environment and have internalized mechanisms for dealing with relevant structure. As an example, Shepard

(1984) drew an analogy between the perceptual system and biological or circadian rhythms. The activity pattern of many animals is guided by day–night cycles that could, in principle, be directly under the control of the sun. Researchers have found, however, that when animals such as hamsters are placed under conditions of constant illumination, a very artificial situation, they continue to show 24-hr activity cycles, plus or minus only a few minutes. In short, the periodicity has become internalized so that it continues in the absence of the external stimulus, allowing the animal to anticipate the future and freeing it from depending directly on the sun. The latter would be advantageous for animals on cloudy days or in environments (e.g., the safety of a burrow) in which cues from the sun are not directly available. These rhythms are not fully independent of illumination, however, and can be "entrained" by patterns of illumination produced in the laboratory. Circadian rhythms, then, behave very much like internalized schemata that are sensitive to relevant information in the organism's environment.

Shepard (1984) suggested that the same situation holds for the perceptual system. Basically, certain structures or constraints associated with the environment (more properly, the interaction of organisms with their environment) may be internalized or embodied in the perceptual system. To observe these constraints, and to evaluate their significance, researchers need to put organisms into artificial situations in which information underdetermines performance. In these ambiguous situations, one may see natural constraints or assumptions emerge, just as circadian rhythms are observed under the uninformative situation of constant illumination.

Shepard's (1984) framework will succeed or fail on its own merits in the area of perception. Our goal is not to defend this position in the domain of perception but rather to examine its viability for higher order cognitive processes such as categorization and reasoning. Later on, we will argue by example that it does provide an effective research strategy. Note that what we call *ecological sensitivity* involves a procedure for understanding the relation of cognitive systems to their environment by using artificial, underdetermined situations and is not a blanket endorsement of artificial situations of and by themselves. Indeed, worrying about real-world circumstances may be critical for interpreting results from these artificial situations.

In short, we believe that a concern with real-world circumstances is important to ensure that laboratory results will be generalizable. Perhaps even more important, ecological considerations are critical for understanding cognition, even cognition in the laboratory. Cognitive psychologists may profitably and explicitly violate ecological validity for certain purposes, but they cannot ignore ecological considerations. As we shall demonstrate, analyses of natural situations may also provide an important source of ideas about constraints that act to guide performance in complex cognitive tasks.

Functions

One way to incorporate ecological sensitivity into our methodology is by concerning ourselves with the functions of different behaviors and processes. Although it makes sense to raise questions about function in the life sciences (as opposed to the physical sciences), these questions have not been wildly popular in cognitive psychology. In some cases, function has been implicitly assumed, and in others, it has been considered to be nothing more than idle speculation. However, Anderson (1990), one of our discipline's preeminent cognitive modelers, has recently described a strategy based on asking questions about function and then formulating computational models that satisfy or optimize this function. One of the major contributions of research on so-called "everyday memory" is that it raises questions about function, the answers to which are leading investigators along some very promising lines of research (e.g., Neisser & Winograd, 1988).

Constraints and Naturalness

Underdetermination

As we have mentioned, the environment surrounding an organism is not the only factor bearing on that organism's behavior. In fact, almost any interesting cognitive task actually involves a shortage of information from the environment. In language acquisition, for example, any linguistic input has to be consistent with the correct grammar (we will ignore the fact that speech is not always grammatical) but will necessarily be consistent with an infinite set of alternative grammars. Further sentences will not rule out many of these incorrect grammars, but any finite set of sentences will always be consistent with an unlimited number of grammars. Indeed, there are formal proofs (e.g., Gold, 1967; Pinker, 1984; Wexler & Culicover, 1980) that in its general form, the language learning problem is insolvable.

Analogous problems in learning arise in a variety of contexts. Consider a rat that eats some contaminated food in the morning, wanders around its environment, sees a cat, hears thousands of sounds, is exposed to innumerable sights and smells, and then gets sick late in the day. To what should the rat attribute its illness? Seeing the cat? The sound of rattling garbage can lids? The water it drank in the early afternoon? There are limitless possibilities, but laboratory research suggests that the rat would associate illness with the smell and taste of the food eaten in the morning and acquire an aversion to it (e.g., Garcia, Ervin, & Koelling, 1966). In general, this bias toward associating tastes and smells with illness serves the rat quite well. However, when the true association conflicts with a bias, learning may be difficult. For example, it is very hard, if not impossible, for a rat to learn to associate illness with visual cues. The general point is that organisms do not often have the luxury of running factorial experiments to determine which correlations are valid and informative. Instead, they have certain assumptions or expectations that allow some things to be readily learned and others not.

Computational Complexity

Even when possibilities can be systematically enumerated, there may be too many of them to allow an exhaustive search. The search issue comes up again and again in AI. Many AI systems are computationally explosive; the time it takes to run the program increases exponentially as the problem size increases. To reduce this problem, AI systems use heuristics and biases to reduce the number of possible choices from which a system must decide.

Complexity problems have important implications for processing models. Consider the problem of category construction in children. Nelson (1974) argued that children learn natural object categories by first constructing their own categories and then learning which labels apply to them. A model of this type of category construction could either generate and then evaluate all possible category partitions or it could be biased to only generate a subset of the possible partitions. Given that the number of ways of partitioning unclassified objects is computationally explosive (one can partition 3 objects in 5 ways, 4 in 15 ways, 5 in 52 ways, and 10 objects in more than 100,000 ways), the latter process seems more likely. Focusing on complexity issues in this way highlights places in theories in which constraints may be necessary.

Naturalness and Implicit Assumptions

What can organisms do in the face of these complexity and underdetermination problems? We see no alternative to the idea that organisms must be biased to learn some things rather than others, to draw some inferences rather than others, and in general to favor some possibilities at the expense of others. Because people cannot consider all the possibilities in a given situation, it should not be surprising that human cognition is interwoven with implicit assumptions about the world (assumptions that oversimplify but often work) and riddled with heuristics and strategies for dealing with problems and situations. In the case of categorization, one could say that people often rely on a "similarity heuristic," that is, the assumption that objects belonging to the same categories will tend to be more similar than objects belonging to different categories. Presumably, the human perceptual and conceptual system has evolved such that the similarity heuristic is usually correct.

More generally, these heuristics and implicit assumptions should render some tasks natural and easy (when people's biases fit the world) and other tasks difficult and unnatural (when their natural biases are not supported by data). Therefore, one can use people's performance in underdetermined situations to identify constraints or biases in learning. Naturalness can also serve as a guideline for evaluating theories of cognition. For example, categorization models make predictions about which kinds of partitionings will be hard for people to learn and which kinds will be easy. Theories may be judged by how well their predictions about naturalness correspond to data.

Theories and Formal Models

There are many distinct perspectives on the value of theories and formal models. Many researchers presuppose their value and importance and question the need for further discussion. On the other hand, we have heard one important branch of formal methods, mathematical psychology, talked about in the past tense (and with an air of "good riddance" at that). We believe that formal methods are of fundamental significance, and that the critical issue is how to use them properly. By formal methods we refer to any of a variety of procedures for developing, testing, and evaluating theories of cognition. These methods include at least logical and mathematical proofs and analyses, mathematical models, and models cast in the form of computer programs or simulations.

Why Formal Models Are Good
Because Intuition Is Bad
Argument by plausibility often drives our intuitions. Unfortunately, plausible argument is a rather blunt tool that often leads to mistakes. Consider, for example, some basic empirical findings from categorization research. In a line of work begun by Posner and Keele

(1968, 1970), investigators have studied the learning of ill-defined or "fuzzy" concepts. The modal procedure involves selecting some prototype (or best example) and then transforming the prototype in different ways to construct learning examples. After learning is complete, transfer tests are given that involve both old and new examples.

Three results from these procedures are very robust. First, typical examples (ones that vary little from the prototype) are more likely to be correctly categorized than are less typical examples. Second, the prototype, which is not presented with the test examples, may be classified more accurately than examples that do appear during training (Homa & Vosburgh, 1976; Medin & Schaffer, 1978; Posner & Keele, 1968). Finally, perhaps the most striking result is that over a delay interval, classification accuracy drops more rapidly for old examples than for the prototype or other new examples (Homa & Chambliss, 1975; Posner & Keele, 1970; Strange, Keeney, Kessel, & Jenkins, 1970).

These results have been interpreted as showing that (a) on the basis of experience with examples, people abstract out the central tendency or prototype for a category, and (b) classification decisions are based on similarity to this abstracted prototype. How else could prototypes be classified better than old examples, and how else could one explain differential retention?

This interpretation of the data stands in contrast to a less intuitive exemplar model. Exemplar models assume that learning involves storing examples and that classification is based on the similarity of the test items to the previously stored examples. Because it did not seem plausible that such a model could account for these data, exemplar models were either never considered or rejected by argument.

It turns out, however, that exemplar theories of categorization readily predict all these results (Hintzman & Ludlam, 1980; Medin & Schaffer, 1978). A prototype can be classified more accurately than an old example because the prototype of a category will tend to be very similar to many category examples and dissimilar to examples from contrasting categories. An old example will be maximally similar to itself but not necessarily similar to other examples from the same category and not necessarily dissimilar to examples from different categories. The same reasoning accounts for differential forgetting. Individual examples may be "on their own," whereas the prototype has many "friendly neighbors." Of course, the real test of this theory depends on whether or not mathematical or simulation models actually produce these results. They do, although not for all assumptions about forgetting (see Hintzman & Ludlam, 1980). If the exemplar model had been formalized and tested, it might not have been rejected so quickly and inappropriately.

Formal Models Indicate Where to Look for Information About Processes

As you can see, prototype and exemplar models of categorization often make similar predictions. Once these models are formalized, one can begin to ask about where to look to discover contrasts between models or, equally to the point, where not to look. For instance, there are some fairly broad conditions under which these two types of models make not just similar but identical predictions (Estes, 1986a; Nosofsky, 1990). Of course, there are other contexts in which the models make distinctive predictions, and these are the predictions to test experimentally. For instance, because prototypes only represent information about central tendencies, prototype models are insensitive to correlational information. Therefore, in a prototype model, knowledge about the average bird will not indicate that large birds are less likely to sing than small birds. Exemplar models, on the other hand, can account for this correlational information because most of the retrieved instances of large birds will not be song birds. The observation that people show sensitivity to correlation (Medin, Altom, Edelson, & Freko, 1982) provides evidence in favor of exemplar models.

Formal Models Help Conceptual Analyses

Models allow formal comparisons, and formal comparisons frequently yield rather surprising results. Consider, for example, the neural network model of category learning developed by Gluck and Bower (1988). This model is on the surface quite distinct from prior categorization models in its assumptions about representation and in its competitive learning rule. Nosofsky (in press), however, has proven that this network model is actually a special case of prototype models. This is a clear case in which formal analysis has illuminated deep underlying similarities that may have been concealed at the level of verbal description.

Formal Models Force Researchers to Be Concrete

Formal models have a built-in safeguard against vagueness. This is especially true for computational models; unless one's assumptions can be translated into steps in a program, the program will not run. Writing a program forces one to face issues and assumptions that otherwise might be hidden in informal verbal descriptions and mathematic formulas.

Formal Models Can Show Where Constraints Are Needed

As discussed in the section on constraints, computational models also serve to heighten our awareness of computational complexity problems. A program might run but take forever to come up with an answer because of the number of possibilities to be considered. In AI programming, a standard question is whether a program will "scale up," that is, continue to perform efficiently when given a larger problem or more knowledge. Programs that do scale up need heuristics (i.e., constraints) to limit the amount of possibilities that they consider.

Why Formal Models May Be Bad
Formal Models May Invite Too Narrow a Focus

To keep models from getting too complex, one may have to simplify the experimental situation so severely that what is truly of interest gets left out. As a consequence, one may end up constructing models that describe the constraints of the situation rather than the constraints of the human mind. In the study of decision making, for example, focusing on how people make choices between alternatives may ignore the problem of how people generate choices to begin with (e.g., Hogarth, 1981). To avoid modeling only task-specific strategies, recent mathematical models have placed a premium on breadth and applicability to a variety of situations (e.g., Hintzman, 1988; Raaijmakers & Shiffrin, 1981).

Even within a domain of analysis, formal models tend to focus on some phenomena at the expense of others. Mathematical models often contain (free) parameters that are estimated as part of the application of the model to data. For example, consider Bower's (1961) one element model for paired-associate learning. This model describes in great detail the consequences of assuming that learning takes place in an all-or-none manner and that the learning probability does not change across trials. At the same time, however, the theory says nothing at all about what would make the learning probability large or small. That is, even successful models are like a slice through a sphere—they reveal some things and conceal others.

Comparisons between models may engender another type of narrow focus. Because one model is often proposed as an alternative to another, the assumptions shared by both may not be questioned. In the flurry of interest in contrasting prototype and exemplar models, for example, one should not lose sight of the fact that both models invoke similarity (rather than other types of knowledge) as the basis for classification.

Formal Models May Be Taken Too Literally

When a model successfully describes a set of data, one should not confuse the explanatory "success" of the formalization with the ideas that led to the formalization. One must recognize that a variety of other ideas, perhaps quite different in character, might have led to the same formalization. For example, the decision rule associated with exemplar models of classification often takes the form of the sum of the similarities of the probe to the examples of the category of interest divided by the sum of the similarities of the probe to all stored examples. Fried and Holyoak (1984) have proposed a different model in which the learner stores information in memory that will allow him or her to make estimates of the likelihood that some probe was generated from the alternative exemplar distributions. It turns out that exemplar models of categorization are closely related to likelihood ratio models and under some conditions are not distinguishable from them (Nosofsky, 1988). In short, these two descriptions of the categorization process produced very similar formalizations. (For further illustrations and recommendations associated with the level at which models are evaluated, see Palmer, 1978.)

Formal Models May Become Opaque

When moving from mathematical models to computational models, one encounters what Smith (1978) referred to as the *sufficiency/transparency trade-off.* Any computational model comprises both a theory and some amount of extra programming necessary to make the model run. The general principles of the theory, however, may be buried in the mass of detail needed to make the model sufficient. Consequently, it may be difficult to isolate individual assumptions or components of a model and evaluate them separately. There may be an unavoidable trade-off between the clarity of a theory and its ability to handle complex problems.

We include connectionist or parallel distributed processing models as a specific type of computational model. For these models in particular, it is often difficult to identify the reason for success and failure (for a clear counterexample to this generalization, see Dell, 1986). Consequently, this area has had to use techniques (such as factor analysis) aimed at figuring out exactly what the model has learned.

Interactions and Examples

So far, we have treated the reader to a pretty abstract diet. In the following section, we link our arguments, observations, and conjectures to some specific examples.

Constraints and Models

Formal Models and Constraints on What Is Learnable

We have described the computational complexity problems that confront any computing device, including algorithms and simulation models. To our knowledge, every model for category learning has constraints or biases associated with it in the sense that the models predict that some kinds of classification problems should be easier to master than others.

One way to evaluate alternative learning models is to see whether the problems that they predict should be easy or difficult are, in fact, easy or difficult for people to master.

One constraint of interest is linear separability. A number of models, including prototype models, imply that categories must be linearly separable to be learnable. Classifying examples on the basis of similarity to a prototype basically involves summing evidence against a criterion. For example, if an instance shows a criterial number of "bird" features, it will be classified as a bird. The key is that there must be some weighted additive combination of properties that can be used to assign instances as members or nonmembers. This means that a prototype process requires that all bird examples be more similar to the bird prototype than to alternative prototypes and that nonbirds must be more similar to their respective prototypes than to the bird prototype. If a bat were more similar to the bird prototype than to the mammal prototype, it would be incorrectly classified.

Figure 1 gives a more intuitive description of linear separability. For examples that have values on two dimensions, the categories they form are linearly separable if there is a straight line that perfectly partitions them (Figure 1a). If no straight line will partition the objects (Figure 1b), then there is no way to construct prototypes such that all examples are closer to their own category prototype than to the prototype for the contrasting category.

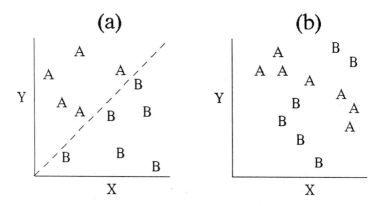

FIGURE 1   Two-dimensional example of a linearly separable category (Panel A) and a nonlinearly separable category (Panel B). (In each graph, members in Categories A and B are denoted by A and B, respectively.)

If linear separability acts as a constraint on human categorization, people should find it easier to learn categories that are linearly separable than categories that are not linearly separable. To make a long story short, studies using a variety of stimulus materials, categories, subject populations, and instructions have failed to find any evidence that linearly separable categories are learned more easily than are nonlinearly separable categories (e.g., Kemler-Nelson, 1984; Medin & Schwanenflugel, 1981).

Many network models are also constrained by linear separability. Like prototype models, single-layered network models involve a weighted integration of input units and, in a sense, add up the evidence favoring a classification decision (Minsky & Papert, 1988). Although more sophisticated network models, those that have "hidden units," can learn categories that are not linearly separable, Gluck (1991) has found that they consistently predict that linearly separable categories will be mastered more easily than nonlinearly separable categories.

We hasten to add that these results are not a problem for network models as an entire class. One can make alternative assumptions about how the input is encoded (e.g., Gluck & Bower, 1988) or how examples are represented (e.g., Kruschke, 1990), neither of which lead to a linear separability bias. The point of our example is that one can compare human performance and theories at the broad level of constraints. Our models of category learning should be as unbiased by linear separability as are people.

Formal Models and Constraints on What Is Learned

In addition to focusing on what people can learn, constraints may also be found by studying what people do learn.

Medin and Ross (1989) have argued that induction should be conservative. By *conservative* they meant that abstractions should preserve more than the minimal information necessary to perform a task. Exemplar models fare better than prototype models mainly because prototype models do not conform to conservative induction (see Nosofsky, in press, for a review of the comparisons made between prototype and exemplar models). For example, a prototype representation discards information concerning category size, variability of examples, and within-category correlations of properties. There is good evidence that people are sensitive to all three of these types of information (e.g., Estes, 1986b; Flannagan, Fried, & Holyoak, 1986; Fried & Holyoak, 1984; Medin & Schaffer, 1978; Medin & Shoben, 1988).

It is important to note, however, that exemplar models do produce abstract information. The key difference between abstraction in exemplar and prototype models is that exemplar models integrate information at the time of retrieval rather than at the time of storage. During a new–old recognition task, for example, an old cue may access both its own representation in memory and those of similar stored exemplars. A new–old judgment for such a cue will be based on a conglomeration of several exemplars, and thus may be incorrect. Indeed, some of the strongest support for exemplar models comes from classification experiments in which new-old recognition is barely above chance (Smith & Medin, 1981).

The moral of this story is not that exemplar models are better than prototype models. Instead, the point is that attention to the information that is preserved or lost in classification tasks provides clues about what constraints exist in categorization processes.

Environmental Sensitivity and Function

Cognitive psychologists often ask people to make similarity judgments, and the standard assumption is that these judgments reflect computations in terms of matching and mismatching features. Goodman (1972), however, has argued that this notion of similarity is too unconstrained to be useful because one always needs to specify the respects in which two things are similar. Indeed, the most prominent theory of similarity to date, Tversky's (1977) contrast model, describes how selected features are evaluated but says nothing about how these features are selected in the first place. An important clue to "establishing respects" may be provided by an analysis of the functions that similarity comparisons serve for organisms in their natural contexts.

Glucksberg and Keysar (1990) suggested that similarity comparisons may act like similes in important ways. Similes are directional comparisons that involve assertions. For example, saying that butchers are like surgeons asserts something very different from saying that surgeons are like butchers. Our recent research on similarity judgments is motivated by the idea that similarity is less a computation across a predefined set of features than a comparison in which the goal is to determine the relevant respects. These respects are an essential part of a speaker's message when he or she asserts that one thing is like another.

Like similes, similarity comparisons may be directional. For example, people rate the similarity of crayons to pencils to be greater than the similarity of pencils to crayons. We interpret this as an example in which the "respects" considered vary with the direction of the comparisons and modify one's impression of similarity. Specifically, in evaluating the similarity of crayons to pencils, one focuses on salient properties of pencils and considers whether these properties are also true of crayons. A salient property of pencils is that one writes with them. One can also write with crayons. In the reverse comparison, a salient property of crayons is that one colors with them, and it is not clear that one can color with pencils. With respect to coloring, then, pencils and crayons are not very similar.

"Discovering" respects may also influence similarity judgments. Medin and Goldstone (1991) recently asked people to rate the similarity of terms on a 9-point scale, with 9 being the highest similarity. Judgments were either made in two separate contexts or in a common context. In isolation, people rated the similarity of skin and hair to be 4.71 and the similarity of skin and bark to be 6.58. In a combined context, however, people rated the similarity of skin and hair to be greater than the similarity of skin and bark. These results support the idea that the comparison of skin and bark in isolation yields a sensible type of respects, leading to correspondingly high ratings. In the combined context, subjects were led to consider a different set of respects, for which skin and bark were less similar than skin and hair.

What do these results tell us about the way people make similarity judgments? We think they mean that people often answer a different question than the one being asked. When the experimenter asks, "How similar are A and B?" the subjects appear to base their answers on "how A and B are similar." That is, similarity judgments are primarily comparisons for establishing respects, not computations over respects that are predefined. If this conjecture is correct, the moral is clear. What people do in normal, more naturalistic contexts may intrude on and heavily influence performance in laboratory contexts. This appears to be as true for similarity judgments by people as it is for the activity patterns of hamsters under conditions of constant illumination.

Constraints, Functions, and Models

In principle, anything might be a constraint. For example, rats could be biased to associate illness with sounds instead of tastes. To guide one's search for constraints, it is often useful to think in terms of natural environments and what functions might be served by a particular bias. Although thinking in terms of adaptation may in principle only shift the problem of constraints from the subject of inquiry to the researcher, we nonetheless believe that questions about adaptation provide a useful heuristic.

Inference

An instructive example of this approach is Anderson's (1990) rational theory of categorization. As we have mentioned, Anderson argued for the general strategy of constructing models on the basis of what would be rational (or even optimal) given an analysis of an organism's goals. The purpose of categorization, according to Anderson, is to maximize the inference potential or predictability of information. The key information for inferences is category validity, the probability of some feature being present in a given category. For example, if one knows that some entity is a bird, one can predict that it has two legs, has wings, may sing, and is unlikely to be dangerous. Anderson's model provides a surprisingly good account of a number of categorization effects, and we take this success as evidence that the inference function of categories is indeed important.

If categories serve to maximize inference potential, people may be biased to produce certain kinds of categories over others. Consider the results from rule induction experiments in which people are asked to develop a rule for categorization based on preclassified examples. In this situation, there are many rules that would correctly partition the examples. Among these rules, however, Medin, Wattenmaker, and Michalski (1987) found that conjunctive rules appeared more than five times as often as disjunctive rules. Conjunctive rules reveal a concern for, or sensitivity to, category validity. For example, a rule of the form A and B allows one to infer from knowledge of category membership that both A and B will be present. In contrast, a rule of the form A or B does not allow any inference to be made with certainty. Because category validity is relevant to drawing inferences from category membership, the preponderance of conjunctive rules is consistent with the inference function of categories.

Communication

In contrast to Anderson (1990) and others who assume that inference is the sole function of categories, we believe that categories serve multiple functions (Matheus, Rendell, Medin, & Goldstone, 1989). For example, concepts play a role in communication. Almost all clustering algorithms, including Anderson's rational theory, perform computations on the properties of examples. The resulting categories tend to maximize either inference potential or some relation of within- and between-category similarity. These methods, however, ignore the form of the category descriptions. If categories serve to ease communication, people should prefer partitions that have straightforward descriptions.

Unfortunately, some distributions of examples do not permit simple descriptions. In these situations, it seems likely that a bias toward easily described categories will lead people to represent their concepts by a simple rule plus a series of exceptions. Models that classify by predictiveness, on the other hand, will tend to develop categories based on overall similarity ("family resemblance"). On the basis of data from their rule induction task, Medin et al. (1987) suggested that subjects develop categories of the latter sort. They found that subjects constructed simple rules, and when these rules did not work perfectly, they "patched the rules up" instead of dropping them. In another experiment, Ahn and Medin (1989) asked subjects to sort examples that were structured so as to make one-rule descriptions impossible. They were able to predict sorting behavior in terms of a two-stage model in which the first stage corresponded to the development of a simple rule and the second stage consisted of strategies for dealing with examples that did not conform to the rule. In short, subjects in these two experiments preferred categories with simple descriptions over the family resemblance categories predicted by inference-based classification models.

Explanation

Categories also play a role in theories and in explanatory structures. Some researchers acknowledge the importance of the explanatory function of concepts but suggest that only the similarity-based aspect of categorization is tractable. This attitude entails a commitment to the view that similarity-based categorization is an isolatable component or module in categorization.

We believe that the explanatory function of categories needs to be integrated with similarity-based categorization (see Medin & Ortony, 1989, for one approach). The relation between similarity-based and explanation-based categorization has recently become a central focus in our research. In one line of work, we have used children's drawings as stimuli (see Figure 2) and introduced knowledge by varying the category labels (Wisniewski & Medin, 1991). For example, in a control condition the categories may be labeled *A versus B* and in the knowledge conditions (drawn by) *high IQ versus low IQ* (children). The task is to induce a rule that will successfully partition the categories.

If similarity can be treated as a separate module, one might account for the influence of knowledge by suggesting that induction occurs in two stages. In Stage 1, knowledge or explanations select and weight features of drawings. Stage 2 involves a similarity-based system that uses these weighted features to induce a rule. Our results, however, undermine the idea that similarity is an isolatable module. When the categories are labeled *A versus B,* people develop rules of the form that Michalski's (1983) similarity-based induction system would produce. For example, a typical rule for Figure 2 might be, "Category A drawings have buttons or stripes on their shirts and dark, thick hair." In the knowledge conditions, the rules were either more abstract (e.g., "The high IQ drawings are more relaxed and free flowing") or consisted of abstract generalizations linked to more specific, supporting predicates (e.g., "The high IQ drawings are more detailed, showing, for example, teeth, extensive shading, and drawing the body underneath the clothes").

Category A

Category B

FIGURE 2   Example of stimuli from Wisniewski and Medin (1991). (Subjects were to decide which group of pictures was drawn by children with high IQs and which was drawn by children with low IQs. Used by permission.)

To condense things quite a bit (see Wisniewski & Medin, 1991, for details), these results lead to two primary conclusions: (a) Knowledge-based rule induction involves developing links between abstract, explanatorily-relevant properties and more specific perceptual features, and (b) knowledge and similarity are tightly coupled and interact in a manner not captured by separate modules. In short, knowledge influences do more than simply select and weight perceptual features. These results, should they generalize, preclude the notion of a distinct similarity-based induction module. To better understand the processes of category learning, the explanatory function of categories must inform the models.

Summary and Conclusions

A true exemplar theorist following his or her model would be much more comfortable with case-based reasoning than with making abstract generalizations. Therefore, we will focus more on summary than on drawing conclusions. Nevertheless, we feel the need to insert a caution or two. The examples we have given are clearly not ideals. Many of our studies could be criticized on the standards that we have just outlined. In several cases, we may have learned something useful despite the fact that our stimuli and procedures may have worked to undermine success.

With this disclaimer in place, we conclude with a summary of the 12 pairwise connections between the four perspectives discussed. Although we do not cover every connection, many of the examples touch on one or more of them.

Beginning with the interaction between environmental sensitivity and function, we note that attention to the environment provides information about the problems that an organism needs to solve. Knowing the obstacles that an organism is likely to meet provides insight into what functions the organism is likely to have. Environmental sensitivity can also highlight the need for constraints. For example, if the language-learning problem is insolvable given the information available, there must be language-learning constraints. Finally, no formal model can adequately describe a process without representing the input to that process.

The interactions between environmental sensitivity and the other perspectives are not simply unidirectional. The environment is a vast place, and observations need to be driven by theory. This theory can be derived by concentrating on the functions that different processes might serve and the constraints that may be inferred from experimental data.

Constraints also affect, and are affected by, formal models. As we have mentioned, formal modeling can indicate which processes will be combinatorially explosive and hence need constraints. In turn, knowledge of what constraints exist in a given process must be included in any model of that process. For example, models of category learning should be as unconstrained by linear separability as are people.

Another interaction exists between constraints and functions. Medin et al.'s (1987) finding that people produce conjunctive rules more often than disjunctive rules provides both a constraint and a clue to the functions that rule induction might serve.

Finally, models interact with all three of the other perspectives. Function, environmental information, and constraints must be included in any model. The model can, in turn, determine whether the information given is sufficient. There may be too few constraints, too little information, or the model may not generalize to account for many functions.

Although we have only discussed pairwise interactions, three-way connections also exist. For example, we have seen how the difference between conjunctive rules and disjunctive rules implies function (predictiveness of concepts is important) and constraints (people produce more conjunctive than disjunctive rules) and bears on models (models that maximize category validity do a good job in predicting subjects' performance in certain tasks).

Abstraction theorists would probably tell us that we are trying to say something like the following: For at least the domain of classification learning and concept formation, a useful research strategy involves a mutually reinforcing interaction of sensitivity to ecological considerations, a constraints framework, questions about function, and formal and computational models. Ecological sensitivity guides and interprets experimental findings. Constraints address computational complexity. Function assists in understanding preferences or biases in underdetermined situations. Formal models help to avoid a host of mistakes and to construct mechanisms that could give rise to observed behavior. We think these four approaches to research, considered individually and in combination, provide an effective framework for thinking about and studying cognition.

References

Ahn, W. K., & Medin, D. L. (1989). *A two-stage categorization model of family resemblance sorting.* Paper presented at the 11th Annual Conference of the Cognitive Science Society, Ann Arbor, MI.

Anderson, J. R. (1990). *The adaptive character of thought.* Hillsdale, NJ: Erlbaum.

Bower, G. H. (1961). Application of a model to paired-associate learning. *Psychometrika, 26,* 255–280.

Dell, G. S. (1986). A spreading activation theory of retrieval in sentence production. *Psychological Review, 93,* 183–321.

Estes, W. K. (1986a). Array models for category learning. *Cognitive Psychology, 18*, 500–549.

Estes, W. K. (1986b). Memory storage and retrieval processes in category learning. *Journal of Experimental Psychology: General, 115*, 155–175.

Flannagan, M. J., Fried, L. S., & Holyoak, K. J. (1986). Distributional expectations and the induction of category structure. *Journal of Experimental Psychology: Learning, Memory, and Cognition, 12*, 241–256.

Fried, L. S., & Holyoak, K. J. (1984). Induction of category distribution: A framework for classification learning. *Journal of Experimental Psychology: Learning, Memory, and Cognition, 10*, 234–257.

Garcia, J., Ervin, F. R., & Koelling, R. A. (1966). Learning with prolonged delay of reinforcement. *Psychonomic Science, 5*, 121–122.

Gibson, J. J. (1979). *The ecological approach to visual perception*. Boston, MA: Houghton-Mifflin.

Gluck, M. A. (1991). Stimulus generalization and representation in adaptive network models of category learning. *Psychological Science, 2*, 50–55.

Gluck, M. A., & Bower, G. H. (1988). Evaluating an adaptive network model of human learning. *Journal of Memory and Language, 27*, 166–195.

Glucksberg, S., & Keysar, B. (1990). Understanding metaphorical comparisons: Beyond similarity. *Psychological Review, 97*, 3–18.

Gold, E. M. (1967). Language identification in the limit. *Information and Control, 10*, 447–478.

Goodman, N. (1972). Seven strictures on similarity. In N. Goodman (Ed.), *Problems and projects* (pp. 437–447). New York: Bobbs-Merrill.

Hintzman, D. L. (1988). Judgments of frequency and recognition memory in a multiple-trace memory model. *Psychological Review, 95*, 528–551.

Hintzman, D. L., & Ludlam, G. (1980). Differential forgetting of prototypes and old instances: Simulation by an exemplar-based classification model. *Memory & Cognition, 8*, 378–382.

Hogarth, R. M. (1981). Beyond discrete biases: Functional and dysfunctional aspects of judgmental heuristics. *Psychological Bulletin, 90*, 197–217.

Homa, D., & Chambliss, D. (1975). The relative contributions of common and distinctive information on the abstraction from ill-defined categories. *Journal of Experimental Psychology: Human Learning and Memory, 1*, 351–359.

Homa, D., & Vosburgh, R. (1976). Category breadth and the abstraction of prototypical information. *Journal of Experimental Psychology: Human Learning and Memory, 2*, 322–330.

Kemler-Nelson, D. G. (1984). The effect of intention on what concepts are acquired. *Journal of Verbal Learning and Verbal Behavior, 23*, 734–759.

Krushscke, J. K. (1990). *A connectionist model of category learning*. Unpublished doctoral dissertation, University of California, Berkeley.

Marr, D. (1982). *Vision*. San Francisco: Freeman.

Matheus, C. J., Rendell, L. R., Medin, D. L., & Goldstone, R. L. (1989). *Purpose and conceptual functions: A framework for concept representation and learning in humans and machines*. Paper presented at the Seventh Conference of the Society for the Study of Artificial Intelligence and Simulation of Behavior. Sussex, England.

Medin, D. L., Altom, M. W., Edelson, S. M., & Freko, D. (1982). Correlated symptoms and simulated medical diagnosis. *Journal of Experimental Psychology: Learning, Memory, and Cognition, 8,* 37–50.

Medin, D. L., & Goldstone, R. (1991). *Respects for similarity.* Manuscript submitted for publication.

Medin, D. L., & Ortony, A. (1989). Psychology essentialism. In S. Vosniadou & A. Ortony (Eds.), *Similarity and analogical reasoning* (pp. 179–195). Cambridge, England: Cambridge University Press.

Medin, D. L., & Ross, B. H. (1989). The specific character of abstract thought: Categorization, problem-solving, and induction. In R. J. Sternberg (Ed.), *Advances in the psychology of human intelligence* (Vol. 5, pp. 189–223). Hillsdale, NJ: Erlbaum.

Medin, D. L., & Schaffer, M. M. (1978). Context theory of classification learning. *Psychological Review, 85,* 207–238.

Medin, D. L., & Schwanenflugel, P. J. (1981). Linear separability in classification learning. *Journal of Experimental Psychology: Human Learning and Memory, 7,* 355–368.

Medin, D. L., & Shoben, E. J. (1988). Context and structure in conceptual combination. *Cognitive Psychology, 20,* 158–190.

Medin, D. L., Wattenmaker, W. D., & Michalski, R. S. (1987). Constraints and preferences in inductive learning: An experimental study of human and machine performance. *Cognitive Science, 11,* 299–339.

Michalski, R. S. (1983). A theory and methodology of inductive learning. *Artificial Intelligence, 20,* 111–161.

Minsky, M. L., & Papert, S. A. (1988). *Perceptrons.* Cambridge, MA: MIT Press.

Neisser, U., & Winograd, E. (Eds.). (1988). *Remembering reconsidered: Ecological and traditional approaches to the study of memory.* Cambridge, England: Cambridge University Press.

Nelson, K. (1974). Concept, word, and sentence: Interrelations in acquisition and development. *Psychological Review, 81,* 267–285.

Nosofsky, R. M. (1988). Exemplar-based accounts of relations between classification, recognition, and typicality. *Journal of Experimental Psychology: Learning, Memory, and Cognition, 14,* 700–708.

Nosofsky, R. M. (1990). Relations between exemplar-similarity and likelihood models of categorization. *Journal of Mathematical Psychology, 34,* 393–418.

Nosofsky, R. M. (in press). Exemplars, prototypes and similarity rules. In S. Kosslyn, R. Shiffrin, & A. Healy (Eds.), *Festschrift for William K. Estes.* Hillsdale, NJ: Earlbaum.

Palmer, S. E. (1978). Fundamental aspects of cognitive representation. In E. Rosch & B. B. Lloyd (Eds.), *Cognition and categorization* (pp. 259–303). Hillsdale, NJ: Erlbaum.

Pinker, S. (1984). *Language learnability and language development.* Cambridge, MA: Harvard University Press.

Posner, M. I., & Keele, S. W. (1968). On the genesis of abstract ideas. *Journal of Experimental Psychology, 77,* 353–363.

Posner, M. I., & Keele, S. W. (1970). Retention of abstract ideas. *Journal of Experimental Psychology, 83,* 304–308.

Raaijmakers, J. G., & Shiffrin, R. M. (1981). Search of associative memory. *Psychological Review, 88,* 93–134.

Shepard, R. H. (1984). Ecological constraints on internal representation: Resonant kinematics of perceiving, imagining, thinking, and dreaming. *Psychological Review, 19,* 417–447.

Smith, E. E. (1978). Theories of semantic memory. In W. K. Estes (Ed.), *Handbook of learning and cognitive processes* (Vol. 6, pp. 1–52). Hillsdale, NJ: Erlbaum.

Smith, E. E., & Medin, D. L. (1981). *Categories and concepts.* Cambridge, MA: Harvard University Press.

Strange, W., Keeney, T., Kessel, F. S., & Jenkins, J. J. (1970). Abstraction over time of prototypes from distractions of random dot patterns: A replication. *Journal of Experimental Psychology, 83,* 508–510.

Tversky, A. (1977). Features of similarity. *Psychological Review, 84,* 327–352.

Wexler, K., & Culicover, P. (1980). *Formal principles of language acquisition.* Cambridge, MA: MIT Press.

Wisniewski, E. J., & Medin, D. L. (1991). Harpoons and long sticks: The interaction of theory and similarity in rule induction. In D. Fisher & M. Pazzani (Eds.), *Computational approaches to concept formation* (pp. 237–278). San Mateo, CA: Morgan Kaufman.

CHAPTER 8

On the Origins of Domain-Specific Primitives

David Premack

R ecent research has changed the view of the infant mind. The infant no longer faces
a booming, buzzing confusion but rather enters the world a domain specialist,
primed to divide the world into categories and able to deal with each category in a privileged way. The special domains of the child that are presently recognized are physical
object, mind, biological kind, and number.

Moreover, the mental processes of the infant are not confined to perception, as
Spelke (1988, in press) eloquently emphasized, using examples from her own work and
that of Baillargeon (1987), Leslie (1988), and others. The infant can reason or make inferences about the events that belong to a domain. For example, the infant who shows surprise when one solid object passes through another shows not merely dishabituation. In
Baillargeon, Spelke, and Wasserman's (1985) clever design, the "impossible" condition
(one that caused the infant's surprise) was more like the condition to which the infant
was habituated than was the "possible" condition that does not surprise the infant at all.
Outcomes of this kind generally suggest inference, not mere dishabituation. To attribute
inference to the infant is part of a more radical shift in the view of cognition. Formerly,

*It is a pleasure to express my indebtedness to Ann James Premack, with whom I discussed the present ideas and many others
over the course of a long period.*

all complex processes such as reasoning and thinking were considered conscious higher order processes; only simple processes were considered "automatic." Research on language processing has helped modify this view. We now recognize that some of the most complex processing is automatic.

Consider three views of domain-specific processing. The first is that processes are unique to a domain and have no counterpart in any other domain. For instance, the categorical discrimination of speech perception is unique and never occurs with respect to nonspeech stimuli. The second is that although the processes are not themselves domain unique, the physical resources for realizing them are; for example, if the processes used in reasoning about biological kinds are habituated, they have no effect on processes used in reasoning about mind or number. The third is that domain specificity is not found at the level of underlying process but at a higher level, as in the kind of hypotheses that are contemplated or the kind of questions that are asked. For example, one does not ask of a mind whether it reproduces or of a physical object whether it has contracted a disease. Although the data necessary for choosing among these views are incomplete, neither of the first two alternatives seems plausible. Only the last alternative seems likely because a domain is not a microlevel entity but an entity at a higher level of organization.

The infant mind has been compared with that of the adult. One hears less about limitations on infant mental representation (e.g., that it is concrete, based on sensory-motor units or images) and more about adult representation, which is formed from units of a vastly more abstract nature. This distinction has always operated under an oppressive handicap. It requires the comparison of two unknowns given that one knows no more about the fundamental representational elements of the adult mind than of the infant mind.

I consider yet another possible comparison between infant and adult: the initial conceptual state. Does the initial state include the basic theoretical concepts that are fundamental to a domain (and individuate it as a domain)? Examples are cause in the case of physical objects; intention, want, and belief in the case of mind; growth and disease in the case of biological kinds; and addition in the case of numbers. Are these concepts part of an initial state in which change owes more to maturation than to experience, or are they acquired later on an experiential basis by the child or even the adult?

I shall present a case for the former by defining the concept of the *domain-specific primitive* by means of examples, both hypothetic and actual. I shall then describe two rules that can be used to distinguish a domain-specific primitive.

Briefly, when an individual is shown an example of a conceptual primitive, his or her mind seeks to explain the example, hence, to assign properties to it that will account for the outcome as shown. As a result, when the individual is subsequently shown a reversal of the original example, he or she demonstrates greater than usual dishabituation because the mind must readjust the properties it previously assigned, accommodating them to the reversed outcome. Reversal does not have this effect in the case of ordinary distinctions because the individual makes no attempt to explain the distinction in the first place and does not assign any properties; hence, there are no properties to adjust to the new outcome. These descriptions will be clearer when I use examples from the several domains to show how the discovery procedure works.

I shall build the case in four steps. First, contrary to appearance, there is no evidence to support the view of ontogenetic differences in conceptual primitives, neither in theory of mind (TOM) or any other domain. I will argue that conceptual primitives are a phylogenetic variable, not an ontogenetic one; apes differ from humans and monkeys differ from apes in conceptual primitives, but members of the same species at different ages do not.

Second, the power of habituation/dishabituation procedures has been grossly underestimated; there is no principled limitation on the complexity of concepts that can be tested with these procedures. Removing this limitation on these procedures, which are the only ones applicable to the study of the infant, eliminates the implication that infants must therefore be conceptually weaker than adults. Perhaps they are, but if so, not because adults have concepts the complexity of which disallows detection by differences in habituation/dishabituation processes.

Third, it is essential to use measurement of habituation/dishabituation to assess the content of the infant's initial state. Tests that rely on explicit processes are at risk. Negative data need not mean that the infant lacks the knowledge but only that the infant lacks the explicit processes required by the test. In addition, positive data that are based on 3- to 5-year-old children are ambiguous because they may not reflect innate concepts (the infant's initial state) but rather that which the child has learned. I shall discuss three explicit processes that infants lack and show that the use of tests that presuppose these processes underestimates the infant's initial state. TOM, as I shall show, is particularly susceptible to inaccurate estimation of initial state because all estimation of initial state in TOM is based on tests that presuppose explicit processes. Actually, the difficulties in TOM are not unique; testing for understanding of biological kind suffers from the same condition. Although Keil (1990) presented interesting positive data, had the data been negative, they could be discounted because his tests presupposed explicit processes (and, as already noted, positive data obtained with 3- to 5-year-old children, as he used, may not reflect initial state but rather knowledge based on learning). Assessment of habituation/dishabituation procedures are long overdue in testing for understanding of biological kind.

Fourth, I will discuss the implications for TOM of a test that apes pass and children fail. This is the kind of anomaly one wishes to find because it suggests that the two species solve the same problem using different (weaker and stronger) mechanisms and that the weaker mechanisms may be available to the ape before the stronger ones are available to the child. The anomaly may help in the comparison of the chimpanzee's weak TOM with the child's stronger one. This comparison could be of special value if, as I argue, there are only phylogenetic and no ontogenetic differences in TOM.

Finally, in the course of developing these points, I shall discuss the recent data of Zaitchik (1990) and the implications of the implicit/explicit distinction concerning what develops in infants. In other words, if the process of maturation is not that of filling in conceptual lacunae, as I argue, what then is its principal work?

Although at least touching all the theoretical domains, I will concentrate on TOM, which is of special interest for the present discussion because it is a domain concerning which all specialists agree. They advocate the weak initial state in which the infant lacks conceptual primitives and in which the infant's TOM is weaker than that of the adult. This view has proceeded without opposition.

For example, Wellman's (in press) child starts with simple "desire psychology," only later attaining the "desire–believe" psychology of the adult. Leslie and Thaiss's (1990) infant understands goals and intentions, a stage at which autism locks the individual, but lacks epistemic states (e.g., believing, knowing, thinking). Finally, in a recent model of the infant's "theory of self-propelled objects" (Premack, 1990), I granted that the infant understands goal and intention but explicitly lacks epistemic states. Here, I shall argue that the former and the theory of maturation that this view presupposes is incorrect and build a case for the latter.

Evidence for Maturation of Conceptual Primitives

Is there any evidence that conceptual primitives mature? Children quite obviously lack knowledge that adults possess. But what is the nature of this knowledge? Does it consist of primitives? At first blush, recent data from Spelke and Baillargeon suggest that there are indeed differences in primitives. Their data came in two installments, the first dealing with the elementary properties of objects (Baillargeon, 1987; Spelke, 1982), the second dealing with inertia and gravity (Baillargeon & Hanko-Summers, 1990; Spelke, in press). A quick comparison of the two sets of data gives the impression of conceptual development, of the maturation of primitives. However, a more thoughtful comparison dispels this view.

In the first set of data, infants as young as age 2½ months showed a convincing grasp of the fundamental nature of an object. The data do not merely refute imprudent claims about object constancy but establish in the infant the analog of a basic physics for solid macro objects. The infants appreciated that objects are solid, move coherently (not in separate parts), cannot pass one through another, and change neither their dimensions nor their positions spontaneously. This uniformly positive set of data was followed by the next installment in which the results were negative.

Turning from object to gravity and inertia, Baillargeon and Hanko-Summers (1990) and Spelke (in press) found that infants as old as age 6 months showed no appreciation for any of the basic implications of these concepts. The infants were not surprised by unsupported objects that stood in midair, headed in one direction but ended up in another, or moved at high speeds but then came to abrupt halts. Although infants possess a fundamental concept of object, they clearly lack the concepts of gravity and inertia. Could one find clearer evidence for development of conceptual primitives?

Moreover, when Spelke (in press) and Baillargeon and Hanko-Summers (1990) studied older infants, they found evidence of their understanding of gravity and inertia. By age 8 months, infants were surprised by unsupported objects and, to some extent, by unprecipitated changes in direction and speed. These data differ from those obtained in the first installment.

Whereas all infants understood the basic nature of an object and performed uniformly, passing or failing the same test conditions, the data for gravity and inertia lacked this uniformity. Even infants who understood gravity or inertia did so in only some circumstances, which varied from one infant to another. The infants' idiosyncratic knowledge of gravity and inertia contrasted with their uniform knowledge of object. The former would be expected if each infant's knowledge of gravity and inertia was learned (rather than based on innate primitives) in a somewhat different, individual way.

Curiously, adult knowledge of gravity and inertia proved to be very like that of infants (McCloskey, 1983). When adults were asked to judge the path of a moving object, many chose paths inconsistent with the effects of gravity or inertia. Their judgments were often uncertain and varied across individuals and situations. As Spelke (in press) noted,

> These observations suggest that no general conceptions of gravity or inertia guide the commonsense reasoning of adults. Abilities to reason about the effects of gravity and inertia may depend instead on a wealth of accumulated knowledge about how objects move under particular conditions.

In other words, the contrast between the infant's firm grasp of object and uncertain grasp of gravity and inertia does not support the maturation of conceptual primitives. The same contrast characterizes the adult. Moreover, if adults know more about gravity and inertia than infants, it is only because they have learned more; gravity and inertia are not innate human concepts. If gravity and inertia were innate concepts, how likely would we be to regard Galileo and Newton as geniuses for having invented these concepts?

The suggestion that not all human physical knowledge is based on innate primitives is extremely encouraging in that the number of primitives, rather than being hopelessly large and unmanageable, may be more determinate and perhaps even manageable. We may yet exhaustively list the primitives.

The Power of Habituation/Dishabituation

Although habituation/dishabituation was once confined to simple concepts (e.g., the infant's ability to distinguish colors), there are, in fact, no principled limits on the complexity of the concepts to which this technique can be applied, as evident by the work of Spelke (1982), Baillargeon (1987), Leslie (1988), and others. Moreover, it is fortunate that there are no such limitations because, as mentioned, this is the only procedure that can provide an unbiased estimate of the infant's initial state, and procedures that rely on explicit processes can grossly underestimate initial state.

Defining Attribution of Epistemic States

I will now discuss the application of habituation/dishabituation to TOM by presenting an argument similar to the previous argument concerning physical objects. I specifically consider the so-called epistemic states of knowing, believing, and thinking—concepts available to the adult's but not the infant's or even the young child's TOM.

Does the normal infant lack epistemic states and acquire them only at a much later age (as late as 4 years of age) when he or she can pass the false-belief test? Is the absence of this concept the basis of autism? Is the concept unique to humans and the lack of such concepts specifically what is weak about the chimpanzee TOM?

Although the test for epistemic states is complex—involving more steps than required for testing intention or desire—it is not different in kind. For purposes of comparison, consider the way in which one might test for a nonepistemic state, for example, the infant's expectancy that reciprocation will preserve valence, an expectancy that I treat as part of the infant's theory of self-propelled objects (Premack, 1990).

In this nonepistemic state, the infant expects that if Object A acts positively on Object B, in the event that B reciprocates, B will act positively on A. That is, the infant expects that reciprocation will preserve valence. If Object B acted negatively, thus failing to preserve valence, this would disconfirm the infant's expectations, leading to greater dishabituation than if Object B had acted positively. Notice that this expectancy does not require that the infant attribute epistemic states. To expect that reciprocation will preserve valence, the infant need attribute nothing more to the object than a behavioral disposition, keeping in mind the difference between instantiation and attribution and the fact that TOM concerns only those mental states that the infant attributes, not those that the infant instantiates.

This assumption could be tested using a procedure involving at least two balls (Object A and Object B) and two steps. First, the experimenter shows the infant Object A acting positively on Object B in one case and negatively in another. Positive and negative can be instantiated by, for example, gentle rubbing versus forceful pounding. That positive and negative can be instantiated so simply suggests, first, that simple cases can be reduced to physical formulae and, second, that an innate coding of simple cases is possible (see Premack, 1990).

Next, the experimenter shows the infant the reverse, Object B acting on Object A, either positively or negatively. Reciprocation that preserves valence should conform with the infant's expectations and result in less dishabituation than should reciprocation that does not preserve valence.

Consider now the kind of test required to establish whether or not infants attribute epistemic states. An infant may be considered to attribute epistemic states if it can be established that the infant believes that Object A follows Object B because A thinks B knows something that A wants to know. Undoubtedly, there are other and probably simpler ways of demonstrating attribution of epistemic states. My point is that the epistemic state is as testable as the nonepistemic state.

Such a test would be strengthened by eliminating competing accounts of Object A's behavior (e.g., A follows B because A likes B or A is curious about B) based on weaker or nonepistemic mental states.

In the positive outcome of this test, the infant believes that Object B knows how to get out of an enclosure (a line drawing on a screen) because it knows that if it bounces three times at a specific spot, the wall of the enclosure will open and it can get out (as well as back in in the same way). The infant believes that Object A would like to do the same thing but does not know how; A suspects that B does know and therefore it follows B.

The test scenario may also include the following features: (a) Object A does not especially like Object B, as shown by the fact that it plays with other objects more often than it plays with B (thus eliminating the conclusion that A follows B because it likes B), (b) A visibly wants to get out of the enclosure, as shown by its struggle to do so (bumping repeatedly against the enclosure wall), and (c) B's knowledge of how to get out and return is not a matter of speculation (B is shown getting out several times). One might even add a motive for B's action (e.g., each time B returns, it is fatter than when it left; objects that never get out of the enclosure progressively shrivel up).

In proving attribution of epistemic states, consider a subject whose attribution of such is not in question and who is habituated to the present scenario. Presumably, in reading the scenario the subject attributes epistemic states to the "actors" and thus habituates these attributions. The questions that follow are how to test for such habituation and what new material can be used to maximize dishabituation for the attribution of believe and know?

Discovery Procedure for Conceptual Primitives

The most potent material we can present is a scenario that involves a reversal of the original attributions. Although other scenarios will also produce dishabituation, none will have so pronounced an effect. Moreover, the special effect of reversal does not hold only for the present case but for all conceptual primitives. It is, in fact, the substance of the first of the two rules previously mentioned: Reversal maximizes dishabituation in the case of conceptual primitives.

Consider two simple examples. First, contrast the effect of reversal on *Mary pushes John down the slide* with *Mary precedes John down the slide*. After first habituating infants to both cases, test them by presenting a reversal: *John pushes Mary down the slide* and *John precedes Mary down the slide*. We can be reasonably certain that the reversal of *push* will produce far greater dishabituation than the reversal of *precede* because *push* implies a conceptual primitive (viz., intention), whereas *precede* implies merely a physical action. Temporal order, unless otherwise specified, is theoretically neutral; it implicates no conceptual primitives, being simply one of indeterminately many physical distinctions that every species can discriminate.

The same distinction is present in an experiment by Golinkoff (1975) in which she contrasted donorship with spatial location. Infants were first habituated to a scene in which Mary gave Jane an apple. Then, half of them were shown a reversal of donorship (Jane now gave Mary the apple), whereas the other half were shown a reversal of spatial location (the left–right position of Mary and Jane was interchanged, but donorship remained the same). The results corresponded with those predicted for push versus precede: Reversal in donorship produced greater dishabituation than reversal in spatial position.

Donorship, who gives to whom, belongs to the same domain as does push; it implicates the same concepts, intentions, and mental states that humans attribute to social agents in accounting for action. Left–right position, on the other hand, is like temporal order in that, unless otherwise specified, it is a theoretically neutral physical distinction, one of indeterminately many that every species makes. It is a perceived, not interpreted, distinction.

Consider a last example, which comes from the domain of physical objects rather than from that of mental events. Leslie and Keeble (1987) showed infants a film of either a standard causal interaction (one object struck another, propelling it forward) or a pseudo-causal interaction (although the first object moved toward the second and the second then moved ahead, there was both a temporal and spatial gap between the action of the two objects). After habituating the infants to one of the two cases, the experimenter then presented a reversal of the film. Reversal produced significantly greater dishabituation in the case of the standard causal interaction than in the case of the pseudocasual interaction.

This outcome is predicted by the principle that causality is to physical objects what intention is to minds or mental events. In the domain of physical objects, causality is the major conceptual primitive, one that underlies all the theoretical distinctions that apply to the domain. One perceives a causal relation between colliding objects only when there is spatial and temporal contiguity between the impact of one and the movement of the other. If there is a temporal or spatial gap between the events, as there was in the case of the pseudocausal interaction, one perceives only temporal order (one object moved before the other), not a causal relation. Temporal order is only a physical distinction; hence, its reversal produces less dishabituation than does that of a causal relation, which is not only a perceived but also an interpreted distinction.

Two general rules can be formulated to help identify conceptual primitives. First, as this last case demonstrates, the reversal of an interpreted relation will produce greater dishabituation than the reversal of an uninterpreted one. Second, the effect of reversing an (old) interpreted relation will be greater than that of presenting a new instance of the relation. By contrast, the effect of reversing an uninterpreted relation will be the same as the effect of presenting a new case. For example, the dishabituation produced by changing from *A pushes B* to *C pushes D* (new case) will be less than that produced by presenting *B pushed A* (reversal of the old relation), whereas that produced by changing *A preceded B* to *C preceded D* (new case) will not be less than that produced by presenting *B preceded A* (reversal of the old relation). Only in the case of interpreted relations does reversal maximize dishabituation.

The principle that dishabituation is maximized by reversing the original interpreted relation also holds for motion. In a previous example, Object A was seen as following Object B because A thought B knew something that it wanted to know. The reversal, in which B follows A because B thinks A knows something that it wants to know should produce greater dishabituation than a new case, for example, in which D follows C because D thinks C knows something that it wants to know. Reversal should force one to change the properties that one ascribes to A and B to account for the original direction of the process, whereas switching to new "agents," as in the new case, should not have this effect.

In addition, it would strengthen the argument if simply presenting the reversed behavior alone (without reversing the accompanying mental states) did not maximize habituation. Object B following Object A for no apparent reason should not maximize dishabituation; maximization would require information supporting the inference that B is not merely following A out of curiosity, liking, or such, but specifically because B believes that A knows something that it wants to know. Only a scenario that establishes the attribution of reversed epistemic states should maximize dishabituation.

Implicit Versus Explicit Processes

Establishing the initial state of the infant requires tests that depend on implicit processes because, as shown by increasing evidence, infants lack explicit processes. Tests that measure explicit processes, rather than habituation/dishabituation seriously underestimate the infant's initial state because positive results from such tests do not univocally characterize the initial state given that the knowledge discerned may be based on what the child has learned. In this section, I will illustrate this point by discussing three explicit processes that infants lack and showing how tests that presuppose them underestimate the infant's initial state.

The first example concerns a disparity in the infant's ability to detect a distinction, on the one hand, and to make instrumental use of it, on the other hand. This disparity is found both in human and chimpanzee infants and concerns the sameness or difference of relations, in this example, the sameness or difference of the relations between the pairs of Objects AA, BB, CD, or EF. The detection of sameness or difference between relations, which is more powerful than the detection of that between objects, is the basis of analogies and provides some of the earliest evidence that primates, both human and nonhuman, can compute equivalence on grounds more powerful than that of simple similarity (Premack, 1988a).

With habituation/dishabituation procedures, Premack (1988a) found that 18-month-old chimpanzees could detect the sameness or difference not only of objects but, more important, of relations. For example, animals were habituated to either AA or CD and then tested on either BB or EF. All animals responded more to the heterogeneous cases (same followed by different or different followed by same) than to the homogeneous cases (same followed by same or different followed by different). That is, the animals responded to BB more when it was preceded by CD than when it was preceded by AA; similarly, they responded to EF more when it was preceded by AA than when it was preceded by CD.

The next example concerns the explicit process of choice, assessed by measuring the ability to match like objects. At age 18-months human infants can spontaneously match like objects, and although chimpanzees do not spontaneously put like objects together, they can be trained to do so (Premack, 1988a).

However, although both species match like objects and both detect the sameness or difference of relations, neither can match like relations. I (Premack, 1988a) tested both 18-month-old human and chimpanzee infants for matching using the same stimuli as in the habituation/dishabituation tests (e.g., either AA or CD as a sample and either BB or EF as an alternative). Not only did both species respond at chance level, but both were completely impervious to differential feedback. Moreover, the failure was not short lived.

Children are between ages 4 and 5 years before they match like relations; chimpanzees, unless given special training, never achieve this ability. In reacting differently to relations that do and do not match, infants of both species demonstrate this type of knowledge, although years pass before either can comprehend analogies.

Notice, incidentally, that children do not spontaneously match relations, for example, pair similar objects (e.g., two dolls, two red blocks) and different objects (e.g., a doll and a block, a spoon and a knife) and then put the pairs of like cases in one place and the pairs of unlike cases in another place. The natural tendency of children is to detect only similarity—sameness or difference of objects—not of relations. Although a biological difference separates children from apes in their treatment of similarity, it does not separate them in their treatment of conceptual equivalence. Children make no more spontaneous use of conceptual equivalence than do apes; cultural not biological evolution separates the two species here. Humans have "invented" education or pedagogy, and part of the human competence in conceptual equivalence depends on the experience that pedagogy guarantees the child.

Baillargeon and Hanko-Summers (1990) recently illustrated another example of an explicit process that the infant lacks. The infant's failure to reach for concealed objects is not, they showed, based on lack of knowledge. Infants aged 4 months were shown hands that reached for objects that were or were not "accessible" (covered or behind a barrier). The infants reacted differently to objects that were accessible than they did to objects that were not accessible. They looked longer if the hands did the "impossible," namely, retrieve an object that was not accessible.

Consider next a comparison of the effect of delay on this test and on a test in which the infant was required to reach for the concealed object (Baillargeon & Hanko-Summers, 1990). In the latter, delay interfered with reaching; the longer the delay, the greater the effect and the older the infant must be to overcome the interference imposed by the delay. Naturally, this interference has been interpreted as a loss of mental representation, a decrement in short-term memory. However, delay does not have a comparable effect on the former test; despite delays that interfere with reaching, the infant still looks longer at the hand that retrieves the inaccessible object.

Clearly, the effect of delay on reaching has been misunderstood. Delay does not impair the mental representation; the infant knows the concealed object is there but does not reach for it. The explanation must be sought in some quarter other than that of the infant's mental representation.

What the infant lacks has to do with the ability to map representation onto action. Although the infant's representation of the concealed object is intact, he or she cannot act satisfactorily on what he or she knows. The infant has some version of the "buried in thought" problem with which Guthrie taunted Tolman and thus cannot properly translate his or her thoughts into action. However, mapping representation onto action requires substantial maturation and learning. To obtain the concealed object, the infant must reach and then lift; Baillargeon and Hanko-Summers (1990) suggested that infants of this age may not yet have the ability to combine responses in this fashion.

Yet another explicit process that the infant lacks is suggested by the infant's success in reaching for a covered object in darkness. When an object that the infant is holding is covered, the infant releases the object (as though it were not there). However, the infant does not release the object if the lights are turned off. Notice the difference between the two conditions. In the first condition, the visual information is negative: There is no object to be found at the location, and this negative visual information is pitted against positive tactual information. In the second condition, darkness eliminates visual information: There is no competition between positive tactual and negative visual information. Given only positive tactual information, the infant does not release the object.

Thus, it appears that infants are unique in their management of competition between visual and tactual information. They give priority to visual information, allowing it to override the tactual information, although not necessarily at the level of representation. That is, contradictory visual information need not eliminate the tactual representation; it simply dominates the control of action.

Premack and Dasser (1991) found a similar outcome in children as old as 3½ years. Information that was based on inference (which they are known to comprehend) failed to supersede information that was based on visual perception at the level of action but, again, not necessarily at the level of representation (what the child knows).

The experiment proceeded in two steps. First, the child was shown that a large pretzel was put into a container on the left and a much smaller one put into a container on the right. On five trials in which the child chose between the containers, all children consistently chose the container with the larger pretzel.

On the sixth trial, the child was asked to defer to a classmate, allowing the classmate to choose first. The child was not allowed to see what his or her classmate actually chose but was quite capable of making the appropriate inference; questions subsequently asked of the children assured that they all knew that their classmates made the same choice that they did. Nevertheless, the children did not adjust their choices to the fact that their classmates always took the larger pretzel and persisted in choosing the empty container. Thus, when shown that the classmate took the larger pretzel, they adjusted their choices but not when they were left to infer this choice. The children chose the wrong container 10 times in a row. Moreover, when the child was not allowed in the initial training to actually take the pretzel but only to observe where it is placed, the classmate's inferred choice had a greater effect, although still only an incomplete one. A representation that is based on inference evidently cannot overpower one based on perception. The child's action is governed by what he or she sees, even more by what he or she does, not by what it inferred.

That the control of action by knowledge is not a simple matter has long been suggested by the difficulty that psychology has had producing theories of action or performance. Tolman is not alone in leaving the rat "buried in thought"; in much of psychology, action is left at a commonsense level (e.g., An individual who wants food and knows where it is will take whatever steps are appropriate to obtain it—hardly an explicit theory of action). We have no good account of the processes that stand between infant knowledge and adult action.

The lesson to be drawn for TOM from this discussion is simple enough. There has been no use of habituation/dishabituation in testing for TOM; all tests assessing the infant's initial state have measured explicit processing; therefore, negative data recently compiled in this busy field tell little about the possible lack of conceptual primitives. This is a disappointing conclusion given the activity level of the field. The simple distinction between implicit and explicit has somehow been lost in all the activity. (This failure applies equally to the animal work. Nonverbal tests do not guarantee implicit processes. The choice between alternatives in matching depends on explicit processes no less than answering questions on the usual verbal test.)

A recent series of experiments by Zaitchik (1990) bears on what is taken to be the initial state of TOM. Zaitchik (1990) showed that young children draw mistaken conclusions about the relation between photographs and the state of the world that they represent. If a change were made in the world after a photograph was taken, the child "updated" the photograph, making it correspond to the world. For instance, the child was shown a photograph of a doll on the floor or wearing a blue sweater. Zaitchik then moved the doll or changed its clothing and asked the child to describe the content of the photograph without showing the child the photograph. Children reported that the photograph showed the doll in its current location and in its current dress.

Zaitchik (1990) presented these data as reflecting inadequacy in young children's representational competence. Leslie and Thaiss (1990) accepted this view but argued that representational competence need not be general; it may be domain specific, there being separate representational competencies for physical objects and mental events. Are there also separate representational competencies for biological kinds and numbers? How many representational competencies are there?

However, Zaitchik's (1990) data may have nothing to do with representational competence. It is psychologists more than children who are preoccupied with representational relations. There are more primitive relations than that of representation, such as similarity matching and causal connection, which in children (although often not in psychologists) take priority over representation.

This phenomenon was suggested in a test of similarity matching in which an apple served as the sample and a photograph of the apple and a second apple served as two alternatives (Premack, 1991). Children between the ages of 4 and 5 years chose the photograph (it was a more likely representation of the apple), but younger children chose the other apple (it was more similar to the sample). Not until children are 4 or 5 years old does representation make inroads on territory controlled by similarity.

Causal connections are presumably as primitive as those of similarity matching, and they may also take priority over representational relations. A 3½-year-old child brought this to my attention some years ago (Premack & Premack, 1983). The child was among the 10 that we brought to the chimpanzee lab to compare with the animals on ability to use a dollhouse as a representation of a room. The performance of animals on this problem had been a total failure. We brought in children so that we could estimate the difficulty of the problem.

As with the chimpanzees, we tested the children, avoiding the use of language (to enhance the comparison between chimpanzee and child). There were three pieces of corresponding furniture in the dollhouse and the room—chairs, tables, and the like—on each of which stood a metal container, large containers in the room and little ones in the dollhouse. We tested the children by placing a candy under a container in the dollhouse and then leading the child to the room and releasing him or her.

I held to the view that children might use the dollhouse as a representation of the room until one of the children, after making his choice in the room, got back to the dollhouse before I did. The child reached into the dollhouse, lifted up one of the three little containers there, and expressed great surprise: How could the candy still be there? He had already taken "this" candy in the room, so how could it still be there in the dollhouse?

Only two of ten children behaved in this manner. After observing this one child's spontaneous exploration, I attempted to inveigle all of the children into similar explorations, indulging their natural curiosity. However, most of the children did not demonstrate any such curiosity: They did not wish to explore the little containers in the dollhouse.

The lesson to be learned came from the two curious children. Although the dollhouse was offered as a representation of the room, they construed the dollhouse differently. For them, the dollhouse was a guide to the room because there was a causal relation between the two. Just as what I did in the dollhouse had a causal effect on the room, so conversely, what they did in the room had a causal effect on the dollhouse. It was, of course, the symmetry of the childrens' assumptions that called attention to this causal, rather than representational, construal of the relation. The dollhouse served the children as a guide to the room, not because it was a representation of the room but because it was both similar to and causally connected to the room. Representations, in contrast, are asymmetrical, and their effect does not depend on either similarity or causal connections.

Following this enlightenment, I made a few further inquiries into the problems of causality and representation (Premack & Premack, 1983). Such investigation was difficult with the chimpanzees because they failed to use nearly everything that was offered as a representation. Finally, we found one that they could use, a kind of *reductio ad absurdum*, namely, one room as a model of another. The location of food hidden in one room was offered as a guide to the location of food hidden in another room (where controls showed that they recognized the presence of two rooms and did not confuse the two).

In the context of this success, I then tested them by requiring that they do on a regular basis what the exploratory child had done spontaneously: make choices in both rooms (Premack, 1991). First, the animal was shown under which container the candy was placed in Room A and then taken to Room B. After making its choice in Room B, it was returned to Room A and allowed to choose among containers (the equivalent of the spontaneous trial by the curious child).

All four animals tested responded like the curious children, largely from the beginning, avoiding repeating in Room A choices that they had made in Room B. For instance, if the animal chose the container on the red chair in Room B, when returned to Room A it avoided the red chair, significantly often choosing containers on other furniture.

This test, with one room standing as the model of another, also pointed up the arbitrariness of what is treated as an external representation in the human case. With the children, we always used a small model to represent a larger item (e.g., a dollhouse to represent a room, a map to represent a city). Is this difference essential or, as one might suspect, strictly practical? Similarly, our representations were always one to one, rather than one to many, many to one, and so on (e.g., we used one dollhouse to represent one room). Presumably, this distinction too is practical rather than essential. The child should be willing to treat the information provided by a dollhouse as indicating the location of candy not in one room but in many. Picture a dollhouse and a house, both with many rooms. After informing the child where things were hidden in the dollhouse, the experimenter would walk her through the house, finding perhaps that the dollhouse successfully guides the child's choices not only in the first room encountered but in all subsequent ones as well. Will the child treat the dollhouse as a one–many representation, thus repeating the same choices in all like rooms, or rather as a representation of only the first room, treating the first room as a representation of the second, the second of the third, and so on (thus never repeating choices from room to room)? The point is obvious: Once the standard features of external representations (e.g., asymmetrical relation, small to large, one to one) are relaxed, the question remains of whether the features are essential or only practical. Is the child primed to accept the standard features or will he or she as readily acquiesce to entirely nonstandard ones?

To return to the point at hand, do the Zaitchik (1990) data tell us about incompetence in the young children's representations of nonmental items or rather about peculiarities in their causal construals of such items? Given the primitiveness of causal construals relative to representational ones, I think it best to eliminate the former before opting for the latter.

One way to do so is to reverse the Zaitchik (1990) experiment: Would changing a photograph cause the child to "update" the world in the same way that changing the world causes the child to update the photograph? For example, one might take a picture of a scene (e.g., a doll sitting on a chair), conceal the scene from the child, change the photograph (e.g., the doll leaving the chair for the floor), and ask the child to describe the doll's present location in the (concealed) real world.

One might find that the updating effect is quite symmetrical, namely, that changes in photographs cause children to update previously photographed scenes no less than changes in scenes cause them to update photographs. If so, Zaitchik's (1990) data would not reflect representational incompetence but rather peculiarities in children's causal construals. In this case, the findings reported by both Leslie and Thaiss (1990) and Leekam and Perner (1990) should not be surprising. Although autistic children fail false belief tests, they did not fail Zaitchik's test. Autistic children should not have failed Zaitchik's test if it concerned causal construals.

But what if the data were not symmetrical? Although children at certain ages think that altering the world changes photographs, they do not believe the reverse. One might then conclude that the relation in question is a representational one and that Zaitchik's (1990) data reflect what she claims, namely, a deficit in representational competence.

But does it then follow that autistic children should fail Zaitchik's (1990) test? If autistic children have a deficient theory of mind, why should they fail a test that concerns a camera? Leslie (1988) claimed that the autistic child's success indicates that representational competence is not general, that there are separate competencies for physical objects and mental events. The logic of that argument, however, escapes me.

If Zaitchik's (1990) test does prove to be one for representational competence (presently a moot point), the success of the autistic child on this test demonstrates that such a child has normal representational competence. It does not tell us, however, that the representation of the attribution of mental events depends on a separate competence. The autistic child, presumably, cannot make such attributions; the social relations perceived by a normal individual as indicating one or another mental state are presumably not perceived by the autistic individual. One cannot ask, therefore, whether the autistic child represents such mental events. I would not use a color blind person to determine whether the representation of color is separate from that of shape, size, and so on any more than I would use an autistic person to determine whether or not the representation of mental states is separate from that of others.

Apes Succeed Where Children Fail

As mentioned, chimpanzees pass a test of TOM that children fail (Premack, 1988b). The test is one of several nonverbal tests that were designed for the chimpanzee and then extended to the child. The individual was faced with a choice between two containers the baiting for which was blocked from view by a barrier. What the individual could see were two "onlookers" standing near the containers. One of them was in exactly the same predicament as the individual: A barrier blocked his or her view of the containers, so that the onlooker could not see the baiting. However, the other onlooker had a perfect view of the containers.

Before the subject was asked to choose between the containers, he or she was given the opportunity to seek the advice of the two onlookers. The children did this by pointing to the onlooker of their choice, the chimpanzees by pulling one or the other of the strings that was tied to each of the onlookers. In both cases, the chosen onlooker then stepped forward and pointed to one of the containers, the correct container if he or she could see the containers or the incorrect one if he or she could not see the containers.

Three of the four young chimpanzees chose the correct onlooker from the beginning, whereas, to our great surprise, the 3½- to 4-year-old children performed at chance level. All attempts to modify the test so that the children's difficulty could be credited to some procedural quirk failed completely (Dasser & Premack, 1991).

There was only one thing that the children did correctly that the apes did not, namely, consistently follow the advice of the onlooker that they selected, always choosing the container to which he or she pointed. Although they chose the right onlooker, the chimpanzees sometimes ignored the onlooker's advice, choosing the other container.

Only once before has my rule of thumb (based on nearly 30 years of comparison) that any cognitive test a chimpanzee can pass will be passed easily by a 3½-year-old child been violated (Woodruff, Premack, & Kennell, 1980).

This kind of anomaly offers either of two lessons. First, apes and children solve this problem in the same way, using the same mechanisms and making the same attributions, but apes succeed earlier because, as human neoteny teaches, apes mature earlier than humans. Second, apes and children do not solve this problem in the same way but use different mechanisms: The states of mind they attribute are not the same. Moreover, the mental events the children attribute (or try to attribute) to the seeing onlooker are more complex than those that the ape attributes to the same onlooker. Finally, the ape's simpler attributions mature earlier than the child's more complex ones.

To do justice to the latter view, one must also consider that if the child "passes through" the ape's simpler state en route to a more complex one, it cannot go back to the simpler state. Despite the child's inability to attribute the more complex states of mind that adult humans attribute, the child cannot revert to an earlier stage and attribute the simpler states of mind that the ape attributes. There is another possibility: The child does not pass through the ape's simple system en route to its more complex one, never attributes the simple states the ape attributes, and hence has no simpler state to which to revert.

What is the simple state of mind that the ape attributes in this situation, and what is the more complex one that the child attributes or rather tries but fails to attribute? For the ape, the problem is simply a distinction between seeing and not seeing; "simply" because in the ape's theory of mind, one can go directly from perception to action. For the child, the distinction is not between seeing and not seeing but rather between knowing and not knowing. The child's TOM has a step that is not part of the ape's TOM. Perception affects knowing or believing, which in turn affects action. Knowing and believing are not part of the ape's theory; the ape goes directly from perception to action.

The second position is more defensible than the first. Children as young as 3 years can tell the difference between seeing and not seeing. At this age, they can be shown people who do and do not have their eyes open, do and do not wear a blindfold, or do and do not stand behind an opaque barrier and can distinguish between those who can see and those who cannot. Children understand the conditions on which seeing depends better, no doubt, than do apes. (I [Premack, 1988b] have so far tested only the more blunt conditions that affect seeing, such as blindfolds and opaque barriers with apes, not the more subtle conditions such as visual orientation or attending; we therefore do not yet know how subtle or complete is the ape's theory of seeing.) In any case, it seems unlikely that the child fails at this problem because he or she is unable to recognize which individual has the unobstructed view; the child fails despite his or her ability to make this discrimination. In the child's TOM, seeing is presumably not a sufficient condition for pointing, rather the individual must see to know and know to point. Additionally, the child at this age is evidently not yet able to manage the attribution of know.

The first position, that apes and children solve the problem in the same way, although at different developmental stages, is additionally untenable. It requires that the mechanisms essential for TOM mature earlier in the ape, when in fact mechanisms far simpler than TOM (ones that may be seen as precursors) do not appear in the ape at all. For example, social pointing is not found in the ape, although it is part of the child's repertoire by as early as age 11 months. Under the special "pressures" of an experiment designed to "invite" them to lie (Woodruff & Premack, 1979), young chimpanzees spontaneously developed—to our great surprise—a kind of pointing. However, the act failed to transfer and departed from human pointing in other essential respects (Premack, 1988c). It seems unlikely, then, that in a species that does not ever develop social pointing, mechanisms essential to TOM would appear earlier than they do in the child.

The animal data are generally compatible with this view. A chimpanzee named Sarah passed tests requiring that a state of desire or intention be attributed to actors shown in a videotape; in addition, both Sarah and younger chimpanzees passed tests that required attributing perception to actors (Premack, 1988b). None of these tests required the animal to attribute belief or knowing. Moreover, Sarah failed a nonverbal version of a false belief test, which definitely required the attribution of belief (Premack, 1988b).

Interestingly, this interpretation of the animal data, which Woodruff and I first proposed in 1978 (Premack & Woodruff, 1978), sparked a debate with philosophers of mind (e.g., Bennett and Dennett) that still continues (e.g., Bennett, 1989). Bennett dismissed our suggestion that desire is computationally simpler than knowing, maintaining that any theory of rational action requires both desire and knowing, one no less than the other. One acts to get x because one wants x and believes that in so acting one can get x. If this theory of action is correct, does it follow that every creature must use this theory? Even if the ape's behavior instantiated this theory, why must the ape attribute this theory to others? As shown by their weak TOM, apes are less able to do so than are philosophers of mind.

(Philosophy of mind is hilariously noncomparative. It entertains only one kind or quality of mind. In this sense, it has never departed from Descartes. For Descartes, only people had minds; animals were automata. Contemporary philosophers of mind do not subscribe to this, of course, but make all the standard obeisances to Darwin. They grant mind to animals almost indiscriminately. The mind that they grant is not only the human one but, being no more troubled by ontogeny than by phylogeny, the adult human mind. For contemporary philosophers no less than for Descartes, there is only one mind, that of the human adult.)

A final point concerns how to maintain that the 3- to 4-year-old child is incapable of attributing epistemic states—thus failing a test that the ape passes—and at the same time propose that even infants may attribute epistemic states. In an earlier section, I not only described tests that could be used to prove that infants have the concept of epistemic states but argued that the scenarios they depicted differed only in complexity from those that proved the existence of nonepistemic states. How, then, can the infant do what the 3- to 4-year-old child fails to do?

The answer lies in the difference between the two tests, one requiring only implicit processes, the other explicit ones. Perhaps the tests could be made somewhat more comparable simply by reducing the demands made on the child. In the tests discussed, the child was required to predict that an onlooker with an unobscured view would be able to point accurately (Premack, 1988b). One might reduce these demands by showing the child onlookers who do and do not point correctly and then require the child to indicate which of them had an unobscured view of the baiting. In any case, the inability of the child to use a concept that is putatively present in the infant is not itself a problem; in other tests discussed, infants recognized the sameness or difference of relations, whereas children were unable to use the distinction in the tests measuring ability to match relations (Premack, 1988b).

Summary

I presented two models of the infant's initial state, one in which the initial state is distinctly incomplete and in which learning fills in the missing concepts and another in which the initial state contains all the basic theoretical primitives of the species.

Although the latter eliminates conceptual primitives as a source of ontological difference, it does not discount differences in primitives; rather, it attributes them to phylogeny. Conceptual differences are what distinguish species. The chimpanzee is conceptually deficient relative to the human, the monkey conceptually deficient relative to the ape, and so on through the evolutionary branches of the primate tree. Maturation does not correct these conceptual deficiencies any more in the case of phylogeny than in that of ontogeny. That is, the adult ape is no less conceptually deficient (relative to the human) than is the infant ape. Nevertheless, maturation makes the same kind of contribution to the ape that it makes to the human, only in a far lesser degree.

In this model, the infant does not suffer from conceptual lacunae. Thus, the infant does not lack the epistemic states (believe, think, know, etc.), having only the concepts of goal, agent, intention, desire, and the like. On the contrary, infants and adults have exactly the same innate conceptual inventory. Infants differ from adults, according to this model, not in their conceptual stock but in what they can do with their concepts, in the instrumental uses they can make of them. They differ, that is, in the size of the gap between their implicit and explicit knowledge. This gap looms large in the infant but is much reduced in the adult.

Infants differ from adults, of course, in learning as well as in maturation. For instance, cultural artifacts can evidently acquire the automatic kind of processing innately associated with a natural domain. An American adult watching two individuals collide may automatically perceive a causal relation between the movement of one individual and that of the other (domain of physical objects), an intentional collision (domain of mind), and the third "out" that retires the side (domain of baseball). Infants differ from adults in that there are no cultural additions; domain-specific processing is confined to the "original" list.

Ironically, it is not in basic aspects of mentation that infants differ from adults but rather in an aspect that has been of much less central concern to psychology, namely action or translating conceptual knowledge into motor knowledge.

Infants are now thought to know about the world, to have adult primitives and adult representations and even to reason about them in relatively adultlike ways. They are not, however, able to map this knowledge onto their motor resources. Because psychology is deficient in theories of action, good accounts of the infant's and young child's deficiencies are not available. The present hypotheses are entirely local, for example that the infant cannot execute motor plans involving a sequence of different responses or that in a competition between different perceptual inputs, the infant and child give peculiar priority to vision, failing to carry out acts that would be indicated by other sources of information such as modality or inference. But this topic cannot enjoy major clarification until a long-standing deficiency in theories of action is corrected. It will be ironic if the infant, long credited with a weak mind, proves to be more weak in body than in mind and thus motivates theoretical work on action and knowledge that is mapped onto action.

References

Baillargeon, R. (1987). Young infant's reasoning about the physical and spatial characteristics of a hidden object. *Cognitive Development, 2,* 179–200.

Baillargeon, R., & Hanko-Summers, S. (1990). Is the object adequately supported by the bottom object? Young infant's understanding of support relations. *Cognitive Development, 5,* 29–54.

Baillargeon, R., Spelke, E. S., & Wasserman, S. (1985). Object permanence in five-month-old infants. *Cognition, 20,* 191–208.

Bennett, J. (1989). Thoughtful brutes. *American Philosophical Association Proceedings and Addresses, 62,* 197–210.

Dasser, V., & Premack, D. (1991). *Instructive anomoly: Chimpanzees pass a test for "theory of mind" that children fail.* Manuscript in preparation.

Golinkoff, R. M. (1975). Semantic development in infants: The concept of agent and recipient. *Merrill-Palmer Quarterly, 21,* 181–193.

Keil, F. (1990, October). Paper presented at the Conference on Domain Specificity, University of Michigan, Ann Arbor.

Leekam, S. R., & Perner, J. (1990). *Do autistic children have a metarepresentational deficit?* Unpublished manuscript, Laboratory of Experimental Psychology, University of Sussex, England.

Leslie, A. M. (1988). The necessity of illusion: Perception and thought in infancy. In L. Weiskrantz (Ed.), *Thought without language.* Oxford, England: Clarendon Press.

Leslie, A. M., & Keeble, S. (1987). Do six-month-old infants perceive causality? *Cognition, 25,* 265–287.

Leslie, A. M., & Thaiss, L. (1990, October). *Domain specificity in conceptual development: Evidence from autism.* Paper presented at the Conference on Domain Specificity, University of Michigan, Ann Arbor.

McCloskey, M. (1983). Naive theories of motion. In D. Gentner & A. L. Stevens (Eds.), *Mental models.* Hillsdale, NJ: Erlbaum.

Premack, D. (1988a). Minds with and without language. In L. Weiskrantz (Ed.), *Thought without language.* Oxford, England: Claredon Press.

Premack, D. (1988b). "Does the chimpanzee have a theory of mind?" revisited. In R. W. Byrne & A. Whiten (Eds.), *Machiavellian intelligence.* London: Oxford University Press.

Premack, D. (1988c). How to tell Mae West from a crocodile. *Behavioral and Brain Sciences, 13,* 518–519.

Premack, D. (1990). The infant's theory of self-propelled objects. *Cognition, 36,* 1–16.

Premack, D. (1991). [Perception overrides inference in young children]. Unpublished raw data.

Premack, D., & Dasser, V. (1991). *Perception overrides inference in the control of young children's behavior.* Manuscript in preparation.

Premack, D., & Premack, A. J. (1983). *The mind of an ape.* New York: Norton.

Premack, D., & Woodruff, G. (1978). Does the chimpanzee have a theory of mind? *Behavioral and Brain Sciences, 1,* 515–526.

Spelke, E. S. (1982). Perceptual knowledge of objects in infancy. In J. Mehler, M. Garrett, & E. Walker (Eds.), *Perspectives on mental representation.* Hillsdale, NJ: Erlbaum.

Spelke, E. S. (1988). Where perceiving ends and thinking begins: The apprehension of objects in infancy. In A. Yonas (Ed.), *Perceptual development in infancy. Minnesota Symposium on Child Psychology* (Vol. 20). Hillsdale, NJ: Erlbaum.

Spelke, E. S. (in press). Physical knowledge in infancy: Reflections on Piaget's Theory. In S. Carey & R. Gelman (Eds.). *Biology and cognition.* Hillsdale, NJ: Erlbaum.

Wellman, H. (in press). *Children's theories of mind.* Cambridge, MA: MIT Press.

Woodruff, G., & Premack, D. (1979). Intentional communication in the chimpanzee: The development of deception. *Cognition, 7,* 333–362.

Woodruff, G., Premack, D., & Kennell, K. (1980). Conservation of liquid and solid quantity in chimpanzee. *Science, 33,* 269–271.

Zaitchik, D. (1990). When representations conflict with reality: The preschooler's problem with false beliefs and "false" photographs. *Cognition, 35,* 41–68.

PART THREE

Learning in the
Larger World

CHAPTER 9

How To Think About Perceptual Learning: Twenty-Five Years Later

Eleanor J. Gibson

I s learning still a respectable topic for a psychologist looking for the answers to questions about the way behavior develops? I hope so, but the cognitive revolution and the present wave of neo-rationalism have removed it from the limelight, where it was in my youth. We are badly in need of a theory of cognitive development (here the majority of my colleagues are with me), but I think we need one that emphasizes perception and learning and is not divorced from developing action. We need to go back to the origins (but not in the sense of rationalism), and we need to look for the dynamics of change. I think the search takes us directly to perception (the grounding for cognition) and to action, to which it is inevitably coupled, and so most of all to a kind of learning that is centered in perception. Infants rely on it; they have to. Adults may rely on it less because linguistic sophistication brings other resources. What I did not know when I began to think about perceptual learning was that infancy is the perfect place to study it.

In the 1930s and 1940s, there was a strong developmental movement in psychology, represented in this country by Gesell, Shirley, McGraw, and others. In Europe, there was Piaget, who was publishing his three volumes of longitudinal observations made on his own children. Of these, only Piaget survived the move to cognitive psychology. For a while, he reigned supreme, until technological revolution occurred in infant research. Researchers learned how to ask infants what they perceived, what they remembered, and even if they had representations of anything. We now have a wealth of facts in infant cognition and appreciate the wonderful competence of infants. Piaget did not know everything after all. However, while researchers were proving that infants are competent cognitively, they neglected a truly developmental approach. There are now many elegant methods and a mass of cross-sectional research results, but we know little more than we did in 1950 about how development proceeds—where the transition points are and what the dynamics of change look like.

I believe that we are about to see a surge of longitudinal research and a burst of theorizing along with it. We need a theory of cognitive development that emphasizes perception and learning (not just memory), one that includes action. My theme is what kind of theory we need. What should we bring to it from the past, and what is new?

Gleanings From the Past

During World War II, it became clear that perceptual learning was a real phenomenon and that the concept was a theoretical necessity. In my first theoretical article on perceptual learning as such, written with James Gibson (J. Gibson & E. Gibson, 1955), I argued against association and inference as mediating or additive mechanisms in perceptual learning, proposing instead that perceptual learning must be characterized as increasing differentiation of what is to be perceived, a developmental change much more in keeping with biological development. I thought of it as a gain in the specificity of what is perceived in relation to what is there in the world. And I thought, unlike many others, that there is plenty of information to specify what the world affords if we have the skill to detect it.

The theory of perceptual learning that I came up with later (E. Gibson, 1969) can be summarized in three parts: (a) what is learned, (b) the mechanisms or principles invoked, and (c) the trends characterizing development. What is learned, I thought, included the distinctive features of things (e.g., objects, graphic symbols, etc.), the invariants of events, and the higher order structure of both. Distinctive features I thought of as relational contrasts characterizing a set of things. I worked out sets of features for letters, borrowing ideas from Jakobson's (1968) distinctive features of phonemes. The idea was that the contrasts, once detected, should render each item unique. Invariants of events—properties that remain invariant over transformation—I illustrated by events such as sudden appearance, disappearance, and collisions. Their meaning would be discovered long before a child could refer to them by words, even spoken ones. Higher order structural variables I illustrated by the complex structure of words and sentences and by nested events such as the rhythmic hierarchical structures of music and spoken language.

Perceiving any of these surely involved a learning process but not an associative one. The process had to produce differentiation of some relation from a hitherto unanalyzed spectrum. The information for specifying something real and meaningful was there, but it had to be detected and extracted from variable context. The processes I considered included, first, *abstraction* from varying context, such as abstraction of phonemic constituent relations from the speech flow of ongoing conversation or from different voices. The second process was *filtering*, a concept in great vogue at the time, figuring prominently in theories of attention. The idea was that irrelevant stimulation was somehow faded out, sloughed off, and disposed of. An example occurring as learning over a period of time might be a child's loss of ability to hear as distinctive phonemic contrasts ones that did not occur in his or her language environment ("use it or lose it" was the popular phrase applied). I called the third process *peripheral mechanisms of attention*, consigning it to a rather lowly status. I would now promote this concept to first place; perception is active, an exploratory process from Day 1 for every perceptual system, prominent especially in infants and resulting in consequences that define what is to be selected.

Selected is in fact the key word. Perceptual learning is first and foremost a process of selection. Exploratory activity by systems that are ready to go or that develop along the way provides potential information. Motivation to use these systems is intrinsic and very strong in infants. It was only when this was realized that researchers developed successful methods for studying infant perception. Preference, habituation, contingent reinforcement are all methods that rely on an infant's ability to search, explore, and seek to control in some way the array of stimulation presented. But what marks the "find" and so terminates the search? I (E. Gibson, 1969) proposed that the key principle is *reduction of uncertainty*, that is, the discovery of predictability, of invariance, and of the specificity of information—all contributing to yield the minimal information that is useful for guiding action. This is an economy or minimum principle, ubiquitous in scientific theory and with respectable antecedents in psychology.

I intend not only to salvage a great deal from this theory but also to introduce changes in it. The theory I envisaged in 1969 failed to capture adequately what happens when an infant learns how to cope with the world and by detecting the information needed to guide appropriate action as his or her capabilities and action systems are maturing. For human infants, whose performatory capacities are minimal at birth, perceptual learning has to be the beginning of knowledge.

An Ecological Approach to Perceptual Learning

My new approach begins with a young animal in an environment to which it is responsive and in which its ancestors have evolved. One can assume that this animal is fairly well prepared as a member of its species to cope with aspects of the environment for which it has adapted. However, that does not mean that it already knows what the world is like and what ongoing events mean for it. It is equipped to find out, and there the learning process starts. There is a new kind of learning theorist, operating under the aegis of an "ecological approach to learning." This approach emphasizes the reciprocity of animal and environment and the importance of considering the animal in its niche. Supporters of this view have for the most part studied learning in animals other than humans (e.g., song learning in birds; learning to forage in various mammals), but there is every reason for extending the view to the human infant. I cite two precepts from a chapter by Johnston (Johnston & Pietrewicz, 1985): first, that we should study the role of learning in adaptations to the natural environment, considering the characteristics of both animal and environment; second, that we should study learning in the context of development because learning occurs in ontogeny as part of the natural experience of the species.

Why do these precepts recommend themselves to me? I am an advocate of the ecological approach to perception as proposed by J. Gibson. Reciprocity between animal and environment is at the heart of that approach. An animal's environment must be described in terms relevant to that animal, and its behavior and the information for it must be described with reference to the environment. The central concept tying this system together, psychologically speaking, is that of *affordance.* One must describe what the environment affords for an animal (i.e., what it offers that has utility and provides support for the animal's actions) and must describe the propensities and capacities for action that make the supports appropriate. This system is sometimes referred to as the *animal–environment fit* (Warren, 1984). The task for the developmental psychologist is to show how the young animal learns about affordances, how it detects the appropriate supports and resources offered it as it lives in the world and matures, and how it knows what can be controlled and used by virtue of its own propensities and potential for action. Perception of affordances is vital for guiding action, making perceptual learning vital to survival.

How does one formulate a theory of perceptual learning that satisfies these requirements? I think that one should begin as I did earlier, by asking what is learned but in so doing revising the content to include what human infants do spontaneously and what they actually learn. Such an account must consider the kind of environment infants inhabit and the changes that take place as they grow. These constraints change from month to month, especially in the first year of life.

What Is Learned?

Species-typical accomplishments that emerge during the first year of life of a human infant include primarily basic communication skills, grasping and handling objects, and locomotion. The researcher's task is to observe and analyze these skills as they develop. One can then ask what information specifies the events and things with which infants interact in the world, what information specifies their own powers to deal with them, and what spurs the changes.

What the infant learns about is the affordances of the events, the objects, and the surrounding layout; that is, what is there to be perceived. This is a large order for the infant and a major phenomenon to unravel. One way to go about it is to take a tip from the infant. The infant goes about it by pursuing a course of exploration, with every means in its power. Exploratory activity has a development of its own (E. Gibson, 1988). I divide the infant's first year into three periods, roughly separated by phases of exploration constrained by the infant's ability to control his or her posture. The following is an examination of what the infant can explore and thus learn in these three periods.

Phase One

In the first period, extending from birth to about the end of the fourth month, the infant progressively controls head movements and such limb movements as it can make in a supine position or when held or firmly propped. Its spontaneous exploratory activity is marked by active looking and listening, which are aided by head turning. Haptic exploration occurs by mouthing substances or objects, such as its fist, that the infant can get into his or her mouth. Neonates' exploratory actions can be extended for research purposes by giving them instrumental aides such as a ribbon tied to a limb that can activate a mobile, tape recorder, or projector (Rovee-Collier & Gekoski, 1979) or a nipple equipped with a transducer so as to activate some display mechanism (Eimas, Siqueland,

Jusczyk, & Vigorito, 1971; Siqueland & DeLucia, 1969). When the infant moves the limb or sucks with sufficient amplitude on the nipple, he or she can explore the consequences of his or her actions. This method, known as *contingent reinforcement*, has proved extraordinarily useful in studying the development of auditory perception, especially perception of speech events.

Looking and listening are apparent at birth and, furthermore, are coordinated. A voice at one side of an infant's head evokes a head turn that brings the speaker into the infant's view. That is as it should be because social events provide both optical and acoustic information. The events that are most accessible to a neonate are social ones that provide an opportunity to observe and interact with caretakers. It is notable that human infants' earliest lessons about the world have to do with communication: They hear adults speaking to them, and we know in fact that a newborn is capable of discriminating his or her own mother's voice from others a few hours after birth (DeCasper & Fifer, 1980; Fifer & Moon, 1988). Neonates (4 days old) can also discriminate messages spoken in the native language from those in another language (Mehler et al., 1988) and even discriminate a passage that was rehearsed aloud by their mothers prenatally from another spoken passage (DeCasper & Spence, 1986). The suprasegmental and prosodic properties of the voice carrying the message are presumably used by the infant for differentiation. An infant listening, even prenatally (Cooper & Aslin, 1989), to these messages may be learning to segment the speech stream into units on the basis of well-stressed prosodic features. "Motherese," or infant-directed language, seems to be particularly effective (Cooper & Aslin, 1990; Fernald, 1985).

Along with the differentiation of spoken messages, neonates may learn ordering and contingency relations within a communication event. A wealth of research now exists on mother–infant communication. Mothers the world over (Fernald et al., 1989) speak to their infants in a special voice and rhythm that engages the infants' attention and soon elicits facial gestures and even vocalization. This event is a sort of turn taking, referred to by some as *protocommunication*. "Protoconversations are intersubjective exchanges in which infant and mother engage in a nonverbal 'dialogue' of visible and audible expressions," wrote Trevarthen (1989). That the infants' responsiveness in such an exchange involves perception of an affordance relating their own actions to control of those of an attentive listener is made clear by an experiment of Murray and Trevarthen (1987). Pairs of mothers and their infants from 6 to 12 weeks old were observed in face-to-face interactions. In addition to normal communication, each pair was observed in a double closed-circuit television situation that retained essential features of the normal face-to-face interchange but permitted timing of the display so as to delay communication and thereby disturb the infant's responsiveness (contingency relations) to the interaction. Live, appropriate televised interactions could in this way be compared with "unresponsive" sequences. In the live and appropriately timed interactions, infants smiled, maintained eye contact, made active movements of tongue and lips, and gestured with their arms. In the replayed unresponsive condition, the infants turned away from the images of their mothers and exhibited signs of distress (frowning, pouting, grimacing, yawning), and their expressions of positive affect decreased. They were described as looking puzzled or confused. It appeared that at 2 months of age, infants expected mutual responsiveness in their communications with their mothers, detected a predictable relation between their mothers' and their own actions, and regulated their own expressive gestures in synchrony with those of their mothers.

Aside from their social encounters, infants witness other events involving movement in which they do not yet participate. Objects loom toward them (e.g., faces, a bottle, a hand). They witness changes in the appearance of their surroundings while being carried or wheeled around. Motion is of the greatest importance at this early age in providing information by means of optical transformations of objects' true size and shape (Kellman, 1984). Motion reveals a permanent structure and arrangement of the layout through occlusion and disocclusion as relative viewing position is changed. Motion of a partly occluded object reveals its actual wholeness or unity and permits contrast with transformations caused by self-movement. Infants appear to be capable at 4 months of differentiating object motion from transformation in the optic array resulting from self movement (Kellman, Gleitman, & Spelke, 1987). Detecting structure through observation of events involving movement is an important avenue of perceptual learning that occurs, although perhaps to a limited extent, before more extended exploration is possible.

Whereas infants learn about predictable contingent relations between their own behavior and that of other people during this neonatal period, learning about objects is limited by the fact that the infant's exploration of them is necessarily relatively passive. Insofar as objects can be gotten to the mouth, an effective way of exploring their substance and shape is available (E. Gibson & Walker, 1984; Rochat, 1983). Raising the hands to the mouth is a typical neonatal gesture (Rochat, Hoffmeyer, & Blass, 1987), and a little later objects are conveyed to the mouth whenever possible. The hands may be extended in the direction of a moving object (Hofsten & Lindhagen, 1979), but contact is only rarely achieved before the end of the fourth month. It is at about that time that mothers begin to report that their infants become less attentive to them and show an interest in objects.[1] Learning about objects characterizes the second phase of exploratory activity.

Phase Two

In this second period, the infant's postural control extends progressively down his or her torso, first permitting use of the arms when well propped in a sitting posture and gradually progressing to unassisted sitting with both arms freed from the necessity of providing a prop or balancing (Fontaine & Pierraut le Bonniec, 1988; Rochat & Senders, 1991). Exploration of objects at this point progresses rapidly, beginning by reaching to grasp with one hand, then with two hands in synchrony, until finally independent coordinated exploration by both hands is achieved. During this period, infants are intensely attracted by objects within reach. Learning is marked at first by increasing perceptual–motor skill in controlling the reach and the grasp but later, from 6 months on, by diversifying exploratory activities that serve to reveal differential and unique properties of objects (e.g., paper is crumpled, pliable objects are squeezed, textured objects are scratched, shakable objects are shaken to test their sounding properties, rigid objects are banged against rigid surfaces, etc.; Palmer, 1989).

Early in this phase, objects are observed visually as they are rotated and translated, providing the infant (by now a viewer with good stereopsis) with opportunities for discovering the visually distinctive features of objects. Objects are generally carried to the mouth during or after viewing, so further haptic information is obtained about their substance, thereby increasing multimodal information for an object's affordances.

Visual–auditory bimodal information is available from birth for communication events, but as auditory properties of objects can be explored by squeezing, shaking, and banging, infants can provide themselves with extended multimodal information for an object's affordances (e.g., the characteristic look, sound, and feel of a metallic object). Here is a rare opportunity for perceptual learning. The infant learns about affordances of objects by varied exploratory actions that provide multimodal information for recognition of the affordance by many avenues. Control of objects is learned about by doing things with them; throwing, for example, has the consequence of landing an object on the floor out of reach. Some things afford throwing and land with a thud; others, more elastic, bounce and there is information to be obtained, in a single event, for properties of the object, the surface on which it lands, and the infant's own biodynamic capacities for perpetrating object events.

---

[1]Sustained interest in objects is reportedly first displayed at about 4 months in other cultures also, for example, the !Kung (Bakeman, Adamson, Konner, & Barr, 1990).

Phase Three

Once an infant has achieved the ability to sit up unaided and to change its posture easily from prone to sitting and vice versa, he or she may assume a crawling posture and attempt to move forward to obtain an attractive object. Locomotion hugely enhances the infant's opportunities for encounters with the world, making possible exploration of the larger layout. Being able to change viewing position at will makes possible the perfecting of "position constancy," that is, perceiving positions of articles in the layout as constant relative to one another despite shifts in one's own viewing point. There is a fair degree of position constancy in precrawlers (McKenzie, Day, & Ihsen, 1984), but it may be limited by the range of the infant's view commands when turning his or her head and torso without changing position in space. As the infant becomes able to move around so as to change his or her viewing point at will, the permanent nonchanging features of its surroundings are revealed in full (e.g., what is behind a wall or even what is behind himself or herself).

Just as mastering the sitting posture extends the infant's knowledge of objects and the ways in which he or she can use them, so mastering self-controlled locomotion extends knowledge of the larger layout and the way it can be used. But like the skilled use of the hands, the skilled use of the legs has a development of its own. Maintaining balance on hands and knees while moving forward and eventually maintaining balance on two legs in an upright position when either still or moving are no mean achievements. What has seldom been understood is the importance of perceptual guidance and learning in achieving them.

How does perception guide locomotion? What information is available? Traditionally, one thinks of "muscle senses" and vestibular stimulation, which surely have their role in locomotor development. But guiding activity is heavily dependent on visual information for relating one's own body to locations of other things that provide destinations and obstacles. J. Gibson's (1950, 1966, 1979) description of flow patterns in the optic array engendered by self-movement, and their role in locomotion, revolutionized our way of thinking about movement. Self-movement through the environment creates continuous optical information for keeping in touch with where we are and where we are going.

Flow patterns are used in a number of ways but especially for steering (given that they specify the direction in which one is heading) and for maintaining balance. A moving object creates a kind of flow pattern, too (e.g., looming), but the flow has properties that differentiate it from the changes in the array created by self-movement. The extent to which learning is involved in using this information to guide action has been little studied, although one study (Schmuckler & Gibson, 1989) suggested that toddlers in the early stages of independent walking progressively differentiate the affordances of information in flow patterns for steering around obstacles, on the one hand, and for staying upright, on the other.

Learning affordances of the terrain (i.e., the surface of support for crawling and walking) is a major task for the newly ambulatory infant. Although crawling infants tend to avoid a major drop-off in the terrain, as studies with the visual cliff have shown (E. Gibson & Walk, 1960; Walk & Gibson, 1961), there are many new affordances to be discovered, such as variations of rigidity and slipperiness, and slopes to be mounted or descended. We still have a way to go in understanding how young crawlers and walkers learn about environmental supports for locomotion in relation to their own abilities to control action. Posture must be safely maintained under varied environmental circumstances while still keeping the goal in sight. This becomes a problem when novice crawlers or walkers must literally turn their backs to the goal to advance safely (e.g., going down stairs). They have to learn that the ground extends around them (or does not) whether they are at that moment viewing it or not.

Until this time, the infant learned about many affordances of things, people, and events, quite directly. Mouthing, grasping, shaking, and so on have consequences that are immediately observable, affordances that are easy to obtain information for once the necessary action system is functional. But as action systems increase, so do the opportunities (and the necessity) for learning what I call *nested affordances*—that is, means by which to realize affordances that require some preliminary step, such as crawling across the room before reaching for and seizing some attractive object. Reaching itself can involve nested affordances, such as pulling on a cloth or other support to bring into reach an object resting on it, an activity that becomes functional at about 8 months of age (Willats, 1985). Exploratory activity in the third phase frequently seems to entail exploring new means to realize an affordance not attainable in a more direct one-step activity.

Just as the two earlier phases brought their own opportunities for learning about multimodal information for affordances, so does locomotion; in this case, perceptual learning implicates vestibular, visual, and haptic information for maneuvering oneself around the layout. Multimodal specification of one's own actions is already available during limb movement when lying prone and when sitting up and reaching, but in the third phase, multimodal guidance of posture poses a major task for development, one that continues throughout the growth and development of highly controlled actions such as jumping, hopping on one leg, or skipping.

An Outline of What Is Learned

I follow this abbreviated review of exploratory development by roughly classifying what is learned perceptually. Generally speaking, the infant learns new affordances, but one needs to be more explicit because one must eventually show where the information is that specifies an affordance.

The Self as Distinct

Differentiation of oneself as distinct from other people and objects in the world goes on throughout the first year of life. Information specifying the self is directly available for perceiving (E. Gibson, in press). An important source is the information for control, for the fact that events in the world can be contingent on one's own actions. An infant's early discovery of such control (and enjoyment of it) is evident in mother–infant "turn taking." Even more convincing evidence is found in the experimental demonstrations with so-called contingent reinforcement. One of the most dramatic demonstrations of learning about such control was given in an experiment by Kalnins and Bruner (1973) in which infants learned to suck on a nipple equipped with a transducer to bring a movie displayed before them into focus and actively maintain the focus.

An infant's early ability to distinguish object motion from self motion is further evidence of learning that one is distinct from external things. Increasing ability to make differential use of flow patterns (Schmuckler & Gibson, 1989) suggests that learning is involved. Finally, as new affordances are learned, learning about the self (its dimensions and capability for action) is always part of what is learned because an affordance is an animal–environment fit, a relation defined not only by the supports offered by the environment but also by the characteristics of the animal that make it a potential user. During development especially, this learning must be frequently updated because a young animal is continually growing in powers and dimensions.

Constancy of the Layout and Permanent Features of the World

Although there is now evidence that even newborn humans do not perceive their retinal images or proximal stimuli but rather pick up information about the sources of stimulation (i.e., the surfaces and things that surround them), what is perceived must nevertheless be originally limited. There is evidence that size constancy holds shortly after birth (Granrud, 1987), but we know that information for depth increases as stereopsis matures around 4 months, and perception of size at a distance may well become more precise with this added information. Shape constancy has also been demonstrated shortly after birth (Slater & Morison, 1985). Research has suggested that transformations yielded by motion are critical information for it (Kellman, 1984). We do not know whether perceptual learning plays a role in picking up this information. It is possible that the information is registered at some level but becomes functional (or more meaningful) as affordances of objects are learned, after exploratory reaching and grasping has begun. Where things are not only in relation to oneself but to one another is perceived to some extent early in the first year, but the salience and precision of the detection of layout information certainly increases along with the extension of exploratory systems, including locomotion. Perceiving permanent features of the layout despite shifts in arrangement is a very general achievement, extending, for example, to numbers of things (van Loosbroeck & Smitsman, 1990).

One kind of information about distances of objects, monocular static information, does not seem to be picked up until age 7 months or so, or if it is, it is not used to guide action. Yonas and his colleagues have performed a number of experiments on the so-called "pictorial cues" for depth—for example, perspective information such as relative size in a projected image (Yonas, Granrud, Arterberry, & Hanson, 1986). This information may function in a situation in which infants look with one eye and a relatively fixed head at 7 months of age but not before. Yonas et al. referred to this acquisition as *perceptual learning* and speculated on how the learning might occur. They suggested that one way might be through a correlation with earlier available information for depth (i.e., retinal disparity and motion information), but these typically occur with both eyes open and/or a moving head, and both override the "pictorial" information in experiments with adults. Motion information even overrides stereopsis in adults (Wallach & Karsh, 1963). The "pictorial cues" are evidently second-string ways of knowing. They provide information for depth portrayed in a picture but not for the picture plane itself. They are another kind of nested affordance, giving information not about the location of the picture as an object but about the location of something portrayed in the picture, that is, about something else.

Features of Objects

Learning about features of objects in one's surroundings should have high priority, and it seems that it does. Learning about human objects who are responsive to an infant's own actions come first, but by age 5 months, when manipulation becomes available, infants can learn about distinctive features of inanimate objects (i.e., what makes them unique in affordances and appearance). At some point, infants may learn not just what features distinguish an object from others, but what gives an arrangement of parts unity and coherence. Objects that are partly occluded by other objects are perceived by the infant as whole at age 4 months if they move or are spatially separated from other things (Kellman & Spelke, 1983). But later on, arrangements of features such as proximity and similarity (the so-called Gestalt laws; Wertheimer, 1923) may also be used as information for unity. This kind of information is not functional before age 7 months (Schmidt, 1985) as are the so-called pictorial cues for depth. Likewise, it seems to be of secondary importance compared with information given by motion. Static arrays are poorer in information and are not a natural way to view the world. Furthermore, there is little in a static array that provides multimodal information; multimodal information is especially likely to come with haptic exploration or with the movement of oneself or an object so as to modulate resulting acoustic and other consequences.

Multimodal Invariants

Multimodal specification for an event leading to perception of amodal invariants can only be learned perceptually. Multimodal information for communication events is normally available to neonates, but for events involving objects the infant must for the most part await manipulatory exploration to obtain the spectrum as a whole.

Multimodal specification is the rule for properties of the self (e.g., dimensions of a limb that constrain reaching), for properties of objects (e.g., substance), and for properties of the layout (e.g., properties of surfaces of support, such as rigidity or slipperiness). It is important for the adaptiveness of behavior that commonality of specification be known and functional. This is a kind of categorization that is very basic in cognitive organization.[2]

Causal Relations in Events

Tolman described what was learned as "what leads to what" or, more elegantly, the "causal texture of the environment" (Tolman & Brunswik, 1935). It may be that infants

---

[2] *I was asked by a colleague who read an early version of this chapter and criticized it for me what it has to say to all of the cognitive psychologists who are concerned with such topics as categories and the way in which mental content is organized in memory. Although I did not prepare this chapter with such an aim in mind, I do think it has something to say to them. I think it tells them about the foundations for categories and the way knowledge gets organized. All of my examples of what is learned perceptually indicate a natural grouping of knowledge in very basic ways and indicate good functional reasons for why and how such groupings come about in development. Awareness of affordances and of the information for animal–environment relations that specifies them does the rest.*

first learn about causal relations when they discover their own efficacy for producing an environmental change (Piaget, 1954, p. 228). But at some point, causal relations in the external world are detected, and we can define the invariant information for this in cases (such as mechanical ones) in which there is conservation of energy manifest in an exchange between objects such as one billiard ball striking another. It is not clear how early infants detect causal relations in external events, but some recent research has suggested that it may be as early as 7 months of age (Baillargeon, 1987). Differentiation of the objects and their roles must take place, however, before the constant property and the causal relation can be detected, a case of differentiating and discovering nested affordances.

Means–End Relations

Nested affordances are detected later than ones more directly perceived. They are of several kinds, but prominent among them are cases of what have been called *means–end relations* (Piaget, 1954; Tolman, 1932; Willats, 1985). Learning to use a lever (e.g., a turn-tablelike affair that must be pushed away to bring an object close enough to seize) is one case that has been studied in children between 12 and 24 months of age. Koslowski and Bruner (1972) found that a direct approach preceded the more advanced strategy and that the children had to differentiate the action of the lever from the total task before solution. Once solved, the strategy was highly generalizable. Exploration of means for accomplishing a task that is not realizable through simply perceiving a direct affordance is a viable and frequent mechanism of learning once the structure of a nested affordance has been detected.

These topics do not end the potential list of what may be learned through perceptual learning, but they should suffice to demonstrate its ubiquity and importance. Above all, these topics identify major problem areas for research.

A Connected Story: Research on Perceptual Learning in Infancy

Much research on learning about control of environmental consequences has been conducted using head turning, sucking, or moving a limb as the action performed. The first informal experiment of this type was done by Piaget when he tied one end of a string to one of his own children's wrist, and the other end to a celluloid toy hanging above it (Piaget, 1954). The child quickly discovered that a wrist motion activated the toy and was able to transfer its action without hesitation to the other arm. Watson (1972) arranged a mobile above his child's head and pointed out that the child smiled and cooed when the mobile was activated by the child's own spontaneous movements but not when it was otherwise set in motion. Rovee-Collier and others have performed many such experiments with careful controls (Finkelstein & Ramey, 1977; Rovee & Rovee, 1969; Rovee-Collier & Gekoski, 1979). Infants quickly learned to operate the mobile as early as 2 months of age; they responded with smiling and cooing when their action and its consequence were contingent; they fussed and cried when the event was made noncontingent, as did yoked controls; and when the mechanism was unhooked, they did not exhibit an extinction curve but tugged even harder and showed anger (Alessandri, Sullivan, & Lewis, 1990). Obviously, the infants detected a relation between their own exertion and an environmental change, a sequence of cause and effect. There is evidence, too, that learning control of an event in one situation will transfer to learning to control a different event, including one that is too difficult without the preliminary learning (Finkelstein & Ramey, 1977).

What could be the information for the affordance that these infants detected in learning to control an external event by their own action? I think it has to be an intermodal proprioceptive–visual invariant relation. But how does one know that an infant can detect this subtle relation between something happening in its own body, a self-directed action, and an event in the world? Bahrick and Watson (1985) showed that this can and does happen. They placed infants before two video screens. On one appeared a display of the infant's own legs, which were free to move and kick. On the other appeared a display of the legs of another infant, identically dressed, or the same infant's legs recorded at a different movement so that the visible motions were not synchronous with the infant's current activity. The infant's limbs, in reality, were screened from his or her view by a bib. Thus, the infant could feel his or her own leg movement and view a synchronous recorded version of the movement or an asynchronous recorded version of his or her own or another infant's legs. Are infants sufficiently aware of their own movements to recognize a visual portrayal of them in action? The answer is yes. The activity is multiply specified by some common amodal invariant information. The infants turned to look preferentially at the nonself-specifying display. It is notable that this detection of proprioceptive–visual invariance occurs long before infants recognize their own facial images in a mirror as a kind of static portrait of themselves. Predicting the effects of their own self-initiated movement is evidently a more directly attainable kind of knowledge and has utility for controlling events.

A comment sometimes made about detection of intermodal relations is that it is just a case of association of two experiences that happen to occur simultaneously. Is it really the result of an arbitrary, perhaps fortuitous associative pairing? Bahrick (1988) compared learning of arbitrary and nonarbitrary intermodal relations by 3-month-old infants. Several groups of infants were familiarized with two visible and audible filmed events. One film depicted a hand shaking a clear plastic bottle containing one very large marble. The other depicted a hand shaking a similar bottle containing a number of very small marbles. Four familiarization conditions varied in their pairings of film and sound track as to whether the appropriate track (one or many marbles) was paired with a film or whether a track was synchronous with the film or not. Only one condition (one group of infants) was familiarized with films paired with their appropriate, synchronized sound track. After familiarization, an intermodal preference test was given too each group with the two films presented side by side and a single centered track played.

Learning did occur as a result of familiarization, resulting in a preference for matching the film specified by its appropriate sound track, but learning was confined to just one group, namely, the group familiarized with the appropriate synchronous pairing of sight and sound. Equal opportunity for association with an inappropriate sound track did not lead to a preference for that combination in the intermodal test.

The infants in the Bahrick (1988) study were only 3 months old. A preliminary experiment had shown that they did not show a preference for the appropriately unified film and sound accompaniment before they were given the opportunity for familiarization. But older infants, 5½ months old, did. What was different? A survey of the development of exploratory behavior revealed that infants at 3 months of age are capable of learning and communicating in a rather complex interchange of facial and vocal gestures with a companion. They are not yet involved in exploratory manipulation of objects to provide themselves with synchronous, multimodal information about objects. But by 5½ months of age, self-initiated events implicating objects occur.

An experiment by Eppler (1990) compared infants at these two periods, giving them an opportunity to look preferentially at pairs of events displaying humans in a communicative event in one series and objects being manipulated in characteristic ways in a second series. The human events portrayed either a woman telling a story with expressive facial gestures or a woman playing a pat-a-cake game. The object events were a clear plastic bottle containing a marble being shaken and a hand beating a spoon on a saucepan. It was expected that all of the infants would show a preference for the unified sound and event when human events and corresponding sounds were presented but that only the infants capable of manipulating objects would show a preference for looking at the appropriately corresponding object event specified by sound. Eppler went further, testing all of the subjects of both groups for ability to handle objects. Their skill at grasping and manipulating several objects was coded and rated so as to reveal an interaction of attention to multimodal object properties and development of manipulatory skill. Within the 5½-month-old group, there were fairly large differences in manipulatory skill, and a significant relation was found between attention to visible–audible object properties and handling skill.

This result shows that perceptual learning of multimodally specified properties of objects is correlated with the development of the exploratory system that characteristically reveals information for them. One can go on to ask whether such a relation holds for the development of locomotor exploratory systems. Does development of self-initiated locomotion give rise to new perceptual learning about properties of the layout, such as the affordance of surfaces of support?

A program of research at Cornell University with a "walkway" compared crawling and walking infants for manifestations of such development, varying surfaces of support (E. D. Gibson et al., 1987). Rigidity of a surface was a major variable. Infants were observed before and during traversal of two surfaces contrasting in rigidity, one a firm plywood surface, the other a waterbed that could be traversed on all fours but that offered poor support for upright locomotion. Crawling and walking infants behaved similarly on the rigid surface, with a minimum of preliminary exploration and little hesitation. A number of walkers walked across it, although they had been placed in a sitting position to start. However, locomotion on the waterbed revealed a difference. Crawlers showed no hesitation in crossing it to a waiting parent, but walkers hesitated, engaged in exploratory testing and prodding, and never attempted to walk across it. Standing upright and walking evidently places a new challenge on maintaining an interactive relationship with one's surroundings; affordances have changed, and learning to predict the consequences of environmental supports for the new action is required.

More recently, research comparing crawlers and walkers on traversal of a sloping terrain was conducted by Adolph, Gibson, and Eppler (1990). Young walkers, 13 months of age, attempted upright traversal of upward slopes without hesitation, even trying surfaces inclined at 40 degrees. Downward slopes were a different matter. Almost no infants attempted upright traversal of downward slopes at a greater than a 10-degree inclination. Downward slopes provoked much hesitation, prodding with hands or feet, and rocking at the brink. The children also searched for new means of traversal, so that a number eventually managed to slide down on their bottoms or stomachs, although none had had previous experience on playground slides. Upward slopes were explored quite differently, by actually embarking and attempting to climb.

When these young walkers were compared with infants still locomoting by crawling, there was a major difference. The crawling infants attempted to scale up the slopes of all the inclinations presented, as did the walkers. But unlike the walkers, they also embarked on the downward slopes, head first, in crawling position, and had to be rescued by the experimenter. When crawlers lift one arm from the surface and push their weight forward, balance is precarious and the uplifted arm cannot reach a downward sloping surface in time to prevent a topple. It seems that crawlers have not yet mastered the art of assessing properties of the terrain that pose a a risk in relation to their own capacity for maintaining equilibrium. There must be a visible surface of support, as we know from research on the visual cliff, but slope in relation to postural control is not yet taken into account.

Do the crawlers lack the means of exploration? They did explore manually, feeling the surface and patting it. But a manually felt slope was apparently not a deterrent. Furthermore, they did not explore other means of descent, such as turning around and sliding down backward. Although all of the crawlers were capable of turning, and often did so, they did not try advancing backward. Some cognitive development apparently intervenes when walking is initiated; it may be the relation of slope to maintenance of postural control that must be mastered

We know that perception and action develop together as affordances are learned, one providing impetus for the other to make learning possible. Can we say anything about how perceptual learning occurs and the mechanisms that might be involved?

The Question of Mechanism

The question of mechanisms of learning, in particular neurological ones, will remain open until we have a fuller description of what happens at a behavioral level over the first year. I think we can confidently make a few generalizations about what happens at that level. We know that learning in infancy depends on self-initiated exploratory activity on the part of the infant and that that activity has a development of its own based on control of posture and limb movements (which are, of course, related). Exploratory activity can be extended artificially by putting instrumental means at the infant's disposal (e.g., a string tied to the ankle, connected to some transducer), so that this development is not so much one of increasing cognitive capacity as it is one of gaining the means of exploring the system relating the infant's actions to the environment. The power to learn would seem to exist all along. This entails, in my opinion, not association, but the power to detect environmental consequences of exploratory action. It is not a cementing of a connection but a differentiation process, a selection of information.

If one must look for a neural process that can accomplish the changes seen in behavior, one needs to look for a selection process in the developing nervous system. I read Edelman's (1987) *Neural Darwinism* with great hopes. Edelman does offer a kind of selection process. An originally very unspecific system of neuronal groups is presumably pushed toward differentiation and specificity by environmental as well as organic forces that amplify some preexisting function, selecting groups of variant neurons the activity of which corresponds to certain "signals." These signals seem to be experiences that are "tuned" to preexisting groups. But the relative clarity of the exposition of how selection of neuronal groups takes place is swallowed up later in an overall mechanism for "perceptual categorization" that is referred to as *global mapping*, a construct that seems to me highly conjectural, quite fuzzy, and without the needed explanatory power.

Greenough's theory also addresses the effects of experience (Greenough, Black, & Wallace, 1987). He divided the role of experience into two kinds, that which is relevant to "expected" development for the species and another relevant to "experience-dependent" information. The first, occurring in early development, assumes that young animals enjoy environments that are so typical for their niche that genetic blueprinting is unnecessary for much of differentiation. Greenough used a "pruning metaphor": Synaptic connections are overproduced in early development, and experience selects those that will survive as others are lost. The animal is described as "acting creatively" in producing this experience itself. Active interaction with the environment is assumed to be necessary for the animal to "extract appropriate information." This early intrinsically generated experience sets the stage for a subsequent experience-dependent process, one dependent on extrinsically originating events. This second kind of learning is supposed to be an additive process rather than a selective one.

I like the emphasis on pruning and selection, on the role of the species-typical environment, and on the infant's active interaction with its environment to produce learning. However, it seems possible that infants observe and learn about extrinsically originating events too, and I am not at all sure that an "additive process" need be invoked to handle the way in which information is extracted from them.

On the whole, I have not found my sallies into the neuropsychological literature very productive. As psychologists, we are still needed as the scientists who know how to study behavior, who can describe the intricate intertwining of perceiving and acting in the adaptive life of a human animal, and who can observe the development of this activity with insight into the constraints, opportunities, and environmental offerings that underlie the dynamics of change. Renewed efforts to formulate an adequate theory of how learning actually occurs as part of the development of a neonate in its own kind of world will pay off for us, as well as for the neuropsychologists, who would do well to listen to the story of what they are eager to explain.

As a final word, I propose that perceiving is itself a mechanism of learning. Detecting the information that specifies an animal–environment interaction that has consequences for adaptive behavior is the key of knowledge and where it all begins.

References

Adolph, K. E., Gibson, E. J., & Eppler, M. A. (1990). *Perceiving affordances of slopes: The ups and downs of toddlers' locomotion* (Report No. 16). Atlanta, GA: Emory University, Emory Cognition Project.

Alessandri, S., Sullivan, M., & Lewis, M. (1990). Violation of expectancy and frustration in early infancy. *Developmental Psychology, 26,* 738–744.

Bahrick. L. E. (1988). Intermodal learning in infancy: Learning on the basis of two kinds of invariant relations in audible and visible events. *Child Development, 59,* 197–209.

Bahrick, L. E., & Watson, J. S. (1985). Detection of intermodal proprioceptive-visual contingency as a potential basis of self-perception in infancy. *Developmental Psychology, 21,* 963–973.

Baillargeon, R. (1987). Young infants' reasoning about the physical and spatial representations of a hidden object. *Cognitive Development, 2,* 179–200.

Bakeman, R., Adamson, L. B., Konner, M., & Barr, R. G. (1990). !Kung infancy: The social context of object exploration. *Child Development, 61,* 794–809.

Cooper, R. B., & Aslin, R. N. (1989). The language environment of the young infant: Implications for early perceptual development. *Canadian Journal of Psychology, 43,* 247–265.

Cooper, R. B., & Aslin, R. N. (1990). Preference for infant-directed speech in the first month after birth. *Child Development, 61,* 1584–1595.

DeCasper, A. J., & Fifer, W. P. (1980). Of human bonding: Newborns prefer their mothers' voices. *Science, 208,* 1174–1176.

DeCasper, A. J., & Spence, M. (1986). Newborns prefer a familiar story over an unfamiliar one. *Infant Behavior and Development, 9,* 133–150.

Edelman, G. M. (1987). *Neural Darwinism.* New York: Basic Books.

Eimas, P. D., Siqueland, E. R., Jusczyk, P. W., & Vigorito, J. (1971). Speech perception in infants. *Science, 171,* 303–306.

Eppler, M. A. (1990). *Perception and action in infancy: Object manipulation skills and detection of auditory–visual correspondences.* Unpublished doctoral dissertation, Emory University, Atlanta, GA.

Fernald, A. (1985). Four-month-old infants prefer to listen to motherese. *Infant Behavior and Development, 8,* 181–195.

Fernald, A., Taeschner, T., Dunn, J., Papousek, M., deBoysson-Bardies, B., & Fukui, I. (1989). A cross-language study of prosodic modifications in mothers' and fathers' speech to preverbal infants. *Journal of Child Language, 16,* 477–501.

Fifer, W. P., & Moon, C. (1988). Auditory experience in the fetus. In W. Smotherman & S. Robinson (Eds.), *Behavior of the fetus* (pp. 175–188). West Caldwell, NJ: Telford Press.

Finkelstein, N. W., & Ramey, C. T. (1977). Learning to control the environment in infancy. *Child Development, 48,* 806–819.

Fontaine, R., & Pierraut le Bonniec, G. (1988). Postural evolution and integration of the prehension gesture in children aged 4 to 10 months. *British Journal of Developmental Psychology, 6,* 223–233.

Gibson, E. J. (1969). *Principles of perceptual learning and development.* New York: Appleton-Century-Crofts.

Gibson, E. J. (1988). Exploratory behavior in the development of perceiving, acting, and the acquiring of knowledge. *Annual Review of Psychology, 39,* 1–41.

Gibson, E. J. (in press). The self perceived. In U. Neisser (Ed.), *The perceived self: Ecological and interpersonal sources of self-knowledge.* Cambridge, England: Cambridge University Press.

Gibson, E. J., Riccio, G., Schmuckler, M. A., Stoffregen, T. A., Rosenberg, D., & Taormina, J. (1987). Detection of the traversability of surfaces by crawling and walking infants. *Journal of Experimental Psychology: Perception and Performance, 13,* 533–544.

Gibson, E. J., & Walk, R. D. (1960). The "visual cliff." *Scientific American, 202,* 64–71.

Gibson, E. J., & Walker, A. S. (1984). Development of knowledge of visual–tactual affordances of substance. *Child Development, 55,* 451–453.

Gibson, J. J. (1950). *Perception of the visual world.* Boston: Houghton-Mifflin.

Gibson, J. J. (1966). *The senses considered as perceptual systems.* Boston: Houghton-Mifflin.

Gibson, J. J. (1979). *The ecological approach to visual perception.* Boston: Houghton-Mifflin.

Gibson, J. J., & Gibson, E. J. (1955). Perceptual learning: Differentiation or enrichment. *Psychological Review, 62,* 32–41.

Granrud, C. E. (1987). Size constancy in newborn human infants. *Investigative Opthalmology and Visual Science, 28* (Suppl. 5).

Greenough, W. T., Black, J. E., & Wallace, C. S. (1987). Experience and brain development. *Child Development, 58,* 539–559.

Hofsten, C. von, & Lindhagen, K. (1979). Observations on the development of reaching for moving objects. *Journal of Experimental Child Psychology, 28,* 158–173.

Jackobson, R. V. (1968). *Child language, aphasia, and phonological universals.* The Netherlands, The Hague: Molton.

Johnston, T. D., & Pietrewicz, A. T. (1985). *Issues in the ecological study of learning.* Hillsdale, NJ: Erlbaum.

Kalnins, I. V., & Bruner, J. S. (1973). The coordination of visual observation and instrumental behavior in early infancy. *Perception, 2,* 307–314.

Kellman, P. J. (1984). Perception of three-dimensional form by human infants. *Perception and Psychophysics, 36,* 353–358.

Kellman, P. J., Gleitman, H., & Spelke, E. S. (1987). Object and observer motion in the perception of objects by infants. *Journal of Experimental Psychology: Perception and Performance, 13,* 586–593.

Kellman, P. J., & Spelke, E. S. (1983). Perception of partly occluded objects in infancy. *Cognitive Psychology, 15,* 483–524.

Koslowski, B., & Bruner, J. S. (1972). Learning to use a lever. *Child Development, 43,* 790–799.

McKenzie, B. E., Day, R. H., & Ihsen, E. (1984). Localization of events in space: Young infants are not always egocentric. *British Journal of Developmental Psychology, 2,* 1–9.

Mehler, J., Jusczyk, P. W., Lambertz, G., Hallsted, N., Bertoncini, J., & Amiel-Tison, C. (1988). A precursor of language acquisition in young infants. *Cognition, 29,* 143–178.

Murray, L., & Trevarthen, C. (1987). Emotional regulation of interactions between two-month-olds and their mothers. In T. M. Field & N. A. Fox (Eds.), *Social perception in infants* (pp. 193–197). Norwood, NJ: Ablex.

Palmer, C. (1989). The discriminating nature of infants' exploratory actions. *Developmental Psychology, 25,* 885–893.

Piaget, J. (1954). *The construction of reality in the child.* New York: Basic Books.

Rochat, P. (1983). Oral touch in young infants: Responses to variations of nipple characteristics in the first months of life. *International Journal of Behavior Development, 6,* 123–133.

Rochat, P., Hoffmeyer, L. B., & Blass, E. M. (1987). *Hand–mouth coordination in newborn human infants.* Paper presented at the meeting of the Eastern Psychological Association, Arlington, VA.

Rochat, P., & Senders, S. J. (1991). Active touch in infancy: Action systems in development. In M. J. Weiss & P. R. Zelazo (Eds.), *Newborn attention: Biological constraints and the influence of experience* (pp. 412–442). Norwood, NJ: Ablex.

Rovee, C. K., & Rovee, D. T. (1969). Conjugate reinforcement of infant exploratory behavior. *Journal of Experimental Child Psychology, 8,* 33–39.

Rovee-Collier, C. K., & Gekoski, M. J. (1979). The economics of infancy: A review of conjugate reinforcement. In H. W. Reese & L. P. Lipsitt (Eds.), *Advances in child development and behavior* (Vol. 13, pp. 195–255). San Diego, CA: Academic Press.

Schmidt, H. (1985). *The development of Gestalt perception.* Unpublished doctoral dissertation, University of Pennsylvania, Philadelphia.

Schmuckler, M. A., & Gibson, E. J. (1989). The effect of imposed optical flow on guided locomotion in young walkers. *British Journal of Developmental Psychology, 7,* 193–206.

Siqueland, E. R., & DeLucia, C. A. (1969). Visual reinforcement of nonnutritive sucking in human infants. *Science, 165,* 1144–1146.

Slater, A., & Morison, V. (1985). Shape constancy and slant perception at birth. *Perception, 14,* 337–344.

Tolman, E. C. (1932). *Purposive behavior in animals and men.* New York: Appleton-Century-Crofts.

Tolman, E. C., & Brunswik, E. (1935). The organism and the causal texture of the environment. *Psychological Review, 42,* 43–77.

Trevarthen, C. (1989, Autumn). Origins and directions for the concept of infant intersubjectivity. *SRCD Newsletter.*

van Loosbroeck, E., & Smitsman, A. W. (1990). Visual perception of numerosity in infancy. *Developmental Psychology, 26,* 916–922.

Walk, R. D., & Gibson, E. J. (1961). A comparative and analytical study of visual depth perception. *Psychological Monographs, 75* (15).

Wallach, H., & Karsh, E. G. (1963). The modification of steroscopic depth perception and the kinetic depth-effect. *American Journal of Psychology, 76,* 429–435.

Warren, W. H. (1984). Perceiving affordances: Visual guidance of stair-climbing. *Journal of Experimental Psychology: Human Perception and Performance, 10,* 683–703.

Watson, J. S. (1972). Smiling, cooing, and "the game." *Merrill-Palmer Quarterly, 18,* 323–339.

Wertheimer, M. (1923). Untersuchungen zur Lehre von der Gestalt, II. *Psychologische Forschung, 4,* 301–350.

Willats, P. (1985). *Development and rapid adjustment of means-end behavior in infants aged six to eight months.* Paper presented at the biennial meeting of the International Society for the Study of Behavioral Development, Tours, France.

Yonas, A., Granrud, C. E., Arterberry, M. E., & Hanson, B. L. (1986). Infants' distance perception from linear perspective and texture gradients. *Infant Behavior and Development, 9,* 247–256.

CHAPTER 10

Learning, Cognition, and Education: Then and Now

Robert Glaser

T his chapter considers the interaction between psychological science and its contributions to educational practice and instructional theory as seen through my eyes as a participant. My long-term engagement in this interaction reflects relentless optimism (with occasional periods of despair) that the study of behavior and cognition should influence and be influenced by changes in the ways society educates its people. As knowledge accumulates in the behavioral sciences, a scientific and technological foundation should be provided for educational practice. Moreover, scientific progress often results from examination of attempts at application and contact with real-world problems. Fortunately, developments in the study of cognition are now encouraging this scrutiny.

A Brief History

The history of the engagement of psychological science with education is a story of inconstancy. At the beginning of this century, figures such as Dewey, Judd, and Thorndike encouraged active relations between psychological science and applications to education. The seeming practicality of association theory and the building of associations appeared to capture the essence of education. For example, in Thorndike's (1922) book *The Psychology of Arithmetic*, the theory of stimulus–response (S-R) bonds and the law of effect underlie the analysis and teaching of arithmetic tasks; Thorndike carefully analyzed learning addition, for instance, in terms of S-R bonds that could be taught and observed by the teacher. Thorndike proceeded very directly from laboratory findings to practice, a style that Skinner later used. In contrast to this direct imposition of theory, Dewey envisioned interaction between scientific work and practice; knowledge obtained from each could be mutually modifying (Dewey, 1900). But soon after Thorndike and Dewey's day, education and psychology went their separate ways. Each field addressed demanding problems of building its own discipline. Psychology aspired to become a natural science and take its place among other sciences. Psychologists studying learning went into the laboratory to work out experimental techniques using tasks designed to illuminate theoretical problems. Education, by contrast, found its challenges primarily in the practical problems of teacher training, teaching methods, curriculum development, and testing for the schools. For the most part, experimental psychologists pursued careers in psychology departments, and educational psychologists joined faculties of education. During this period, the field of testing and psychometrics developed a strong technology (Carroll, 1982); theories of mental tests were bolstered by factor analysis but were unsupported by underlying psychological theories of learning and performance (Anastasia, 1967; Cronbach, 1957). For the most part, investigators studying learning, memory, and problem solving carried out their work with little inclination to explore applications to education, and problems that might have been uncovered through applied studies were not available to challenge theories and findings from the laboratory. Little force was generated either to move scientific knowledge into practice or to have the intuitive principles of schooling interpreted as issues and concepts for scientific study.

After War World II, during the 1950s and early 1960s, two major events stimulated rapprochement between psychology and educational research and technology. One was the movement of Skinner and operant psychology into the educational scene (Glaser, 1978; Skinner, 1954, 1958). The surge of interest in teaching machines and programmed instruction has been well documented (Glaser, 1965; Lumsdaine & Glaser, 1960). Within a decade, hundreds of instructional programs were published, numerous different kinds of teaching machines were offered for sale, and societies for programmed instruction were founded in a dozen countries. However, in the rush to technology in education and training, applications were quickly separated from the theory underlying them. A mutually correcting system in which failures and limitations in both application and theory could be confronted never developed.

The second event was the large postwar research effort that this country sponsored on problems of military training. Many well-known psychologists of the time and many who later became well-known were involved (Melton, 1957). There was a vast increase in research on complex performance, much of which focused on the kinds of performances involved when individuals controlled human–machine systems that were generally concerned with the detection and transmission of information for human and machine decision making. Human cognitive capacities were modeled in terms of the hardware with which they interacted, and the results later contributed to modeling of human performance and mental processes in terms of information processing systems.

In the late 1950s, psychologists who addressed problems of training emphasized the acquisition of complex skills (Glaser, 1965) and turned scientific interest to the long-term requirements for the development of high levels of proficiency. Reference was made to the "phantom plateau" or "phantom asymptote" in a learning curve (Fitts, 1965; Keller, 1958) that masked the continued improvement in performance over long periods, over days and months of practice. Attention was called to the artificial limits on improvement of performance that were inherent in short-term studies of learning; this signaled future study of high levels of competence and expertise that develop with extensive experience and that are relevant to the objectives of education and training.

With the growth of interest in complex performance, psychologists expressed concern with the level of knowledge in their science. For example, when the *Annual Review of Psychology* first included instructional psychology in 1969, the authors, Gagne and Rohwer, limited their attention to studies in experimental psychology that had some relevance to the design of instruction, but, they wrote,

> Remoteness of applicability to instruction, we note with some regret, characterizes many studies of human learning, retention, and transfer, appearing in the most prestigious of psychological journals.... The conditions under which the learning is investigated, and the tasks set for the learner are often unrepresentative of conditions under which most human learning occurs.... This is not to imply that such studies do not further an understanding of the learning process. However, it would seem that extensive theory development centering upon learning tasks and learning conditions will be required before one will be able to apply such knowledge to the design of instruction. (p. 381)

In the decade before, Sputnik had stimulated real concern about our educational accomplishments in the federal government. In addition to major curriculum efforts, such as the new math, there were psychological stirrings. Bruner's (1960) report of the proceedings of a landmark conference, titled *The Process of Education*, elaborated on themes that were to contribute to an agenda for educationally relevant research on cognitive processes. One theme was the role of structured knowledge in learning, particularly knowledge that entails the principles and problem representation capabilities that underlie effective problem solving and transfer. A second theme was readiness for learning. Attention was called to young children's capabilities and intuitions that are generative in developing qualitative models for thinking, particularly in science and arithmetic, in their early years of schooling. In addition, the development of prescriptive theories of instruction that were complementary to theories of learning was explored (Atkinson & Paulson, 1972; Bruner, 1966).

In the second *Annual Review* chapter on instructional psychology, Resnick and I (Glaser & Resnick, 1972) noted that experimental and developmental psychologists had turned increasing attention to instructional problems. In so doing, they faced the necessity of studying tasks that were considerably more complex than those typically studied in the laboratory. New ways of analyzing human performance and specifying the content of learning were needed (Gagne, 1962, 1965). The emphasis in the past had been how learning occurs, but techniques for determining what constitutes competent performance were not well worked out. The focus of cognitive psychology on analyses of complex performance intersected with this requirement for instructional psychology, and task analyses became a central endeavor. What is it that an expert in a subject matter has learned? What distinguishes a skilled reader from an unskilled one? These were significant questions for both education and a science of cognitive performance.

In the mid-1970s, well-known cognitive researchers held a conference on the contributions that current research was beginning to make to instructional theory and design, and a stimulating volume was published (Klahr, 1976). The significant theme was the analysis of complex performance. Applying the concepts of cognitive psychology to such educational goals as understanding, comprehension, and reasoning was a first order of business. A related theme was how schemata, semantic networks, and memory representations are built and modified in the course of learning. Understanding of the nature of human memory and how knowledge structures are acquired, modified, and used would come to enrich teaching and students' use of knowledge (Lesgold, Pellegrino, Fokkema, & Glaser, 1978).

By 1980, instructional psychology had become an integral part of mainstream research on human cognition and development (Resnick, 1980). Cognitive psychologists were investigating domains of schooling, such as reading, in studies of word recognition, sources of difficulty in learning to read, and reading comprehension. Work on mathematical problem solving included cognitive models of story problems that children find difficult to solve and studies of children's concept of number and other early mathematical competencies. Work on scientific problem solving examined the knowledge structures and problem representations that differentiate novices' from experts' performances. Information-processing analyses were pursued on the nature of intelligence and aptitude for learning. Almost all of this work applied cognitive theory to the analysis of performance; less work was devoted to analyzing how these complex behaviors are acquired and optimized by instruction.

The Progress of Instructional Psychology and Its Current State

The progress of the past three decades in cognitive instructional psychology can be traced in more detail through four components (Glaser, 1976). These components can be seen as the major categories of analysis needed for the articulation of a prescriptive theory of learning: (a) description of the state of knowledge to be achieved—task analysis and the analysis of competence, (b) description of the learner's initial state and prior capabilities, (c) specification of instruction and conditions for learning, and (d) assessment of the outcomes of learning. Work in each of these categories is described in the remainder of this chapter, as outlined in Table 1.

The State of Knowledge To Be Achieved: The Analysis of Competence

Behavioral Objectives and Taxonomies of Performance

For instructional psychology in the 1960s, the specification of behavioral objectives and the analysis of behavioral hierarchies became important endeavors. Psychologists applied then-current knowledge of learning to designing forms of practice that aimed to produce associative strength, progressive reinforcement to effect behavioral change, presentation of concepts that could be discriminated or subsumed to produce a principle or rule for generalized performance, and conditions of training for building skills and procedures from component parts. Learning theory was fitted to such behavioral outcomes.

TABLE 1
Changing Concepts of the Four Major Components of an Instructional Psychology

Competence to be achieved	Initial state and prior capabilities	Conditions for learning	Assessment of learning outcomes
Behavioral objectives and learning taxonomies	Aptitudes and learning	Behavioral learning theory	Atheoretical test design
Cognitive objectives	Processes of aptitude and intelligence	Emphasis on performance and learning outcomes	Cognitive theory and assessment
Knowledge structures and expertise	Cognitive development: Knowledge structures and capabilities	Reemergence of learning theory in the context of instruction • Procedural skill acquisition • Self-regulatory executive strategies for learning • Acquiring expert knowledge structures	Integration of testing and teaching

Note.   Each column shows changing conceptions of the categories from past to present.

Advances in task analysis took several directions. One was a concern with differentiating categories of learning. The need for a taxonomy of the varieties of human performance was highlighted by Melton's (1965) *Categories of Human Learning*. In discussing the role of taxonomies in the development of a science, Melton pointed out that efforts to develop a technology of human learning brought taxonomical issues to the fore. The identification of psychologically isomorphic tasks could assist in determining which tasks shared similar optimal conditions for learning. Gagne (1965, 1970) made a major effort to categorize tasks according to learning requirements in *The Conditions of Learning*. He described eight varieties of learning and the different conditions required to bring them about. For each of these categories, Gagne presented hierarchies of states of knowledge and skills that are prerequisites in learning more complex performances. The notion of learning hierarchies led to an extensive series of studies of transfer relations that investigated the effectiveness of learning component subordinate tasks as prerequisites to acquiring a superordinate task.

Cognitive Objectives

A second direction for task analysis that accompanied the growth of cognitive psychology was the experimental study of the information structures and processing requirements of proficient performance. The relatively simple surface aspects of performances that older theories could address now seemed trivial in the light of complexities of the competences that had to be understood before instruction could be meaningfully designed. The study of memory structures, problem solving and problem representation, the constructive capability of children, language development, and text processing began to reveal the knowledge structures and mental processes that are entailed in highly proficient human performance. The focus here was not on learning and acquisition but on the products or resulting steady state of learning and experience over time, that is, the properties that characterize highly competent performance. Cognitive psychology and its application to problems of instruction needed to profit from fundamental investigations into the general tasks of problem solving and into specific domains of knowledge and skill. As Newell and Simon (1972) wrote,

> Turning to the performance–learning–development dimension, our emphasis on performance ... represents a scientific bet.... It is our judgment that in the present state of the art, the study of performance must be given precedence, even if the strategy is not costless. Both learning and development must then be incorporated in integral ways in the more complete and successful theory of human information processing that will emerge at a later state in the development of our science. (pp. 7–8)

The experimental and model-based analysis of competence grew rapidly. For example, psychologists such as James Greeno (1976) who were interested in education took seriously the importance of analyzing instructional objectives. Greeno contrasted the formulation of behavioral objectives with what he identified as cognitive objectives and cognitive task analysis, which involved applying the concepts of cognitive psychology to analyzing the structures of knowledge and the intellectual skills and processes that instruction was trying to foster. He pointed out that specifying the kinds of cognitive structures that are involved in performing criterion tasks might reveal otherwise unnoticed components of performance that instruction did not promote yet are necessary for the kinds of thinking and understanding that are its aim. He also provided cognitive definitions of understanding for topics such as fractions and Euclidean geometry by identifying representations of procedural concepts and the knowledge structures involved in solving problems. Greeno attempted to exemplify the kinds of representations that fostered meaningful solutions and, thereby, to reveal why the rote mechanical procedures frequently learned in the classroom fail to produce real learning (see also Resnick, 1976).

Knowledge and Expertise

As scientific findings from cognitive psychology, artificial intelligence (AI), and cognitive science studies of complex performance emerged, the significance of integrated knowledge became clear. The focus earlier, in the pioneering work on problem solving and thinking on relatively knowledge-lean tasks, shifted to work in knowledge-rich domains that addressed how structures of knowledge were generated by, and interacted with, cognitive processes. It appeared that a significant characteristic of individuals who display higher order ability in complex performances is the possession of an organized, accessible body of conceptual and procedural knowledge. Evidence from a variety of sources converged on this conclusion, including findings in developmental psychology on children's reasoning strategies, experimental and AI studies of expert and novice problem solving, and process analyses of intelligence and aptitude test tasks (Glaser, 1984). Cognitive task analysis now incorporated techniques for depicting the structure and utilization of the organized knowledge stored in memory in production systems, semantic and procedural networks, and schema representations. For scientists who were interested in learning and development, it became a pressing matter to understand how complex cognitive structures were modified and restructured (Glaser, 1989).

A fruitful program in the analysis of the role of domain knowledge in performance has been the extensive work contrasting experts with novices on various dimensions of performance (Chi, Glaser, & Farr, 1988). A fundamental issue in accounting for expertise has been describing specific structural knowledge as well as the domain-specific and more general heuristic processes that interact with this knowledge. Studies of expert problem solving in domains ranging from chess, physics, medical diagnosis, computer programming, and skilled memory has led, in little more than a decade, to reasonably well-defined characterizations of expertise. Across these results, certain features have proved typical of proficient performance (Glaser, 1990). Chi and I (Chi & Glaser, 1988) have summarized these features in six overlapping categories:

1. Structured, principled knowledge: Experts' knowledge is well integrated. Proficient individuals store coherent chunks of information in memory that enable them to access meaningful patterns and principles rapidly.

2. Effective problem representation: Experts qualitatively assess the nature of a problem and build a mental model or representation from which they can make inferences and add constraints to reduce the problem space.

3. Proceduralized knowledge: Experts know when to use what they know. In proficient individuals, declarative and propositional knowledge are bound to conditions of applicability and procedures for use.

4. Skilled memory: Proficient individuals draw on their knowledge base in ways that reduce the role of memory search and circumvent limits of short-term memory capacity.

5. Automaticity: In expert performance, component skills are automatically executed, so that conscious processing capacity can be devoted to decision making with minimal interference in the overall performance.

6. Self-regulatory skills: Experts develop a critical set of self-regulatory or executive skills, which they use to monitor and control their performance.

In addition to the research contrasting experts' performances with novices', which has explicated these features of expertise in detail, a great deal of experimental and theoretical effort is now providing knowledge about levels of proficiency in the various domains of schooling (Glaser & Takanishi, 1986; Resnick, 1989). The growing understanding of competence that this work yields will undoubtedly have important implications for new theories of learning and instruction; in it a basis is being laid for description of those changes that cognitive science must explain and that must be considered in the design of conditions for education.

Initial State and Prior Capabilities

Aptitudes and Learning

In the history of psychology, the study of individual differences and the experimental investigation of learning and performance have had only fleeting contact; however, the requirements of a theory of instruction have made consideration of such contact mandatory. The problem of adapting alternative learning conditions to individual differences received a burst of attention in the 1960s when a set of studies appeared on *aptitude–treatment interaction*; the working thesis for this research was that current measures of aptitudes and traits could be useful in designing adaptive instruction. If measures of individual differences and instructional variables could be shown to interact differentially, students could be assigned one of a set of alternative treatments to obtain optimal instructional payoff. As a result of this research, little evidence was found, however, to suggest that individual differences in general ability and aptitude were useful in choosing instructional conditions for students, although the measures correlated generally with achievement in most school-related tasks. In general, low-aptitude students did better under structured instruction, which appeared to reduce the burden of information processing (Bracht, 1970; Cronbach & Snow, 1977; Snow, 1977). An explanation for these results appeared to be that, in most of the studies reported, aptitude measures were selected from available tests and then learning treatments were chosen on the basis of the variables then being investigated in experimental studies of learning. Individual differences were not analyzed in terms of systematic descriptions of the psychological processes that would be called on, nor were alternative instructional treatments generated by analyses of these processes. These negative results underlined the fact that aptitude constructs had grown out of a psychometric, selection-oriented tradition that was separate from the analyses of processes of learning and performance. But, during the 1960s, a notion was developing that promised to be more fruitful; individual difference variables were beginning to be conceptualized in terms of the process constructs of contemporary theory of human performance.

Processes of Aptitude and Intelligence

With the growth of cognitive information processing analyses, the tasks that assessed performance on aptitude and intelligence tests were subjected to theoretical and empirical analyses (Carroll, 1976; Hunt, 1978; Hunt, Frost, & Lunneborg, 1973; Pellegrino & Glaser, 1982; Sternberg, 1977, 1985). The two main approaches were characterized as *cognitive correlates* and *cognitive components* (Pellegrino & Glaser, 1979). The first sought to correlate the differences between high- and low-verbal ability groups, as measured on aptitude and intelligence tests, with key variables studied in models of information processes in short- and long-term memory (Hunt, 1978). The components approach (Estes, 1974) directly focused on aptitude and intelligence test items as tasks to be analyzed in a search for the component processes of performance. The tasks studied were memory span, as presented in the Stanford-Binet and Wechsler tests, and analogy and series completion items, which loaded on a general inductive reasoning factor early identified by Spearman (1923). Sternberg (1985) emphasized this approach, which he called *componential analyses*. His work led to a theory of intelligence that has become the basis for the design of instructional programs that attempt to develop component skills of intelligent performance (Sternberg, 1986). From a different perspective, Gardner (1983; Gardner & Hatch, 1989) argued for domain-specific intelligences—linguistic, musical, logical-mathematical, spatial, bodily-kinesic, and personal. This perspective highlights the significance of multiple approaches to learning.

The process analysis of aptitude and intelligence tasks, as well as the research on problem solving and the components of competence and expertise, have been accompanied by increased emphasis on improvements in teaching learning and thinking skills in school programs (Chipman, Segal, & Glaser, 1985; Glaser, 1984; Resnick, 1987; Segal, Chipman, & Glaser, 1985). Theoretical and educational issues center around teaching problem-solving strategies and heuristics that could enhance both learning abilities and the outcomes of education (Bransford, Sherwood, Vye, & Rieser, 1986; Perkins & Salomon, 1989; Resnick, 1987).

Cognitive Development

The view that knowledge plays a major role in even early learning has been encouraged by modern theories of human development that hypothesize that even young children's abilities depend on the extent of their knowledge. It is a view that stands in contrast to Piagetian and other stagelike theories that posit qualitative changes in general logical capacities. It is now clear that gains in children's knowledge in specific content domains may underlie changes in their reasoning that were previously attributed to the development of general capabilities. Much developmental research now focuses on establishing the relations between prior knowledge and such cognitive activities as accessing memory (Chi, 1978), organizing and coordinating information (Scardamalia & Bereiter, 1989), making inferences (Carey, 1985; Crisafi & Brown, 1983; Gobbo & Chi, 1986), discovering new strategies (Siegler & Jenkins, 1989), and categorizing objects (Smith, 1989). In addition, models of development no longer represent thinking ability as being added on after specific knowledge has been acquired. Rather, it is widely acknowledged that domain knowledge and intellectual skill develop coordinately at all stages of competence.

In developmental psychology, growing attention to the role of knowledge has encouraged three intertwined strands of research that influence instructional theory. First, over the past 20 years, an impressive body of information has emerged about competences that infants and young children possess that were long believed to develop much later in childhood. A very wide array of capabilities have been studied, including understanding speech sounds (Eimas, 1982), recognizing faces (Barrera & Maurer, 1981), grouping by number (Antell & Keating, 1983), and making causal inferences (Borton, 1979; Leslie, 1982). This work provides insight into how early knowledge is organized, including constraints on its development (Keil, 1981). Second, an important line of developmental research has described, particularly in the past decade, the naive conceptions and misconceptions that affect formal learning, sometimes supporting it, as in young children's understanding of number and principles of counting (Ginsberg, 1977; Resnick, 1986), and sometimes impeding it, as in science learning (Carey, 1985; West & Pines, 1985). Because misconceptions are not only present before instruction but also may persist long after students receive relevant instruction, this work is particularly important for understanding conceptual change and for designing teaching tactics that foster lasting changes in knowledge.

The third emphasis in research in this area has been the metacognitive or executive control strategies that children and adults use to access task-relevant information and to oversee its use. People vary in the facility with which they check their progress in learning, judge problem difficulty, apportion attentional resources, allocate time, ask questions to elaborate their knowledge, and predict the outcomes of their performance. These skills boost learning because they enhance knowledge use. Cultivating them, in concert with the acquisition of school subject-matter skill and knowledge, is a current focus of studies of major instructional interventions (Brown & Palinscar, 1989; Cognition and Technology Group at Vanderbilt, 1990; Scardamalia & Bereiter, in press).

The contributions of developmental psychology to description of initial states and prior capabilities can be of significance to educational practices. Equally important, the study of development, by definition, is concerned not primarily with states but with change over time, and a mainstream issue in developmental psychology is providing findings and theoretical accounts on the mechanisms that are responsible for cognitive change.

Instruction and Conditions for Learning

In the 1950s, psychologists knew more about learning than about the competence and expertise that learning produces. Since then, the situation has reversed. Cognitive psychology has focused on the structures and processes of human competence and on the nature of the performance system as a consequence of learning and development, and less attention has been given to processes of acquisition. But at present, theories of learning are emerging, interestingly enough, from experimental attempts at instruction. Scientists are designing instructional programs to teach complex forms of knowledge and skill, and in the course of these "engineering" attempts, are articulating learning theory and instructional principles. Although other forms of experimental study and investigation of machine learning are contributing, it appears that learning theory is emerging from studies that take principled approaches to application.

What is common to exemplary work in this area is grounding in cognitive task analysis; that is, the objectives of instruction are based on current knowledge of the characteristics of competent performance on a task (Glaser & Bassok, 1989). The three examples described here address different forms of competence, in separate domains of knowledge, each deriving from a somewhat distinct research tradition. Each program emphasizes one of the three forms of competence: (a) the compiled, automatized, and proceduralized knowledge characteristic of a well-developed cognitive skill; (b) the effective use of internalized self-regulatory control strategies for fostering comprehension; and (c) the integrating and structuring of knowledge for explanation and problem solving. The domains include mathematical problem solving, computer programming, reading comprehension, and medical diagnosis.

Proceduralized Knowledge and Skill

A widely discussed set of instructional programs, in which the objective is the acquisition of efficient procedural cognitive skill and in which learning theory is unusually explicit, has been developed by a group led by John Anderson. Computer tutoring programs for three complex, well-defined skills have been designed: programming in LISP (Anderson, Farrell, & Sauers, 1984), generating geometry proofs (Anderson, Boyle, & Yost, 1985), and solving algebraic equations (Lewis, Milson, & Anderson, 1988). The major learning mechanism posited by Anderson's ACT* theory is *knowledge compilation*, which accounts for the transition process that turns declarative knowledge, initially encoded from text or from the teacher's instruction, into proceduralized, use-oriented knowledge. The theory holds that effective procedural knowledge can be acquired only by actually using declarative knowledge in solving problems. First, during solution, it is assumed that learners draw on declarative knowledge as they apply general problem-solving processes, using domain-general methods such as means–ends search or analogy to an example. Subsequently, the process of knowledge compilation creates efficient, domain-specific productions (condition–action rules) from the trace of the initial problem-solving episode. Compilation consists of two major submechanisms, *proceduralization* and *composition*. Proceduralization results from comparing the problem states before and after generating the solution and creates production rules— the building blocks of the skill. Composition, analogous to chunking, collapses a sequence of productions into a single, efficient action. This process of knowledge compilation is assumed to be an automatic learning mechanism, and the major instructional principles involved in the design of the tutors are derived from theoretical assumptions about this process.

The production-rule architecture explicates how students execute the skill that is to be taught and comprises a performance model that corresponds to an ideal student's performance and to "buggy" variations of the student's rules at various stages of skill development. The learner's actual performance is compared in real time with the rules in the model, and the tutoring system tries to keep the student on a correct solution path. The student's history of correct and incorrect applications of productions gives an estimate of the availability and the strength of the productions comprising the skill. Tracking changes across problems enables the tutor to select problems appropriate to the student's knowledge state to optimize learning.

In general, Anderson's (Anderson et al., 1984, 1985; Lewis et al., 1988) theory and work are continuous with a learning tradition in experimental psychology. The tutor's close control of the learning process, the immediate feedback during problem solving, the focus on minimizing errors, and the gradual approximation of the expert's behavior by accumulating components of the skill are reminiscent of Skinnerian shaping and successive approximation. The cognitive sophistication of Anderson's theory, however, further requires organizing the productions according to the problem-solving structure of goals and subgoals, as well as introducing an intelligent component to the instructional system to trace the student's performance.

Self-Regulatory Skills and Performance Control Strategies

Another set of instructional studies focuses on self-regulatory strategies and apprenticeship experiences as means for studying knowledge and skill acquisition. Instructional programs in reading comprehension (Brown & Palinscar, 1984, 1989), writing (Scardamalia,

Bereiter, & Steinbach, 1984), and mathematics (Cognition and Technology Group at Vanderbilt, 1990; Schoenfeld, 1985) have been designed to foster the development of self-regulatory skills (Collins, Brown, & Newman, 1988). Brown and Palinscar's program for reading comprehension is an excellent representative. Students in this program, which is called reciprocal teaching, acquire specific knowledge and also learn a set of strategies for elaborating and monitoring their understanding. Three major components of the program are (a) provision, initially by a teacher, of an expert model of executive strategies—questioning, summarizing, clarifying, and predicting in the course of reading text; (b) instruction and practice with these metacognitive processes, which enable students to monitor their understanding; and (c) a social setting that enables joint negotiation for understanding and apprenticeship experiences. With the help of a teacher who provides expert scaffolding, the collaborative group maintains a mature, nondecomposed version of a target task. By sharing it, a complex task is made more manageable without simplifying the task itself. Each learner contributes what he or she can and gains from the contributions of those more expert. In the Vygotskian (1978) sense, a *zone of proximal development* is created where learners perform within their range of competence while being assisted in realizing higher levels of performance.

Several general concepts from developmental psychology influence this approach. The first is that conceptual change is self-directed in the sense that humans are intrinsically motivated to understand the world around them and to explain events to extend their knowledge (Gelman & Brown, 1986). The second general concept derives from theories that emphasize learning's social genesis. Conceptual development in children involves internalizing cognitive activities originally experienced in social settings. Thus, the process of generating explanations is believed to be internalized gradually, and *internalization* (Vygotsky, 1978) is considered a key mechanism of learning. In general, the view that learning and thinking are essentially the individual's enactment of activities experienced in social participation underlies the focus on group activity. Cooperative learning provides social support and rewards for individual efforts. The group extends the locus of cognitive activity by providing sources of dissatisfaction outside the individual and by supplying both expert models and alternative points of view that challenge current understandings.

The procedural skill programs and the metacognitive programs present very different views of the learner. The knowledge compilation approach sees the learner as striving for efficiency in performing a well-defined skill, whereas the metacognitive programs conceive of the learner as motivated to explore and seek explanations. Those who adhere to the metacognitive approach fault current modes of schooling because students often acquire skills mechanically; although efficient, these skills remain inert knowledge, inaccessible except in the circumstances in which they were learned. An interesting issue is whether the extensive practice required to attain reasonable efficiency and automaticity in basic procedural skills might be achieved not only in highly structured environments in which students practice subcomponent procedures but also in the context of the mature task format of a cooperative learning group.

Interrogating Expert Knowledge Structures

A third approach uses a model of expert knowledge to guide the design of an intelligent tutoring system. It is reminiscent of earlier research by Carbonell and Collins (1973) that made the analysis of information structures in the form of knowledge networks a basis for instruction. This work assumed an ideal model of the organization of knowledge as it might exist in human memory. Instruction proceeded as the student interrogated this structure and the program provided information about errors that reflected differences between the student's knowledge structure and the ideal structure.

A more recent effort is an instructional system designed by Clancey (1986) that has evolved into the AI tradition of knowledge engineering and the construction of expert systems. The base of expertise is a structure of knowledge, in this case for medical diagnosis, that represents an expert's understanding of the domain as well as a large number of problem-solving routines (Clancey & Letsinger, 1984). This knowledge base is organized into categories of general principles that underlie domain knowledge (e.g., definitions, taxonomic relations, causal relations) and includes heuristic rules and strategies. The reasoning strategies revolve around the management of hypotheses, including grouping hypotheses into more general cases, refining them into special cases, differentiating them, and so forth. The instructional objective is not only specific expertise in medical diagnosis but also a set of interrogation and inference processes used to construct an organized body of functional knowledge.

The learning process in this approach is driven by detection and explanation of problem-solving failures that result from the learner's efforts to apply existing knowledge. The learning objective is to acquire new knowledge in the context of generating a causal explanation that links conclusions to findings. This conception emphasizes the learner's role in directing learning, which requires generating plausible conjectures about missing knowledge and posing focused questions to an expert teacher. Given a case, the student acts as a diagnostician, gathering data to guide hypothesis generation and testing. The system displays attempts at solution as a progressive extension of a graph that links conclusions to findings until the graph represents all of the relations for the case. After detecting a failure, which is indicated by the lack of a link in the solution graph, the student has to generate possible repairs by reasoning about additional domain knowledge. She or he then articulates the nature of the deficiency by posing a specific question to the system. If the information provided in response proves sufficient to generate the desired link, the student updates his or her knowledge base accordingly. This approach makes the acquisition of new declarative knowledge a conscious process of error detection and repair. Knowledge acquisition is engineered by teaching strategies for observing and interrogating the expert and by displaying the knowledge updating and restructuring that occur during learning (see also White & Frederiksen, 1986).

Commentary

In the programs just described, different views of the learning process are apparent, raising the question of whether such differentiation of learning theory is necessary to account for different kinds of performance. Even if we accept that it will be difficult to achieve a unified theory of learning, we should attempt to discover grounds for integrating the key aspects of human competence that are considered separately in these programs. The programs for proceduralization of declarative knowledge allow only minimal attention to the structuring of knowledge and do not deal with self-regulation. The instruction that focuses on self-regulatory skills in cooperative learning or on knowledge restructuring attend less to issues of efficiency and automaticity. It is good science to avoid confounded effects, but the eventual objective in these studies is obviously not isolated phenomena. Competence is characterized by both efficiency and principled understanding, by both fast pattern recognition and conscious monitoring. The processes of knowledge and skill acquisition and the various learning mechanisms involved do not operate in isolation.

A major instructional research task may be to design programs that test approaches to the integration of competent performance. For example, a developmental study with children has shown that the ability to establish an appropriate conceptual representation constrains acquisition of strategies and procedures but, at the same time, that the degree of procedural efficiency constrains the complexity of children's representations (Case & Sandieson, 1988a, 1988b). In other research, training studies have shown that procedural skill is effectively acquired in the context of a supporting mental model of organized knowledge (Gott, 1988; Kieras & Bovair, 1984; White & Frederiksen, 1986).

Attempts at integration promise to provide new grounds for the development of encompassing theories of learning.

Finally, on the issue of learning, investigation of instruction now seems to be a significant tool for building and applying learning theory. In an expanding array of school domains, researchers together with teachers are designing and studying new environments for learning (Brown & Campione, 1990; Cognition and Technology Group at Vanderbilt, 1990; Lampert, 1986; Minstrell, 1989; Scardamalia & Bereiter, 1989). In a mature science, work on basic theory is often invigorated by goal-oriented technology, and perhaps at this time in the history of the study of learning, the close coupling of theorizing and practical development will encourage fundamental science, as well as improvements in education and training.

Assessment of the Outcomes of Learning

In contrast with the technology of aptitude and intelligence testing, the underlying theory of the assessment of achievement in subject-matter learning is poorly developed and derives primarily from behavioral objectives that have not adequately focused on complex processes of reasoning, problem solving, and expertise. In addition, techniques for measuring achievement and the growth of competence have relied on the psychometric technology that emerged in the context of selection and aptitude testing and is not particularly appropriate for assessing levels of learning. To ascertain the critical differences between successful and unsuccessful student performance, we need to assess the knowledge structures and cognitive processes that reveal degrees of competence in a field of study. Much of current testing technology is post hoc and focuses on statistical test properties after artful designers construct test items. Recognizing this, a number of researchers have begun to think about how theories of cognition and performance might underpin item design and new forms of assessment that are responsive to educational practices (Frederiksen, 1984; Glaser, 1981; Linn, 1986; Mislevy, 1989; Snow & Lohman, 1989).

Integration of Teaching and Testing

A concept that illuminates a new attitude toward testing has been given new form in a recent article by Gardner (1990). Gardner calls his approach to education *individually configured excellence.* In the context of modern theory of human development, individually configured excellence bears some resemblance to a notion that I attempted to describe some years ago, *adaptive education,* in which I contrasted a selective educational mode with one designed to support inclusiveness and the cultivation of talent (Glaser, 1972, 1977).

Adaptive education assumes that the educational environment can provide a range of opportunities. Conditions for learning and modes of teaching are adjusted to individuals—their backgrounds, talents, interests, and the natures of past performances and experiences. Assessments occur so that information about progress toward instructional goals is available to both the teacher and the student as learning proceeds and, in turn, is related to subsequent alternate opportunities for problem solving and learning. The effect of the student's choice or assignment to a learning opportunity is evaluated on the basis of the progress that he or she makes in realizing goals of competence and potential for future learning. This adaptive mode is especially relevant to today's aspirations for schooling and the requirements of education. As we become a more pluralistic society than at any time in our history, aspects of schooling that make sense in relatively homogeneous societies will not be workable.

In adaptive education or individually configured excellence, learning and achievement are regularly monitored as an integral part of schooling. Assessment has a certain naturalness; meaningful competence is displayed regularly in the context of the activities of a community of learners, as contrasted with the decontextualized, isolated, and competitive performances currently required by testing. Students learn to assess their own performances and to rely on group feedback and commentary about their work as a form of assessment. Although students have flexibility in acquiring knowledge and skill, the criteria for attainment can be rigorous and require increasing competence and expertise.

Assessment instruments and procedures that are integral to instruction rather than stand outside of it are now being developed. Various lines of research on instruction are laying the grounds for testing practices that will be geared to the design of adaptive learning opportunities in which students monitor their performances and observe the performances of more competent individuals. The emphasis on cognition suggests the increasing salience, in the future, of certain features that can assure that new assessment procedures enhance learning (California Mathematics Council, 1989; Frederiksen & Collins, 1989; Gardner, 1991; R. Linn, personal communication, March 12, 1990; Wiggins, 1989).

1. Testing will involve more extended tasks and contextualized skills. Assessment will be more representative of meaningful tasks and subject-matter goals. A testing exercise will provide a worthwhile instructional experience that illustrates the relevance and utility of the knowledge and skill being acquired and its transferability to different circumstances. Traditional tests may provide adequate content coverage, but they can neglect many significant processes of competence. Increasingly, assessments will employ situations in which students write about their approach to a problem, the questions that come to mind, and the explanations for their solutions.

2. Knowledge and skills, in the future, will be measured so that the processes and products of learning are openly displayed. There will be fewer examples of indirect measurement procedures that use formats for multiple choice or controlled scoring. The criteria of performance by which students will be judged will be transparent so that these criteria can motivate and direct learning.

3. Testing will involve the teaching of self-assessment. Because assessment and instruction will be integrally related, instructional situations will provide coaching and practice in ways that help students reflect on their performance and acquire the self-regulatory skills to do this. Such occasions for assessment will enable students to set incremental standards by which they can judge their own achievement and develop self-direction for attaining higher performance levels.

4. Testing will be more socially situated. Assessment situations in which the student participates in group activity will be used. Performance in a social setting in which students contribute to a task and assist others has the advantage of encouraging students to develop and question their definitions of competence. The student can observe how others reason and receive feedback on his or her own efforts. In this context, not only performance but also the facility with which a student adapts to help and guidance can be assessed.

5. Tests will be judged in terms of their effectiveness in leading teachers to devote time to certain concepts, content, and cognitive skills in the curriculum. Scores will be interpreted in terms of their instructional effects; they should inform the development of classroom activities that are conducive to expressed learning goals.

Overall, the development of a theory of assessment will necessitate the analysis of the cognitive aspects of a task and the processes of performance that are entailed. At present, a significant research agenda is emerging for integrating cognitive psychology and psychometrics, and it should have a formative influence on the nature of testing in education.

Summary and Conclusions

Two criteria can be used for judging the status of the relation between psychological science and education. One is scientific advances made in the four components of instructional theory, if these are, indeed, the right rubrics for analysis. A second criterion is the extent to which psychological knowledge enables the development of theory to guide teaching and education, as well as to describe the processes of learning. Given the growth of research on instructional innovations that also promise advances in learning theory, psychological science and education can now be seen as having entered a period of mutually beneficial relationship (Bransford & Vye, 1989). If one looks at advances in the various components of instructional theory, it is apparent that rich descriptions are becoming available of the cognitive processes of skilled performance, of thinking and understanding, and of the dimensions of competence in various domains. Considerable progress also is now being made in describing abilities for learning, initial states of competence that contribute to individual differences, and self-regulatory strategies on which learning can build.

With respect to learning theory, cognitive instructional psychology is embarking on a new enterprise; learning must now be described in terms of modern conceptions of cognition, including the constructive capabilities of learners and the processes of knowledge and skill acquisition that are assisted in problem solving and social interaction. Although experimental studies of human and artificial learning are proceeding, educationally relevant experiments are being carried out through attempts at instructional intervention. In this work, scientists are applying hypotheses about the acquisition of knowledge and skill to contribute to change in educational practices and, at the same time, define theory through application. We may have entered a phase in the study of cognition in which the interplay between theory and application can yield significant contribution to both.

New conceptions for the assessment of learning outcomes seem likely to have rapid payoff. Theories and techniques for the measurement of human performance can be built from rich findings in the analyses of competence and initial state. At the same time, assessment in the context of innovative conditions for learning can be studied. The improved measurement of human attainment should contribute to a science of instruction because appropriate measures will be available to evaluate the successes and shortfalls of our knowledge of competence, initial state, and conditions of acquisition, given that this knowledge shapes educational systems. Finally, on the basis of cognitive descriptions of competence, assessments will indicate where integrated knowledge, thinking and problem solving skills, and abilities for new learning can be better developed by instruction.

References

Anastasia, A. (1967). Psychology, psychologists, and psychological testing. *American Psychologist, 22,* 297–306.

Anderson, J. R., Boyle, C. F., & Yost, G. (1985). The geometry tutor. In *Proceedings of the International Joint Conference on Artificial Intelligence* (pp. 1–7). Los Angeles; CA: International Joint Conference on Artificial Intelligence.

Anderson, J. R., Farrell, R., & Sauers, R. (1984). Learning to program in LISP. *Cognitive Science, 8,* 87–129.

Antell, S. E., & Keating, D. P. (1983). Perception of numerical invariance in neonates. *Child Development, 54,* 695–701.

Atkinson, R. C., & Paulson, J. (1972). An approach to the psychology of instruction. *Psychological Bulletin, 78,* 49–61.

Barrera, M. E., & Maurer, D. (1981). Perception of facial expression by the three-month-old. *Child Development, 52,* 203–206.

Borton, R. (1979, March). *The perception of causality in infants.* Paper presented at the meeting of the Society for Research in Child Development, San Francisco, CA.

Bracht, G. H. (1970). Experimental factors related to aptitude-treatment interactions. *Review of Educational Research, 40,* 627–645.

Bransford, J. D., Sherwood, R., Vye, N., & Rieser, J. (1986). Teaching thinking and problem solving. *American Psychologist, 41,* 1078–1089.

Bransford, J. D., & Vye, N. (1989). A perspective on cognitive research and its implications for instruction. In L. B. Resnick & L. E. Klopfer (Eds.), *Toward the thinking curriculum: Current cognitive research* (pp. 173–205). Alexandria, VA: Association for Supervision and Curriculum Development.

Brown, A. L., & Campione, J. C. (1990). Communities of learning and thinking, or a context by any other name. In D. Kuhn (Ed.), *Contributions to human development: Vol. 21. Developmental perspective on teaching and learning thinking skills* (pp. 108–126). Basil, Switzerland: Karger.

Brown, A. L., & Palinscar, A. S. (1984). Reciprocal teaching of comprehension-fostering and monitoring activities. *Cognition Instruction, 1,* 175–177.

Brown, A. L., & Palinscar, A. S. (1989). Guided cooperative learning and individual knowledge acquisition. In L. B. Resnick (Ed.), *Knowing, learning, and instruction: Essays in honor of Robert Glaser* (pp. 393–451). Hillsdale, NJ: Erlbaum.

Bruner, J. S. (1960). *The process of education.* Cambridge, MA: Harvard University Press.

Bruner, J. S. (1966). *Toward a theory of instruction.* New York: Norton.

California Mathematics Council. (1989). *Assessment alternatives in mathematics: An overview of assessment techniques that promote learning.* Berkeley, CA: EQUALS.

Carbonell, J. R., & Collins, A. (1973). Natural semantics in artificial intelligence. In *Proceedings of the Third International Joint Conference on Artificial Intelligence* (pp. 344–351). Stanford, CA: Stanford University Press.

Carey, S. (1985). *Conceptual change in childhood.* Cambridge, MA: MIT Press.

Carroll, J. B. (1976). Psychometric tests as cognitive tasks: A new "structure of intellect." In L. B. Resnick (Ed.), *The nature of intelligence* (pp. 27–56). Hillsdale, NJ: Erlbaum.

Carroll, J. B. (1982). The measure of intelligence. In R. J. Sternberg (Ed.), *Handbook of human intelligence* (pp. 29–120). Cambridge, England: Cambridge University Press.

Case, R., & Sandieson, R. (1988a). A developmental approach to the identification and teaching of central conceptual structures in middle school science and mathematics. In M. Behr & J. Hiebert (Eds.), *Research agenda in mathematics education: Number concepts and operations in the middle grades* (pp. 236–259). Hillsdale, NJ: Erlbaum.

Case, R., & Sandieson, R. (1988b). *General conceptual constraints on the acquisition of specific procedural skills (and vice versa).* Paper presented at the annual meeting of the American Educational Research Association, New Orleans, LA.

Chi, M. T. H. (1978). Knowledge structures and memory development. In R. Siegler (Ed.), *Children's thinking: What develops?* (pp. 73–96). Hillsdale, NJ: Erlbaum.

Chi, M. T. H., & Glaser, R. (1988). Overview. In M. T. H. Chi, R. Glaser, & M. J. Farr (Eds.), *The nature of expertise* (pp. xv–xxviii). Hillsdale, NJ: Erlbaum.

Chi, M. T. H., Glaser, R., & Farr, M. (Eds.) (1988). *The nature of expertise.* Hillsdale, NJ: Erlbaum.

Chipman, S. F., Segal, J. W., & Glaser, R. (Eds.). (1985). *Thinking and learning skills: Research and open questions* (Vol. 2). Hillsdale, NJ: Erlbaum.

Clancey, W. J. (1986). From GUIDON to NEOMYCIN and HERACLES in twenty short lessons: ONR final report 1979–1985. *AI Magazine, 7,* 40–60.

Clancey, W. J., & Letsinger, R. (1984). NEOMYCIN: Reconfiguring a rule-based expert system for application to teaching. In W. J. Clancey & E. H. Shortliffe (Eds.), *Medical artificial intelligence: The first decade* (pp. 361–381). Reading, MA: Addison-Wesley.

Cognition and Technology Group at Vanderbilt. (1990). Anchored instruction and its relationship to situated cognition. *Educational Researcher, 19,* 2–10.

Collins, A., Brown, J. S., & Newman, S. E. (1988). Cognitive apprenticeship: Teaching the craft of reading, writing, and mathematics. In L. B. Resnick (Ed.), *Knowing, learning, and instruction: Essays in honor of Robert Glaser* (pp. 453–494). Hillsdale, NJ: Erlbaum.

Crisafi, M., & Brown, A. L. (1983, April). *Flexible use of an inferential reasoning rule.* Paper presented at the meeting of the Society for Research in Child Development, Detroit, MI.

Cronbach, L. J. (1957). The two disciplines of scientific psychology. *American Psychologist, 12,* 671–684.

Cronbach, L. J., & Snow, R. E. (1977). *Aptitudes and instructional methods: A handbook for research on interactions.* New York: Irvington.

Dewey, J. (1900). Psychology and practice. *Psychological Review, 7,* 105–124.

Eimas, P. D. (1982). Speech perception: A view of the initial state and perceptual mechanisms. In J. Mehler, E. C. T. Walker, & M. Garrett (Eds.), *Perspectives on mental representations* (pp. 339–360). Hillsdale, NJ: Erlbaum.

Estes, W. K. (1974). Learning theory and intelligence. *American Psychologist, 29,* 740–749.

Fitts, P. M. (1965). Factors in complex skilled training. In R. Glaser (Ed.), *Training research and education* (pp. 177–197). New York: Wiley.

Frederiksen, N. (1984). The rest test bias: Influences of testing on teaching and learning. *American Psychologist, 39,* 193–202.

Frederiksen, J. R., & Collins, A. (1989). A system's approach to educational testing. *Educational Researcher, 18,* 27–32.

Gagne, R. M. (1962). The acquisition of knowledge. *Psychological Review, 69,* 355–365.

Gagne, R. M. (1965). *The conditions of learning.* New York: Holt, Rinehart & Winston.

Gagne, R. M. (1970). *The conditions of learning* (2nd ed.). New York: Holt, Rinehart & Winston.

Gagne, R. M., & Rohwer, W. D., Jr. (1969). Instructional psychology. *Annual Review of Psychology, 20,* 381–418.

Gardner, H. (1983). *Frames of mind: The theory of multiple intelligences.* New York: Basic Books.

Gardner, H. (1990). The difficulties of school: Probable causes, possible cures. *Daedallus: Journal of the American Academy of Arts and Sciences, 119,* 85–113.

Gardner, H. (1991). Assessment in context: The alternative to standardized testing. In B. R. Gifford & M. C. O'Connor (Eds.), *Changing assessments: Alternative views of aptitude, achievement, and instruction* (pp. 77–120). Norwell, MA: Kluwer Academic.

Gardner, H., & Hatch, T. (1989). Multiple intelligences go to school. *Educational Researcher, 18,* 4–10.

Gelman, R., & Brown, A. L. (1986). Changing competence in the young. In N. J. Smelser & D. R. Gerstein (Eds.), *Behavioral and social science: Fifty years of discovery* (pp. 175–209). Hillsdale, NJ: Erlbaum.

Ginsberg, H. P. (1977). *Children's arithmetic: The learning process.* New York: Van Nostrand Reinhold.

Glaser, R. (Ed.). (1965). *Training research and education.* New York: Wiley. (Original work published 1962)

Glaser, R. (1972). Individuals and learning: The new aptitudes. *Educational Researcher, 1,* 5–13.

Glaser, R. (1976). Components of a psychology of instruction: Toward a science of design. *Review of Educational Research, 46,* 1–24.

Glaser, R. (1977). *Adaptive education: Individual diversity and learning.* New York: Holt, Rinehart and Winston.

Glaser, R. (1978). The contributions of B. F. Skinner to education and some counterinfluences. In P. Suppes (Ed.), *Impact of research on education* (pp. 199–265). Washington, DC: National Academy of Education.

Glaser, R. (1981). The future of testing: A research agenda for cognitive psychology and psychometrics. *American Psychologist, 36,* 923–936.

Glaser, R. (1984). Education and thinking: The role of knowledge. *American Psychologist, 39,* 93–104.

Glaser, R. (1989). Expertise and learning: How do we think about instructional processes now that we have discovered knowledge structures? In D. Klahr & K. Kotovsky (Eds.), *Complex information processing: The impact of Herbert A. Simon* (pp. 269–282). Hillsdale, NJ: Erlbaum.

Glaser, R. (1990). Expertise. In M. W. Eysenck, A. Ellis, & E. Hunt (Eds.), *The Blackwell dictionary of cognitive psychology*. Oxford, England: Basil Blackwell.

Glaser, R., & Bassok, M. (1989). Learning theory and the study of instruction. In M. R. Rosenzweig & L. W. Porter (Eds.), *Annual review of psychology* (Vol. 40, pp. 631–666). Palo Alto, CA: Annual Reviews.

Glaser, R., & Resnick, L. B. (1972). Instructional psychology. In P. H. Mussen & M. R. Rosenzweig (Eds.), *Annual review of psychology* (Vol. 23, pp. 207–276). Palo Alto, CA: Annual Reviews.

Glaser, R., & Takanishi, R. (Eds.). (1986). Psychological science and education [Special issue]. *American Psychologist, 41*(10).

Gobbo, C., & Chi, M. (1986). How knowledge is structured and used by expert and novice children. *Cognitive Development, 1,* 221–237.

Gott, S. (1988). Apprenticeship instruction for real-world cognitive tasks: The coordination of procedures, mental models, and strategies. In E. Z. Rothkopf (Ed.), *Review of research on education* (pp. 97–169). Washington, DC: American Educational Research Association.

Greeno, J. G. (1976). Cognitive objectives of instruction: Theory of knowledge for solving problems and answering questions. In D. Klahr (Ed.), *Cognition and instruction* (pp. 123–159). Hillsdale, NJ: Erlbaum.

Hunt, E. (1978). Mechanics of verbal ability. *Psychological Review, 85,* 109–130.

Hunt, E., Frost, N., & Lunneborg, C. (1973). Individual differences in cognition: A new approach to cognition. In G. Bower (Ed.), *The psychology of learning and motivation* (Vol. 7, pp. 87–122). San Diego, CA: Academic Press.

Keil, F. (1981). Constraints on knowledge and cognitive development. *Psychology Review, 88,* 197–227.

Keller, F. S. (1958). The phantom plateau. *Journal of Experimental Analysis of Behavior, 1,* 1–13.

Kieras, D. E., & Bovair, S. (1984). The role of a mental model in learning to operate a device. *Cognitive Science, 8,* 225–273.

Klahr, D. (1976). *Cognition and instruction.* Hillsdale, NJ: Erlbaum.

Lampert, M. (1986). Knowing, doing, and teaching multiplication. *Cognition and Instruction, 3,* 305–342.

Lesgold, A. M., Pellegrino, J. W., Fokkema, S. D., & Glaser, R. (Eds.). (1978). *Cognitive psychology and instruction.* New York: Plenum Press.

Leslie, A. M. (1982). The perception of causality in infants. *Perception, 11,* 173–186.

Lewis, M. W., Milson, R., & Anderson, J. R. (1988). Designing an intelligent authoring system for high school mathematics ICAI: The teacher apprentice project. In G. Kearsley (Ed.), *Artificial intelligence and instruction: Applications and methods* (pp. 269–300). New York: Addison-Wesley.

Linn, R. (1986). Barriers to new test design. In E. E. Freeman (Ed.), *Proceedings of the 1985 ETS Invitational Conference: The redesign of testing for the 21st century* (pp. 69–79). Princeton, NJ: Educational Testing Service.

Lumsdaine, A. A., & Glaser, R. (1960). *Teaching machines and programmed learning: A source book.* Washington, DC: National Education Association.

Melton, A. W. (1957). Military psychology in the U.S.A. *American Psychologist, 12,* 740–746.

Melton, A. W. (Ed.). (1964). *Categories of human learning.* San Diego, CA: Academic Press.

Minstrell, J. A. (1989). Teaching science for understanding. In L. B. Resnick & L. E. Klopfer (Eds.), *Toward the thinking curriculum: Current cognitive research* (pp. 129–149). Alexandria, VA: Association for Supervision and Curriculum Development.

Mislevy, R. J. (1989). *Foundation of a new test theory.* Princeton, NJ: Educational Testing Service.

Newell, A., & Simon, H. A. (1972). *Human problem solving.* Englewood Cliffs, NJ: Prentice-Hall.

Pellegrino, J. W., & Glaser, R. (1979). Cognitive correlates and components in the analysis of individual differences. In R. J. Sternberg & D. K. Detterman (Eds.), *Human intelligence* (pp. 187–214). Norwood, NJ: Ablex.

Pellegrino, J. W., & Glaser, R. (1982). Analyzing aptitudes for learning: Inductive reasoning. In R. Glaser (Ed.), *Advances in instructional psychology* (Vol. 2, pp. 269–345). Hillsdale, NJ: Erlbaum.

Perkins, D. N., & Salomon, G. (1989). Are cognitive skills context-bound? *Educational Researcher, 18,* 16–25.

Resnick, L. B. (1976). Task analysis in instructional design: Some cases from mathematics. In D. Klahr (Ed.), *Cognition and instruction* (pp. 51–80). Hillsdale, NJ: Erlbaum.

Resnick, L. B. (1980). The role of invention in the development of mathematical competence. In R. Kluwe & J. Spada (Eds.), *Developmental models of thinking* (pp. 213–244). San Diego, CA: Academic Press.

Resnick, L. B. (1986). The development of mathematical intuition. In M. Perlmutter (Ed.), *Perspectives on intellectual development: The Minnesota Symposium on Child Psychology* (Vol. 19, pp. 159–194). Hillsdale, NJ: Erlbaum.

Resnick, L. (1987). *Education and learning to think.* Washington, DC: National Academy Press.

Resnick, L. B. (Ed.). (1989). *Knowing, learning, and instruction: Essays in honor of Robert Glaser.* Hillsdale, NJ: Erlbaum.

Scardamalia, M., & Bereiter, C. (1989, October). *Schools as knowledge-building communities.* Paper presented at the workshop on development and learning environments. University of Tel-Aviv, Israel.

Scardamalia, M., & Bereiter, C. (in press). Schools as knowledge-building communities. In S. Strauss (Ed.), *Human development* (Vol. 5). Norwood, NJ: Ablex.

Scardamalia, M., Bereiter, C., & Steinbach, R. (1984). Teachability of reflective processes in written composition. *Cognitive Science, 8,* 173–190.

Schoenfeld, A. H. (1985). *Mathematical problem solving.* San Diego, CA: Academic Press.

Segal, J. W., Chipman, S. F., & Glaser, R. (Eds.) (1985). *Thinking and learning skills: Relating instruction to research* (Vol. 1). Hillsdale, NJ: Erlbaum.

Siegler, R. S., & Jenkins, E. (1989). *How children discover new strategies.* Hillsdale, NJ: Erlbaum.

Skinner, B. F. (1954). The science of learning and the art of teaching. *Harvard Educational Review, 24,* 86–97.

Skinner, B. F. (1958). Teaching machines. *Science, 128,* 969–977.

Smith, L. B. (1989). From global similarities to kinds of similarities: The construction of dimensions in development. In S. Vosniadou and A. Ortony (Eds.), *Similarity and analogical reasoning* (pp. 146–178). Cambridge, England: Cambridge University Press.

Snow, R. E. (1977). Research on aptitude for learning: A progress report. In L. S. Shulman (Ed.), *Review of research in education* (Vol. 4, pp. 50–105). Itasca, IL: Peacock.

Snow, R. E., & Lohman, D. F. (1989). Implications of cognitive psychology for educational measurement. In R. L. Linn (Ed.), *Educational measurement* (3rd ed., pp. 263–331). Washington, DC: American Council on Education.

Spearman, C. (1923). *The nature of "intelligence" and the principles of cognition.* London: Macmillan.

Sternberg, R. J. (1977). *Intelligence, information processing, and analogical reasoning: The componential analysis of human abilities.* Hillsdale, NJ: Erlbaum.

Sternberg, R. J. (1985). *Beyond IQ.* Cambridge, England: Cambridge University Press.

Sternberg, R. J. (1986). *Intelligence applied.* San Diego, CA: Harcourt Brace Jovanovich.

Thorndike, E. L. (1922). *The psychology of arithmetic.* New York: Macmillan.

Vygotsky, L. S. (1978). *Mind in society: The development of higher psychological processes.* Cambridge, MA: Harvard University Press.

West, L., & Pines, A. (Eds.). (1985). *Cognitive structure and conceptual change.* San Diego, CA: Academic Press.

White, B. Y., & Frederiksen, J. R. (1986). *Progression of quantitative models as a foundation for intelligent learning environments* (Report No. 6277). Cambridge, MA: BBN Laboratories.

Wiggins, G. (1989). A true test: Toward more authentic and equitable assessment. *Phi Delta Kappan, 70,* 703–713.

CHAPTER 11

Preliminaries to a Theory of Culture Acquisition

Claudia Strauss and Naomi Quinn

C ulture is shared understanding, as well as the public customs and artifacts that embody these understandings (Quinn & Strauss, 1989). In the more exact terms of modern cognitive science, shared understandings are shared schemata. The question is how culture comes to be shared. How do different individuals come to have the same or similar schemata?

It may surprise outsiders to learn that this problem has been little studied, that there exists no cumulative, substantial field of culture acquisition comparable to the well-defined and flourishing field of language acquisition. There has been research on this topic, but most studies have taken a partial perspective, illuminating one aspect of culture acquisition without relating it to an overall theory. The result is that, with the exception of the landmark studies of the Whitings and their collaborators (J. Whiting, 1941; B. Whiting & J. Whiting, 1975; B. Whiting & Edwards, 1988), the terrain of culture acquisition

William Charlesworth, Katherine Ewing, Amy Sheldon, Julie Tetel, Albert Yonas, and the students in Claudia Strauss's "Language and Culture Acquisition" course at Duke University provided helpful comments on earlier versions of this chapter. We are grateful to the conference cochairs, Herbert Pick and Paul van den Broek, for organizing the stimulating conference at which this report was delivered. Most of all, we appreciate the willingness of our three young interviewees to talk to us about marriage.

resembles a vast plain on which have been built a few, scattered huts.[1] There are at least two reasons for this.

First, there has been little study of how culture learners arrive at shared understandings because the majority of cultural anthropologists do not even agree that culture involves shared understandings. For the past 15 years or so, most of our colleagues have defined culture as codes of meaning expressed in public events and objects, and they have disdained psychological questions about the knowledge and feelings of the people who enact those events, make those objects, and use those codes. According to this still influential view, there is no need to ask how culture is acquired; it is just there. This approach is starting to lose favor, but its unquestioned preeminence for many years helps explain why so little work has been done on the study of culture acquisition.

There is another reason as well, one that has less to do with the field of anthropology than with the distinctive properties of culture as a phenomenon and one at the heart of this chapter. Our aim in this chapter is to show that the process of culture acquisition is much more complex and problematic than that of language acquisition or some of the other sorts of learning discussed in this volume, such as learning motor skills or learning about perceptual invariances of various sorts. We will use pilot interviews we have conducted with three U.S. children on the topic of marriage to inform and illustrate our arguments.

A Schema-Theoretic View of Culture Acquisition

By *culture acquisition* we mean the acquisition of cultural models (Quinn & Holland, 1987), which are learned, shared schemata. Two clarifications of this definition are necessary. First, we take cultural models to include only those learned schemata that are held in common by some members of a social group or subgroup but not by all adult humans. (Learned object constancies, for example, are not an example of a cultural model.) Second, just as *schema* can be used to refer to a relatively simple cognitive representation (e.g., of the letter *A*) or to a complex representation (e.g., of ideas about war or honor),

---

[1] Some of this scattered research has been interesting. See, for example, Harkness and Kilbride (1983), Hollos and Leis (1989), Jahoda and Lewis (1988), Leiderman, Tulkin, and Rosenfeld (1977), LeVine (1977), Mayer (1970), Mead and Macgregor (1951), Mead and Wolfenstein (1955), Miller and Moore (1989), Schwartz (1976, 1981), Shweder and Much (1987), Shweder, Mahapatra, and Miller (1990), Skinner (1990), Skinner and Holland (1990), Super and Harkness (1980), and Weisner (1979, 1982). This list does not include relevant work on the anthropology or psychology of education, the numerous ethnographies that include information about culture acquisition, or much of the voluminous anthropological literature on child development. Another important subfield includes works such as Heath (1983), Miller (1982), Ochs (1988), Ochs and Schieffelin (1984), and Schieffelin and Ochs (1986), which focus on the acquisition of communicative competence, broadly defined, as a way of providing insight into culture acquisition.

we use *cultural model* to refer to anything from a simple, shared schema to a more complex shared cluster of linked schemata. Our's is a neoassociationist view consonant with one attempt, currently influential in cognitive science, to provide a foundation for schema theory (Rumelhart, McClelland, & the PDP Research Group, 1986; McClelland, Rumelhart, & the PDP Research Group, 1986). In this view, schemata are patterns of associations among various features of experience. We assume a basically Hebbian (Hebb, 1949) model in which learning consists of neural changes that result from exposure to repeated (or emotionally salient) co-occurring features of one's experience. Quite often, this process of schema formation takes place without any conscious effort on the learner's part and leads to representations that are in no sense sentential or rulelike. We argue that even in societies with formal schooling, most cultural models are learned in this way, largely without awareness, and retained in nonsentential form. We consider this process to be the prototype of cultural learning.

The sorts of repeated and salient inputs that form the basis of cultural schemata can come from a variety of sources such as patterns implicit in the arrangements of objects and practices in the culturally constructed world, patterns implicit in creative representations of the everyday world (e.g., songs, history lessons, paintings, stories, television shows), and the way words are used in varied contexts to classify and link culturally relevant objects and practices. Talk is also used to direct, guide, and correct learning (D'Andrade, 1981).

To give an example of a cultural model that U.S. adults know but U.S. children need to learn from these various inputs, all adults sometime before or (at the latest) soon after they are married have acquired considerable knowledge of what marriage is about. They know, for instance, that you fall in love and then get married, that you are supposed to marry the person you love and love only the person you marry. Ideally, you will love each other forever, but if one of you falls out of love with the other (typically because of falling in love with someone else), you should divorce and marry the one you love. Even if it does not turn out that way, most people intend their marriages to be lasting and expect marriage to involve a life that is shared in substantial ways. Most also expect marriage to be mutually fulfilling, and lack of fulfillment felt by one or both spouses is another reason for divorce. You may be incompatible, or grow incompatible, not fulfilling each other's needs. If your marriage is to be a lasting and hence successful one, you may have to put a good deal of effort into learning to meet each other's needs and achieving compatibility.

Because this model is such a taken-for-granted part of our everyday understanding, it may not be immediately obvious how wholly cultural, and culturally distinctive, are these ideas about marriage. Yet, there are societies in which what we might gloss as marriage has nothing to do with love; in which marriages are not expected to last; in which, far from being an exclusive relationship between two people who share a life together, marriage is polygamous, for example, or a means of linking two families or descent groups; and in which our very idea of "need fulfillment" or "success" would be met with incomprehension.

In what follows, we pursue the case of the U.S. cultural model of marriage. We chose this topic because one of us has completed an extensive investigation and derived a model of U.S. adult's understandings of marriage (Quinn, 1982, 1986, 1987, 1991, in press). The claim that the model of marriage summarized above is shared in U.S. society rests on an average of 15 hr-long interviews apiece with 22 interviewees, both the husband and the wife in 11 marriages. These men and women were chosen for diversity of age, length of marriage, geographic origin, occupation, education, and racial and ethnic identity. We will use parts of the model of marriage shared by these adults as the "well-formed" standard against which to measure what children know and say.

Anthropologists have not substantially investigated either what children do and do not know or how children's knowledge compares with adult understanding. From our pilot data, we have highlighted a variety of ways in which children's understandings deviate from adults'. These divergences, in turn, open up windows on the process by which adult cultural understandings are attained and point to complexities in this process.

A Pilot Investigation

Our pilot interviews about marriage were conducted with three U.S. girls: Rachel V. (RV), age 8 years; Leanna (L), age 11 years; and Rachel Q. (RQ), nearly a young woman at age 14 years.[2] The youngest and oldest are our own daughters, and the middle girl is the daughter of a friend. Although we do not plan to rely so heavily on our own children and the children

---

[2] The interviews with Rachel V. and Rachel Q. covered the following topics: What is marriage? (How would you explain it to a Martian?) Why do people get married and divorced? Do you want to get married some day? What traits would you want your spouse to have? How is being married different from your relationship with your parents or a friend? What do you think about the following: arranged marriages, marriages of convenience, repeated divorces and remarriages, commuter marriages, noncompanionate marriages (i.e., wife and husband spend leisure time in separate pursuits), extramarital affairs, polygamous marriages, and homosexual marriages? Questions on these topics were phrased in colloquial terms, adapted to the child's age, with a consistency of topics pursued rather than standardization of wording as our goal. Leanna's interview came earlier and included fewer questions about possibly deviant types but more elicitation of personal narratives. Each interview session was about a half-hour long and was tape-recorded and transcribed verbatim. The interviews were conducted, separately, by the ' authors of this paper.

of friends in our future research on this subject, doing so was appropriate for this preliminary study because our intimate knowledge of these children's lives gave us some insight
into the developmental and environmental factors that may account for their ideas.

These interviews suggest that what our interviewees did not know is as interesting
as what they did know. As a brief illustration, a fundamental assumption about marriage,
known to all U.S. adults and saturating popular imagery of the institution, is that love and
marriage are closely linked. Indeed, this is such a strong assumption that it led the adult
transcribing Rachel Q.'s interviews to mishear her at one point. When asked if she
wanted to get married someday, Rachel responded, "I don't know. I mean, if I found
somebody that I want to be with." What the transcriber typed instead was, "If I found
someone to love." In fact, neither this Rachel nor the other one ever brought up love in
their interviews about marriage (although it was a theme in Leanna's interview).

Perhaps both Rachels knew that love and marriage go together but simply failed to
mention this. Although we cannot say for certain what they did and did not know, it is
still a striking finding that the love–marriage link was not salient enough to have emerged
during the approximately 90-min of their combined interviews, even in response to some
questions that were designed to elicit discourse about love (e.g., "How about the feeling
you have for a friend? And the feeling you'd have for the person you're married to? Is
that about the same? Or do you think it might be different?"). More striking was that
questions such as these elicited responses from the two Rachels that were inconsistent
with adult notions of marital love.

It does not matter that these particular responses may not be common to all or
even most children their age. Our aim at this point is not to arrive at general descriptions
of what U.S. children of different ages know about marriage. (We cannot even begin to
do that with such a small, skewed sample.) Instead we hope to show some of the complexities of the relation between the cultural information that children receive and the
understandings that they construct out of this information.

Culture Acquisition, Language Acquisition, and Other Learning

The rest of this chapter will argue that culture acquisition is quite different from language
acquisition and other forms of learning described in this volume in at least four important

respects, outlined briefly in this section and then illustrated with our interview material in following sections. We will also describe two further differences in this section. Although we expect them to be equally important to a theory of culture acquisition, these last two differences are not illustrated by our pilot study. (We should note at the outset that by *language acquisition* we mean primarily the acquisition of syntactic and phonological structures. Much of pragmatics and semantics overlaps with cultural understanding.)

Some Cultural Information is Unavailable to Young Learners

All information needed to learn phonology and syntax in the speaker's native tongue (leaving aside prestige dialects and special registers) is available to children at an early age (at least by age 5 years). Characteristics of the world such as object, event, position constancies, and the effect of gravity on body movement are likewise available to young children. By contrast, much of their culture is not available to them because of the way their environment is structured or because adult culture-bearers deliberately suppress it (see, e.g., Barth, 1975).[3]

Culture Learners Make Up for Unavailable Information About One Cultural Model by Analogy With Another

Analogizing is a pervasive property of cognition: No two circumstances are ever exactly the same, thus, intelligent beings constantly have to ignore differences and highlight similarities if they are to use their knowledge in new situations. The kind of analogizing that takes place in culture learning, however, is different from that which occurs, for example, in simple generalization. What is at stake is not the correctness of the move from particulars to generalities or vice-versa but the aptness of one domain to serve as a basis for understanding another domain. This makes the sorts of analogies used in culture learning different from those used in language learning. When language learners overgeneralize (e.g., saying "goed" and "sheeps"), they simply mistake the scope of application of their rules. By contrast, when culture learners mistakenly think of the flow of electricity through a wire as being like a crowd of lemmings rushing through a chute, evaporation as being like popcorn popping (Collins & Gentner, 1987; Gentner & Gentner, 1983), or, as

---

[3]*Furthermore, the kinds of information available to children varies cross-culturally depending on socializers' cultural models of how children learn (see, e.g., Lutz, 1983). This is a complication for learning language (Ochs & Schieffelin, 1984) and some cognitive skills as well but may not be as significant in these latter cases. Although we do not have the space to illustrate this point with cross-cultural evidence, the cultural environment in which children learn can be very different depending on the adult model of learning that structures that environment.*

in the example presented below, the feelings and motives of married partners as being like the feelings and motives of best friends, their error is not one of scope but of appropriateness. It is like trying to play baseball on a cricket field (to use another analogy).

This last analogy hides an important difference between the would-be ball player and the culture learner. The ball player is likely to enact his or her understandings and receive corrective feedback. By contrast, children's erroneous hypotheses about their cultural world can remain unenacted and hence uncorrected for much of the early part of life and, sometimes, beyond. Some cultural knowledge, as well, remains the province of experts and is never mastered by the majority of adults. Unless and until they reach a time in life when they have to put their cultural knowledge of marriage and other adult concerns into action and bear the consequences of these acts, children can make do with their partial, approximate, and in some ways mistaken, immature models of these things. Some adults report that they do not learn the entire adult model of marriage or, indeed, even realize that there is something missing from their naïve model of it, until after they get married and find themselves at sea.

Cultural Inputs Bearing on a Given Model Are Unevenly Available

This subtle source of complexity in culture acquisition arises from the way in which some kinds of inputs lag behind others in contributing to a learner's developing understanding. An important example of this that we will describe is that learners may command a knowledge of patterns in the world before they command an abstract vocabulary for talking about those patterns, or they may learn an abstract vocabulary before they have learned very much about the referents of these words. These different kinds of lags lead to different kinds of naïveté.

The Motivation to Learn Cultural Knowledge Is Often Uneven

Even when the relevant information is present in the learner's environment to fill in gaps, correct mistaken understandings, and provide labels for observed patterns or explanations for abstract words, culture learning is complex because, as we will show, learners do not automatically use all the knowledge to which they have been exposed in their developing understandings. Information is sometimes not absorbed at all and is sometimes learned but "encapsulated" rather than integrated into what else is known. This is not a problem in the study of language acquisition or early perceptual and motor learning, probably because children are uniformly highly motivated to pay attention to, remember, and integrate inputs that are relevant to their understandings of language, motor skills, and physical invariances in their world.

Cultural Models Are Often Acquired Without the Motivation to Enact Them

Learning what is culturally typical, correct, or otherwise expected does not automatically impart the motivation to do the expected thing. For linguistic competence and other cognitive skills, this does not seem to be an issue, probably both because of uniformly high motivations to enact the knowledge acquired and because of lack of knowledge of other alternatives. To the extent that they must do so in order to be understood, speakers are highly motivated to observe the speech norms of their community. (The situation is essentially the same for bi- or multilingual speakers.) By contrasting example, people can learn their subgroup's expectation that adults get married but decide not to get married themselves.

Inconsistent Cultural Models Are Sometimes Inferrable From Alternative Inputs

In contrast with earlier estimates that much speech is ill-formed, newer studies show that most speech that children hear is fluent and well-formed (Pinker, 1989). Thus, for grammar and phonology, at least, there is no radical disjuncture between the system to be learned and the system observed. This is not to say that the underlying rules or patterns are directly evident but only that whatever the competence to be acquired, it corresponds to available evidence. The same is true for the relation between perceptual information and the physical structure that is to be inferred from that information. For culture acquisition, the situation is much more complicated in part because culture learners are presented with a variety of "ill-formed" examples. The very categories of well- and ill-formed are somewhat less apt when applied to cultural enactments than linguistic ones because our native intuitions about cultural correctness typically are fuzzier than our native intuitions about linguistic correctness. Adults' everyday behaviors may contradict their stated values. Media presentations and other creative representations (e.g., myths and morality tales) differ from everyday behavior and among themselves as a result of their goals (e.g., to entertain or instruct), their conditions of creation (e.g., by ritual specialists or for commercial television), and their differing genres (e.g., oral legend, ritual reenactment, situation comedy). Both linguistic structures and cultural understandings change over time, but culture can change much faster than language can change, so the common understandings that learners imbibe as children or adolescents may be quite different from the common understandings that they face as adults. All of these variations go beyond subcultural differences—still another source of confusion but one that does have a direct linguistic analog in dialect differences.[4]

Unfortunately, the material that we analyze here will not allow us to pursue any further the last two differences between culture learning and other forms of learning— that motivations to enact understandings may not be acquired with those understandings and that the inconsistency of cultural messages complicates our understanding of culture acquisition (however, see D'Andrade, in press; Ewing, 1990; Quinn, 1986, in press; Strauss, 1990, 1991, in press). We hope, however, that these two points do not require much argument. That cultural understandings do not necessarily carry motivational force should be obvious (but, see Shweder, in press) and could be supported by many examples in addition to that of marriage: People can know what competition, fidelity, and piety are, for example, without being motivated to act competitively, faithfully, or piously.

This disjuncture between learning models and wanting to enact them in turn helps create the problem of inconsistent cultural messages because it means that to the extent that adults are unmotivated to enact cultural models, the next generation of culture learners will observe behaviors that differ from those models. However, inconsistency is not limited to differences between models and their enactment (which has its linguistic analog). For some domains, such as marriage, there are at least five dimensions along which culture learners acquire information. In particular, learners may be presented with information about the typical, the good ("natural" or morally right), heroic or other ideals, variant roles, or cultural alternatives. To take the example of marriage, the statistically typical (average or modal) marriage in this society will probably be shorter and less happy than our model of a good marriage. That good marriage, in turn, is something that anyone is supposed to be able to attain, unlike an exceptional ideal, represented, for example, by the faithful Penelope of Homer's *Odyssey*. Variant roles are represented, for example, by priests and nuns, who abstain from marriage. At present, some examples of cultural alternatives are open marriages and commuter marriages. Part of the task of culture acquisition is learning to sort instances along these dimensions, and part of the complexity of the process is that the behaviors represented in a model in one dimension will

---

[4]*Even this analogy breaks down, however. Although the syntax and phonology of a dialect tends to be learned as a system, cultural models are not learned as a system but in a more fragmented way, leaving culture learners freer than language learners in the kinds of syncretisms they can construct. Finally, to the extent that learners have the option of choices among the syntactic and phonological structures of different dialects and registers, they will be guided by cultural models of the social and situational identities associated with those linguistic differences, which make such linguistic choices (e.g., between standard and nonstandard English) subtypes of the sort of cultural variation we are describing.*

be inconsistent with the behaviors represented in a model in another dimension, necessitating a (conscious or nonconscious) choice among models to enact. This is not even counting the diversity of cultures usually present in a society, the counteralternatives introduced by contact with geographically distinct cultures, or the fantasy worlds, for example, of myth or science fiction. All of this makes the very term *culture acquisition* problematic because it suggests obtaining a fixed, well-defined object rather than learning from changing, diverse practices. To retain the parallelism with "language acquisition," we will continue to speak of "culture acquisition," but the differences between these kinds of learning need to be kept in mind. In another simplification we will frequently refer to culture learners as children, although, in fact, culture learning continues throughout life.

Unavailability of Cultural Information

The structure of everyday objects and practices determines that much adult cultural knowledge is simply inaccessible to children. This was strikingly evident in our pilot interviews about marriage. Not being able to observe the internal thoughts, feelings, and motives of others and having no equivalent internal experiences of their own from which to infer those of married adults, the girls seemed unable to divine the psychological part of marriage. For example, not only did two of these girls appear ignorant of the role of love in marriage, but none of them gave any indication of knowing about other equally key features of the U.S. adult model of marriage such as that it is supposed to fulfill the individual needs of spouses, that the typical spouses are not entirely compatible in terms of their abilities to meet each other's needs, that marital difficulties are typically engendered by this incompatibility, that such difficulties can only be overcome with effort, and that the success of the marriage rides on the couple's ability to overcome these difficulties and achieve this compatibility. Although a large portion of what Quinn's (1987, 1991) adult interviewees said about marriage consisted of narratives on these topics, the child interviewees offered almost no discussion of them. It was, for these young girls, as if the guts of the model of marriage were missing. This surprising quality of knowing a great deal about marriage while missing what, for adults, are some of its most essential features will be evident in many of their responses quoted below.

Although none of the girls understood that marriage was supposed to be need fulfilling, all knew that marriage was supposed to be neolocal and shared in various other ways. This is not, we argue, because neolocality and sharedness are more central to our cultural model of marriage than need fulfillment. A better explanation is that the girls knew about neolocality and certain kinds of marital sharing largely because they were able to observe them in their everyday life. Thus, the youngest interviewee, Rachel V., had a fine sense of the shared social identity that marriage, by comparison with other types of relationships, entails (I = interviewer):

I: Do you want to get married some day?

RV: Yes, of course.

I: Uh huh. Why?

RV: Well... Because I'd be lonely by myself.

I: 'Cause you'd be lonely by yourself?

RV: Yeah.

I: Uh huh. Of course, you could just live with somebody. You could just live with a friend. You wouldn't have to get married to anybody, just so you wouldn't be lonely.

RV: (pause) If I was with a friend, we wouldn't always be together. [I: Um hm.] That friend might have other friends. If I was married, I would probably get to know the friends of whoever I got married to.[5]

Rachel had never been told, "When you get married, you and your husband will have the same friends." The assumption that this would be so is likely to have been inferred from the highly joint social life of her own parents. Yet, conspicuously missing from her talk about motives for marriage were other, more intangible kinds of sharing between spouses that adult interviewees never failed to mention, such as common goals, common values, and, above all, emotional closeness. These are no more difficult to comprehend, as concepts, than neolocality or joint social identity but are much harder to observe than common residences and jointly hosted dinner parties.

When we refer to what the structure of children's everyday world makes accessible and inaccessible to them, we mean not the physically given structure of the world so much as the culturally determined structure. It is true that others' feelings are less observable than their behavior, but parents could conceivably tell their children, or talk in front of them, about their own needs and how well each spouse was fulfilling the other's needs, from which the children could learn about these unobserved inner states and their links to observable behavior. Or, children could learn about these matters from books or

---

[5] *Rachel V's answer, "Because I'd be lonely by myself," along with an earlier response that people get married "to have company" may reflect some idiosyncrasies of her experience. At the time this interview was conducted, not only was she an only child with no playmates in the house, but she had only 5 months earlier moved to a new state where she was just beginning to make friends.*

television. In fact, however, cultural ideas about what is ordinarily too private and intimate for a married couple to share with their children, and other ideas about what constitutes sufficiently dramatic material for fairy tales, soap operas, and other creative
representations of marriage, seem to ensure that these particular unobservables remain
inaccessible.

Analogy to Known Cultural Models

It does not follow from the inaccessibility of information about the emotional work of marriage that children have nothing at all on which to go in formulating understandings of the
motivations and concerns of married people. As active theorizers, these girls did their best to
make sense of marriage by filling in the blanks in their knowledge of it with what they did
know from their own experiences. Two of the girls, Rachel V. and Rachel Q., seemed to have
formulated the hypothesis that the relationship between partners in a marriage is essentially
the same as the relationships that they have with their good friends. This is an example of a
not-quite-right (from the adult's perspective) understanding that can persist for years if learners do not need to enact their understandings and confront disconfirming social feedback.
(Although many U.S. adults may believe that one's spouse should be one's best friend, their
understanding of what is involved in being best friends does not adequately characterize
their model of the marital relationship. Adults typically hold that romantic love and sexual
attraction between married partners result in a more intense relationship than that between
two people who are "only" friends.)

    We have some quite direct evidence about the two Rachels' equations of friendship
with partnership in a marriage: Each was asked whether the relationship that she would
have with her husband would be the same as or different from the relationship that she
would have with a friend, and each replied in terms that indicated that she saw little
difference. Although 8-year-old Rachel V. maintained that there would be a difference, this
turned out to be a matter of how long the two people, married or not, had known each
other:

> I: How about the feeling you have for a friend? And the feeling you'd have for the person
> you're married to? Is that about the same? Or do you think it might be different?
> RV: Different.
> I: How?

RV: Well, you might have known a friend a little longer than you were married to that person, that you're married to. So you might feel closer to them.

I: Feel closer to the friend?

RV: Um hm.

I: Um hm.

RV: But after you've been married for a while, I don't know.

At 14-years-old, Rachel Q. had advanced only marginally beyond this understanding:

RQ: Well, maybe closer [i.e., between married partners], I don't know. It shouldn't be less.

Indirect evidence that the two girls used their knowledge about friendships to hypothesize about the marital relationship came from the ways in which the girls reasoned in response to questions about such matters as what makes a marriage good or bad, what they would want in a spouse, and whether they thought that extramarital affairs were all right. A careful examination of this talk suggests something even more interesting: Although Rachel Q. held the same culturally erroneous assumption as did the younger Rachel V. about the similarity of friendship to marriage, the more nearly adult friendships of the older girl provided her with a closer analogy to the adult cultural model of marriage than did the younger girl's friendships.

Asked what she would want her husband to be like, Rachel V. provided details about doing things and going places together, revealing the source of her ideas about marital goings-on in her own 8-year-old playmate relationships:

RV: [My husband should] Like the same *names* as me.

I: (laughs) What do you mean, like the same—what do you mean?

RV: Well, if we have a baby, then, we'll be able to agree on a name.

I: Huh! Uh huh.

RV: Like the same kinds of places as me.

I: What do you mean places?

RV: Or foods.

Quizzed further about what she meant by places, she elaborated, "Places like where I like to go. Like places sort of like playgrounds. Places like, *neat* places." Asked next about whether she cared what work her husband did, she responded, "Something that wouldn't be all messy [like working in a restaurant]." She said, when prodded further about this criterion, "Well, if he has a messy job then that might mean he likes messy things. And that probably means he doesn't like the same kind of things as me." Married people must not only like the same kinds of things, they must do these things together, a necessary condition of marriage for her. Asked whether two people who lived in the same house but did not spend too much time together because they do not like to do the same things would have a good marriage, she declared, "That probably would not be good because they would—they would just get married to live together and to support each other and they wouldn't really, like—wouldn't be— really be able to do anything together." Tellingly, the older Rachel responded very differently to the same question: "I just think it's up to them. They're the people getting—I mean, they're the people married. It wouldn't really matter. If they like two different things, they don't have to do everything together." The very different model in terms of which Rachel Q. casts the marital relationship did not foreground common preferences and activities in the way that Rachel V.'s playmate model did. Doing things together is the essence of the playmate relationship. Hence, having the same preferences for activities, objects, and settings are desiderata of a good playmate—ones on which Rachel V. unfailingly commented after she had a new friend over to play.

When Rachel Q. talked about what marriage involves, she seemed to draw on the very different experience of teenage girls' friendships. Her concerns echoed the themes, identified in studies of social cognition (reviewed in Shantz, 1983), that have come to characterize other children's talk about friendship by the time that they are her age. To the degree that these themes begin to incorporate some adult social concerns, such as understanding what the other person wants and working at relationships, Rachel Q.'s talk about marriage sounded quite a bit more grown up than did 8-year-old Rachel V.'s. But to the extent that adolescent girls are preoccupied with certain interpersonal issues, while at the same time unaware of other motives and feelings that distinguish marriage, Rachel Q.'s description of marriage had unexpected emphases and gaps, sounding slightly odd as a result.

Rachel Q. extended to marriage the logic that teenage friends are people who like each other, and if they do not like each other any more, they break up.

I: Why do you think people get divorced?

RQ: They don't want to live together or be tied to this other person any more.

I: Why?

RQ: When you marry a person, it is to someone you like. If you don't like the person you are married to any more, you get divorced so you can find someone else you like to live happily ever after.

Asked exactly the same question about divorce, Rachel V. replied, "Because of not being able to agree on things," such as what to name the baby, what school to send the children to, or what to have for supper. The fate of 8-year-old playmate relationships rests on such agreements and disagreements about what the playmates like, rather than on whether they like each other. Teenage friendships are more like marriages in being based on stable affectional bonds. Marriages, like teenage friendships, can be jeopardized by dislike, as they can by breach of loyalty or trust. But there is distinctly more to marriage. Unlike either Rachel, adults almost always report that when people get divorced, it is because they do not love each other any more or because they are no longer fulfilling each other's needs.

All the girls talked about the necessity of married people agreeing and getting along, but Rachel Q. was the only one to exhibit the further understanding that getting along requires work and apply this understanding to marriage. A good marriage "just goes really easily," she said, "and you don't have to work very hard to get along," whereas a bad marriage is one in which getting along is a struggle. But all marriages require some work; asked to expand on a comment that people get married "to show each other that they are willing to stay together and work to live happily every after," she continued,

> RQ: If you want to be happy with somebody else you'll have to work, to be happy with someone else.
> I: Because ... Why is it work?
> RQ: It's not bad work, I mean....
> I: No, I didn't mean that.
> RQ: I mean, just 'cause people are always going to be different and so you don't want to—and if everybody does a little bit to get along with the other person and everybody will live happier.

Rachel V. did not discuss working at the relationship at all. Presumably, in her mind, if two people are unable to agree on things, little can be done about it—they simply do not play together again.

In this respect Rachel Q.'s ideas about marriage were considerably closer to those of adults interviewed on the subject, who invariably stressed the work that it involves. Once again, however, there was a crucial difference. "If everybody does a little bit to get along with the other person and everybody will live happier" is advice one might give to girls bunking together at summer camp. That the central work of marriage is the work of achieving a kind of compatibility in which the married couple has learned to fulfill each other's psychosocial needs was as foreign to Rachel Q.'s way of thinking as to the younger Rachel V.'s.

A final set of concerns that Rachel Q. brought to the topic of marriage, we argue, from her understanding of friendship, was displayed in her reaction to extramarital sex:

> I: What about sex—having sex with other people while you are married?
>
> RQ: Well, I mean, I don't think—I think that if you were married that you would be loyal to that person. I mean, why would the person that you are married to want you to go out and have sex with other people?

The interviewer pursued the topic after a short digression:

> I: What if you had sex with other people and didn't tell the other person? Would that be okay?
>
> RQ: Why? I mean why would that be ok?
>
> I: I don't know.
>
> RQ: That'd be—that other person would be—I mean the other person probably went by the marriage, I mean. That— it wouldn't be being married because being married is—i—c—(frustrated sigh)—is being with this person that you want to be with. It's not anything else. I mean, it's being with the person that you want to be with, and being friends and being loyal and honest with this person, and you wouldn't go out and see other people. If—I mean, if you were married. Don't get married, then, if you are the kind of person that would do that, because I don't think that's what marriage—what anybody else would want in a marriage.

Like other children her age, Rachel Q. had learned to take the perspective of the other, worrying about what the other person wants, and "being friends and being loyal and honest with this person," presumably all high priorities among the things that teenagers want from their friends. Of course, adults too value these qualities in their spouses. But it is likely, for instance, that loyalty at Rachel's age has certain resonances that it does not have for adults due to the importance that teenagers place on acceptance and popularity: Loyalty is sticking up for your friend, refusing to gossip about her behind her back, including her in social activities, and so forth. Rachel Q. may have assumed that loyalty means just the same to marriage partners. As adult sounding as it is, her language can also mislead us into thinking that she knows more about what people actually do want out of marriage than she really knows. Thus, she recognized that married people do not want an unfaithful spouse. She also seemed to have an appreciation of the more general expectation on which this concern for marital fidelity is founded, that the marital relationship as a whole be an exclusive one. Thus, for example, she said of married people that "they don't, like, go out on dates with anybody else because they're married," and she considered bigamy bad because "people are usually looking for a whole husband, not just an eighth." But she seemed to have no idea that marital exclusivity, including sexual exclusivity, follows from the exclusivity of the love relationship. She appeared to lack that part of the model of marriage having to do with love.

Teenage friendships introduced Rachel to concerns that helped her understand marriage by analogy. These concerns are part of her experience of friendship because they are generic to voluntary relationships of all kinds from adolescence on—paying attention to what the other person wants, liking that person, and working at the relationship. This is what made Rachel Q.'s discussion sound so much more mature than Rachel V.'s, although her talk was still remarkable for what is left out. Her discussion of extramarital affairs and bigamy made no mention of sex, her discussion of divorce completely overlooked falling out of love, and her discussion of working at a relationship said nothing about fulfilling each other's needs. In these areas, the analogy to friendship failed her because teenage friendship does not encompass these matters; sex, love, and need fulfillment are particular to marriage and a narrow range of other adult relationships. This is what made her discussion of marriage sound so unadult. At the very end of her interview, when the interviewer observed, "You haven't mentioned love," Rachel Q. responded, "Oh ... well, I just thought—I think love would be friendship, caring, and everything like that." Nothing could be more diagnostic of her assimilation of marriage to her own experience of friendship.

Whether or not this particular analogy to friendship is atypical—and we have no reason to expect it to be—these interviews suggest that analogy, more generally, is an important source of children's cultural understandings. Rachel Q.'s example also illustrates that such analogies, and their attendant misunderstandings and partial understandings, persist long past the point at which children have learned perceptual invariances, Piagetian concrete operations, the essential features of the grammar of their languages, and the like.

Uneven Availability of Cultural Inputs

First, we showed a patterning of insight and ignorance shaped by the availability and unavailability to young learners of information about a given aspect of the U.S. cultural model of marriage. Then, in the previous section, we showed a somewhat different pattern to be the outcome of analogizing from other domains of the interviewees' experience. Now we will discuss a still different pattern, one that follows not from which models or aspects of a model are known but from the source of available information. In particular, we will focus on the relation of verbal knowledge, especially abstract verbal labels, to experientially acquired knowledge of the referents of these labels. Learners sometimes acquire knowledge of patterns in the world before learning how to describe these patterns, and sometimes vice-versa.[6]

When children have only isolated observations on which to go and do not command the terms for classifying and grouping what they know, they are recognized as beginners. Rachel Q. knew that married people live in the same house, spend time being with each other, enjoy each other's company, and do not go out on dates with other people. She used an abstract label when she grouped together all of these dispersed observations by saying that marriage is "a legal way of two people sharing life." By contrast, Rachel V. had extensive knowledge that marriage involves sharing preferences, friends, living quarters, and activities but never summarized all of this as "sharing a life." That was one more respect in which her talk sounded less mature than did Rachel Q.'s.

When children begin to command abstract terms, they sound much more adult. But discursive sophistication that has outstripped any empirical referent typically has an empty constitutive ring to it. Thus, Rachel Q., when asked how she would tell a visiting Martian what marriage was, responded, "Joining of two people in holy matrimony." Just a few weeks before her interview, she had attended her older sister's wedding, at which she was exposed to a heavy dose of symbolic language from the realms of church and law. But she did not know what it means to think of marriage as a sacrament; "holy matrimony" was just a jargoned-up synonym of marriage for her. This was evident as she continued:

> RQ: Joining of two people in holy matrimony. I guess it would be two people under—I don't know. Certified together, I don't know.
>
> I: Certified together.
>
> RQ: Well it would just—it's a—umm, a legal way of two people sharing a life.

---

[6]*Of course, if patterns in the world are unobservable and relevant discourses unavailable, then cultural knowledge may be truly difficult to come by and late of acquisition. This would seem to be true, for example, in the case of marital need fulfillment and its difficulty.*

Finding herself unable to explain "holy matrimony," she abandoned that language and tried another tack.

Similarly, Leanna knew that if one is married to someone, one is supposed to love them, which she has doubtless learned from discourse linking the terms *love* and *marriage* (or cognates). Not having experienced marital love herself, however. Leanna had a great deal of trouble explaining her strong objections to loveless marriage and extramarital sex:

> I: What if they have totally different interests? Like one of them likes to go out dancing and the other one likes to stay in and read books and so you know they basically love each other and the're happy together but most of the time they're doing things separately. Is that okay too?
>
> L: Yeah. Just as, I mean, it's—it's really important they still love each other because if they don't then that's—that's bad.
>
> I: Okay, what if they actually have, you know, extramarital affairs. Like one of them has a boyfriend of girlfriend on the side. Is that okay?
>
> L: That's bad, no.
>
> I: That's bad.
>
> L: That's bad.
>
> I: Why?
>
> L: Because people really—they shouldn't—that's—that's like—umm—that would be—I would be very upset if, like, my husband or wife was doing that to me because— just—you're not—you're not, like—you're—to love each other you have to—you have—well—(sigh) I mean, you're—you're supposed to—you're supposed—you're not supposed to have another girlfriend or boyfriend if you're—if you're married to each other, because that—that would mean that they—they love someone else, and if you're married to someone you have to really love them and—and almost, like— you know, you can't just have—if you don't—if you only, like, love them a little bit, but then you love this other person a little, but mo—you know—it doesn't—doesn't— can't really—you can't really do that. I don't know really how to explain it.

It is interesting to compare this with what Rachel Q., who was quoted on the very same subject of extramarital sex, had to say about it. In the older girl's answer there was some of the same "just-so" quality as in the 11-year-old's: Sex outside of marriage "wouldn't be being married" and marriage is "not anything else." But mingled with this constitutive language was another, very different, empathic kind of talk about loyalty to one's spouse and consideration of what the other person wants that was only hinted at in Leanna's "I would be very upset if my husband or wife was doing that to me." This other-oriented reasoning, quite typical of 14-year-old Rachel's Q.'s interview, is drawn from a realm of social experience (teenage friendships) that she knows well. Lacking this or any other relevant experience on which to draw, 11-year old Leanna had no recourse but to offer permutations of the sentence, "If you're married to someone, you have to really love them."

Other children or adults might have answered the question about extramarital affairs differently, for example, declaring them against the teachings of their church. Leanna, however, said, "That's bad" and "you're not supposed to," but did not go on to defend her stance in terms of religious or other moral values; rather, what seemed to have been violated, in her mind, was a definition of terms. Strictly constitutive arguments are based on the belief that the essence of y is x and rest in the end on appeals to natural law or logical finality. Adults make arguments of this sort too but are capable of adding to this language arguments and explanations that draw on a richer, more detailed set of understandings than children can muster. Because children lack crucial understandings, the limits of what is constitutive and not explicable are generally much broader for them than for adults. Leanna's unqualified disallowance of extramarital sex, as much as her halting attempts and ultimate inability to justify her stand against it, illustrates this. Because she had more than words on which to draw, Rachel Q.'s developing understanding seems to be somewhere between Leanna's and the understanding that an adult might have.

Uneven Motivation to Learn Cultural Models

Eight-year-old old Rachel V. has seen movies, read stories, and heard ditties that make it clear that love and marriage are linked. One of her favorite books about a year before she was interviewed was a collection of short fairy tales, including a story in which Li-Ho loved and wanted to marry Wang and another in which a prince fell in love with and married Cinderella. When she was 6 years old, she listened to and read to herself from a larger story book[7] that included six stories in which characters were described as having fallen in love and married. (For neither of these books are we counting the many other

[7]The first fairy tale collection is *Antique Fairy Tales*, (Parsipanny, NJ: Unicorn Publishing House, 1988). The second is *My Giant Story Book: Famous Fairy Tales, Animal Stories, Adventure Stories*, (New York: Westport Corporation, 1972).

stories in which poor but beautiful and good-natured girls married princes or poor but lucky or intrepid boys married princesses without it being explicitly stated that love was involved—although that might have been inferred.) Also, in the year preceding the interview, Rachel V. saw the movie *The Little Mermaid* three times. In the middle of the film, it is repeatedly said of the mermaid Ariel, and she says of herself, that she loves a handsome prince. In the final frames of the film, still another character sighs and says, "She really loves him," and seconds later Ariel and her prince appear together in wedding clothes. The love–marriage link could not be clearer. Furthermore, about 3 months before the interviews, Rachel V. came home reciting, "Philip and Paula sitting in a tree, K-I-S-S-I-N-G. First comes love, then comes marriage, then comes Carol in the baby carriage." About a week after the interviews, her mother casually asked her, in the midst of dinner conversation, how that poem goes, the one that starts "So-and-so and so-and-so sitting in a tree..." Rachel finished it without difficulty. Finally, she had been in the habit of saying, whenever she was enthusiastic about something, that she "loved" it but had been met on the school playground with the testing retort, "If you love it, why don't you marry it?" As a result, she had developed a defensive reaction: "I love yoghurt" (or some other favorite item), she would say, quickly adding, "but I don't want to marry it."

Given all this, it was very interesting that in 21 interviews, each a ½ hr long, about marriage Rachel V. never talked about love. Not only did she never once use the word *love*, but her discussion of marriage was inconsistent with the idea that romantic love is involved:

> I: Do you think you'd feel any different about the person you're married to than you'd feel about your par—[starting to say *parents*, a continuation of the previous topic]
>
> RV: (Interrupting) *Yes*.
>
> I: Yes? How?
>
> RV: Um ... Well, you probably don't feel *quite* as close to them.
>
> I: Which one don't you feel as close to?
>
> RV: The person you're married to.

We saw earlier that Rachel V. similarly said that she saw no essential difference between the feelings between friends and the feelings between married partners.

Children do not always ignore fictional or folkloric representations in trying to understand their everyday worlds. Leanna's 7-year-old brother, Jason, complained recently that he wanted more than anything to have his own mother and father both living in the same house with him like other people. When his mother pointed out to him that few of the other children he knew actually lived in "intact" families, he was surprised and interested. Jason's cultural model of the family as one in which mothers and fathers live in the same house with their children was doubtless decisively shaped by movies, television shows, and stories about intact nuclear families.

Why was 7-year-old Jason so influenced by *Cosby Show*–style creative representations of intact nuclear families, whereas 8-year old Rachel V. was not influenced by creative representations linking love and marriage? The difference probably lies in the motivations that each of them brings to learning these cultural models. Although we do not know for sure, it is plausible that Jason was more likely than another child would have been to use fictional images of intact families to interpret his everyday experience of families because the former images were especially compelling for him as the child of divorced parents. Rachel V., on the other hand, did not yet find stories and ditties about love and marriage personally compelling, and as a result, seemed to learn them in an encapsulated way, unconnected to her cultural model of real-life marriage. She could pay attention to and remember such representations (a few weeks after the interviews she produced a plot summary of *The Little Mermaid* that included the ideas that Ariel loved the prince and married him), but her *Little Mermaid* schema had not been integrated with her model of real-world marriages.

In a parallel case, Rachel Q. and her friends are avid followers of the daytime soap operas, watching them whenever they got a chance after school, filling each other in on missed episodes, comparing notes on their favorite characters, and discussing the meanings and motives behind new developments in the story lines. Declarations of love and revelations of infidelity are staples of soap opera marriages. Yet Rachel Q. did not consider love relevant enough to real-life marriage to mention in the interview and when asked about real-life marital infidelity, deemed it not just disloyal but unthinkable. These two concerns, of course, are patently absent from the teenage girls' friendships on which she drew so heavily for her understanding of marriage. Like the romantic love in Rachel V.'s story books, the soap operas' depictions of marital love and sexual infidelity were at odds with everything in Rachel Q.'s own social and inner experience. Just as Rachel V. was uncompelled, we have speculated, to connect what she read and heard about love and marriage to her model of the latter, Rachel Q. was unmotivated to connect her knowledge of soap opera marriage, love, and infidelity to her model of real marriage.

What is intriguing about Rachel Q.'s interest in soap operas was that she and her friends seemed to be so highly motivated to attend to depictions of marriage and other adult heterosexual relationships. What do teenage girls find so engrossing in the soaps?

The probable answer is that these shows satisfy their intense new thirst for knowledge about the intricacies of social relationships. Yet, if Rachel Q.'s talk is typical, the girls absorb only that information that fits their friendship model of social relationships, setting aside themes that occur in the same stories but that are irrelevant and unassimilable to their model. Casual conversation with her suggested that Rachel Q. remained genuinely puzzled about much that goes on in the soaps.

We conclude that, although a good part of the girls' ideas about marriage can be explained by the inputs available to them, not all of their ideas can be so explained. In particular, the nonsalience of the love–marriage link for two of them cannot be attributed to missing or sparse information in their environment. As we have shown, even the youngest of the girls had already been exposed to many creative representations explicitly linking love and marriage. Dominant cultural messages do not automatically imprint themselves on impressionable young minds.

Instead, the concerns of a given person at a given point in life seem to shape what information that person will notice, remember, and link to other relevant information. Those concerns are, in turn, the result of a combination of idiosyncratic, social, and developmental factors. In the two cases we have just considered, it appears that the girls were not simply disinterested in connecting what they learned from creative representations about love, in the first case, and marital infidelity, in the second case, to their immature models of marriage. It may have been that the overwhelming developmental importance in these girls' lives of playmates or teenage friends dictated that they actively exclude information inconsistent with their models of those relationships from the understandings of marriage that were founded on analogy to these other models.

Conclusions

We have argued that there are some factors that are much more problematic in a theory of culture acquisition than they are in theories of language acquisition or many other sorts of learning, such as perceptual learning or the learning of physical skills, that are the focus of several other chapters in this volume. These are the sometimes unavailable, uneven, and inconsistent sources of cultural information; use of analogies to fill in missing information; and uneven motivations to learn cultural information and to enact the understandings one attains.

Although we do not have the data to comment on the latter motivation and its sources, it should be obvious that the motivation to enact cultural understandings is centrally implicated in the various conditions that promote lack of understanding. If learners are not motivated to enact their knowledge, they will be unlikely to seek out information that is not readily available, integrate information that is available, or push for an understanding of the referents of abstract terms. Furthermore, knowledge that is not enacted is less likely to be corrected; thus, incorrect hypotheses founded on inapt analogies can persist. Also, if lack of motivation to enact understandings is an obstacle to acquisition of those understandings, lack of understanding is sure to be an obstacle to enactment. Of course, lack of understanding is not an insuperable barrier to enactment: Many cultural understandings are acquired in a "bootstrapping" process as initial, bumbling action leads to greater insight, which leads in turn to more culturally appropriate actions, and so on (Holland, in press).

Both lack of understanding and lack of motivation to enact understandings were evident in our interviewees' talk about marriage. In this respect, their knowledge of marriage departed from their knowledge of some other domains such as gender, friendship, family, school, sports, and the like. In contrast to these topics but more like others such as national politics or adult occupations, marriage is likely to be a distant and abstract concern to most children and to remain so until at least late adolescence. Because it is so distant and abstract, it does not become a part of children's self understanding. As a consequence, it is neither highly motivating to them (Quinn, in press) nor are they highly motivated to learn about it, and they therefore remain relatively ignorant about it. Their ignorance provides an excellent window onto the way in which these children's cultural knowledge departs from that of adults. However, that marriage was more mystifying than motivating to these young learners was an unanticipated obstacle to anything we might have hoped to discover about the important question of how cultural models, more than being acquired by individuals, gain their motivation for so many of these individuals by the time they are adults.[8]

Although there are many topics about which U.S. children learn that are more directly relevant than marriage to their lives, marriage is certainly not alone in its lack of immediacy among theses topics. How typical, more generally, is marriage of the cultural

---

[8] We would expect that cultural understandings can be linked to different kinds of motivation, with widely different long-term consequences, that are learned at different times of life from different experiential sources. Some examples are modeling, empathy, reward and punishment, trauma, as well as desires for social approval, competence, and expertise. That each of these sources of motivation is represented by one or more different subspecialties in academic psychology reflects the current lack of a unified theory of motivation.

models that children learn? Although we cannot answer that question at this point, the structure that we provide here gives a way of thinking about how to answer it. For any given domain of cultural understandings, we should investigate the extent to which cultural inputs are available or unavailable to learners of different ages (hence, the likelihood that learners will need to fill in by analogy), the kinds of inputs that are available to learners at a given age (e.g., the relation of discourse to observable patterns), the range of diversity in cultural information bearing on a domain of knowledge, and, again, whether learners of different ages and in different life circumstances are motivated to acquire and enact cultural understandings. We suspect marriage will turn out to be fairly typical in these respects. It may be that marriage, more than many other shared schemata, is bound up with psychically fraught issues (in this case, of sexuality and love, both romantic and parental), although all culturally significant models are sure to carry strong emotional valences. In any case, whether marriage is typical or not, and whether our interviewees were typical or not, the complexities of culture acquisition that we have described here deserve to be further investigated.

Culture is pervasive. It figures importantly in many of the topics of the other chapters of this book. For example, it shapes what we talk about and the meaning of what we say, the way we categorize the world, the way we move about in it, and above all, our motives and intentions in doing so. It is time that culture has a place in psychological theories of cognition and learning.

References

Barth, F. (1975). *Ritual and knowledge among the Baktaman of New Guinea.* New Haven, CT: Yale University Press.

Collins, A., & Gentner, D. (1987). How people construct mental models. In D. Holland & N. Quinn (Eds.), *Cultural models in language and thought* (pp. 243–265). Cambridge, England: Cambridge University Press.

D'Andrade, R. (1981). The cultural part of cognition, *Cognitive Science, 5,* 179–195.

D'Andrade, R. (in press). Schemas and motives. In R. D'Andrade & C. Strauss (Eds.), *Human motives and cultural models.* Cambridge, England: Cambridge University Press.

Ewing, K. (1990). The illusion of wholeness: Culture, self, and the experience of inconsistency. *Ethos, 18,* 251–278.

Gentner, D., & Gentner, D. R. (1983). Flowing waters or teeming crowds: Mental models of electricity. In D. Gentner & A. L. Stevens (Eds.), *Mental models* (pp. 99–129). Hillsdale, NJ: Erlbaum.

Harkness, S., & Kilbride, P. L. (Eds.) (1983). *The socialization of affect* [Special issue], *Ethos 11*(4).

Heath, S. B. (1983). *Ways with words: Language, life, and work in communities and classrooms.* Cambridge, England: Cambridge University Press.

Hebb, D. O. (1949). *The organization of behavior: A neuropsychological theory.* New York: Wiley.

Holland, D. (in press). How cultural systems become desire: A case study of American romance. In R. D'Andrade & C. Strauss (Eds.), *Human motives and cultural models.* Cambridge, England: Cambridge University Press.

Hollos, M., & Leis, P. (1989). *Becoming Nigerian in Ijo society.* New Brunswick, NJ: Rutgers University Press.

Jahoda, G., & Lewis, I. M. (Eds.). (1988). *Acquiring culture: Cross-cultural studies in child development.* London: Croom Helm.

Leiderman, P. H., Tulkin, S. R., & Rosenfeld, A. (Eds.). (1977). *Culture and infancy: Variations in the human experience.* San Diego, CA: Academic Press.

LeVine, R. A. (1977). Child rearing as cultural adaptation. In P. Leiderman, S. Tulkin, & A. Rosenfeld (Eds.), *Culture and infancy: Variations in the human experience* (pp. 15–27). San Diego, CA: Academic Press.

Lutz, C. (1983). Parental goals, ethnopsychology, and the development of emotional meaning. *Ethos, 11,* 246–262.

Mayer, P. (Ed.). (1970). *Socialization: The approach from social anthropology.* London: Tavistock.

McClelland, J. L., Rumelhart, D. E., & the PDP Research Group. (Eds.). (1986). *Parallel distributed processing: Exploration in the microstructure of cognition: Vol. 2. Psychological and biological models.* Cambridge, MA: MIT Press.

Mead, M., & Macgregor, F. C. (1951). *Growth and culture: A photographic study of Balinese childhood.* New York: Putnam.

Mead, M., & Wolfenstein, M. (Eds.). (1955). *Childhood in contemporary cultures.* Chicago: University of Chicago Press.

Miller, P. J. (1982). *Amy, Wendy, and Beth: Learning language in South Baltimore.* Austin: University of Texas Press.

Miller, P. J., & Moore, B. B. (1989). Narrative conjunctions of caregiver and child: A comparative perspective on socialization through stories. *Ethos, 17,* 43–64.

Ochs, E. (1988). *Culture and language development: Language acquisition and language socialization in a Samoan village.* Cambridge, England: Cambridge University Press.

Ochs, E., & Schieffelin, B. B. (1984). Language acquisition and socialization: Three developmental stories and their implications. In R. A. Shweder & R. A. LeVine (Eds.), *Culture theory: Essays on mind, self, and emotion* (pp. 276–320). Cambridge, England: Cambridge University Press.

Pinker, S. (1989). Language acquisition. In M. Posner (Ed.), *Foundations of cognitive science* (pp. 359–399). Cambridge, MA: MIT Press.

Quinn, N. (1982). "Commitment" in American marriage: A cultural analysis. *American Ethnologist, 9,* 775–798.

Quinn, N. (1986, September). *Love and the experiential basis of American marriage.* Paper presented at the conference Love in Social and Historical Perspective, Charlottesville, VA.

Quinn, N. (1987). Convergent evidence for a cultural model of American marriage. In D. Holland & N. Quinn (Eds.), *Cultural models in language and thought* (pp. 173–192). Cambridge, England: Cambridge University Press.

Quinn, N. (1991). The cultural basis of metaphor. In J. Fernandez (Ed.), *Beyond metaphor: Trope theory in anthropology* (pp. 56–93). Stanford, CA: Stanford University Press.

Quinn, N. (in press). The motivational force of self understanding: Evidence from wives' inner conflicts. In R. D'Andrade & C. Strauss (Eds.), *Human motives and cultural models.* Cambridge, England: Cambridge University Press.

Quinn, N., & Holland, D. (1987). Cognition and culture. In D. Holland & N. Quinn (Eds.), *Cultural models in language and thought* (pp. 3–40). Cambridge, England: Cambridge University Press.

Quinn, N., & Strauss, C. (1989). *A cognitive cultural anthropology.* Paper presented at the 88th Annual Meeting of the American Anthropological Association, Washington, DC.

Rumelhart, D. E., McClelland, J. L., & the PDP Research Group (Eds.). (1986). *Parallel distributed processing: Exploration in the microstructure of cognition: Vol. 1. Foundations.* Cambridge, MA: MIT Press.

Schieffelin, B. B., & Ochs, E. (Eds.). (1986). *Language socialization across cultures.* Cambridge, England: Cambridge University Press.

Schwartz, T. (Ed.). (1976). *Socialization as cultural communication: Development of a theme in the work of Margaret Mead.* Berkeley: University of California Press.

Schwartz, T. (1981). The acquisition of culture. *Ethos, 9,* 4–17.

Shantz, C. U. (1983). Social cognition. In P. H. Mussen (Series Ed.) and J. H. Flavell & E. M. Markman (Vol. Eds.), *Handbook of child psychology: Vol. 3. Cognitive development* (pp. 495–555). New York: Wiley.

Shweder, R. A. (in press). Ghost busters in anthropology. In R. D'Andrade & C. Strauss (Eds.), *Human motives and cultural models.* Cambridge, England: Cambridge University Press.

Shweder, R. A., Mahapatra, M., & Miller, J. G. (1990). Culture and moral development, In J. Stigler, R. Shweder, & G. Herdt (Eds.), *Cultural psychology: Essays on comparative human development* (pp. 130–204). Cambridge, England: Cambridge University Press, 1990.

Shweder, R. A., & Much N. C. (1987). Determinations of meaning: Discourse and moral socialization. In W. Kurtines & J. Gewirtz (Eds.), *Moral development through social interaction* (pp. 197–244). New York: Wiley.

Skinner, D. (1990). *Nepalese children's understanding of self and the social world: A study of a Hindu mixed caste community.* Unpublished doctoral dissertation, University of North Carolina at Chapel Hill.

Skinner, D., & Holland, D. (1990). *Good selves, angry selves: Formation of gender identities in a mixed caste Hindu community in Nepal.* Paper presented at the 19th Annual Conference on South Asia, University of Wisconsin.

Strauss, C. (1990). Who gets ahead? Cognitive responses to heteroglossia in American political culture. *American Ethnologist, 17,* 312–328.

Strauss, C. (in press-a). Models and motives. In R. D'Andrade & C. Strauss (Eds.), *Human motives and cultural models.* Cambridge, England: Cambridge University Press.

Strauss, C. (in press-b). What makes Tony run? Schemas as motives reconsidered. In R. D'Andrade & C. Strauss (Eds.), *Human motives and cultural models.* Cambridge, England: Cambridge University Press.

Super, C. M., & Harkness, S. (Eds.). (1980). *New directions for child development: Vol. 8. Anthropological perspectives on child development.* San Francisco: Jossey-Bass.

Weisner, T. S. (1979). Some cross-cultural perspectives on becoming female. In C. Koop (Ed.), *Becoming female: Perspectives on development* (pp. 313–331). New York: Plenum Press.

Weisner, T. S. (1982). As we choose: Family life styles, social class, and compliance. In J. Kennedy & R. Edgerton (Eds.), *Culture and ecology: Eclectic perspectives* (pp. 121–141). Washington, DC: American Anthropological Association.

Whiting, B. B., & Edwards, C. P. (1988). *Children of different worlds: The formation of social behavior.* Cambridge, MA: Harvard University Press.

Whiting, B. B., & Whiting, J. W. M. (1975). *Children of six cultures: A psycho-cultural analysis.* Cambridge, MA: Harvard University Press.

Whiting, J. W. M. (1941). *Becoming a Kwoma: Teaching and learning in a New Guinea tribe.* New Haven, CT: Yale University Press.

CHAPTER 12

Liberation Thereology

Gerald M. Siegel

I n the field of communication disorders, concerns are dictated by the practical problems presented by adults or children who are unable to communicate in a socially appropriate way. We tend to focus on practical methods to identify and help children and adults with communication problems. We focus on problems and solutions. This is true of any applied field. I was attracted to the Center for Learning, Perception, and Cognition at the University of Minnesota because everyone there was a story teller. The data were never enough; they had to be woven into an explanatory tale. Skinner (1957), a failed novelist, called these tales *explanatory fictions*, but they were often more interesting than the data—and sometimes more credible.

I became involved with the Center because, although I came from an applied field, I too wanted to be a storyteller. However, I soon discovered that storytelling has special consequences in an applied field. The current story about any particular communication disorder can liberate therapists to devise imaginative, creative therapy methods or it can have the opposite effect and severely limit the range of clinical methods that seem appropriate, ethical, or even possible. Any theory, in fact, usually influences its field in both constraining and liberating ways. It is this role of storytelling that I will explore in this chapter.

I may have first become sensitized to the unsettling effects of stories soon after the publication of Chomsky's (1957) *Syntactic Structures*, when I began to hear discussions of language development that started with what became a mandatory professional mantra that implied in one form or another that language is "special" and deeply biologically determined, that only the most severe neurological damage can interfere with natural development of language (e.g., Lenneberg, 1967). This story troubled me because I knew that across the country thousands of children were being seen in special education classes and speech and language therapy sessions for language disorders—children who failed to assemble words into coherent sentences, master the grammar or the phonology of the language, or develop adequate vocabularies. These children are puzzling precisely because most often they do not have severe neurological or any other deficits that anyone can discover. In the clinic, one soon learns that not all apparently normal children develop adequate language.

In the field of communicative disorders, the influences of theory and methodology are perhaps nowhere so dramatic and transparent as with respect to stuttering. Stuttering is the communication disorder that is probably the best researched (although not the best understood) and that laypersons usually conjure up when I mention that I am a speech pathologist.

The stories that have been told about stuttering cover an amazing gamut, and the cures that have been offered are no less amazing. (For an early history, see Klingbeil, 1939; for a comprehensive review of more contemporary theories, see Bloodstein, 1987). Moses stuttered because he put hot coals in his mouth. Demosthenes treated stuttering by speaking with pebbles in his mouth. In the name of therapy, stutterers have had portions of their tongues excised. They have been discouraged from playing a musical instrument because music is purportedly localized in the right cerebral cortex and it was thought that stutterers needed to establish dominance in the left cortex (Delcato, 1963). A variant of that theory, promulgated at the University of Minnesota by Bryngelson (1956) suggested that stutterers needed to practice unilateral-handedness exercises. Stutterers have been taught to speak slowly, in a monotone, and to wiggle their fingers rhythmically while talking. They have been treated by snake potions and hypnotism. As powerful as these treatment methods may be, stuttering is more powerful, and it continues to elude adequate explanation and treatment.

Starting in the late 1930s, and for many decades afterward, the reigning theory of stuttering was Wendell Johnson's "diagnosogenic" theory (Johnson, 1956, 1959; Johnson & Leutenegger, 1955). Johnson felt that there were no biological or physical differences between stutterers and nonstutterers. Instead, stutterers had come to the conclusion that they were not able to speak normally and had to be careful to avoid speech errors or bobbles and struggle with these errors when they occurred. Johnson felt that stuttering almost always began in childhood, when the child's parents inadvertently taught the child to fear speech and to be anxious about what were really ordinary, benign nonfluencies of the sort that occur in the speech of all developing children. Stuttering runs in families, according to Johnson, because the attitudes toward speech that lead to stuttering are handed down from parents to child, not because of genetic transmission. Most stutterers are capable of perfectly fluent speech when they sing, during choral reading, or when they are by themselves. According to Johnson, it is the stutterer's attitudes that are maladaptive, not the stutterer's speech mechanism. Stutterers struggle with phantoms when they really need only to talk, stumble occasionally, but simply go on talking. Johnson's was clearly an environmental theory of stuttering and in the common polarity of the day that pitted organic against learning theories, stuttering, by default, was said to be learned. At the core of the child's problem was increasing anxiety about making mistakes.

The consequences of Johnson's theory of stuttering were profound. It followed that there was no need to focus on the child's handedness and that drawing attention to the child's stuttering would cause the problem to increase. Similarly, it would be unacceptable to praise or compliment the child for periods of fluency because, by implication, the child might reason that if fluency is approved, nonfluency must be objectionable. Treatment for stuttering consisted of admonitions to the parents to not pay attention to the child's speech, to try not to cause the child stress, to create a relaxed atmosphere in the home, and to make speech a pleasurable activity. It did not allow direct treatment of the stuttering behavior itself. Even conducting experimental research on conditions that led to the development of stuttering was unthinkable because the research or the treatment was thought to exacerbate the problem by increasing the child's anxiety.

During this period, Johnson was convinced that he had liberated theories of stuttering from the oppressive idea that the stutterer was a disordered or inferior organism. I suspect that he did not recognize that he had also narrowly constricted the range of treatments and even research that one would dare attempt with stutterers.

In the 1960s Israel Goldiamond, in the flush of the success that behavior modification had earned in dealing with a great variety of intractable behavioral problems, turned to stuttering, one of the last behavioral frontiers (Goldiamond, 1965). He claimed that stuttering was operant behavior and that adult stutterers could be taught a new, fluent form of speaking by the careful application of operant methods of behavior analysis. Most researchers in speech pathology responded skeptically at first because so many pronouncements of a cure for stuttering had been offered over the years, and they rarely had enduring value for the clinical enterprise.

At the University of Minnesota, Dick Martin and I were attracted to Goldiamond's ideas not so much because they offered a treatment for stuttering but because they revealed a fascinating paradox. As students of Johnson, we had absorbed the idea that stuttering is environmentally determined—a form of learned behavior. Conventional wisdom in the field argued that events that called attention to stuttering, such as punishment or reinforcement, would increase the stutterer's anxiety and thereby exacerbate the problem (Wischner, 1952). At the same time, learning theorists who studied punishment (e.g., Solomon, 1964) indicated that behavior that is punished should decrease, at least temporarily. Why then should stuttering, unlike other behaviors, increase when it is punished? Goldiamond's (1965) work stimulated us to think that something was wrong with the conventional wisdom about stuttering, that stuttering was not really learned behavior, or that not all behaviors responded to punishment in the same way. Any one of these possible explanations of our paradox invited exploration.

For a period of 7 or 8 years, Dick Martin and I performed a systematic series of studies on the effects of various forms of punishment on stuttering and nonfluent behaviors, and Martin and Haroldson and their students continued to make important contributions to this literature long after I switched to other research problems (for reviews, see Bloodstein, 1987; Ingham, 1984; Martin, 1968; Siegel, 1970). Martin and I used mild electric shock, the word "wrong," time out from speaking, and loss of points or money as events that could be made contingent on stuttering. The initial studies were with adults, not children, and involved both normal speakers and stutterers (Martin, 1968; Siegel, 1970, 1973). The findings were dramatic. The conventional wisdom about the effects of punishment on stuttering and nonfluency was not upheld. When punishing events were made contingent on stuttering or nonfluent behaviors of normal speakers, the behaviors decreased. Punishment did not cause stuttering to increase in frequency or severity. Armed with these data, we looked back at the studies that had supposedly established the harmful effects of punishment on stuttering (e.g., Brutten & Shoemaker, 1967; Hill, 1954; Sheehan, 1958; Van Riper, 1937) and found that in a variety of ways they violated the conditions for a test of punishment as defined in the learning literature. Our predecessors had been so convinced about the harmful effects of punishment that they had not looked carefully at their own designs. Most often, the so-called punishment studies did indeed involve some unpleasant stimulus, but the studies did not require that the stimulus be presented as the immediate consequence of any particular behavior. There was no concern for the contingency between the response and its punishment. In some studies, a supposedly punishing event was presented on a predetermined schedule, with no necessary relation to the speaker's nonfluencies (Stassi, 1961); in others, it was threatened but not delivered (Van Riper, 1937), and so on.

At one point in the research program, Martin and his colleagues became uncommonly bold. They dared to test the effects of punishment on the speech of two stuttering children. Martin, Kuhl, and Haroldson (1972) asked the children to speak with a puppet who sat on a small stage and whose mouth could be manipulated by an unseen experimenter who also provided the puppet's voice. When the child stuttered, the puppet's voice stopped and the stage darkened for a few seconds so that the child could no longer see the puppet. The children were effectively being given time out for stuttering—perhaps the first direct experimental attempt to manipulate a child's stuttering. In both children, the procedure accomplished substantial reductions in stuttering frequency.

Something had happened. The story about stuttering was changing. The dominant diagnosogenic theory was no longer satisfying. A new theory that viewed stuttering formally as learned behavior was promulgated, and research and clinical practice was once again liberated from what had become the constraints of the old theory. It became possible to contemplate and to implement procedures that were unimaginable while Johnson's theories held sway. The liberation was both in the realm of research and treatment of stuttering. Theory had constrained, and eventually, theory liberated the field.

However, this new theory, too, finally succumbed. Using the methods of behavior modification, it was indeed possible to make substantial changes in the speech behaviors of stutterers, but they did not stick. It was an old problem that speech pathologists know too well. Innumerable procedures are temporarily effective with stutterers, but they do not succeed in the whole range of situations in which the stutterer has to function. Goldiamond (1965) dismissed the problem of obtaining enduring changes by considering it a matter of simple behavioral engineering—a problem in generalizing gains accomplished in one setting to a wide range of novel situations. But, in fact, the failure of the learning approach is much broader. Ultimately, the research generated from the operant framework was abandoned because it was not a well-constructed story. It concentrated on the end of stuttering, but it did not have a good beginning and middle. It focused on how to change stuttering but not on stuttering's basic underlying nature; it did not explain where or how stuttering developed (but see Shames & Sherrick, 1963, for an unsuccessful attempt), why some people become stutterers and others do not. It did not connect the variables that could modify stuttering with those that caused it to occur in the first place. It was not a good story, with a beginning that connected to a middle and an end. Nonetheless, I believe that it transformed our understandings of the relation of stuttering to its consequences in ways that clearly repudiated older theories and made it possible for therapists and researchers to use methods with stutterers that could not have been attempted under previous theories.

In stuttering treatment and theory, I believe we are currently in a dark place that even Kuhn (1970) could not illuminate. Our old theories have been largely abandoned but not through scientific revolution. We do not have compelling alternatives. We are rummaging around for a new theory. Physiological variables have become popular again, quite predictably after the demise of the learning approaches. New technology has made it possible to examine the activity of the vocal system in exquisite detail, particularly in the larynx. Genetic theories are enjoying new popularity. But none of these approaches is as broad and embracing as was Johnson's (1956, 1959) diagnosogenic theory. In some ways, the world of stuttering was a more comfortable place in which to do research back in earlier days. We at least knew where to look for important variables and where not to bother looking. Now there is theoretical anarchy and, consequently, a lack of any truly coherent program of research or therapy. There are therapists still using methods from the Johnson era and even before. Behavior modification still is used in some form. Systems of rate control have found favor, incorporating features that at the turn of the century might have been labeled quackery.

We need a new story. Freed from the shackles of a dominant theory, we lack the kind of sweet paradox that energized the research that Dick Martin and I embarked on 25 years ago. I know that for most cognitive researchers, stuttering is not a central concern. I offer it as a case history, however, of how theory interacts with practice in a clinical field.

I am currently developing another analysis, of the same general sort, that shows how simple methodological decisions on how to measure stuttering also has had a profound effect on how we conceptualize the disorder. Until 1933, stuttering was measured primarily by assigning severity scores to samples of speech, based on the listener's subjective impression of the extent of the disorder. In 1933, Johnson proposed that it might be possible to identify stuttering episodes—moments of stuttering—in the flow of speech and that stuttering could be quantified by counting these moments. This simple discovery set the stage for an abundance of studies that could now specify how stuttering frequency varied as a function of the listener, the reading material, the situation, practice, and so on. It was an enormously empowering idea that made possible the scientific study of stuttering behavior. But it also encourages us to think of stuttering as though, in fact, it consists of discrete events that were imposed on the flow of speech, rather than as a way of speaking that may suffuse the entire speech episode. It causes us to talk about stuttering as occurring "on" words as though speech and stuttering are independent events with one overlaid on the other. In this account, stuttering is different from speaking as well as from nonfluency. It is a qualitatively distinctive behavior that, by definition, can only occur in stutterers and so is discontinuous with the nonfluent behaviors found in normal speakers.

Only recently have we begun to recognize the consequences of this measurement decision for the very ways in which we conceptualize the basic nature of the disorder, and only recently have we begun to challenge these assumptions. Thus, methodological decisions, too, have the power both to liberate and to shackle our understanding of natural phenomena.

As cognitive scientists consider new theories and methods for understanding and explaining human behavior, I suggest that they add another criterion to the usual array of evaluative criteria that greets each new theory—and that they consider, too, how the theory will play in the clinic, what implications it will have for the therapist or teacher. This is different from suggesting that we might learn something about normal behavior from studying its disruption. Cognitive scientists already know that lesson very well and have made rich use of data from brain-damaged and other disordered populations. I am suggesting something more. I am suggesting that cognitive theorists ask also what implications their theories might have for the management or remediation of abnormal behavior—how the theory encumbers the teachers and clinicians who must, if they are intellectually alert, pay attention to the theories that are generated in the basic sciences.

Of course, I do not really expect cognitive scientists to do that; it is the job of those of us in clinical fields, who must challenge researchers to consider the implications of theory for the domain of real human problems.

In conclusion, I would like to leave you with a quotation from Dana's absorbing book, *Two Years Before the Mast*. I read the book with great interest while I was on sabbatical at the University of California in Santa Barbara because a good part of Dana's voyage took place along the shores of that lovely city. In *Two Years Before the Mast*, Dana (1840) seems to have anticipated my concern for the articulation of that which lies between theory and the lives of the ordinary people on whom the theory impinges. He concluded his book with an admonition that might have been addressed to both cognitive scientists and theory makers:

We must come down from our heights, and leave our straight paths, for the byways and low places of life, if we would learn truths by strong contrasts; and in hovels, in forecastles, and among our own outcasts in foreign lands, see what has been wrought upon our fellow-creatures by accident, hardship, or vice.

References

Bloodstein, O. (1987). *A handbook on stuttering.* Chicago: National Easter Seal Society.

Brutten, E. J., & Shoemaker, D. J. (1967). *The modification of stuttering.* Englewood Cliffs, NJ: Prentice-Hall.

Bryngelson, B. (1956). In E. Hahn (Ed.), *Stuttering: Significant theories and therapies* (pp. 14–23). Stanford, CA: Stanford University Press.

Chomsky, N. (1957). *Syntactic structures.* The Hague, The Netherlands: Mouton.

Dana, R. H., Jr. (1840). *Two years before the mast.* New York: Harper.

Delcato, C. H. (1963). *The diagnosis and treatment of speech and hearing problems.* Springfield, IL: Charles C Thomas.

Goldiamond, I. (1965). Stuttering and fluency as manipulable operant response classes. In L. Krasner & L. P. Ullman (Eds.), *Research in behavior modification* (pp. 106–156). New York: Holt, Rinehart & Winston.

Hill, H. (1954). An experimental study of disorganization of speech and manual responses in normal subjects. *Journal of Speech and Hearing Disorders, 19,* 295–305.

Ingham, R. J. (1984). *Stuttering and behavior therapy: Current status and experimental foundations.* San Diego, CA: College Hill.

Johnson, W. (1933). An interpretation of stuttering. *Quarterly Journal of Speech, 19,* 70–76.

Johnson, W. (1956). Stuttering. In W. Johnson, S. J. Brown, J. C. Curtis, C. W. Edney, & J. Keaster (Eds.), *Speech handicapped school children* (pp. 202–300). New York: Harper.

Johnson, W. (1959). *The onset of stuttering.* Minneapolis: University of Minnesota Press.

Johnson, W., & Leutenegger, R. (Eds.). (1955). *Stuttering in children and adults: Thirty years of research at the University of Iowa.* Minneapolis: University of Minnesota Press.

Klingbeil, G. M. (1939). The historical background of the modern speech clinic. *Journal of Speech Disorders, 4,* 115–132.

Kuhn, T. (1970). *The structure of scientific revolutions* (2nd ed.). Chicago: University of Chicago Press.

Lenneberg, E. H. (1967). *Biological foundations of language.* New York: Wiley.

Martin, R. R. (1968). The experimental manipulation of stuttering behaviors. In H. N. Sloane & B. D. MacAuley (Eds.), *Operant procedures in remedial speech and language training* (pp. 325–407). Boston: Houghton Mifflin.

Martin, R. R., Kuhl, P., & Haroldson, S. (1972). An experimental treatment with two preschool stuttering children. *Journal of Speech and Hearing Research, 15,* 743–752.

Shames, G. H., & Sherrick, C. E. (1963). A discussion of nonfluency and stuttering as operant behavior. *Journal of Speech and Hearing Disorders, 28,* 3–18.

Sheehan, J. (1958). Conflict theory of stuttering. In J. Eisenson (Ed.), *Stuttering: A symposium* (pp. 121–166). New York: Harper.

Siegel, G. M. (1970). Punishment, stuttering, and disfluency. *Journal of Speech and Hearing Research, 13,* 677–714.

Siegel, G. M. (1973). Studies in speech fluency. *Journal of Communication Disorders, 6,* 259–271.

Skinner, B. F. (1957). *Verbal behavior.* New York: Appleton-Century-Crofts.

Solomon, R. L. (1964). Punishment. *American Psychologist, 19,* 239–253.

Stassi, E. J. (1961). Disfluency of normal speakers and reinforcement. *Journal of Speech and Hearing Research, 4,* 358–361.

Van Riper, C. (1937). The effect of penalty on frequency of stuttering spasms. *Pedagogical Seminary and Journal of Genetic Psychology, 50,* 193–195.

Wischner, G. (1952). An experimental approach to expectancy and anxiety in stuttering behavior. *Journal of Speech and Hearing Disorders, 17,* 139–154.

CHAPTER 13

Expertise and Fit: Aspects of Cognition

Paul E. Johnson, Laura K. Kochevar, and Imran A. Zualkernan

F or a number of years, we have investigated problem solving in business and professional settings. We have studied domains ranging from medical diagnosis and computer troubleshooting to financial statement auditing and process diagnosis in semiconductor manufacturing (e.g., Johnson, Duran, Hassebrock, Moller, & Prietula, 1981; Johnson, Grazioli, Jamal, & Zualkernan, in press; Volovik, Zualkernan, Johnson, & Matthews, 1990).

In the course of this work, we have often received comments from subjects, and from our collaborators (who are usually also experts in fields we are studying), that suggest that all is not well with our understanding of what they know. These comments range from those such as, "Keep in mind that when I do this problem normally, I would

The research in semiconductor manufacturing reported here is currently supported by a grant from the IBM Yorktown Research Center in Yorktown, NY, and the IBM Semi-Conductor Manufacturing Facility in East Fishkill, NY. The work in auditing has been supported by grants from the KPMG Peat Marwick Foundation and the SEC Financial Reporting Institute, School of Accounting, University of Southern California. The work in medicine is currently supported by Grant SES-9009267 from the National Science Foundation.

We would like to thank the many individuals who have contributed to the work reported here. We are especially grateful to Cathy Caswell and her colleagues at IBM, Eash Fishkill, NY, and Steve Campbell from the University of Minnesota who gave generously of their time and energy to the work on process diagnosis. Glen Berryman from the Department of Accounting and James Moller from the Department of Pediatrics at the University of Minnesota have been instrumental, respectively, in making possible the work in auditing and medical diagnosis. Our work could also not have been done without the contributions of Dean Briesemeister, Stefano Grazioli, Karim Jamal, Gail Nelson, Kip Smith, and Dmitry Volovik.

ask a colleague for her opinion on the X-ray" (medical diagnosis) to, "We don't see many instances of fraud in our firm, because we screen our client's heavily up front" (from a study of financial statement fraud detection in auditing).

In each case, what the individuals who made these comments seemed to be saying was that we were missing important aspects of their behavior in the tasks that we had constructed for them to perform. Although we could usually manage to extract from such tasks a model of problem-solving activity that was consistent with what we understood problem solving to be, our model often lacked both the richness and contextual links that were part of the settings in which our subjects worked.

As we struggled with ways to represent these other aspects of the individuals' behavior, it became increasingly clear that our vocabulary and conceptual tools were incomplete. As we searched for a means of conceptualizing the knowledge constructed to meet the demands of real-world tasks, we were increasingly driven to the concept of *adaptation.*

The concept of adaptation, as used by others in the study of cognition (e.g., Anderson, 1990; Simon, 1980, 1981), has provided an explanatory basis for describing the mechanisms of cognitive change as well as a source of analogies for shaping problems for scientific study and evaluation. More recently, it has also provided a link between research in cognition and work in sociobiology and the neurosciences (Dupré, 1987).

In this chapter, we use past work on adaptation in biology to identify a potentially fruitful invariant for guiding the study of problem solving in complex, semantically rich environments. We call this invariant *fit.*[1] It is based not on an agent's knowledge per se but rather on the relation between features of this knowledge and features of the environment to which the knowledge constitutes an adaptation.

We use the concept of *fit* as the basis for constructing a framework within which both the success and failure of problem-solving knowledge can be understood. In what follows, we briefly describe this framework and then illustrate it with examples drawn from a variety of fields. We then provide a more extensive example of application of the framework in a specific environment that we have studied for the past year. We conclude with a brief consideration of some methodological and conceptual consequences that follow from this approach.

---

[1] *The concept of fit has its roots in evolutionary biology (Darwin, 1859; Wilson, 1975). The biological concept of fit addresses the capacity of the individual to contribute to the gene pool of subsequent generations, thereby fulfilling an inherent goal of survival. The psychological use of fit that we propose also addresses the attainment of goals but goals as defined by task demands and agent capacities (see also Rosenberg, 1980; Sober, 1984).*

Framework for the Study of Expertise

We define *expertise* as the operative knowledge that enables an agent to perform tasks in specific environments.[2] Fit, then, characterizes the degree to which an agent's expertise (a) reflects the requirements for success in these performing tasks and (b) is in accordance with the structure of available task information. We develop each of these concepts after first defining more precisely what we mean by *environment*.

The *physical environment* is a description of objectively observable characteristics. The units of measurement for this description are determined by an observer's theory of the environment. For example, the environment of the physicist might be described using oscilloscopes and galvanometers, the carpenter's in terms of feet and inches, and the physician's in terms of signs and symptoms. Regardless of scale, the units and their interrelations are potentially observable separate from the agent's behavior.

Specific characteristics of the physical environment (e.g., disease or defect) may require specific action by the agent (e.g., diagnosis or repair). There are, in fact, lawful relations between the information in the physical environment and potentially successful actions. A task can be performed by an agent only because the information contained in the task is lawfully related to some physical occurrence (Turvey, Carello, & Kim, 1989). Specific occurrences in the physical environment generate specific detectable information. For example, a smooth, highly polished object reflects most of the incident light, an upper respiratory infection causes sniffles, a short circuit alters measurable voltage. Specification of the physical environment, however, is not sufficient to understand an agent's performance. Different agents can occupy the same physical environment and display radically different behaviors. These differences can be attributed to between-agent differences in goals and sensitivity to information.

The description of the *task environment* is an attempt to specify the subset of the physical environment that is relevant to a class of agents who share common goals and sensitivity to available information. The task environment in this sense is a specification of the physical environment for a class of agents. It is a subset of the physical environment subject to the function of a class of agents (e.g., orthopedic surgeons).[3] The information in the task environment must necessarily be accessible to the class of agents

---

[2] *The term* agent *is used here to refer to any entity that acts autonomously in the world, including humans, other animals, biological organisms, and machines.*

[3] *The distinction between physical and task environments is analogous to the biological distinction between habitat and niche. Whereas habitat is the physical environment of the organism, niche is the organism's function within the habitat (Elton, 1927).*

(Newell & Simon, 1972). For example, infrared radiation is a source of information for honey bees but not for taxi drivers. The task environment also specifies the actions that are required in the environment to which the agents are adapted. For example, if performing surgery is the function of a class of physicians, then precisely locating the physical defect is a required action.

The *functional environment* is a subset of the task environment that is specific to an individual agent and its goals. It is constituted of the information that is used by a specific agent and those potential actions that comprise that agent's behavioral repertoire (Kochevar & Johnson, 1988). The functional environment is also a reflection of the adaptation of an agent to the task environment. This adaptation is the agent's expertise.

Fit is reflected in the degree to which an agent is competent in a task environment and how well the agent's adaptation reconciles the capacities and goals with the information and demands of the task environment. Fit is a description of the relation between the task environment and the adaptation. Because adaptations develop under both environmental and agent constraints, the fit estimates from each perspective should be related (see Figure 1).

Regardless of the perspective, fit varies along two dimensions: semantic and structural (see Figure 1). Semantic fit refers to the degree to which actions in the adaptation reflect the agent's goals and the requirements for action in the task environment. We have seen this kind of fit most clearly in our work on medical diagnoses (Johnson et al., 1981). Initially in this work, we failed to appreciate the fact that the experienced clinician and the less experienced resident often approach the diagnostic task differently because they have quite different goals. The experienced physician tends to perform a diagnosis with treatment in mind. As one of our subjects remarked, "I always try to come up with a treatable condition." In some cases, the goal linking diagnosis to treatment is used as an aid to diagnosis (i.e., using the patient's response to treatment as a means of arriving at a final diagnosis). The resident (and medical student), on the other hand, is much more likely to approach diagnosis as a challenging intellectual puzzle, with the goal of coming up with a correct answer.

Semantic fit also reflects the degree to which the agent's adaptation meets requirements for performance in the task environment. The experienced physician's ability to generate a good response from the perspective of treatability (e.g., Chase & Simon, 1973; Johnson et al., 1981) is also a consequence of being well fit to the task environment of diagnosis.

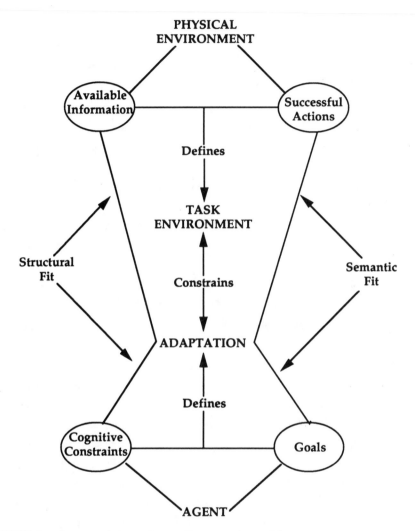

FIGURE 1   Framework for understanding expertise and fit.

Although the concept of *semantic fit* tends to be fairly apparent, the idea of structural fit is not. *Structural fit* is the degree to which the structure of information in the agent's adaptation reflects optimal utilization of the agent's cognitive capacities and is aligned with the structure of information in the task environment. When structural fit is high, the agent accepts the tasks as meaningful and belonging to the environment over which the agent has achieved mastery. When structural fit is low, the agent often rejects the task as something that is appropriate to work on. Low structural fit occurs when experts in the field refuse to accept tasks as ones to which their expertise applies. Examples of this kind of response vary from that of the federal judge who said to us, "I'll do it for you, but I doubt it will tell you anything about what I know," to the engineer who wanted to know how the device we asked him to troubleshoot was created because he did not believe that it was possible for a typical manufacturing line to create a device with these properties.

Structural fit also reflects the congruence between the adaptation and the agent's cognitive capacities. Assuming a general adaptive strategy consisting of the optimal use of limited cognitive processing resources supposes that a high degree of structural fit is reflected in the fluency of the agent's performance and in the agent's ability to make a direct intuitive response (Dreyfus & Dreyfus, 1986; LaBerge, 1973; Larkin, McDermott, Simon, & Simon, 1980). One of our more interesting examples of degree of structural fit in this sense occurred in our work in medical diagnosis (Swanson, 1978). When we first began to work with physicians at the University of Minnesota Medical School, one of them would regularly say after going through only a few pieces of data in a case, "I know what the answer is." For this physician, the cases we had constructed were ones to which he was literally able to "perceive" an answer on the basis of only a few cues.

Although an agent's response in a given task environment can be direct and intuitive, this form of behavior may not appear in the way tasks are done in the world. Because the consequences of errors are often substantial, and because of the way in which information is requested and received, tasks in the world are often carried out in a sequential problem solving–like form. In many instances in which we have studied these kinds of environments, agents nevertheless achieved high degrees of structural fit that was apparent when the tasks we gave them permitted it to be revealed (Johnson, Jamal, & Berryman, 1991).

In what follows, we examine the concept of fit in more detail in an environment of complexity and change for which there nevertheless exist adaptations with high levels of both structural and semantic fit.

Expertise and Fit in a Changing Environment

The environment we describe here is semiconductor manufacturing. In this environment, the products (chips) created by a manufacturing process are undergoing continuous evolution because of changes in design and advances in technology. The problem we investigated was that of diagnosing breakdowns in the manufacturing process that gave rise to specific faults on chips. We investigated this problem by creating tasks for expert process diagnosticians (engineers) to perform from which we could infer properties of the expertise they had used in performing the tasks. We describe this expertise in terms of problem-solving methods (Newell, 1973) and then show how such methods establish various types of fit to the task environment that they support.

In the process diagnosis task, a diagnostician uses as input a faulty chip (at some stage of processing) and the results of tests on the chip (Lukazek, Grambow, & Yarbreough, 1990) to determine the parameters of the manufacturing process that may be causing the fault. Faults occurring in the manufacturing environment can be classified according to the level of diagnosis that is carried out. The process of diagnosis always starts with measurement deviations, which lead to a diagnosis of physical anomalies, which eventually leads to diagnoses of process anomalies or root causes (Dishaw & Pan, 1989). The experiments described here present results of an investigation of the expertise used by two agents to assess faults at the level of physical anomalies given a set of measurement deviations.

Experiment 1: Evidence of Fit

In semiconductor manufacturing, it is possible to define the physical environment of the chip (device) by means of computer simulation models based on the physics of the device (such simulations are regularly used by designers of devices). In this experiment, one such simulation of a bipolar device (see Figure 2) was used as a surrogate for the physical transistor on a chip. In this context, the physical environment was defined by the physics equations that constituted the simulation. These equations describe relations between the various input and output parameters. The simulation takes six input parameters of a bipolar transistor cell and uses a set of physics equations to generate various electrical measurements of a bipolar device, such as sheet resistance of the various layers, junction capacitances, and current and gain characteristics.

The task environment of the diagnostician adds the constraint of diagnosis to the physical environment defined by the simulation. Agents who perform the process diagnosis task are required to determine physical anomalies (represented as faulty inputs to the simulation) given a specific set of measurement deviations (represented as outputs from the simulation). In the task environment we examined, the measurements provided to the

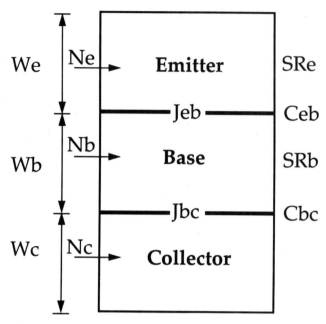

FIGURE 2   Model of simulated bipolar transistor. (Parameters: We = width of emitter, Wb = width of base, Wc = width of collector, Ne = concentration of emitter, Nb = concentration of base, Nc = concentration of collector, Jeb = emitter–base junction, Jbc = base–collector junction. Electrical characteristics: SRe = sheet resistance of emitter, SRb = sheet resistance of base, Ceb = emitter–base capacitance, Cbc = collector–base capacitance.)

agents were restricted to sheet resistances, junction capacitances, punch-through voltage, base and collector currents, and beta (current gain).

An expert in the design of bipolar devices and a collaborator in our research was asked to determine how product anomalies could be represented in the simulation. Product anomalies investigated included pipe faults, leakage faults, and pinholes in dielectric insulation layers (see Mahajan, 1989). On the basis of parameters identified by the expert informant, an initial set of 11 test problems was constructed using runs of the simulation to develop data for each problem. Each test problem represented a change in one of the physical parameters of the device (e.g., width of the base; Wb) and consisted of a consistent set of symptoms (i.e., measurement deviations) and an expected outcome (i.e., a product anomaly). For example, Test Problem 1 was constructed by increasing the width of the base from 1.5E-5 cm to 1.75E-5 cm in the simulation. Simulating the device caused this change in Wb to decrease the sheet resistance of the base (SRb) from 3.08E03 to 2.52E03 ohms/square and increase the punch-through voltage (Vpt) from 16.1 V to 22.2 V. Similarly, Test Problem 10 was an example of a fault in which the junction between the base and the collector (Jbc) moves up. This fault was introduced by simultaneously decreasing Wb and increasing the width of the collector (Wc) by the same amount.

A diagnostic expert (E1) working at a commercial fabrication facility, who had more than 10 years of experience in both design and development of semiconductor devices and manufacturing processes, was given the 11 test problems. Each problem was represented as a process recipe for a bipolar process (a sequence of steps in a manufacturing process), a set of design parameters, expected electrical characteristics of the transistor, and a set of actual measurement deviations from the simulation. The expert was asked to determine the cause of the measurement deviations.

Thinking-aloud verbal protocol was collected as the expert solved each problem. The protocols were analyzed to determine the methods used by the expert to perform the task. These methods were identified from problem-solving data using a previously developed protocol analysis schema based on the assumption that diagnosis can be viewed as a hypothetico-deductive task (Johnson et al., 1981; Johnson et al., in press; Reed, Stuck, & Moen, 1988). The methods are an indicator of the agent's adaptation or expertise (Johnson, Garber, & Zualkernan, 1987).

The expert's methods were validated by constructing an additional set of seven problems. Each problem in this set was constructed to either replicate or explore complementary problem types not covered in the first set of problems. For example, whereas the first set included a problem of emitter–base junction (Jeb) moving down, the second set included the complementary problem of Jeb moving up. An analysis of E1's protocol on the second set of problems confirmed the methods that we developed based on the first set of problems (the first set of 11 problems and the second set of 7 problems will henceforth be referred to as the set of 18 problems).

E1's methods were further validated by constructing a problem-solving model that embodied each method.[4] The output of the model was compared with E1's behavior on

---

[4] *E1's methods were implemented as a production system model (using NEXPERT, a software shell published by Neuron Data, Inc.). In this model, all methods are executed on each problem. Because each method uses a different cue for its invocation (i.e., SRb, SRe, Cbc), in some problems only one method reaches a final conclusion; the other methods simply fail the first condition of the method. For other problems, multiple methods reach a conclusion to diagnose problems that look like multiple faults in the output space of the methods (Davis, 1984). An example of such problems in semiconductor*

the set of 18 test problems. The model was then further evaluated by testing its outcomes on 30 systematically generated additional problems. The model showed 100% correspondence with the outcomes arrived at by E1 on the original set of 18 problems and 80% success on a systematically generated set of 30 additional problems.

Methods Used by the Expert Diagnostician

The three methods identified from E1's protocols on the set of 18 problems are presented in Figure 3. Each method represents an adaptation by E1 to the task of diagnosing semiconductor devices. Although each method is based on a hypothetico-deductive strategy of diagnosis, each has a unique, specific structure. For example, Method 1 represents a closely related set of hypotheses arranged in a specific structural configuration. Each node in this structure represents an operation on a hypothesis or on data.

Method 1 indicates observation of a measurement deviation in the sheet resistance of the base (SRb) leading to the proposal of two alternative hypotheses: Either the concentration of the base (Nb) is high or low, or Wb is low or high. The emitter–base capacitance (Ceb) is then used as evidence to decide between the two competing hypotheses. As Method 1 shows, if Ceb does not change, then the hypotheses about changes in Nb are rejected, which leaves Wb as the only candidate. The hypothesis about a change in Wb is further confirmed by ensuring that the Vpt has moved in the appropriate direction. A move in the correct direction leads to acceptance of a change in Wb as the product anomaly that led to the observed measurement deviation. This sequence of activities, shown in Figure 3, can be clearly seen in Steps 15 through 26 of E1's protocol for Test Problem 1:

15. the ahm
16. the base resistivity went down
17. so obviously there's more in
18. there's more boron in the base
19. total
20. but since the capacitance didn't change
21. means that
22. the concentration at the junction didn't change

---

manufacturing are junction move problems. In a junction move problem, two sets of width measurements (i.e., Wb and We to simulate Jeb move, see Figure 1) are changed and hence require Method 3 and Method 2 simultaneously to arrive at a correct outcome.

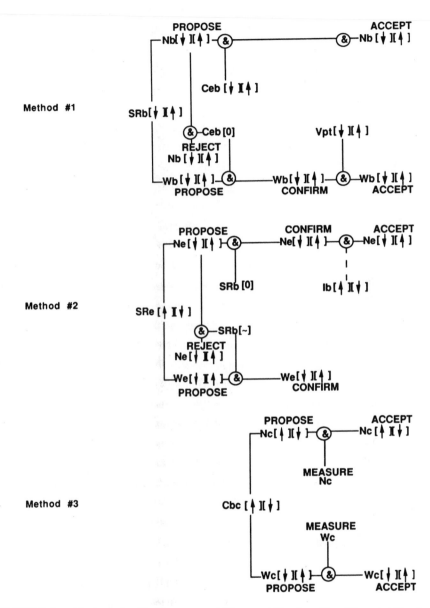

FIGURE 3   Methods for E1. (Parameters: We = width of emitter, Wb = width of base, Wc = width of collector, Ne = concentration of emitter, Nb = concentration of base, Nc = concentration of collector. Electrical characteristics: SRe = sheet resistance of emitter, SRb = sheet resistance of base, Ceb = emitter–base capacitance, Cbc = collector–base capacitance, Vpt = punch-through voltage, Ib = base current.)

23. so the only thing that could have happened is it [base] got wider

24. um now

25. and that's also consistent with the punch-through voltage

26. going up

It is important to notice that only the direction of change (if there is a change) is represented in this excerpt of E1's protocol. The methods described in Figure 3 do not represent the quantitative values of the variables themselves or changes in variables.

Method 2 in Figure 3 is very similar in structure to Method 1 and is also based on a hypothetico-deductive strategy. In Method 2, SRb is used as the discriminating piece of evidence. This method leads to the acceptance of either a change in Nb or in the width of the emitter (We) as the cause of the deviation.

Figure 3 also shows the third method used by E1, which is initially triggered by a change in the expected value of the collector–base capacitance (Cbc). Method 3 is different from Method 1 and Method 2 in its treatment of the confirmation of proposed hypotheses. Whereas Method 1 and Method 2 use additional cues (such as Ceb) to discriminate and confirm a hypothesis, Method 3 relies on direct measurements from the world. This method shows that it is difficult for E1 to discriminate between the changes in the width of the collector (Wc) or the concentration of the collector (Nc) without taking direct measurements, which are usually available through destructive testing.

In summary, E1 used SRb, sheet resistance of the emitter (SRe), and Cbc as data to trigger various hypotheses about possible physical anomalies (such as increased Wb). In addition, E1's methods used precise discriminating cues (such as Ceb and SRb) to distinguish among the various competing hypotheses. Additional data such as Vpt was then used to confirm and accept a plausible hypothesis.

Fit of Expert Methods

The methods described above represent the adaptation or the expertise developed by an agent to cope with the demands of a specific task environment. In what follows, we discuss properties of these methods and how they reflect fit to the task environment.

The structural fit of the expert's methods to the task environment is defined by the correspondence between information represented in the methods and information found in the task environment. The methods in Figure 3 show a complete reliance on binary differential relations between key sets of variables. All methods depend only on directional changes in a variable (i.e., increase or decrease), constancy of variables, or change in variables regardless of direction. Because the methods are independent of the absolute values of the various parameters of the device, they are stable in an environment within which changes in the specific device being diagnosed regularly occur.

Because the methods are also based on the use of only a few specific cues, the selectivity of the expert's adaptation is a reflection of structural fit to the task environment. The information that is taken into consideration is highly functional and closely tied to the demands of the diagnostic task. This is reflected both in what individual measurements (i.e., cues and events) are paid attention to and in the form of the relations that are considered. For example, the methods are selective in ignoring beta (the current gain) and the collector currents. Both beta and currents are considered crucial factors from the perspective of designing a device (e.g., see Wolf, 1990, p. 464) but are of little diagnostic value in differential diagnosis because they depend on too many factors.

The semantic fit of the expert's methods is revealed by examining the functional dependencies between the parameters of the physical environment and the actions that are useful to the expert. These relations express the lawful relations between available information (i.e., values of symptoms such as SRb) and successful action (such as a decrease in Wb). Figure 4 is a functional dependency network that abstracts out the functional relations among variables of the physical environment while suppressing their exact form (as given by the physics equations in the simulation). The functional dependency network represents a stable structure in this task environment. It clearly shows the functional relations among the potential action components (changes in concentration of emitter [Ne], Nb, Nc, We, Wb, or Wc) and potential cues (changes in SRe, SRb, Ceb, Cbc, or Vpt).

E1's methods exhibited semantic fit by exploiting the functional dependency network shown in Figure 4 in a manner that relates symptoms to appropriate actions. In all three methods, E1's initial hypothesis can be explained by following the functional dependency network backward from observed measurement deviations to what can generate these deviations. For example, on observing a deviation in SRb, Method 1 hypothesizes that the problem may be with Nb or Wb. Figure 4 shows that this is done by following SRb's functional dependencies to the source (Nb and Wb).

The next step in Method 1 consists of discriminating between the hypothesized faults. This is done by using Ceb as a discriminating cue and Vpt as confirming evidence. The use of these two variables as discriminating and confirming evidence, respectively, can be predicted from the functional description of the environment by running the functional dependencies forward from Nb and Wb through Equations 5 to Ceb and Vpt,

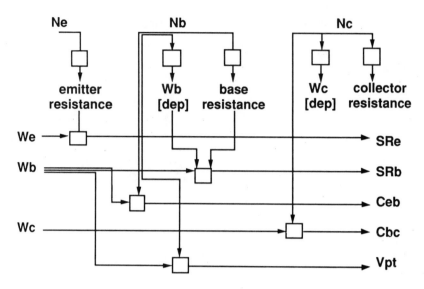

FIGURE 4 Functional relationships embedded in the simulation model. (Boxes represent specific equations, not given here, that collectively make up the simulation model. Parameters: We = width of emitter, Wb = width of base, Wc = width of collector, Ne = concentration of emitter, Nb = concentration of base, Nc = concentration of collector. Electrical characteristics: SRe = sheet resistance of emitter, SRb = sheet resistance of base, Ceb = emitter–base capacitance, Cbc = collector–base capacitance, Vpt = punch-through voltage. Wb[dep] and Wc[dep] = widths of depleted regions.)

respectively. This, however, does not explain why Method 1 uses Ceb as discriminating evidence and Vpt as only confirming evidence.

To explain this, we used the results of a sensitivity analysis shown in Figure 5 to determine how a change in Nb and Wb (while other parameters are kept constant) affects Ceb. Both Nb and Wb were varied on a scale from one quarter ($\times$ 0.25) to four times ($\times$4) their baseline values. Figure 5 shows clearly that a change in Wb does not have an effect on Ceb, whereas such a change is directly proportional to the change in Nb. This property of Ceb makes it an excellent candidate for discriminating between Wb and Nb as possible fault hypotheses. The use of this property in E1's methods shows a high degree of semantic fit over a wide range of faults (changes in Wb and Nb).

A sensitivity analysis of the effect of the Wb and Nb also clearly shows that, although Vpt is functionally dependent on both Nb and Wb, it does not represent a good

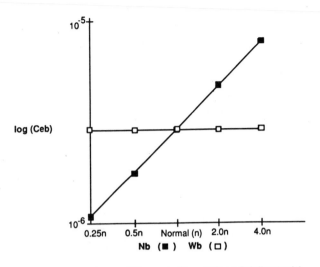

Effect of Change in Nb and Wb on Ceb (log scale)

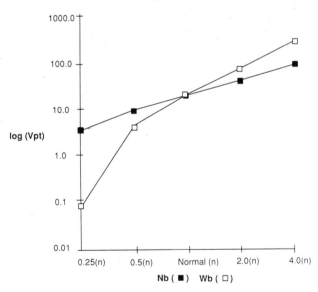

Effect of Change in Wb and Nb on Vpt (log scale)

FIGURE 5 Sensitivity analysis of E1's methods. (Parameters: We = width of emitter, Wb = width of base, Wc = width of collector, Ne = concentration of emitter, Nb = concentration of base, Nc = concentration of collector. Electrical characteristics: SRe = sheet resistance of emitter, SRb = sheet resistance of base, Ceb = emitter–base capacitance, Cbc = collector–base capacitance, Vpt = punch-through voltage.)

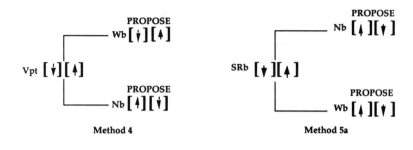

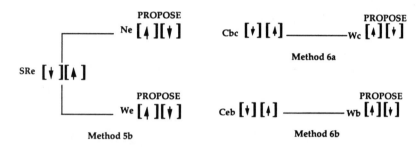

FIGURE 6 Methods for E2. (Parameters: We = width of emitter, Wb = width of base, Wc = width of collector, Ne = width of concentration of emitter, Nb = concentration of base. Electrical characteristics: SRe = sheet resistance of emitter, SRb = sheet resistance of base, Ceb = emitter–collector capacitance, Cbc = collector–base capacitance, Vpt = punch-through voltage.)

candidate for discriminating between Nb and Wb because it varies directly with both Wb and Nb (also shown in Figure 5). It is interesting to note, however, that over the wide range of variation, Vpt responded more (in absolute terms) to Wb than to Nb. This makes Vpt a candidate for confirming evidence for Wb and not for Nb.

The sensitivity analysis in Figure 5 also shows how the functional dependencies among components of the device and electrical characteristics of the device were used by E1 in conjunction with a propose–confirm–discrimination diagnostic scheme to establish semantic fit. The relations (e.g., the ones shown in the sensitivity analysis) in the methods are invariant over wide variations in possible faults (e.g., changes in Wb) within bipolar technology. This property of the E1's methods served to establish a high degree of semantic fit with the task environment of bipolar technology by ensuring that the methods diagnosed wide variations in faults on a specific device. The reliance of E1's methods on differential relations also showed that they were not tied to a specific device and therefore should have displayed a high semantic fit to an environment with changing devices as a task requirement.

We have characterized both the structural and semantic fit of one agent's adaptation to this task environment. Although we have described the mechanisms that established fit (both structural and semantic) for this agent, E1's methods represent one adaptation to the task environment. In what follows, we explore the properties of fit of another agent (E2) to the same task environment.

A Second Adaptation in a Changing Environment

E2 was given the same 18 problems as was E1, presented in the same manner. E2, a testing expert, had 7 years of experience working in the VLSI fabrication environment. At the time of the experiment, he worked in the testing department that diagnoses faulty chips that cannot be readily diagnosed "on the line" by individuals such as E1. The protocol analysis of E2's thinking-aloud comments resulted in methods that appear similar to those used by E1 but with interesting differences in establishing structural and semantic fit. The methods used by E2 in solving the 18 problems are shown in Figure 6.

In terms of structural fit, E2's methods were similar to those of E1. Both were selective and considered only binary, qualitative relations among the device parameters. However, the methods of E1 and E2 differed in how they established semantic fit. The device parameters had different meanings or functioned differently within each expert's methods.

Although both E1 and E2 exploited functional dependencies from the task environment in their methods, they differed along two dimensions: the actual equations that comprised the functional dependency and the corresponding diagnostic schema (i.e., propose–discriminate–confirm for E1). Although the functional dependency in the methods of E1 was aligned with that of the equations underlying the simulation, the functional dependency in E2's methods was based on equations that represented a subset of those used by E1.

The second dimension of difference in the mechanism establishing semantic fit between E1 and E2 was in the methods they used. E1 used information in a propose–discriminate–confirm scheme, whereas E2 used information in a propose–confirm-by-contradiction scheme. We next examine this difference in methods by comparing how the two experts arrived at the same answer on the same test problem (Test Problem 12) and then how they arrived at different answers on another test problem (Test Problem 3).

In Test Problem 12, SRb increased, Vpt decreased, and Ceb remained the same. E1's behavior on this problem is explained by Method 1. The increase in SRb led E1 to hypothesize that either the Wb was too shallow or Nb had gone down. Because there was no change in the Ceb, the hypothesis about the change in the concentration was rejected, which left the change in Wb as the only alternative. This hypothesis was confirmed by noticing that the Vpt had moved in the appropriate direction.

E2's behavior is explained by the methods given in Figure 6. Because Vpt went down, Method 4 proposed two hypotheses: Either the Wb had gone down or the Nb had gone up. Method 5a generates the hypothesis that based on the change in SRb, either Nb or Wb had gone down. Because there is a contradiction between the two hypotheses claiming an increase in Nb (from Method 4) and a decrease in Nb (from Method 5a), the hypotheses about the change in Nb were eliminated. This left only the hypothesis about the decrease in Wb as the possible answer. E2 did not use the "no change" in Ceb (as did E1) as a clue to discriminate between the hypotheses about Nb and Wb but was nevertheless able to arrive at the same result.

In Test Problem 3, the E1 used Method 3 to propose two hypotheses: Either Wc had gone down or Nc had gone up. E1 stated that he could not discriminate between the two hypotheses because in his task environment such a discrimination is done through measurement (e.g., of the concentration profile). He concluded, therefore, that he needed more data (from testing) to arrive at the final conclusion. For E2, Method 6a led to a direct conclusion (see Figure 6), namely that Wc had gone down—the correct answer.

The second case that led to different outcomes between the two experts was Problem 8. In this case, E1 arrived at the correct conclusion, whereas E2 arrived at an incorrect conclusion. The presenting symptoms in this case were that Ceb had gone down, SRb had gone up, and Vpt had gone down. In response, E1 followed the propose–discriminate–confirm scheme in Method 1 to conclude that Nb had gone down. The discrimination between Wb and Nb was based on using "no change in Ceb" as the discriminating cue.

On Problem 8, E2 generated the two hypotheses that either Wb or Nb had gone down. A decrease in Vpt led E2 to propose the hypotheses that either Wb had gone down or Nb had gone up (Method 4). The contradiction in the hypotheses about Nb led E2 to reject this hypothesis, which left the decrease in Wb as the remaining hypothesis.

Method 6a, on the other hand, proposes a hypothesis that Wb should go up. Because the hypotheses generated by Method 4 and Method 6a contradict each other, this leads to rejection of the hypothesis about the change in Wb, which leads to a complete deadlock in which no hypotheses are left. E2 said, "I am stuck," and could not arrive at any conclusions.

The cases discussed above show that in one case, E2 arrived a better outcome than did E1 (correct outcome vs. needed more data, respectively), and in another, E1 did better than did E2 (correct outcome vs. "stuck," respectively). Overall, for the 18 problems given to both experts, E1's methods showed a better semantic fit to the task of diagnosis than did E2's methods. E1 was correct on 13 problems (72%), was incorrect on 1 problem (5%), and requested more data on 4 problems (23%). By contrast, E2 was correct on 9 problems (50%), was incorrect on 4 problems (22%), and requested more data on 5 problems (28%). When E1 asked for more data, he had actually generated the correct hypotheses. This was not true for E2; on most of these cases, he was simply stuck.

A comparison of the two sets of methods clearly indicates that although the structural fit of both sets was established by similar mechanisms (i.e., the use of binary differential relations), the semantic fit was established very differently. The E1 (the diagnostic expert) relied on a highly contextual, conservative propose–discriminate–confirm schema based on a rich functional dependency network that was well suited to diagnosing faulty devices on the spot using available information. E2 (the testing expert) used methods that were less contextual and relied on a propose–confirm-by-contradiction schema and a much sparser functional dependency network that was suited to an environment in which more data are available through the testing process. In this sense, each expert's methods reflected the goals appropriate to his environments.

Experiment 2: Breakdown of Fit

On the basis of E1's performance on the 18 problems developed from the simulation model, we concluded that the expertise of this individual was well fit to the task of physical device diagnosis. To further explore the nature of the fit of E1's expertise in this environment, we created five additional problems. In each problem, a manipulation was introduced that would result in a breakdown in the structural fit of E1's methods but would preserve their semantic fit to the task environment.

To verify that semantic fit had been preserved, each problem was run through the problem-solving model to determine that E1's methods would reach a correct conclusion (given that the problem-solving model is based on semantic fit and effectively ignores structural fit). If structural fit was an independent property of E1's adaptation to the task environment of device diagnosis, we would expect him to indicate this even though the semantic properties of fit were preserved. The five problems and E1's response to them are discussed below.

Fit Problem 1

Fit Problem 1 is a "control" problem that is perfectly consistent with how E1's methods established both structural and semantic fit. This problem was constructed by increasing Nb by 15%. When run through the simulation model, this resulted in an 11% reduction in SRb, a 7% increase in Ceb, and a 16% increase in Vpt. This problem was solved using the model in Method 1. As expected, E1 used this method and solved the problem.

Fit Problem 2

Fit Problem 2 represents a mutation of a normal problem that was constructed by reducing Wb by 33%. When run through the simulation model, this change increased SRb by 78% and lowered Vpt by 59% (to 6.62 V). Because one observation of E1 was that the methods did not use absolute values of the parameters, this problem was artificially mutated from its normal "state" by decreasing Vpt by 16% (to 14 V) rather than 59%. The direction of change remained the same. Method 1 generated a correct response.

On Fit Problem 2, E1 arrived at the correct outcome but commented that the problem seemed atypical. It would seem that the manipulation (artificial reduction of Vpt) was responsible for evoking this response. From analysis of his protocol, however, it was obvious that the change was not an issue; rather, E1 was concerned with the fact that the capacitances had not changed. E1 indicated that he expected the capacitances to change "a little bit" because in a typical fabrication process it was unusual to see a change in Wb without a small change in Nb, which would lead to a slight change in the Ceb.

We first detected a potential breakdown in the structural fit of E1's methods in Fit Problem 2. The breakdown was structural in that E1 was able to generate a correct solution, although the problem seemed atypical. It is important to point out that, as shown by the functional dependency diagram underlying the simulation model, no direct relation was assumed between a change in Wb and Nb, each of which could be manipulated independently. This, however, is not the case in the real fabrication process, in which the two are not independent; Nb (in conjunction with other concentration profiles) defines the effective Wb.

Fit Problem 2 evoked an unexpected breakdown in the structural fit for E1's adaptation defined in terms of the task environment of the physical device. In this problem, E1 suddenly changed the task environment he was considering to include process fabrication (i.e., the process that generates the device) as well as the device itself. This indicated that our model of E1's adaptation (based on the methods derived from his protocol) was fit to the task environment defined by the simulation of the device (which was used as a surrogate for the physical world) but not to an environment that successfully constrained actions with respect to the process that generated the device (i.e., the process of fabrication). The breakdown of structural fit led E1 to consider the task as belonging to a different class of problems.

Fit Problem 3

Fit Problem 3 represents a mutation of another normal problem. This problem was constructed by reducing Ne by 15%. When run through the device simulation model, this resulted in a 15.75% increase in SRe. Method 2 generated the hypotheses that either Ne or We had gone down. Because SRb remained the same, Method 2 gave the correct conclusion that Ne had gone down.

In solving Problem 3, E1's Method 2 did not consider Ceb. This presented a potential breakdown in E1's expertise based on missing information in E1's adaptation to the task environment. This happened because any value could have been assigned to Ceb without changing the outcome of E1's methods; his adaptation reflected the independence of Ceb and SRe.

A problem in which an interaction between SRe and Ceb was meaningful for the task of diagnosis could have potentially led to a breakdown of E1's structural fit to the task of device diagnosis. Fit Problem 3 tested the potential for such a breakdown by synthetically increasing Ceb in the original problem by 7.2%. The problem-solving model reached the correct conclusion, as before, because it ignored changes in structural fit.

On Fit Problem 3, E1 generated the initial observation (as explained by Method 2) that because SRe was high, Ne may have been lowered or We may have been shallower. On his first attempt, E1 noticed but ignored the capacitance cue and falsely concluded that We had gone down. E1's performance on Fit Problem 3 is an example of the typical response evoked by a garden-path case (Thompson, Johnson, & Moen, 1983) in which the expert is misled by a critical cue. E1's behavior is explained in this problem by a combination of Method 2 and Method 1. He proposed two initial hypotheses based on Method 2, but because the capacitance cue was present, used SRb and an argument similar to that in Method 1 as a basis for discrimination and arrived at the wrong conclusion.

After several minutes of deliberation, E1 withdrew his first hypothesis that Wb had changed and then indicated that he would like to see how the data presented to him were generated by the fabrication process so that he could review additional data such as concentration profiles.

Fit Problem 3 is interesting because it shows a breakdown of both the structural and the semantic fit of E1's adaptation to the task of device diagnosis. A breakdown in the semantic fit was evidenced by E1's arriving at the incorrect solution. However, E1 was also able to recognize a breakdown in the structural fit, as indicated by his apparent nonacceptance of the conditions of the problem. The breakdown in the structural fit was severe enough for him to withdraw his initial incorrect conclusion. The problem-solving model arrived at the correct conclusion because it effectively ignored structural fit.

Fit Problem 4

Fit Problem 4 was constructed to explore the effect of yet another aspect of the structural fit of E1's adaptation to the task of diagnosis. Because each of E1's methods arrived at a single conclusion (e.g., Wb is too high), two methods can result in multiple conclusions (e.g., Wb base is too high and We is too low). For example, junction move problems can be detected by simultaneous application of either Method 1 and Method 2 (for Jeb moves) or Method 2 and Method 3 (for Jbc moves).

Although junction moves are physically allowed actions (i.e., they occur in the physical environment), some problems can potentially generate multiple conclusions that are not supported by physical environment. A problem that presents a physically unusual configuration of information can, therefore, potentially lead to a breakdown in structural fit.

Fit Problem 4 was constructed to be such a problem. In this problem, the Nb was lowered by 15%, and at the same time. We was lowered by 13.6%. When run through the simulation model, this resulted in an increase of 16.7% in SRb, a 15.68% increase in SRe, a 7.67% decrease in Ceb, and a 16.08% decrease in Vpt. The problem-solving model correctly concluded that We and Nb had gone down at the same time.

In solving Fit Problem 4, E1's initial behavior is explained by Method 1. He determined that an increase in SRb was consistent with a decrease in Ceb. However, he observed that it was strange that Ceb and SRb had both increased at the same time (an indication of a breakdown in structural fit). On seeing this, he concluded that somehow multiple things had changed in the fabrication process to generate the data, which was not generally the case in a closely monitored semiconductor manufacturing environment. As in Fit Problem 3, he indicated that he could not tell what was wrong and would require more data on the process used to create the chip. When pushed for an answer, he indicated that a very "uncertain guess" would be that Nb and Ne were lowered at the same time.

Fit Problem 4 indicated that, as in Fit Problem 3, a breakdown in structural fit led E1 to refuse to offer a conclusion, despite the fact that he was clearly capable of generating plausible answers, as shown by the accuracy of his previous "uncertain guess." The breakdown in structural fit, however, prevented him from committing to this response.

Fit Problem 5

Fit Problem 5 explored another potential breakdown in structural fit of expert adaptation due to the generation of multiple conclusions (by two methods) that were not physically plausible. A normal event was constructed by first reducing Wb by 33%. Cbc was then artificially reduced by 2%. Method 1 concluded that Wb had gone down. Method 3 concluded that either Nc had gone up or Wc had gone down. Like Fit Problem 4, either of the two hypothesized outcomes could only have occurred simultaneously with a change in Wb, provided that multiple faults were present in the fabrication process.

On Fit Problem 5, E1 noted that although SRb had gone up, it was strange that Vpt was only a half of what it was in Fit Problem 1 for the same change in SRb. This was a case of breakdown in structural fit in which E1 expected a consistent relation between SRb and Vpt (see Method 1).

E1 noticed noticed the artificially introduced cue (i.e., Cbc going up) and developed the correct hypothesis that Wb may have been substantially decreased, but he concentrated more on the discrepancy between Fit Problem 1 and Fit Problem 5. Although in this case, the mutation had been a change in the capacitance, E1 unexpectedly discerned the cross-case discrepancy (also a breakdown of structural fit) and concluded that he needed to see how the data given to him had been generated. He refused to offer any conclusions about the outcomes.

Summary

We have presented an analysis of two experts performing a complex diagnostic task. Because a significant property of the task environment in this case was rapid change due to changing technology, the adaptation of both experts was based on approximate measures (e.g., the use of qualitative differentials) as well as on organization for processing specific cue values. We have shown that although the degree of structural fit seemed to be similar for both experts, E1 had a better semantic fit (based on a propose–discriminate–confirm processing scheme) to the task of diagnosing faults using information from the manufacturing line. E2, on the other hand, used methods (based on a propose–confirm-by-contradiction processing schema) that were adapted to the task of diagnosis in an environment in which there was additional information available from the destructive testing of the faulty chip.

The five additional fit problems further suggest how fit affects task performance. On Fit Problem 1 and Fit Problem 2, E1 arrived at the correct outcome in a fairly short period of time. On the three other problems, he generated plausible and correct answers but rejected all of them in the end. This suggests that the structural fit of E1's method to a given task played a key role in his willingness to accept it as an appropriate instance of work of which he is capable.

This analysis shows that E1's methods achieved structural fit to a task environment by relying on stable relations among cues in the environment and by being selective and functional in what information was considered. The methods achieve semantic fit by relying on stable relations among the agent's goals, cues, and actions in that same environment. In semiconductor manufacturing, the expertise of the agent is both general and powerful when understood in terms of these methods.

Conclusion

A fundamental question to ask about an agent's expertise is what can be done with it. One answer to this question has been to focus on the content of the adaptation and its capacity to successfully support performance on tasks (Feigenbaum, 1989). What we have attempted to show is that the power of expertise lies only partly in its content. Structure plays a major role as well, depending on the degree to which properties of the task reflect the structure of information seen in previous tasks. For many tasks in the world, semantic and structural fit are related, so that having a good response seems to go hand in hand with a familiar configuration of information.

As shown, however, there are tasks for which the structural fit of an agent's adaptation is low. In these cases, the agent's actions seem especially variable. At extremely low levels of structural fit, for example, the agent may simply reject the task. In less extreme cases, the structural fit shapes the form of the agent's performance. This may result in the variability that leads to the capacity to deal with novel circumstances. Much of the behavior associated with creativity and learning may be a result of the way in which agents respond to discrepancies between the structure of information expected and the structure of information given.

The picture of expertise that emerges from our attempt to study it using the framework proposed here is one in which the power of an agent's adaptation resides in relatively small sets of methods that are organized to take advantage of specific functional dependencies in the task environment and the agent. When the relation between the agent's adaptation and these dependencies breaks down, the agent either shifts to another set of similar methods or develops new ones. In this sense, expertise appears much more as a set of locally organized methods designed to perform specific tasks (what Levi-Strauss, 1962, called a *bricolage*; see also Jacob, 1977), rather than a global theory of the task environment (see also Compton & Jansen, 1990; Denning, 1990).

Although much more work needs to be done, we conclude that an agent's expertise depends on both the tasks observed and the agent's adaptation to them. From the perspective described here, for example, we conclude that the novice can be well fit, both structurally and semantically, to tasks in an environment. Although not able to solve the same kinds of problems as a professor or teaching assistant (or necessarily be able to solve them in the same way), there is an important sense in which the undergraduate student who does consistently well on tests in, for example, physics courses can be said to be well adapted to undergraduate physics. The student's adaptation "works" in the task environment of undergraduate physics, just as the adaptation of the paralegal in the law firm works (sometimes better than that of the attorney) in finding precedent cases in an online case database.

Our ability to understand the nature of expertise may be enhanced by examining more carefully the relation between individuals and their environments. The concept of fit allows us to understand each individual's adaptation to a given task environment. From this perspective, each individual is an expert. Rather than attributing observed performance to expert–novice differences, we can understand how variations in fit to a task influence each individual's performance.

References

Anderson, J. (1990). *The adaptive character of thought*. Hillsdale, NJ: Erlbaum.

Chase, W. G., & Simon, H. A. (1973). Perception in chess. *Cognitive Psychology, 4*, 55–81.

Compton, P., & Jansen, R. (1990). A philosophical basis for knowledge acquisition. *Knowledge Acquisition, 2*, 241–257.

Darwin, C. (1859). *On the origin of species by means of natural selection or the preservation of favoured races in the struggle for life*. London: Murray.

Davis, R. (1984). Diagnostic reasoning based on structure and behavior. *Artificial Intelligence, 24*, 347–410.

Denning, P. J. (1990). The science of computing: Modeling reality. *American Scientist, 78*, 495–498.

Dishaw, J. P., & Pan, J. Y. (1989). AESOP: A simulation-based knowledge system for CMOS process diagnosis. *IEEE Transactions on Semiconductor Manufacturing, 2*, 94–103.

Dreyfus, H. L., & Dreyfus, S. E. (1986). *Mind over machine.* New York: Free Press.

Dupré, J. (1987). *The latest on the best.* Cambridge, MA: MIT Press.

Elton, C. (1927). *Animal ecology.* London: Sidgwick & Jackson.

Feigenbaum, E. (1989). What hath Simon wrought? In D. Klahr & K. Kotovsky (Eds.), *Complex information processing: The impact of Herbert A. Simon* (pp. 165–182). Hillsdale, NJ: Erlbaum.

Jacob, F. (1977). Evolution and tinkering. *Science, 196,* 1161–1166.

Johnson, P. E., Duran, A. S., Hassebrock, F., Moller, J., & Prietula, M. (1981). Expertise and error in diagnostic reasoning. *Cognitive Science, 5,* 235–283.

Johnson, P. E., Garber, S., & Zualkernan, I. A. (1987). Specification of expertise. *International Journal of Man–Machine Studies, 26,* 161–181.

Johnson, P. E., Grazioli, S., Jamal, K., & Zualkernan, I. A. (in press). Success and failure in expert reasoning. *Organizational Behavior and Human Decision Processes.*

Johnson, P. E., Jamal, K., & Berryman, R. G. (1991). Effects of framing on auditor decisions. *Organizational Behavior and Human Decision Processes, 50,* 75–105.

Kochevar, L., & Johnson, P. (1988). Problem solving is what you do when you don't know what to do. In M. Ringle (Ed.), *Proceedings of the Tenth Annual Conference of the Cognitive Science Society* (pp. 615–622). Hillsdale, NJ: Erlbaum.

LaBerge, D. (1973). Attention and the measurement of perceptual learning. *Memory and Cognition, 1,* 268–276.

Larkin, J., McDermott, J., Simon, D. P., & Simon, H. A. (1980). Expert and novice performance in solving physics problems. *Science, 208,* 1335–1342.

Levi-Strauss, C. (1962). *The savage mind.* Chicago, IL: University of Chicago Press.

Lukazek, W., Grambow, K. G., & Yarbreough, W. J. (1990). Test chip based approach to automated diagnosis of CMOS yield problems. *IEEE Transactions on Semiconductor Manufacturing, 3,* 18–27.

Mahajan, S. (1989). Growth and processing-induced defects in semiconductors. *Progress in Material Science, 33,* 1–84.

Newell, A. (1973). You can't play 20 questions with nature and win: Projective comments on the papers of this symposium. In W. G. Chase (Ed.), *Visual information processing* (pp. 283–308). San Deigo, CA: Academic Press.

Newell, A., & Simon, H. (1972). *Human problem solving.* Englewood Cliffs, NJ: Prentice-Hall.

Reed, N. E., Stuck, E. R., & Moen, J. B. (1988). Specialized strategies: An alternative to first principles in diagnostic problem solving. *The Seventh National Conference on Artificial Intelligence, 1,* 364–368.

Rosenberg, A. (1980). *Sociobiology and the preemption of social science.* Baltimore: Johns Hopkins University Press.

Simon, H. A. (1980). Cognitive science: The newest science of the artificial. *Cognitive Science, 4,* 33–46.

Simon, H. A. (1981). *The sciences of the artificial* (2nd ed.). Cambridge, MA: MIT Press.

Sober, E. (1984). *The nature of selection.* Cambridge, MA: MIT Press.

Swanson, D. B. (1978). *Computer simulation of expert problem solving in medical diagnosis.* Unpublished doctoral dissertation, University of Minnesota, Minneapolis.

Thompson, W. B., Johnson, P. E., & Moen, J. (1983). Recognition-based diagnostic reasoning. In A. Bundy (Ed.), *Proceedings of the Eighth International Joint Conference on Artificial Intelligence* (pp. 236–238). Karlsruhe, Federal Republic of Germany: William Kaufman.

Turvey, M. T., & Carello, C. (1981). Cognition: The view from ecological realism. *Cognition, 10*, 313–321.

Turvey, M. T., Carello, C., & Kim, N. (1989). Links between active perception and the control of action. In H. Harken & M. Stadler (Eds.), *Synergetics of cognition* (pp. 269–295). Heidelberg, Federal Republic of Germany: Springer Verlag.

Volovik, D., Zualkernan, I. A., Johnson, P. E., & Matthews, C. E. (1990). A design-based approach to constructing computational solutions to diagnostic problems. *Proceedings of the Ninth National Conference on Artificial Intelligence, 1*, 835–836.

Wilson, E. O. (1975). *Sociobiology: The new synthesis.* Cambridge, MA: Harvard University Press.

Wolf, S. (1990). *Silicon processing in the VLSI era* (Vol. 1). Sunset Beach, CA: Lattice Press.

Two Themes in the Study of Cognition

Ulric Neisser

S ometimes the study of cognition seems to be all trees and no forest. The topics presented in these chapters constitute an impressively diverse array. There are so many of them, and at first glance they seem to have so little in common: speech perception, stick-wielding, infants and affordances, categories, cognitive psychology applied to education, conceptions of marriage, social insight in chimpanzees, fabricating transistors in fine-tuned factories, qualitative analysis. Obviously, Premack (chapter 8) is right: This is no time for parsimony.

All of these topics are parts of cognitive psychology, but what is that? A quarter of a century ago, I tried to define cognition as "all the processes by which the sensory input is transformed, reduced, elaborated, stored, recovered, and used" (Neisser, 1967, p. 4). Although that definition still works for much of what is discussed in these chapters, it also leaves out a lot. The processes I had in mind in 1967 all took place inside the head, which, as it turns out, is not the right starting point for the study of all aspects of cognition. Fortunately, I offered another definition on the same page of that book, namely that cognitive psychology was the study of "stimulus information and its vicissitudes" (ibid.). Although shorter, this latter formulation is actually more complete. It includes the notion of stimulus information, an idea that I did not really understand in 1967 but that now seems fundamental to the study of both perception and action.

The distinction between these two conceptions of cognition—one beginning with stimulus information, the other focusing on processing—may help bring some faint semblance of order to our diverse field. Although I have introduced it as a distinction between two theoretical approaches, I also mean it as a distinction between two cognitive systems: Each has its own tasks, makes use of its own forms of stimulus information, learns in its own way, has its own neural mechanisms, and is worth studying in its own right. The first system is engaged in what James J. Gibson (1966, 1979) liked to call "direct perception." The second, not at all Gibsonian, carries out many forms of recognition and mental representation. Before elaborating on the distinction between them (see Neisser, 1989), it may be appropriate to review some recent history.

Cognitive psychology began to take shape in the 1960s at about the time when the Center for Research in Learning, Perception, and Cognition was founded in Minneapolis. Before it appeared, the major forces on the psychological scene had been behaviorism, psychoanalysis, and the Gestalt movement. (I am stretching a little to include Gestalt psychology, which really was already over by 1960.) Each of these was a scientific theory, based on evidence, but was also a particular vision of human nature and how it should be investigated. The behaviorists insisted that behavior must be studied scientifically, which for them meant exclusively from the outside. The psychoanalysts believed that the unconscious motives they had uncovered were the real forces behind every action. For the Gestalt psychologists, both physical and psychological processes were ultimately governed by a single elegant principle—the law of good form, or *Prägnanz.*

History has not been kind to any of these schools. With the advantage of hindsight, we now know that they were all more wrong than right. Nevertheless, there is something admirable about the goals they set for themselves. The hope of the behaviorists, for example, was nothing less than to establish psychology as a physical science, one just as objective, lawful, and from-the-outside as chemistry or physics. It now seems obvious (at least to me) that they chose the wrong scientific model—psychology is a branch of biology, not of physics—but we can still admire the boldness of that vision. Psychoanalysis is admirable too: The analysts believed that they could make sense of even the most bizarre and abnormal behaviors in terms of a well-defined set of underlying motives. The Gestalt idea—more explicitly aesthetic and perhaps even more grandiose than the others—was that a single, elegant set of forces governs the mind, the brain, and the physical world. The tendency toward *Prägnanz* was as apparent in the symmetry of the soap bubble as in the laws of visual grouping. Beautiful ideas, all of them.

Then came cognitive psychology. We promised a lot less at first, perhaps because we were grateful to be allowed to study cognition at all in the behaviorist world of the 1960s. Some of us were up front about our limitations: The last sentence of the book in which I proposed the previous definitions was, "The study of cognition is only one fraction of psychology, and it cannot stand alone" (Neisser, 1967, p. 305). Nevertheless, the impulse to propose a more general theory was hard to resist. It soon became commonplace to claim that most or even all human behavior could be modeled in information-processing terms. Unfortunately, the upshot of this theoretical move was to make people seem very much like computers—not a very attractive image. For one thing, it is openly "nonholonomic," to use Turvey's term (chapter 4). Moreover, it leaves out much of what is most attractively human about human beings. Many have pointed out that the information-processing model does little justice to development, culture, or social life. James Gibson showed, at first surprisingly, that it is also inappropriate for much of perception. But much still remains; that is, there is a wide range of behaviors for which the information-processing model works fairly well. Most of them can be found on the list that Simon presents in chapter 5. Although Simon and I have different senses of what is beautiful, I hope to show that there is room for both of our preferences.

In the 1970s, cognitive psychology was an enormous success; one information-processing paradigm after another was developed, explored, and more or less successfully modeled. This very success, however, soon produced a kind of fragmentation. Many distinct research areas took shape: pattern recognition, attention, language, memory, problem solving, and so on. Each seemed to grow at an exponential rate, as they continue to do. The result was a sense of a field that is moving rapidly but with no clear sense of where it is going. Even more important, there is no clear sense of where it ought to be going. Unlike the earlier schools of psychology, we are not driven by any single vision of human nature, by any conviction of what success in our enterprise would bring in its wake.

At the same time, another powerful centrifugal force has come into play. This is the growing progress of neuroscience, with its deluge of remarkable findings about the brain. Valuable as it is, this new body of knowledge has increased our sense of fragmentation still further. It has created yet another specialized field, with yet another technical language and yet another range of background disciplines to be mastered. It has established a new array of facts—more of them almost every day—that seem to have very little coherence. We learn that one part of the brain may be specialized for face recognition, another for spelling. There are neurons with center-surround receptive fields, other neurons sensitive to the widths of gratings, and still other neurons responsive to signals in several different modalities. There are neurotransmitters and endorphins and a whole range of new biochemical phenomena, all with specialized locations and functions. Although this luxurious and undisciplined growth of new findings is just what we should have expected—the early reports of explorers are never smoothly coordinated—it does serve to increase our confusion about where we are going.

Finally, it is beginning to look as if the incoherence of modern neuropsychology is not entirely a methodological artifact or just a result of our still-incomplete understanding. On the contrary, it may be rooted in the very nature of the structure we are studying. The central nervous system turns out not to be a unified system but more like a patchwork of quasi-independent mechanisms. There seem to be a substantial number of separate modules, all performing different tasks in different ways. Human behavior may be coherent, but one would never know it to look at the brain.

With all this going on, can we do anything but make lists of phenomena? Certainly, I am not bold enough, or smart enough, to propose a genuine integration of all this material. But I can at least suggest a direction, or more exactly two directions, that hold out some faint promise of coherence. At a minimum, it seems possible to assign most of the topics discussed in these chapters to one or the other of two distinct categories. These categories are grounded in the history of our discipline, but they may also be related to a curious fact about the cortical basis of perception. That curious fact was established by Ungergleider and Mishkin (1982), who discovered two distinct neural systems in the visual brain of the monkey. These are called, respectively, the *where system* and the *what system*. When these two systems are independently lesioned, the result is a dissociation between two aspects of visually guided behavior. The where system enables the monkey to locate objects in space and reach for them effectively, independent of any previously associated responses. To use Gibsonian language (which Ungergleider and Mishkin definitely do not), the where system deals with the perception of layout and affordances. The what system, in contrast, enables the monkey to identify and discriminate between objects. To use information-processing language, the what system seems to enable comparisons between current input and previously stored mental representations.

For the moment, however, I will put neural speculation aside and base my categories on the history of cognitive psychology. As everyone knows, there have been two very different approaches to the study of cognition. The first of these, and the one with which I am now most comfortable, is based on what James Gibson called the *ecological approach.* Gibson first proposed this approach in 1966, just about when information-processing psychology was building up a head of steam. (Partly for that reason, mainstream cognitive psychologists largely ignored it for a number of years.) Although Gibson was first of all a perceptionist, his work offered more than a theory of perception. It was really a new conception of human nature, different from any that had ever been proposed in psychology, although clearly related to modern biological thought.

To be sure, Gibson's critics complained that it was not even a theory of perception. Where were the models of mental processes? But for the kind of perception in which Gibson was interested, mental models were exactly the wrong place at which to begin. In the ecological approach, people and other animals are seen as embedded in their environments. This notion has a number of strong implications:

1. Neither perception nor behavior can be understood without simultaneously understanding the environment and the information it makes available.
2. Effective action is possible because animals can perceive how the environment really is and what possibilities for action it affords.
3. Animals are not controlled by their environment; rather, they explore it and take advantage of its affordances.
4. There is no need to "represent" that environment because it is immediately at hand.
5. Animals perceive themselves as well as the environment; the self is part of the world, not outside of it.
6. The processes of cognitive development and learning make the fit between animal and environment increasingly appropriate over time.

It is an elegant set of ideas, as beautiful as the underlying conceptions of any of the older schools. (The wise editors of this volume certainly appreciate it; otherwise, they would not have invited so many Gibsonians to contribute chapters.) However, the ecological approach also leaves a great deal out. Although people are indeed embedded in their environments, they also "dis-embed" from those environments in important ways:

1. What they perceive here and now may remind them of other situations, absent friends, or faraway places.
2. They read (and understand) texts that have nothing to do with their immediate ecological situations.
3. In school, they engage in systematically decontextualized forms of learning.

4. They create and maintain cultures, and occasionally rebel against those cultures as well.

5. They make theories, invent science, and develop expertise in exotic and abstract domains.

These activities are not easily incorporated into the ecological approach. For one thing, Gibson's theory of perception is perhaps too free of "speciesism": It applies just as well to many other animals as it does to humans. Nevertheless, people do a lot of things that animals do not; some of which are on the list just above. (And many of which are also on Simon's list in chapter 5). These things seem to require what Turvey (chapter 4) calls *nonholonomic systems,* and the construction of such systems is an almost uniquely human activity. Because they are not embedded in the local environment as directly as are holonomic systems, nonholonomic structures often result in inappropriate or misdirected behavior. This does not make them unimportant. On the contrary, the fact that there is so little room for error or misunderstanding in ecological psychology may be evidence of its inadequacy for as an account of many aspects of human life. Mistakes may be rare in the perception of layout, but other forms of cognition are all too full of them.

Gibson insisted that direct perception does not depend on mental representations, in any ordinary sense of that term. I think he was right, but only about direct perception. Many other behaviors obviously do rely on representations of some kind. We need explanations of those behaviors—recognition, recall, symbol manipulation, school learning, and expertise, to name just a few—at least as urgently as we need perceptual theories. Fortunately, mainstream cognitive psychology has been busy developing just such explanations since the 1960s. This is, in fact, the other side of the distinction I am trying to draw.

I suggest that one broad class of cognitive activities is best understood holonomically (ecologically) in terms of direct perception and affordances. The proper study of those behaviors must begin with an analysis of the stimulus information that makes them possible; it is usually unproductive to begin with models of mental processes and representations. A second broad class of behaviors, however, cannot be understood without modeling the internal representations on which it depends. This is not a clash between theories, one right and the other wrong. Rather, it is a distinction between two sets of problems that require distinct and different approaches.

Let me return briefly to the neural analog of this dichotomy, Ungergleider and Mishkin's (1982) distinction between where and what mechanisms in the visual brain. I do not mean, of course, that all forms of direct perception are mediated by the dorsal cortical subsystem that controls reaching in the monkey. Still less do I mean that all significant representational processes are localized in the ventral cortical subsystem that serves visual object discrimination; that would be absurd. The neural model shows us, however, that the distinction between direct perception and matching to representations may be more than an accidental phase of the history of psychology. Perceiving layout and identifying objects are two quite different survival-relevant tasks, so different that—in at least one case—distinct neural mechanisms have evolved to deal with them. If ecological and representational cognitive psychologists have found it hard to talk to one another, it may be because they have been talking about quite different things.

Both modes of cognition have elegant accomplishments to their credit. More precisely, it is we humans who should take credit for those accomplishments; it is we who have both kinds of systems in our heads and both kinds of behavior in our repertoires. Of course, they do not work in isolation from each other. In most situations, they are smoothly and jointly active; there is no introspectively given seam between direct perception and recognition, between the outer and inner determinants of action. As long as the environment is basically coherent, both physically and culturally, their joint activity can be counted on to produce coherent and appropriate behavior.

Viewed from this perspective, the study of cognition is not so fragmented after all. It is more like a piece of music with two principal themes that keep weaving in and out, each with its own submelodies and cadenzas. If some of it seems discordant, that may be because we do not quite know how to listen to it yet; if some of it seems raw and unfinished, that is only to be expected from a work in progress. Described in this way, what has been going on for the past 25 years may not be as chaotic as a superficial inventory would suggest. Maybe there is a vision here too, one just as elegant as any of those offered by our predecessors. If it is taking longer to come into focus, it may end by showing us more that is worth seeing. In the next 25 years, we may find ways of bringing out both themes more sharply and clearly.

References

Gibson, J. J. (1966). *The senses considered as perceptual systems.* Boston: Houghton Mifflin.

Gibson, J. J. (1979). *The ecological approach to visual perception.* Boston: Houghton Mifflin.

Neisser, U. (1967). *Cognitive psychology.* New York: Appleton-Century-Crofts.

Neisser, U. (1989, August). *Direct perception and recognition as distinct perceptual systems.* Paper presented to the Cognitive Science Society, Ann Arbor, MI.

Ungergleider, L. G., & Mishkin, M. (1982). Two cortical visual systems. In D. J. Ingle, M. A. Goodale, & R. J. W. Mansfield (Eds.), *Analysis of visual behavior* (pp. 549–586). Cambridge, MA: MIT Press.

Index

Abstraction, and perceptual learning, 217
Action
  cognitive development and, 215
  cognitive theory and, 86, 92–94
  information and, 88
  knowledge and, 201–202, 300–321
  locomotive, 98
  mental representation and, 200–201
  optic flow patterns and, 223–224
  perception and, 232
  perceptual control of, 90
  perceptual learning and, 217
  requirements of, 208–209
  situated, 132
  visual perception and, 201
Action capabilities
  cognitive theory and, 88
  reductionism and, 86–87
ACT models, 144
ACT program, 251
Adaptation
  cognition and, 306, 308–309
  problem solving and, 308–310, 313, 323,
    323–325, 327–329
Adaptive education, 257
Adolph, K. E., 231
Adults
  communication disorders and, 298
  conceptual primitives and, 193–194
  culture acquisition and, 269–270, 276–278
  speech perception of, 13–17, 22–25
Affordance
  ecological approach and, 338

  infant perception and, 222, 224–225
  perceptual learning and, 218–219, 226, 228–229,
    232
Ahn, W. K., 181
AI. *See* Artificial intelligence
Analogy
  culture acquisition and, 272–273,
    278–283, 289
  learning theory and, 249, 252
  problem shaping and, 306
  relations matching and, 199
Anderson, J. R., 3, 144, 169, 179–180
  cognitive architecture and, 145
  Cognitive Psychology, 12, 124
  learning theory and, 251–252
Animal–environment fit, 218–219
  perceptual learning and, 225
  Annual Review of Psychology, 28, 241–242
"Anosognosia," 36–47
Anthropology, culture acquisition and, 267–268
Applied psychology, impact of theory on, 295–302
Aptitude, learning and, 247–249, 256
Aptitude–treatment interaction, learning theory
  and, 248
Arnold tongues, 102–104, 108–109
Artificial intelligence (AI), 167
  computational models and, 173–174
  expert systems and, 254
  problem solving and, 123
  qualitative reasoning and, 113
Assessment procedures, teaching and, 256–258
  See also Evaluation; Testing
Association, perceptual learning and, 216

About the Editors

H erbert L. Pick, Jr., Paulus van den Broek, and David C. Knill are all members of the interdisciplinary Center for Research in Learning, Perception, and Cognition of the University of Minnesota.

Pick, former director of the center, is currently director of graduate studies for the Graduate School Cognitive Science Program. He received his PhD from Cornell University in 1960 in experimental psychology. His major research interests are perception, perceptual–motor development, and spatial cognition.

Van den Broek, associate director of the center, is associate professor in educational psychology. He received a PhD in educational psychology from the University of Chicago in 1985 and doctoral degrees in experimental psychology (1981) and developmental psychology (1980) from the University of Leiden, the Netherlands. His major research interests concern the inferential processes and cognitive limitations that contribute to reading comprehension and reasoning in adults and children.

Knill is a postdoctoral research associate in the Department of Psychology at the University of Minnesota. He received his PhD in experimental psychology from Brown University in 1991. His research focuses on computer and human vision and on the application of analytical and computational techniques developed for computer vision to the study of human visual perception.